Mastering America

Southern Slaveholders and the Crisis of American Nationhood

Mastering America recounts efforts of "proslavery nationalists" to navigate the nineteenth-century geopolitics of imperialism, federalism, and nationalism, and to articulate themes of American mission in overtly proslavery terms. At the heart of this study are spokesmen of the southern "Master Class" who crafted a vision of American destiny that put chattel slavery at its center.

Looking beyond previous studies of the links between these "proslavery nationalists" and secession, the book sheds new light on the relationship between the conservative Unionism of the 1850s and the key formulations of Confederate nationalism that arose during the war in the early 1860s. Bonner's innovative research charts the crucial role these men and women played in the development of American imperialism, constitutionalism, evangelicalism, and popular patriotism.

Robert E. Bonner earned his A.B. at Princeton University and his Ph.D. at Yale University. He has held teaching positions at the University of Southern Maine, Michigan State University, and Amherst College and currently teaches at Dartmouth College. He is the author of *Colors and Blood: Flag Passions of the Confederate South* (2002) and *The Soldier's Pen: Firsthand Impressions of the American Civil War* (2006), as well as articles in the *Journal of Southern History, Civil War History,* and *Reviews in American History.*

CAMBRIDGE STUDIES ON THE AMERICAN SOUTH

Series Editors:

MARK M. SMITH

University of South Carolina, Columbia

DAVID MOLTKE-HANSEN

Center for the Study of the American South,
University of North Carolina at Chapel Hill

Interdisciplinary in its scope and intent, this series builds upon and extends Cambridge University Press's long-standing commitment to studies on the American South. The series will offer not only the best new work on the South's distinctive institutional, social, economic, and cultural history but also works in a national, comparative, and transnational perspective.

Mastering America

Southern Slaveholders and the Crisis of American Nationhood

ROBERT E. BONNER

Dartmouth College

CAMBRIDGE
UNIVERSITY PRESS

CAMBRIDGE UNIVERSITY PRESS
Cambridge, New York, Melbourne, Madrid, Cape Town, Singapore, São Paulo, Delhi

Cambridge University Press
32 Avenue of the Americas, New York, NY 10013-2473, USA

www.cambridge.org
Information on this title: www.cambridge.org/9780521541770

First published 2009

Printed in the United States of America

A catalog record for this publication is available from the British Library.

Library of Congress Cataloging in Publication Data

Bonner, Robert E., 1967–
Mastering America : Southern slaveholders and the crisis of
American nationhood / Robert Bonner. – 1st ed.
p.cm.
Includes index.
ISBN 978-0-521-83395-0 (hardback) – ISBN 978-0-521-54177-0 (pbk.)
1. Slavery – Political aspects – United States – History – 19th century.
2. Slaveholders – Southern States – Political activity – History – 19th century.
3. Slavery – United States – Justification – History – 19th century. 4. United States –
Territorial expansion. 5. Imperialism – History – 19th century. 6. Geopolitics –
History – 19th century. 7. Federal government – United States – History – 19th
century. 8. Nationalism – United States – History – 19th century. 9. Nationalism –
Southern States – History – 19th century. 10. Secession – Southern States. I. Title.

E449.B7155 2009
326.0973–dc22   2008043676

ISBN 978-0-521-83395-0 hardback
ISBN 978-0-521-54177-0 paperback

Contents

List of Illustrations   *page* vii

List of Abbreviations   ix

Prologue: Confederate Common Sense   xi

PART I: THE GEOPOLITICS OF MASTERY

1. Slaveholders' Stake in the American Empire   3

2. The Compound Republic and the Cause of the South   41

PART II: THE CONTOURS OF PROSLAVERY AMERICANISM

3. Republican Masters and American Mission   81

4. Reformed Slaveholders and the Gospel of Nationhood   114

5. Fragments from the Past, Histories for the Future   149

6. Yankee Apostates and Allies in the American 1850s   184

PART III: CONFEDERATE NATIONHOOD AND
THE REVOLUTIONS OF WAR

7. The Anatomy of Confederate Nationhood   217

8. Reckoning with Confederate Purpose   252

9. Liberty, Slavery, and the Burdens of
    Confederate Nationhood   286

Epilogue: "A People Brought to the End of a Given Cycle"   323

Acknowledgments   329

Index   333

Dedicated to Patricia Bigbee and Leslie Butler

List of Illustrations

1.1 "The Noble Virginians in the Heat of Battle!" *from William Hillhouse, Pocahontas; A Proclamation: With Plates (New Haven: J. Clyme, 1820). Courtesy of Duke University. Rare Book Manuscript and Special Collections Library.* *page* 17

1.2 David Hunter Strother, "A Southern Planter Arming His Slaves to Resist Invasion," *Harper's Weekly, November 19, 1859. Courtesy of Dartmouth College Library.* 22

1.3 Memucan Hunt, Jr., *from De Bow's Review, October 1853. Courtesy of Dartmouth College Libraries.* 24

2.1 John C. Calhoun, *from James Herring, National Portrait Gallery of Distinguished Americans (Philadelphia, PA: Henry Perkins, 1835). Courtesy of Dartmouth College Library.* 59

3.1 Detail from Edward Williams Clay, *"America" (1841), lithograph held by Library of Congress.* 95

4.1 Frank Vizetelly, "Family Worship in a Plantation," *Illustrated London News, December 5, 1863. Courtesy of Dartmouth College Library.* 125

5.1 "Richmond Washington Monument," *Harper's Weekly, February 20, 1858. Courtesy of Dartmouth College Library.* 168

6.1 "Meeting of the Friends of the Higher Law," *from "Vidi," Mr. Frank: The Underground Mail-Agent (Philadelphia: Lippincott, 1853). Courtesy of Duke University Rare Book, Manuscript, and Special Collections Library.*   193

6.2 Image of Mount Vernon and slaves, *from Benson Lossing, Mount Vernon and its Associations (New York: W.A. Townsend and Co., 1859). Courtesy of Dartmouth College Library.*   197

7.1 "Prospectus," in *Augusta Daily Constitutionalist, April 21, 1861. Courtesy of American Antiquarian Society.*   230

7.2 *Pray, Maiden, Pray,* Sheet Music cover (1864). *Courtesy of Duke University Rare Books and Manuscript Libraries.*   245

8.1 Masthead showing soldier and slave, *from Southern Illustrated News, January 1865. Courtesy of Houghton Library, Harvard University.*   280

9.1 Georgia notices for army deserters and runaway slaves, *Augusta Daily Constitutionalist, April 25, 1861. Courtesy of American Antiquarian Society.*   295

9.2 "The Yankee Soldiers' Nightmare: A Vision of the Black-Horse Cavalry," *Southern Illustrated News, February 20, 1864. Courtesy of Gilder-Lehrman Collection.*   315

List of Abbreviations

AHR	*American Historical Review*
AQR	*American Quarterly Review*
Annals	*Annals of Congress*
BLY	Beinecke Library, Yale University, New Haven, CT
CG	*Congressional Globe*
CMPC	James D. Richardson, *A Compilation of the Messages and Papers of Jefferson Davis and the Confederacy, Including Diplomatic Correspondence, 1861–1865* (Nashville: United States Publishing Company, 1905)
CMPP	James D. Richardson, *A Compilation of Messages and Papers of the Presidents* (Washington, D.C., 1897)
CWH	*Civil War History*
DBR	*De Bow's Review*
DHFFC	Charlene Bangs Bickford, Kenneth R. Bowling, and Helen E. Veit, eds. *The Documentary History of the First Federal Congress* (Baltimore, MD: John Hopkins University Press, 1992)
HEH	Henry E. Huntington Library, San Marino, California
JAH	*Journal of American History*
JCCSA	*Journal of the Congress of the Confederate States of America, 1861–1865* (Washington, D.C.: Government Printing Office, 1904–05)
JDC	Dunbar Rowland, ed. *Jefferson Davis, Constitutionalist: His Letters, Papers and Speeches* (Jackson: Mississippi Department of Archives and History, 1923)

ix

JER	*Journal of the Early Republic*
JSH	*Journal of Southern History*
LSW	Abraham Lincoln, *Speeches and Writings*, ed. Don Fehrenbacher (New York: Library of America, 1989)
LVR	Library of Virginia, Richmond
LWGS	Mary C. Oliphant, et al., eds. *The Letters of William Gilmore Simms* (Columbia: University of South Carolina Press, 1952–82)
OR	U.S. War Department, *Official Records of the Union and Confederate Armies* (Washington D.C., 1880–1901)
OR-N	U.S. War Department, *Official Records of the Union and Confederate Navies* (Washington, D.C., 1903)
PJCC	Robert Lee Meriwether, et al., eds. *The Papers of John C. Calhoun* (Columbia: University of South Carolina Press, 1959–2003)
PJD	Lynda Crist, et al., eds. *The Papers of Jefferson Davis* (Baton Rouge: Louisiana State University Press, 1971)
PMBL	Charles Adams Gulick Jr., ed. *The Papers of Mirabeau Bonaparte Lamar, Edited from the Original Papers in the Texas State Archives* (Austin: A.C. Baldwin & Sons and Von-Boeckmann-Jones, 1921–7)
SHSP	*Southern Historical Society Papers*
SIN	*Southern Illustrated News*
SLJ	*Southern Literary Journal*
SLM	*Southern Literary Messenger*
SPR	*Southern Presbyterian Review*
SQR	*Southern Quarterly Review*
SR	*Southern Review*
TSC Corresp.	Ulrich B. Phillips, ed. *Correspondence of Robert Toombs, Alexander H. Stephens, and Howell Cobb* (Washington, D.C.: American Historical Association, 1911)
VMHB	*Virginia Magazine of History and Biography*
WMQ	*William and Mary Quarterly, 3rd Series*

Prologue: Confederate Common Sense

On the last Thursday of November 1860, as the worst political crisis in American history intensified, the churches of New Orleans filled to capacity. The slave South's largest and most vibrant city had marked Thanksgiving with sermons and prayers on earlier occasions. But never before had men and women left that city's noisy streets and squares with the same sort of expectancy, nor had they ever bowed their heads with such grave questions about their future. A wrenching presidential election had just raised fundamental doubts about the fate of American slavery. With a daily influx of news detailing South Carolina's sprint to secession, white New Orleanians had an understandable appetite for transcendent perspective.

Those who gathered in the Lafayette Square Presbyterian Church that November afternoon received a clearer message than they might have expected. Not long into his hour-long oration, the Rev. Benjamin Morgan Palmer cast aside his typical disavowal of "political" preaching and provided secessionists across the Deep South with the highest sanction he could muster. The native South Carolinian championed slavery, as he had when earlier speaking of Christian duties. His Thanksgiving address went much farther, however, in insisting that white mastery of black dependents involved a distinctive providential mission, which could only be pursued through radical political action. The highest responsibility of America's master class was "to preserve and transmit our existing system of domestic servitude, with the right, unchanged by man, to go and root itself wherever Providence and nature may carry it." With a Republican presidency of the United States now a certainty, Palmer urged his fellow slaveholders to heed his call for action. He wanted them to understand that their proslavery mission would no longer be possible within a United States governed by Lincoln of Illinois.[1]

In coming weeks, Palmer's words became the most influential expression of a sacred understanding of masters' proslavery national mission. The New Orleans press circulated the address with the assurance that it rose "infinitely above the usual thought and rhetoric of a political speech" and was nothing less than "sacramental in its fervor." A Mississippi editor who published the entire speech the week after its delivery speculated how the thirty paragraphs might be "printed in letters of gold, and spread widecast among the people." Before the secession crisis was complete, Palmer's words would have been available to any of his 400,000 fellow slaveholders who sought the comfort of his prophecy. Nearly 100,000 copies of the sermon would ultimately appear in pamphlet form. These were less influential than the republication of his remarks in such important southern periodicals as *De Bow's Review*, the *Southern Planter*, and the *Southern Field and Fireside*. Several leading newspapers reprinted his entire address. Many others stitched together those choice passages that conveyed the sermon's main thrust. In towns, cities, and plantations across the region, men and women of the master class reflected in their diaries and letters upon the electrifying effect of Palmer's intervention.[2]

Palmer realized that far more people would encounter his message in print than hear it at the Lafayette Square Church. He thus emulated the revolutionary-era pamphleteer Thomas Paine by packing as much

[1] There was no one "title" for Palmer's sermon, which would variously be printed as: *The South, Her Peril and Her Duty* (New Orleans, LA: True Witness and Sentinel, 1860), *The Rights of the South, Defended in the Pulpits* (Mobile, 1860); "Why We Resist and What We Resist," *DBR* 31 (February 1861); "The Trust Providentially Committed to the South in Relation to the Institution of Slavery," *Southern Planter* 21 (February 1861) 115–19; *Thanksgiving Sermon, Delivered at the First Presbyterian Church, New Orleans, on Thursday, December [sic] 29, 1860* (New York, 1861), and *Slavery a Divine Trust. The Duty of the South to Preserve and Perpetuate the Institution as It Now Exists* (New York, 1861). There are no major textual discrepancies between these printings, each of which largely match the text that has been conveniently reprinted as "The South: Her Peril and Her Duty" in Jon Wakelyn, ed. *Southern Pamphlets on Secession, November 1860–April 1861* (Chapel Hill: University of North Carolina Press, 1996) 63–77.

[2] New Orleans *Sunday Delta*, December 2, 1860; Thomas Carey Johnson, *The Life and Letters of the Rev. B.M. Palmer* (Richmond, VA: Presbyterian Committee, 1906), 196–223. Specific details on the context and response to Palmer have been taken from Haskell Monroe, "Bishop [sic] Palmer's Thanksgiving Day Sermon," *Louisiana History* 4 (1963), 105–18; Wayne C. Eubank, "Benjamin Morgan Palmer's Thanksgiving Sermon, 1860" in J. Jeffery Auer, *Antislavery and Disunion: Studies in the Rhetoric of Compromise and Conflict, 1858–1861*; and Mitchell Snay, *The Gospel of Disunion: Religion and Separatism in the Antebellum South* (New York: Cambridge University Press, 1993), 175–81.

meaning as possible into the key phrases he offered up that afternoon. He dramatized the "crucifying test" that faced all Americans and speculated how masters' current actions would color "the complexion of our destiny." Some clever writing helped him to hit upon a remarkably wide range of themes, as he took up the burden of civilization, the racial inferiority of blacks, the theological nature of providence, the harmonizing tendencies of slaveholders' republicanism, and even a discussion of the constitutional right of secession. There was just enough of reassurance in his tone to keep the pastoral dimension in evidence. What was by turns a treatise, a sermon, and a message of consolation closed with the simple assertion that "The Position of the South is sublime."

Palmer's sudden fame as the South's most notorious disunionist was unlikely. His prior career had been marked by political moderation and a scrupulous avoidance of fire-eating politics. Though he was raised in South Carolina, a hotbed of separatist sentiment, Palmer had shown little evidence during the 1850s that he would produce the nearest Confederate equivalent to Thomas Paine's *Common Sense*. His national stature came as the sort of theologian, pastor, and orator who could appeal to congregations in the free states as well as in the slave states. During the late antebellum period, he had received calls from prestigious pulpits in the urban North and was unanimously elected in 1860 to the faculty of the Princeton Theological Seminary. Palmer's decision to decline such overtures resulted not simply from his regional loyalties but from his appreciation of what might follow a successful ministry to those New Orleans merchants and planters in whose hands the seat of a continental American empire rested. In political terms, Palmer's Unionist credentials matched those of most of his fellow Presbyterian clergy, who had formed a particularly potent mix of proslavery dogma and American nationalism over the first six decades of the nineteenth century. It was thus with a distinct tone of melancholy that Palmer turned to the cause of disunion. One of the most arresting images of the speech conveyed his genuine regret at breaking ties with the United States and his desire to continue with the work begun in its name. "If we cannot save the Union, we may save the blessings it enshrines," he explained. "If we cannot preserve the vase, we will preserve the precious liquor it contains."[3]

News of Palmer's sermon quickly traveled through an increasingly nationalized network of print to reach New York City, where outrage rather than enthusiasm was the prevailing response to his separatist

[3] Johnson, *Life and Letters*, 147, 235.

ultimatum. The withdrawal of Louisiana from the Union would have drastic implications for the partisan system that had connected New York to the slave South, and for those increasingly intricate commercial, financial, and cultural ties on which the city's future viability depended. The Rev. Henry Ward Beecher of Brooklyn was aware of these dangers, though he had more personal reasons to pause over Palmer's apparent apostasy. The two men had played chess with each other when they were fellow students at Amherst College in the 1830s, and each had since attained celebrity status as their region's most spellbinding pulpit orators. While Beecher's memories of Palmer surely tinged his readings of the New Orleans Thanksgiving sermon, he was unlikely to have followed the sermon's arguments with particular care or noted its tone of pathos and regret. Like many in the North, Beecher traced the current crisis to the failings of aberrant Southerners, who mocked the free states' more genuine version of American republicanism. Beecher noted in 1861 that he had "never heard a man from the South speak of himself as an American" and that "men from the South speak of themselves as Southerners." A year later, he explained how the rebels' overly narrow identities had even more sinister roots, reasoning that "men brought up under the influence of slavery" were "contaminated to the very root, and cannot make good citizens."[4]

Beecher spoke for the common sense of the free-state majority in joining the Confederacy's rebellion against the federal government with slaveholders' more long-standing rebellion against civic morality and global progress. With the outbreak of war in 1861, more and more Union partisans joined Senator Charles Sumner of Massachusetts in arraigning white Southerners for a "triple-headed treason" that united their defiance of government sovereignty, their betrayal of national ideas, and, in their disregard for global progress toward universal freedom, their rejection of "those commanding principles of economy, morals, and Christianity without which civilization is changed into barbarism." The Union soldiers who captured New Orleans early in 1862 displayed similar understandings. For those enlisted under the

---

[4] "Thanksgiving Sermon of Dr. Palmer," New York *Evangelist*, December 20, 1860; "Dr. Palmer's Sermon," New York *Independent*, January 17, 1861; Beecher, "The Battle Set in Array" (first delivered April 14, 1861), "The Success of American Democracy," (first delivered April 13, 1862) both in *Patriotic Addresses in America and England, 1850–1885, on Slavery, the Civil War, and the Development of Civil Liberty in the United States* (New York: Fords, Howard and Hulbert, 1887), 276, 353; Johnson, *Life and Letters*, 48. Trish Lougren, *The Republic in Print: Print Culture in the Age of U.S. Nation Building, 1770–1870* (New York: Columbia University Press, 2007) offers important new perspectives on the relationship between networks of publishing and communications and the mid-nineteenth-century conflicts over nationalization, slavery controversy, and sectionalism.

Stars and Stripes, driving Palmer and his ilk into exile was a means of meting out punishment to selfish traitors and demonic brutes.[5]

These Union publicists and soldiers anticipated the judgment of many later historians, who have tended to conflate an understandable revulsion at proslavery ideology with a willful disassociation of bondage from prevailing American norms.[6] The popular sanction given to secession during the winter of 1860–1 has drawn attention away from dramatic reversals such as that taken by Palmer and toward long-term patterns through which southern slaveholders seemed to have become increasingly alienated from national ideas. Their cultivation of narrow identities that caused them to "speak of themselves as Southerners" has repeatedly been held up as the key problem to be solved.[7] Scholars who have documented the thoroughly "American" self-conception of Confederates have provided a cautionary note about such teleological assumptions and have reminded us how easily the fluid dynamics of nineteenth-century nationalism can be smoothed over in the quest to chart gradual developments. The following study of proslavery nationalism as it operated from the American founding through the Civil War builds on such work and thus

[5] Charles Sumner, *The Rebellion: Its Origins and Its Mainspring* (New York: Young Men's Republican Club, 1861), 6; Chandra Manning, *What This Cruel War Was Over: Soldiers, Slavery, and the Civil War* (New York: Knopf, 2007).

[6] Among those who posit a basic incompatibility between slavery and American nationhood are Liah Greenfeld, *Nationalism: Five Roads to Modernity* (Cambridge, MA: Harvard University Press, 1992) and Gordon Wood, *The Radicalism of the American Revolution* (New York: Knopf, 1992), 186–7. James McPherson provides an intriguing alternative in "Antebellum Southern Exceptionalism: A New Look at an Old Question," *CWH* 50 (December 2004) 418–33, though a stance closer to Greenfield and Wood is evident throughout *Ordeal by Fire: The Civil War and Reconstruction* (New York: McGraw-Hill, 2001). The prevalence of proslavery republicanism across the South (a phenomenon distinct from proslavery nationalism) has been addressed by J. Mills Thornton, *Politics and Power in a Slave Society: Alabama, 1800–1860* (Baton Rouge: Louisiana State University Press, 1977); Lacy K. Ford Jr. *The Origins of Southern Radicalism: The South Carolina Upcountry* (New York: Oxford University Press, 1988); Stephanie McCurry, *Masters of Small Worlds: Yeoman Households, Gender Relations, and the Political Culture of the Antebellum South Carolina Low Country* (New York: Oxford University Press, 1985); and, from a slightly different angle, by James Oakes, *The Ruling Race: A History of American Slaveholders* (New York: Knopf, 1982).

[7] Such tendencies are most evident in the literature on "Southern Nationalism" associated with classics such as John M. McCardell, *The Idea of a Southern Nation: Southern Nationalists and Southern Nationalism, 1830–1860* (New York: W.W. Norton, 1979); Rollin Osterweiss, *Romanticism and Nationalism in the Old South* (New Haven, CT: Yale University Press, 1949); and Jesse T. Carpenter, *The South as a Conscious Minority, 1789–1861: A Study in Political Thought* (New York: New York University Press, 1930). Whether pursuing the development of "identity" independent of other forces obscures more than it reveals about historical processes is a point helpfully addressed in Rogers Brubaker and Frederick A. Cooper, "Beyond Identity," *Social Theory* 29 (2000), 1–47.

remaps the relationship among nationalizing currents of the 1850s, the
crisis of disunion, and the avowedly proslavery Confederacy of the early
1860s.[8]

At the heart of this book is the story of how slaveholders both before
and after Lincoln's election in 1860 contributed to the American project of
"becoming national." As was the case in other modern societies, this
enterprise involved a "complex, uneven, and unpredictable process, forged
from an interaction of cultural coalescence and specific political intervention," as two historians have recently put it. In approaching the slippery
category of nationhood, there is always a temptation to focus more on
issues of self-understanding than of power. In the case of American masters, it was the potential antislavery threats posed at the national, subna-
tional, and international levels that predominated. My desire to address
the high stakes involved in this maneuvering for advantage has led me to
devote the first section of this study to those geopolitical issues that informed considerations of nationhood as well as of empire, state, and sectional initiatives. Only after establishing the intricacy of slaveholders'
attempts to secure power within a federal Union do I turn in the second
section to cultural developments, and in particular to assessing the increasingly ambitious plans to "nationalize" American slavery through variants
of proslavery republicanism, evangelicalism, historical memory, and
domesticity.[9]

---

[8] Drew Faust, *The Creation of Confederate Nationalism: Ideology and Identity in the Civil
War South* (Baton Rouge: Louisiana State University Press, 1988); George Rable, *The
Confederate Republic: A Revolution against Politics* (Chapel Hill: University of North
Carolina Press, 1994); and Anne Sarah Rubin, *A Shattered Nation: The Rise and Fall of the
Confederacy, 1861–1868* (Chapel Hill: University of North Carolina Press, 2005); Paul
D.H. Quigley, "Patchwork Nation: Sources of Confederate Nationalism, 1848–1865"
(PhD dissertation, University of North Carolina – Chapel Hill, 2006).

[9] Geoff Eley and Ronald Grigor Suny, "Introduction: From the Moment of Social History to
the Work of Cultural Representation," in *Becoming National: A Reader* (New York:
Oxford University Press, 1996), 8. These scholars go on to explain how if "politics is
the ground upon which the category of the nation was first proposed," then "culture is
the terrain where it is elaborated." I have found such a formulation a compelling alternative to John Breuilly's overly stark emphasis on the political nature of nationalist claims (as
set forth in *Nationalism and the State* [Chicago: University of Chicago Press, 1992]) and
Benedict Anderson's more influential overview, whose search for alternatives to state-
centered narratives at times obscures the workings of politics and power (see *Imagined
Communities: Reflections on the Origin and Spread of Nationalism* [Verso: London,
1983]). An older, but still relevant, warning about the connections between cultural analysis and the "hard surfaces" of those "political, economic, stratificatory realities within
which men are everywhere contained" can be found in Clifford Geertz, *The Interpretation
of Cultures: Selected Essays* (New York: Basic Books, 1973), 30.

My analysis of the nationalist visions of proslavery Southerners relies on three discrete bodies of scholarship. Most notable has been that ever more sophisticated work on the intellectual life of the antebellum master class. By recovering important texts and recasting critical episodes, this work has set a new standard in American intellectual history.[10] By demonstrating slaveholders' dexterity in shuttling between "American" and "southern" identities as they navigated the crisis of Union, historians such as Drew Faust, Eugene Genovese, and Michael O'Brien have also demonstrated anew the wisdom of David Potter's justly influential insight that Americans, by 1860, were "separated by a common nationalism."[11]

A second body of works has helped me to consider American slaveholders as one among several "master classes," who together witnessed the loss of their human property over a century-long "age of emancipation." Studies that compare American masters to their colonial counterparts in other plantation zones have helped me more fully to appreciate advantages that came with access to governmental power and to a series

[10] William Freehling, *Road to Disunion*, 2 vols. (New York: Oxford University Press, 1991 and 2007); Eugene Genovese, *The Slaveholders' Dilemma: Freedom and Progress in Southern Conservative Thought, 1820–1860* (Columbia: University of South Carolina Press, 1992); Michael O'Brien, *Conjectures of Order: Intellectual Life in the American South, 1810–1860* (Chapel Hill: University of North Carolina Press, 2004); Elizabeth Fox-Genovese and Eugene Genovese, *The Mind of the Master Class: History and Faith in the Southern Slaveholders' Worldview* (New York: Cambridge University Press, 2005). For a wider cataloguing of recent work in southern intellectual history, see Robert E. Bonner, "Ordering Southern Thought," *Reviews in American History* 33 (2005), 54–63.
[11] David Potter, *The Impending Crisis: 1848–1861* (New York: Harper and Row, 1976), 484; and "The Historians Use of Nationalism, and Vice Versa," in *The South and the Sectional Conflict* (Baton Rouge: Louisiana State University Press, 1968). O'Brien, *Conjectures of Order* delineates the alternately imperial, national, and colonial frameworks for proslavery efforts, as does Peter S. Onuf "Federalism, Republicanism, and the Origins of American Sectionalism," in Edward L. Ayers, ed. *All Over the Map: Rethinking American Regions* (Baltimore, MD: Johns Hopkins University Press, 1996) and Peter S. Onuf and Nicholas Greenwood Onuf, *Nations, Markets, and War: Modern History and the American Civil War* (Charlottesville: University of Virginia Press, 2006). The dynamic between the national, sectional, and federal issues beyond the slave South furnishes a central theme of Anne Norton, *Alternative Americas: A Reading of Antebellum Political Culture* (Chicago: University of Chicago Press, 1986); Lewis Simpson, *Mind and the American Civil War: A Meditation on Lost Causes* (Baton Rouge: Louisiana State University Press, 1989); David Waldstreicher, *In the Midst of Perpetual Fetes: The Making of American Nationalism, 1776–1820* (Chapel Hill: University of North Carolina Press, 1997); Harlow Sheidley, *Sectional Nationalism: Massachusetts Conservative Leaders and the Transformation of America, 1815–1836* (Boston: Northeastern University Press, 1998); and Susan-Mary Grant, *North over South: Northern Nationalism and American Identity in the Antebellum Era* (Lawrence: University Press of Kansas, 2000).

of signal triumphs in defining the United States' burgeoning republican
order. We take for granted the extent to which slaveholders tried to
shape the Confederate States of America in their own self-image. Both
hindsight and a certain national provincialism obscure how successful
men like Palmer were during the 1850s in framing a proslavery version of
American nationhood that sought to assimilate bondage to republican
norms.[12]

Scholarship on the contours of modern nationalism has provided me
a final means of honing my understanding of proslavery Americanism and
its place within larger networks of power and meaning. Social scientists
who write in a comparative vein have helped me to appreciate the depth of
slaveholders' commitment to the "nationalizing states" of both the Union
and the Confederacy. This perspective helps to remind how little masters
had in common (except on perhaps a rhetorical level) with such classic
"state-seeking nations" as Ireland, Poland, and other colonized peoples
excluded from the meaningful exercise of political and cultural power.[13]
Historians of nationalist projects in other times and places have similarly
helped me better to understand the central role that politics, religion,

[12] David Brion Davis, *The Problem of Slavery in the Age of Revolution, 1770–1823*
(Ithaca, NY: Cornell University Press, 1971) and *Slavery and Human Progress* (New York:
Oxford University Press, 1994) remain essential, though masters' remarkable power to
shape federal policy is probed by Don E. Fehrenbacher, *The Slaveholding Republic: An
Account of the United States' Governments Relation to Slavery* (New York: Oxford
University Press, 2001) and Steven Hahn, "Class and State in Postemancipation Societies:
Southern Planters in Comparative Perspective," *AHR* 95 (February 1990), 75–98. Recent
studies that reveal the comparatively marginal political role assumed by other slaveholders include Christopher Schmidt-Nowara, *Empire and Antislavery: Spain, Cuba, and
Puerto Rico, 1833–1874* (Pittsburgh: University of Pittsburgh Press, 1999); David Lam-
bert, *White Creole Culture, Politics, and Identity During the Age of Abolition* (New
York: Cambridge University Press, 2005); and Jeffrey D. Needell, *The Party of Order:
The Conservatives, the State, and Slavery in the Brazilian Monarchy, 1831–1871* (Stanford, CA: Stanford University Press, 2006).
[13] I borrow terminology first used by Charles Tilly, "States and Nationalism in Europe,
1492–1992," *Theory and Society* (February 1994), 133, and later refined in Rogers
Brubaker, "Myths and Misconceptions in the Study of Nationalism," in John A. Hall, *The
State of the Nation* (Princeton, NJ: Princeton University Press, 1998). My own attempt to
pair power (in its multiple forms) with the articulation of meaning has been informed by
Michael Mann, *The Sources of Social Power: The Rise of Classes and Nation-States,
1760–1914* (Cambridge: Cambridge University Press, 1993); Craig Calhoun, *National-
ism* (Minneapolis: University of Minnesota Press, 1997); Rogers Brubaker, *Nationalism
Reframed: Nationhood and the National Question in the New Europe* (Cambridge:
Cambridge University Press, 1996); and John A. Hall, "Structural Approaches to Nations
and Nationalism," in Gerard Delanty and Krishan Kumar, eds. *The Sage Handbook of
Nations and Nationalism* (London: Sage Publications, 2006), 33–43.

racial stratification, and war making played in the consolidation of modern nation-states.[14]

The men and women featured in this book were "representative" of the southern master class in one basic sense – as a group, they helped to fashion a powerful set of ideas, images, and political programs that represented to the world at large a collectivity variously known as the "slave interest," the "slave power," or, most simply and most effectively, "the South." As public figures, these individuals enjoyed unusual access to power and publicity and they displayed a rare talent for systematic and nuanced expression. These qualities made them no more "typical" of the approximately 400,000 slaveholders as a class than Beecher and other free labor "nationalizers" were "typical" of the even larger white middle-class populace of the North. Making this basic distinction between "representativeness" and "typicality" helps to clarify a crucial point and to shed light on a related matter – the need to assess the historical significance of individual nationalists not only according to the cogency of their programs but also according to their effectiveness in touching a chord with a broader constituency of fellow masters.[15]

Proslavery Americanism circulated far from the bustle of southern cities, and beyond the realm of printed polemics (the two most important sites of "master class nationalism"). Its image of the world-historical significance of modern "Christianized" bondage increasingly shaped the sensibilities of a plantation world where a complex blend of challenges, struggles, vulnerabilities, and assertions confronted slaveholders on a daily basis. One particularly resonant locale for considering the links between widely shared ideas and particular practices was the costal rice-growing community of Midway, Georgia, where Lincoln's election was felt as deeply as it was in Palmer's New Orleans, or in Beecher's New York. Here, a remarkable testimonial record left by the prominent Jones family reminds us of how many intricate dramas and dilemmas emerged during the closing days of 1860. Such dramas need not have driven broader

---

[14] Linda Colley, *Britons: Forging the Nation, 1707–1837* (New Haven, CT: Yale University Press, 1992); David Bell, *The Cult of the Nation in France: Inventing Nationalism, 1680–1800* (Cambridge, MA: Harvard University Press, 2001); Nancy P. Appelbaum, et al. *Race and Nation in Modern Latin America* (Chapel Hill: University of North Carolina Press, 2003); Don H. Doyle and Marco Antonio Pamplona, eds. *Nationalism in the New World* (Athens: University of Georgia Press, 2006).

[15] It is important to note that while proslavery nationalists spoke to fellow masters, they employed language capable of appealing to southern white yeomen and to northern allies as well. These dimensions of proslavery discourse deserve further attention.

historical development in order to exemplify deeper currents of shifting allegiances and understandings.

We know from surviving correspondence that the fifty-two-year-old Mary Jones reacted to Lincoln's election with every bit as much alarm as her slaveholding husband (and first cousin) Charles, who had made a name for himself as the South's most celebrated white evangelist to southern African-Americans. The Joneses' Unionism had a sentimental dimension, reaching back to the patriotic martyrdom suffered by their grandfather, who had died while defending Savannah from the British assault in 1779. At least as important, however, was their intuitive sense of how much they had benefited from a Union that assured the viability of their world of slaves and rice and cotton. In the half-century that followed American independence, Low Country Georgia had profited as much as any region from the political stability fostered by a federalized American Union. Seen from the Jones plantation residences of "Liberty Hall," "Retreat," and "Montevideo" there was little contradictory about amassing republican wealth on the basis of rice cultivated by enslaved workers, nor was there any real incongruity in the fact that the Joneses' chief slave driver, Pulaski, had been named in honor of one of those revolutionary patriots whose actions had created North America's most powerful federal state.[16]

Wielding power in the realm of national politics was something that the Jones family largely left to others, however. Their contributions as nationalists came less in the establishment of a federal polity friendly to slavery than in the imperatives of American religious life and of patriotic culture. A counterpart to Charles' efforts to gain national support for his evangelical campaign could be seen in Mary's work on behalf of George Washington's Mount Vernon during the 1850s. It was altogether natural for her to join other "Southern Ladies" to preserve a working plantation as a national shrine. Having invested her energies in such patriotic endeavors made it just as natural that the crisis of 1860 would tug at Mary's heartstrings and force her to renegotiate commitments that had not only connected the North and the South but also unified a sense of Unionist political obligation within her white household. In 1860, Mary

---

[16] My understanding of the Jones family comes from the remarkable letters reprinted in Robert Manson Myers, ed. *The Children of Pride: A True Story of Georgia and the Civil War* (New Haven, CT: Yale University Press, 1972) and in Myers, *A Georgian at Princeton* (New York: Harcourt Brace Jovanovich, 1976) and from the still more remarkable context reconstructed in Erskine Clarke, *Dwelling Place: A Plantation Epic* (New Haven, CT: Yale University Press, 2005) and discussed in Lacy K. Ford Jr. "A Paternalist's Progress: Insurgency, Orthodoxy, and Reversal in the Old South," *Reviews in American History* 35 (2007), 46–56.

Jones set about an especially difficult task in writing to her oldest son, Charles C. Jones Jr., who was then serving a term as the mayor of Savannah. She asked him to remember the day "when your brother and yourself were very little fellows" and had taken a trip to Independence Hall in Philadelphia. "At the foot of Washington's statue," Mary Jones had "pledged you both to support and defend the Union." With a full appreciation of imminent changes, Mary Jones assured her son that "*That Union* has passed away and you are free from your mother's vow." With this release came validation of her son's enthusiastic support for the state militia forces that the previous day had captured federal installations in Savannah harbor.[17]

The gesture of family unity must have been appreciated by Charles Jones Jr., whose secessionist leanings had become well known by this time. He reciprocated his mother's generosity a few weeks later, when he enclosed in a letter five chestnuts he had recently gathered from Washington's Mount Vernon estate. After suggesting that transplantation to Low Country Georgia would allow new trees to thrive, the young Jones explained his actions lest his mother mistake his broader meaning. "The memory of Washington is still as dear and . . . as sacred, as ever it was; and I know that no one more patriotically cherishes that memory or those relics than you." Moving into the future need not break all historical ties, he continued, noting that "the dissolution of the Union cannot silence those consecrated voices of the past, nor can it rob us of the relationship which we bear to . . . the Father of our Country." He closed with the simple observation that Washington "was one of us."

The fate of those chestnuts was uncertain. If Virginia transplants did survive the Low Country's summertime heat, they would grow to maturity amidst a world of free black labor rather than plantation slavery. In dissolving a union they had helped to shape, the Jones family followed other southern masters in precipitating a revolution that accomplished their own destruction. Mayor Jones suppressed all discussion of this possibility in 1861 and instead focused on how his mother, in rearing new trees, might maintain connection to a shrine suddenly separated from Georgia by a new international border. The family was elated by news in April that Virginia had finally joined the Confederate States of America and had thus brought Washington's home, along with the rest of that state's historical associations, into a new slaveholding nation. The day that Virginia

---

[17] All quotations from correspondence of Mary and Charles Jones Jr. appear in Myers, ed. *The Children of Pride*, 38, 48, 51.

seceded, Charles Jones shared his hopes once more with his mother and imagined how "a great Southern army" might make a Mount Vernon pilgrimage of its own before long. Jones spoke of the impending war in terms of national integrity rather than of slavery, though his diagnosis clearly rested on anxieties about the menace posed by a free-soil Republican party. Looking forward from 1861, he imagined how an invigorated Confederate populace might transform the process of "becoming national" from the traditional political, diplomatic, religious, and cultural initiatives toward a military effort. Southern masters seemed to be on the brink of a campaign for a new American nation, destined to enshrine elements of the past within a bracing new polity. To do so required making war on apostate Yankee Republicans, and thus to "redeem the tomb of Washington from the dominion of that fanatical rule."

PART ONE

THE GEOPOLITICS OF MASTERY

A t the close of the revolutionary war, the political relations of the independent colonies were much perplexed. Having not yet arrived at a conviction of their common interest nor being freed from the influence of their common position, they found themselves, to use a fanciful illustration, like the immense masses of ice that sometimes congregate in northern seas, floating in such immediate contact that they must close into one compact body or be tossed by the restless motions of the waters in rude and ruinous collision. But in the nature of things it was impossible that a nation could be made in one generation.

Before the action of national sympathy had given to our union the sacredness of national existence, at the very moment we assumed the responsibility of independence, there came the necessity for a national government. And here is the great anomaly in the political history of the country – the existence of a national government before we were a nation.

William Henry Trescot, *Oration Delivered Before the Washington Light Infantry*, 1847

We became a nation by the Constitution; whatever is national springs from the Constitution; and national and constitutional are convertible terms.

Jefferson Davis, "Speech at Faneuil Hall, Boston," October 11, 1858

I

Slaveholders' Stake in American Empire

Southern masters would not have worked so hard to shape American nationhood had they not done so well within a growing federal Union. The economic prosperity enjoyed by American slaveholders in 1860 set them apart from their counterparts in the rest of the hemisphere, as did the enormous authority they wielded within the U.S. government. Most proslavery Southerners appreciated how the Union's combination of security and opportunity had created a slave system that the Charleston editor Richard Yeadon described in 1857 as "imperial in extent." Despite slaveholders' growing disagreement about their collective future, few could effectively rebut Yeadon's claim that the Union had proved "the great bulwark of the institution of Southern slavery" and that the federal government had "nursed and fostered" the institution from "a feeble and rickety infancy, into a giant manhood and maturity and a self-sustaining power."[1]

A few figures and some basic geography dramatize slavery's growth within the United States between American independence and the Civil War. In 1770, fewer than half a million slaves – or one out of every five enslaved workers in the New World – lived in those mainland colonies that would win their independence from Great Britain. American slaves were concentrated along the Atlantic coast, at the fringes of a plantation complex centered in Caribbean sugar islands that were the oldest and most dynamic parts of the Atlantic economy. By the time of the secession crisis of 1860–61, the number

---

[1] Richard Yeadon, Jr., "Slavery and Its Federal Relations – The Influence of the Union on the Institution of Slavery," Charleston *Courier*, February 8, 1858; see also Benjamin F. Perry, *Speech of Benjamin F. Perry of Greenville District Delivered in the House of Representatives of South Carolina* (Charleston: J.B. Nixon, 1851), 8–10.

of slaves within the United States had increased by nearly 1,000 percent to
more than 4 million. This represented fully two-thirds of all bound laborers
across the Western Hemisphere. Emancipations in the Caribbean and in South
America reshaped the geography of New World slavery, as did that global
demand for short-staple cotton grown most profitably on mainland plantations. By the 1830s, slavery's center of gravity had shifted to the Mississippi
River Valley, where masters concentrated slaves in what became the wealth-
iest counties in the entire United States. This area's cotton boom revitalized
slavery in Virginia, the Carolinas, and Georgia; helped ensure that bondage
would flourish in the postrevolutionary Gulf coast states of Florida and Alabama; and soon spilled over into the frontier societies of Missouri, Arkansas,
and Louisiana's Red River watershed. By the 1850s, ambitious planters were
looking toward Texas and beyond, imagining the sweep of an even more
spectacular Cotton Kingdom.[2]

Economic forces – especially the global demand for short-staple cotton –
worked in tandem with a federal state that equipped slaveholders to exploit
virgin land and to continue what seemed to be a never-ending series of
profit-maximizing migrations. Southern representatives secured their interests by backing a newly powerful government late in the 1780s, thus achieving a more stable Union by 1790, just as viability in the international realm
became the most important factor in the preservation of chattel bondage.
Over the following tumultuous decade, the military and diplomatic apparatus of nationhood insulated U.S. plantations from the radicalized Caribbean
rocked by black revolution. Having secured the mainland from the threat of
"contagion," this same government ensured internal order by relocating
native inhabitants from the interior South, which in turn cleared the way
for an expansionist war during the 1840s. The constitutional structure of
Americans' "compound republic" unleashed these full federal powers in
"external" affairs while it checked most federal involvement in "internal"
matters of slavery and racial hierarchy, where the jurisdiction of the separate
states would be supreme.

Despite the suspicions of later critics, no coordinated "slave power conspiracy" designed this imperial republic to project bondage across North
America. Those who established the basis of the Cotton Kingdom in the early
decades of American nationhood were neither as grasping nor as confident as
those who, during the 1850s, sought to extend their sway to the Pacific coast,

---

[2] Figures are from Robin Blackburn, *The Overthrow of Colonial Slavery* (London: Verso,
1988), 5, 544. Don E. Fehrenbacher, *The Slaveholding Republic: A History of the United
States Government's Relations to Slavery* (New York: Oxford University Press, 2001).

across the Caribbean, and perhaps even to Brazil's Amazon Valley. Prior to 1820, slaveholding men and women could scarcely have imagined a future defined by the wealth and power accumulated by their children and grand-children. Still suffering from British military disruption of coastal plantations, masters in the early American republic tended to be more anxious than ambitious and were less intent on gaining an empire than on preventing catastrophe. Their preference for stronger federal government in the late 1780s stemmed from their perceived vulnerability. As the South Carolina Congressman William Smith put it, "when we entered this confederacy we did so from political, not moral motives," and chief among these was a desire to make American nationhood a mechanism of self-preservation.[3]

Slaveholders' effective use of federal power both secured their mastery and established their credentials as guardians of the national interest. Accomplishments that stabilized plantations simultaneously bolstered the pride of white Americans across the Union. The distinctive quality of this first stage of proslavery imperialism was its ability to entwine the interests of masters and the rest of white America and to make national heroes out of leaders like Thomas Jefferson and Andrew Jackson. Masters' association of their own interests with larger national purposes continued through the 1850s, even if these began to seem hollow to many erstwhile northern allies. In moments of candor and at times of crisis, slaveholders tended to admit that their American patriotism had always been backed up by an element of calculation. Late in 1861, the crusty James Chesnut, Sr., summed up a perspective he had developed over a long life, which made him skeptical of those intent on making war against the Union. "Without the aid and countenance of the whole United States, we could not have kept slavery," he insisted, adding, with some sense of vindication, that he "always knew that the world was against us." There was nothing mysterious or sentimental about Chesnut having been a "Union man." He simply "wanted all the power the United States gave me – to hold my own."[4]

FEDERAL UNION AND JEFFERSONIAN EMPIRE

In his public campaign for the new federal Constitution, James Madison argued, "if we are to be one nation in any respect, it clearly ought to be in respect to other nations." By framing American nationhood in avowedly

---

[3] William L. Smith in *DHFFC*, 10: 310.
[4] Chesnut quoted in C. Vann Woodward, ed., *Mary Chesnut's Civil War* (New Haven: Yale University Press, 1991), 241.

international terms, Madison drew attention to the primary challenges that Americans faced in 1788 and accurately foresaw the Union's chief preoccupation for the thirty years that followed. Unifying control of the interior and asserting a presence along the Atlantic coast were the main achievements of these years, though close behind was the quite unexpected extension of the national domain across the Mississippi River to the Rocky Mountains. Fears rather than hopes prevailed for these Jeffersonian architects of American empire, who worried about how the Union might become a European client state or fall victim to intrigues between Native peoples, slaves, and hostile imperial powers. Such scenarios would be all the more likely if the North American Union splintered into several partial confederacies or, worse still, if dozens of separate republics reintroduced the uncertainties of the European state system to North America. The "peace pact" adopted by 1790 thus helped not only to preserve a Union but also to create a federal state capable of setting American boundaries, policing who might and might not cross these frontiers, and accommodating competing sectional interests during a necessarily destabilizing process of territorial growth.[5]

Madison's fellow slaveholders had a particular interest in supporting an American nation that could be a viable presence "in respect to other nations." The occupying armies of the Revolutionary War liberated tens of thousands of slaves and thus suggested how another incursion might end the institution altogether.[6] Most realized how the vulnerabilities of plantation zones precluded an exclusively "Southern" Union. Charles Pinckney was prescient in warning his state's ratifying convention that "without Union with the other states, South Carolina must soon fall." He added that only a "Quixote" would assume that a state with such a dense slave population "could long maintain her independence if she stood alone, or was only connected with the southern states." Edmund Randolph similarly

---

[5] Madison "Federalist No. 42" in Jacob E. Cooke, ed., *The Federalist* (Middletown, CT: Wesleyan University Press, 1961), 279; David C. Hendrickson, *Peace Pact: The Lost World of the American Founding* (Lawrence: University Press of Kansas, 2003); Francois Furstenberg, "The Significance of the Trans-Appalachian Frontier in Atlantic History," *AHR* 113 (June 2008).

[6] For Madison's worries about slaveholders' vulnerability see Lance Banning, *The Sacred Fire of Liberty: James Madison and the Founding of the Federal Republic* (Ithaca, NY: Cornell University Press, 1995), 179–80, 259–61, 300. For the broader context, see Sylvia R. Frey, *Water from the Rock: Black Resistance in a Revolutionary Age* (Princeton: Princeton University Press, 1991); John Shy, "British Strategy for Pacifying the Southern Colonies, 1778–1781," in *The Southern Experience in the American Revolution* (Chapel Hill: University of North Carolina Press, 1978); and Ira Berlin, *Generations of Captivity: A History of African-American Slaves* (Cambridge: Harvard University Press, 2003), 99–157.

warned his fellow Virginians against allying with only Carolina and Georgia, two states that were "diminished in their real force, by the mixture of an unhappy species of population." A "southern confederacy" would simply not be viable, Randolph continued. "As soon would a navy move from the forest, and an army spring from the earth, as such a confederacy, indebted, impoverished, in its commerce, and destitute of men, could, for some years at least, provide a simple defense for itself."[7]

The federal government that was inaugurated in 1789 quickly proved its ability to shore up this weak southern flank. George Washington's administration signed treaties to open the Georgia backcountry to white settlement and began a process that brought free trade to the Spanish-controlled Mississippi River, which had been the most divisive sectional issue of the 1780s.[8] Then, between 1791 and 1803, the federal government successfully insulated the mainland from a series of crises that rocked the French colony of Saint Domingue, formerly the most stable and prosperous of all New World slave regimes. U.S. policymakers initially formed a unified response to the massive slave rebellion there, as rivals Thomas Jefferson and Alexander Hamilton cooperated to provide three-quarters of a million dollars in American aid to the island's planters. Shifting struggles on Saint Domingue and in France soon resulted in a partisan split that divided the American master class against itself. Federalists, who were especially strong in the Carolina Low Country, strove to increase British ties; the Jeffersonian Republicans, whose chief base of support lay in the Chesapeake, actively sympathized with the French Republic, even after the National Assembly issued an emancipation decree in 1794. By the late 1790s, as war raged in both Europe and the Caribbean, the staunchly proslavery Federalists of the Deep South began to consider how accepting the island's black governors might calm and contain the island's revolutionary turmoil. Jefferson

---

[7] Pinckney in *Debates Which Arose in the House of Representatives of South Carolina* (Charleston: A.E. Miller, 1831), 28; Randolph in Jonathan Elliot, ed. *The Debates in the Several State Conventions, on the Adoption of the Federal Constitution* (Washington, 1836), 1: 487. Jeffrey Robert Young, *Domesticating Slavery: The Master Class in Georgia and South Carolina, 1670–1837* (Chapel Hill: University of North Carolina Press, 1999), 91–98.

[8] Arthur Preston Whitaker, *The Spanish American Frontier: 1783–1795: The Westward Movement and the Spanish Retreat in the Mississippi Valley* (Boston: Houghton-Mifflin, 1927); D.W. Meinig, *The Shaping of America: A Geographic Perspective on Five Hundred Years of History, Vol. 2, Continental America, 1800–1867* (New Haven, CT: Yale University Press, 1993), 23–41; Drew McCoy, "Madison and American Nationality" in *Beyond Confederation: The Constitution and American National Identity* (Chapel Hill, NC: University of North Carolina Press, 1988). Interest in the Mississippi River in Virginia, North Carolina, and Georgia followed from the fact that of the original thirteen states, these were the last to relinquish claims to territory on the eastern shore of the river.

established a countervailing Republican position by warning how rapprochement with a government of former slaves would lead to "black crews, & supercargoes & missionaries" whose "free ingress & intercourse with their black brethren" in the United States would lead to certain disaster.[9]

The Caribbean crisis remained unresolved as the Jeffersonians concluded a successful political campaign for the presidency in 1800. During the fall of that year, a plot by the Richmond slave Gabriel to kidnap Virginia governor James Monroe suggested that slaves were being "taught to regard the French as patrons to their cause." Governor Monroe and President Jefferson responded to this jarring event by coordinating state and federal efforts to deport rebels beyond American borders, a measure that both men hoped might lay the basis for a broader program of relocating all free blacks as far away as possible from the United States. To their alarm, the Jeffersonians discovered not long after taking office that Napoleon Bonaparte hoped to accomplish very near the opposite in his initiative to restore French authority. His plans would purge Saint Domingue and Guadeloupe of its most dangerous black rebels by sending them northward to a proposed French penal colony near New Orleans. While France's strategic interest in the trans-Appalachian region would have created friction under any circumstance, the geopolitics of black revolution and forced relocation injected a new urgency in the Jeffersonian quest for control of the Mississippi Valley. While Jefferson at first asserted his willingness to cooperate with Napoleon to isolate Saint Domingue and "starve" the black leadership there, he changed course once the issue was entangled with white American control over the Mississippi Valley backcountry. If reintroducing slavery to the French colonies might eliminate a powerful example to southern slaves, doing so seemed likely to unleash massive violence, spur furious black resistance, and, worst of all for slaveholders, bring a flow of black Jacobins into Louisiana, a locale dangerously near U.S. territory. President Jefferson and Secretary of State Madison witnessed how volatile slavery's restoration in Guadeloupe could be when the French navy carried a relatively small group of black rebels disturbingly close to the U.S. coastline. The panic that resulted caused Deep South planters to seek federal aid and led the South

---

[9] Tim Matthewson, *A Proslavery Foreign Policy: Haitian–American Relations During the Early Republic* (Westport: Praeger, 2003), 24–51, 83–4; Jefferson to James Madison, February 12, 1799 in *Papers of James Madison* (Charlottesville, VA: University Press of Virginia) 17: 230–31; Laurent Dubois, *Avengers of the New World: The Story of the Haitian Revolution* (Cambridge, MA: Harvard University Press, 2004); Alfred N. Hunt, *Haiti's Influence on Antebellum America: Slumbering Volcano in the Caribbean* (Baton Rouge,: Louisiana State University Press, 1988).

Carolina governor to order the immediate execution of any "french Negro incendiary prisoners" who might be brought ashore.[10]

Bonaparte's proposals, and the accompanying specter of relocating black rebels along the Atlantic and within the Mississippi Valley, were resolved as unexpectedly as this episode had begun. Heavy losses in an attempted military campaign against Saint Domingue caused France to abandon the island and to offer the country's entire interest in the Louisiana territories to the United States. In the long term, this doubling of the national territory would be a critical moment in the formation of the American Cotton Kingdom. Yet its announcement initially caused a great many masters to fear how such a sudden extension of frontiers might embroil the country in international difficulties, give rise to a separate Mississippi Valley Confederacy, and undermine the economic viability of their own plantations (this last concern persisted among those planters who would remain wary of southwestern migration through the 1840s).[11] In 1802, the American diplomat Robert Livingston of New York systematized these geopolitical anxieties when he noted how "the unproductive labor of clearing the immense forests" seemed to be "ill calculated for slaves, since it requires long habit in the use of an ax, and a strength and activity seldom found in slaves." Dim economic prospects seemed hardly worth the risk, he continued, since collaboration between Indians and slaves would follow any introduction of slavery into what was widely considered to be a tropical frontier. "The establishment of new colonies in a marshy country and warm climate" required black as well as white labor, but this necessity held the seeds of its undoing. In all probability, expansion would produce little more than "the inroads of savages, the

---

[10] Douglas Egerton, *Gabriel's Rebellion: The Virginia Slave Conspiracies of 1800 and 1802* (Chapel Hill, NC: University of North Carolina Press, 1993); Madison to Rufus King, September 28, 1801, in *State Papers and Correspondence Bearing on the Purchase of the Territory of Louisiana* (Washington: Government Printing Office, 1903), 7; Winthrop Jordan, *White over Black: American Attitudes toward the Negro, 1550–1812* (New York: W.W. Norton, 1968), 375–402; Matthewson, *A Proslavery Foreign Policy* 106, 109. For the Guadeloupe scare, see Wade Hampton and Fontaine Maury to James Madison, August 21, 1802 in *Papers of James Madison, Secretary of State Series* (Charlottesville, 1993–) 2: 503 and Gov. John Drayton's instructions, quoted in Young, *Domesticating Slavery*, 125. Furstenburg, "The Significance of the Trans-Appalachian Frontier," provides an excellent summary of the interconnections between control of the Mississippi Valley and Napoleon's French Caribbean policies.

[11] Robert L. Paquette, "Saint Domingue and the Making of Territorial Louisiana," in David Barry Gaspar and David Patrick Geggus, eds., *A Turbulent Time: The French Revolution and the Greater Caribbean* (Bloomington: Indiana University Press, 1997), 204–225; James David Miller, *South by Southwest: Planter Emigration and Identity in the Slave South* (Charlottesville, VA: University of Virginia Press, 2002).

insurrection of slaves, the insubordination of troops, and the abuses of officers when far removed from the superintending eye of the Sovereign."[12]

Disaster remained a possibility well after a treaty transferred Louisiana to
the United States; only at the end of the six successive presidential administrations of the Virginia planters Jefferson, Madison, and Monroe would American
control of the Mississippi River Valley be firmly established and the sectional
tensions accompanying this expansion be defused. The job of cultivating the
loyalty of white Louisianans was entrusted to the Virginia native William
Claiborne, who served as territorial governor after James Monroe twice
declined the position. Claiborne's duties included enforcing the ban on slave
imports into Louisiana and helping to suppress the largest attempted slave
revolt in American history, which South Carolina planter Wade Hampton,
one of the country's largest slaveholders, crushed while serving as a U.S. general
in 1811. A foreign invasion of the region remained a threat until the Tennessee
planter Andrew Jackson defeated the British at New Orleans four years later.
Then, in 1821, Monroe brought a perspective honed as Paris negotiator and as
secretary of state to the presidency, where he authorized a treaty with the
considerably weaker power of Spain that brought all of the Florida territories
under U.S. control, thus securing the last in a series of American acquisitions
around the eastern Gulf of Mexico. The leverage of statesmen and military
leaders was greatly enhanced by a major population influx and by the arrival of
masters and slaves who replaced sugar with cotton as the region's most lucra-
tive staple. While the loyalty to the United States of these southwestern planters
owed something to their earlier residence in the Atlantic republic, what mattered most was the American government's ability to secure plantation property far more effectively than the weak Spanish, the destabilized French, or the
seemingly untrustworthy British. Options beyond these alternatives were
sparse, since any white settlement on such a dangerous frontier needed the
protection of a more powerful guardian state.[13]

---

[12] Robert Livingston memoir presented August 10, 1802 in *State Papers and Correspondence
Bearing on ... Louisiana*, 36–50. Similar concerns had hindered French development of
Louisiana slavery in the early 18th century, as Ira Berlin explains in *Generations of Captivity*,
88–96. For broader American anxieties about the purchase, see Peter Kastor, *The Nation's
Crucible: The Louisiana Purchase and the Creation of America* (Yale University Press, 2004).

[13] Kastor, *The Nation's Crucible*; James E. Lewis, Jr., *The American Union and the Problem
of Neighborhood: The United States and the Collapse of the Spanish Empire, 1783–1829*
(Chapel Hill, NC: University of North Carolina Press, 1998); Roger G. Kennedy, *Mr.
Jefferson's Lost Cause: Land, Farmers, Slavery, and the Louisiana Purchase* (New York:
Oxford University Press, 2003), 206–7; Adam Rothman, *Slave Country: American Expansionism and the Origins of the Deep South* (Cambridge, MA: Harvard University Press,
2005).

Slaveholders valued these early southwestern additions primarily because of the security they provided. Compared to later periods of territorial expansion, masters in this formative period of American empire were relatively unconcerned with the need for more plantation land and put little emphasis on the need for greater representation in the federal government. What mattered was blocking European incursions with the creation of new forts along American borders and the securing of white domination over potentially disruptive free people of color on the margins of plantation zones. Andrew Jackson's military campaigns in Creek territory and in Florida in the late 1810s effectively neutralized the threat of those Indians and free blacks who had troubled planters by harboring fugitive slaves and presenting the British with a potential alliance. Jackson's attempt to assert American control over these areas set the stage for his more controversial Indian removal policies of the 1830s, whose total cost of $68 million was more than twice the amount the federal government paid for the Louisiana territories and the Mexican Cession combined. The first stage of this process further insulated the United States from the influence of free people of color, a matter that had become a federal responsibility in 1803, when Congress passed legislation that enforced state restrictions against the entry of free blacks from the Caribbean.[14]

In a string of territorial accomplishments, the "Virginia dynasty" thus simultaneously strengthened the plantation order and protected all white Americans from potential enemies. In some respects, the Jeffersonians' emphasis on collective security was quite similar to that of earlier imperial administrators who had monitored the growth of slavery primarily in terms of better governance of distant territories.[15] The diverse consequences

---

[14] R.S. Cotterill, "Federal Indian Management in the South, 1789–1825," in *Mississippi Valley Historical Review* 20 (December, 1933), 333–52. In "Separate Interests: The Washington Administration and the Nation-State," *JAH* 79 (June 1992), Andrew R.L. Cayton contends that the Washington administration's attention to the Northwest secured that region's greater allegiance to the nation-state, though the subsequent pursuit of Indian policy was just as vigorous in the southwest, as is evident in Ronald N. Satz, *American Indian Policy in the Jacksonian Era* (Lincoln: University of Nebraska Press, 1975) (who gives the figure for expenditures at 97), Robert Remini, *The Legacy of Andrew Jackson: Essays on Democracy, Indian Removal and Slavery* (Baton Rouge: Louisiana State University Press, 1988), and Kenneth Wiggins Porter's various essays on the Seminole Wars in *The Negro on the American Frontier* (New York: Arno Press, 1971). For the restriction of free black immigrants, see Jordan, *White over Black*, 383.

[15] David Brion Davis, *The Problem of Slavery in Western Culture* (New York: Oxford University Press, 1966), 125–64; Warren R. Hofstra, "'The Extension of His Majesties Dominion's': The Virginia Backcountry and the Reconfiguration of Imperial Frontiers" *JAH* 84 (March 1998), 1281–312; Christopher Brown, "Empire Without Slaves: British Concepts of Emancipation in the Age of the American Revolution," *WMQ* 56 (April 1999), 273–306.

of their policies blunted attacks upon Jeffersonians as planter-friendly agents whose antislavery sentiments were hypocritical cant. When James Monroe negotiated with Napoleon for a clause protecting the property rights of Louisianans, his agreement might well have bolstered slaveholders' claims. But more important was this measure's effectiveness in attaching new citizens to the Union. Similarly, when Jefferson first explained the beneficial results of slavery's westward "diffusion" in an 1807 aside, his plans to "whiten" plantation districts in the East was motivated more by international viability than by sectional prerogatives. The imperial context of these measures faded in importance as later pleas for this "diffusion" solution became increasingly beholden to sectional agendas.[16]

The key event in sectionalizing Jeffersonian expansionism was the battle over Missouri statehood that roiled Congress between 1819 and 1821. Virginia Republicans took an active role in this first prolonged crisis over slavery, associating their own preferred policies with their traditional concern for the West and linking their opponents to the Northeast's willingness during the 1780s to close the Mississippi River to American traffic and to New England's more recent threats of disunion at the Hartford Convention. Madison and Jefferson each offered alarmed responses to the proposal of the New York Congressman James Tallmadge to require Missouri to adopt a gradual plan of abolition before joining the Union. Such a measure threatened the Jeffersonians' sense of how Americans' constitutional order should operate while it undermined their hope that "natural" movements of population would replace central planning as the primary force in the expansion of Americans' imperial federation.[17]

[16] Roger G. Kennedy offers a more sinister reading of Monroe's actions in *Mr. Jefferson's Lost Cause* 188, 294; Jefferson to John Dickinson, January 13, 1807, in Paul Leicester Ford, *The Works of Thomas Jefferson* (New York: G.P. Putnam's Sons, 1904–5) 9:8; see also Tench Coxe to James Madison, December 12, 1801 in *Papers of James Madison, Secretary of State* 2:306–9. For the case that Jeffersonian diffusion was disingenuous from its inception, see Robert McColley, *Slavery and Jeffersonian Virginia* (Urbana: University of Illinois Press, 1964) 173; John Chester Miller, *The Wolf by the Ears: Thomas Jefferson and Slavery* (New York: Free Press, 1977), 234–42; Donald L. Robinson, *Slavery and the Structure of American Politics, 1765–1820* (New York: Harcourt Brace Jovanovich, 1971), 439; and William Freehling, *The Road to Disunion Vol. I Secessionists at Bay 1776–1854* (New York: Oxford University Press, 1990), 151–2.

[17] Robert P. Forbes, *The Missouri Compromise and Its Aftermath: Slavery and the Meaning of America* (Chapel Hill: University of North Carolina Press, 2006); Lewis, *The American Union*; Peter S. Onuf, *Jefferson's Empire: The Language of American Nationhood* (Charlottesville, VA: University Press of Virginia, 2000), 109–17; John M. Murrin, "The Jeffersonian Triumph and American Exceptionalism," *JER* 20 (Spring 2000), 1–25.

The nation's first slavery-induced geopolitical crisis was ultimately resolved through a bundle of measures that paired Missouri's entrance with that of Maine, that established much of the remaining Louisiana territory as "free soil," and that, the following year, lent Congress' tacit approval of Missouri's restriction of free blacks from its borders. This formula, which would be in place until Congress opened these territories to slavery in 1854, continued Americans' internal "pattern of boundary making" that had begun in 1787, when the Northwest Ordinance also accommodated sectional and federal issues by dividing sparsely settled territories between slavery and freedom. The measures taken in 1787 and in 1820–21 were strikingly more successful than the two other geopolitical struggles over the North American interior, when wartime territorial gains produced more intractable internal disputes over the spoils of victory. The conquest of New France by colonists and British troops in 1763 had generated a conflict over access to the Ohio River Valley, which would be the first in a series of conflicts that led to Americans' separatist war for independence in 1775. Then, in the late 1840s, a successful war against Mexico similarly removed a foreign rival and set in motion a struggle between victors representing northern and southern interests. The legislation passed in 1820 and 1821 was thus, for all its considerable moral shortcomings, an enormously successful program of territorial consolidation. Besides securing American control of the Mississippi Valley (which was itself only made possible by victory against England in 1815), this accord forestalled sectional clashes over the west until another destabilizing series of acquisitions forced what would be the Union's decisive crisis.[18]

Yet if the Missouri compromise resolved an immediate political threat, it also laid the basis for future discord by institutionalizing sectional interests at the longitudinal line of 36′30″. Jefferson himself famously explained how "a geographical line, coinciding with a marked principle" might lead to future conflict, since "once conceived and held up to the angry passions of men" the awareness of divergent sectional interests would "never be obliterated." Shortly before the northern Louisiana territories were pledged to "free soil," Madison similarly saw danger in

---

[18] David Brion Davis, "The Significance of the Northwest Ordinance of 1787," in *In the Image of God: Religion, Moral Values, and Our Heritage of Slavery* (New Haven: Yale University Press, 2001), 201; Glover Moore, *The Missouri Controversy, 1819–1821* (Lexington: University of Kentucky Press, 1954); Forbes, *The Missouri Crisis*; D.W. Meinig, *The Shaping of America: a Geographical Perspective on 500 years of History Vol. 1: Atlantic America, 1492–1800* (New Haven, CT: Yale University Press, 1986).

differentiating between slave and free territories. "Should a state of
parties arise founded on geographical boundaries, and other physical
and permanent distinctions which happen to coincide with them, what is
to control those great repulsive masses from awful shocks against each
other?" Madison found antislavery sensibilities to be mainly at fault, as
was clear in the allegory he wrote at the time that featured a husband
(who represented the North) whose growing hatred for his wife (who
represented the South) resulted from a black stain on her arm, caused by
"a certain African dye."[19]

In 1850, William Henry Trescot spoke as a disunionist rather than an
imperialist when discussing the consequences of the 1820 legislation. With
none of Jefferson's and Madison's sense of alarm, this South Carolina
planter perceived a sign of the future in a "compromise" that marked

a broad declaration that in the American Union there are two people, differing in
institutions, feelings, and in the basis of their political faith – that the government
could not legislate for both on the same principles and on the same subject, and
therefore that as to certain matters of political interest, they must, by an imaginary
line, be separated.

Trescot followed with the provocative question: "Shall this imaginary
line become a real boundary and the two people, bidding each other a
friendly but firm farewell, enter upon their paths as separate and independent nations?" The separate proslavery republic that Trescot imagined would
be only a fragment of what had become a transcontinental United States.
That mattered little, however, since by this time the slave South alone had
become larger than the entire Union had been in 1790. Thanks to a string of
national figures, the slaveholding nation Trescot imagined stretched from
his Sea Island plantation westward for more than a thousand miles. What
had been a precarious southwestern frontier for Jefferson's republic had
been brought within the Union and made into a key node of the global
economy.[20]

---

[19] Jefferson to John Holmes in Andrew Lipscomb and Albert Ellery Bergh, eds., *The Writings
of Thomas Jefferson* (Washington, 1903–4) 10: 157–8; Madison quoted in Drew McCoy,
The Last of the Fathers, 157; Madison, "Jonathan Bull and Mary Bull: A Political
Apologue," *SLM* 1 (March, 1835), 342–45; "Mr. Madison's Allegory of North and
South," *DBR* 21 (October 1856), 369–75.
[20] William Henry Trescot, *Oration Delivered Before the Beaufort Volunteer Artillery* (Charleston: Walker and James, 1850), 7. See also Robert E. Bonner, "Empire of Liberty, Empire
of Slavery: The Louisiana Territories and the Fate of American Bondage" in Peter Kastor,
ed., *The Louisiana Purchase: The Emergence of an American Nation* (Washington: Congressional Quarterly 2003), 129–38.

FROM FLANK TO FORTRESS

In the first two decades of the nineteenth century, as Jeffersonian actions gradually alleviated the plantation South's susceptibility to foreign invasion, Jeffersonian words perpetuated assumptions about the region's military weaknesses. During the 1820 debate over Missouri statehood, antislavery advocates relied time and again on the passage from *Notes on the State of Virginia* that featured a trembling Jefferson considering how a just God might sanction the "extirpation" of southern masters by the sort of "revolution of the wheel of fortune" that Saint Domingue's whites had experienced first-hand. Jefferson updated this imagery with a new, equally arresting explanation of how American slaveholders had "the wolf by the ears" and were thus unable either to hang on or safely to let go.[21]

Shared assumptions about slavery's volatility and the South's corresponding weakness gave a political advantage to representatives of areas where free labor prevailed. As early as the Constitutional Convention of 1787, representatives of non-plantation states based their opposition to the slave trade on the burdensome duties of suppressing slave revolt. Congressional debates over the Louisiana Purchase and then over the admission of Missouri similarly elicited predictions that slavery's spread into the west would invite frontier insurrections and require a federal intervention. In 1819, Charles Rich of Vermont hearkened back to the recent war with England to conclude that it was "admitted by all . . . that some danger exists" in slave society. Such a claim informed his unwillingness to "entail [slavery] on the inhabitants of the West, and with it the obligations of protecting them against 'domestic violence.' "[22]

Masters' own self-perception of weakness led to varied results, depending on the circumstances involved. Anxieties could help to produce radical action, as was the case for at least some planters at the outset of the American Revolution and among a far wider segment of them during the 1860–61 secession crisis. But the perception of masters' vulnerability could also encourage slaveholders to defend the political status quo, as was the case

---

[21] The antislavery portions of Jefferson's *Notes* were quoted at greatest length by David Morril and Clifton Clagget of New Hampshire, Joseph Hemphill of Pennsylvania, Charles Rich of Vermont, and Joshua Cushman of Massachusetts; all in *Annals*, 16th Congress (1819–1821), 135, 1042, 1135, 1401, 1617; Jefferson to Holmes, *op cit.*

[22] Max Farrand, *Records of the Constitutional Convention* (New Haven, CT: Yale University, 1911) 2:220–1, 306–7; James Hillhouse remarks in Everett S. Brown, ed., *William Plumer's Memorandum of Proceedings in the United States Senate, 1803–1807* (New York: Macmillan, 1923), 113–25; Madison's 1789 critique of the slave trade appears in *DHFFC* 1: 649; Charles Rich, *Annals* 16th Congress, 1st session (February, 1820) 1399.

for those Caribbean planters who rejected radical political action in 1776 and for the reliably Unionist cotton planters of Natchez, Mississippi, throughout the antebellum period. The actions of the Virginia dynasty showed how deep-seated fears could shape policy-making at the highest levels. The successful resolution of the Missouri Crisis inspired James Monroe to revisit the program of African colonization he had first contemplated during the Gabriel plot twenty years earlier, to enforce with greater vigor the slave trade ban implemented in 1808, and to present programmatic opposition to European colonization in the New World. Yet for the first time in his life, Monroe also backed away during his second presidential term from further territorial expansion. In writing to General Andrew Jackson of Tennessee, Monroe explained how the fragile sectional accord reached over Missouri made it unwise to secure any new land beyond the Mississippi Valley. During his retirement in 1828, Monroe directly linked such cautious Unionism to misgivings about slavery. He warned South Carolina's John C. Calhoun (who had served in his administration as Secretary of War) that any southern attempt to forge "partial confederacies" would involve them in "a scene of the most frightful calamities, because their slaves would be excited to insurrection."[23]

There were generational as well geographical lines separating Monroe and his fellow Virginian Republicans from Andrew Jackson and John C. Calhoun. Southern leaders of Monroe's era had grown accustomed to northern attacks upon their vulnerability and had done less than one might expect to counteract them. Calhoun, by contrast, led a newly energized group of proslavery nationalists who asserted southern military strength as a new orthodoxy. Andrew Jackson, whose nationalist inclinations proved to be far more consistent than those of Calhoun, displayed confidence in action rather than theory. Along with the southwestern planter-politicians who imagined a destiny apart from the Union, Jackson dispelled anxieties by demonstrating military prowess. If frontier militarists did not deny the continuing existence of grave dangers, they increasingly doubted that slave societies were as vulnerable as their critics made them out to be. Some even began to question whether the Union was really still needed to confront threats from beyond American borders.

Over the first third of the nineteenth century, Deep South representatives had intermittently – and somewhat half-heartedly – taken to the floor of

---

[23] Monroe to Calhoun, August 4, 1828, Stanislaus Murray Hamilton, ed., *The Writings of James Monroe* (New York: G.P. Putnam's 1898–1903) 7: 173–7; Monroe to Calhoun; January 7, 1828, *PJCC* 10: 547.

THE NOBLE VIRGINIANS IN THE HEAT OF BATTLE!
They who have "wit to run away.

FIGURE 1.1. In 1820, as memories of a second British invasion of the Chesapeake were still fresh, a New England poet used this image to convey the military vulnerabilities of slave society. *From Hillhouse, Pocahontas: A Proclamation (1820), Courtesy of Duke University: Special Collections Rare Book, Manuscript, and library.*

Congress to vindicate their region's military strength. They often did so in response to the wavering of other masters, as was the case in a testy 1811 exchange that pitted Calhoun's conviction about white control against the Virginian John Randolph, who offered the more traditional warning about the menace of slave revolt. During the Missouri debates of 1820, Senator William Smith of South Carolina insisted that it was mostly ignorant out-siders, who considered his state to be "in a constant state of alarm" and "in constant danger." Despite his protests, restrictionists continued to appeal to a trembling Jefferson, to a bloodied Haiti, and to the flight of slaves to the British both during the Revolution and the war fought between 1812 and 1815 (see Figure 1.1). A decade later, with southern military embarrass-ments fading in memory, Senator Robert Y. Hayne delivered a forceful critique of "the impression which has gone abroad of the weakness of the South, as connected with the slave question." In a debate with Daniel Web-ster circulated more widely than any previous Congressional oratory, Hayne was candid about his motives, noting how such sentiments had "exposed us to such constant attacks" and done us "so much injury and is calculated to produce such infinite mischiefs."[24]

---

[24] William Smith, *Annals* 16th Congress, 1st session (January 1820), 267–70; Hayne speech of January 21, 1830 in *Webster and Hayne's Speeches in United States Senate* (n.p., 1850), 14. The unprecedented circulation of these speeches is noted in Harlow W. Sheidley, "The Webster–Hayne Debate: Recasting New England's Sectionalism," *NEQ* 67 (March 1994), 5–29.

Slaveholders were partly responsible for the vivid imagery of plantation vulnerability. In 1823, Edwin Holland adopted the memorable language of the *Edinburgh Review* in noting that slaves were "truly the Jacobins of the country," adding that they were "the anarchists and the domestic enemy; the common enemy of civilized society, and the barbarians who would IF THEY COULD, become the DESTROYERS of our race." In 1827, William Branch Giles of Virginia portrayed the murderous upheaval that would follow the mere discussion of ending slavery. Lazy freedmen would produce wide-scale starvation, he wrote, assuring a crisis in which "one part must cut the throats of the other, for the inadequate pittance which must be raised." Recalling the racial warfare of Haiti, Giles wrote "there will be no necessity for mounting the old federal black cockade to mark the reign of terror. Nature has done that work: every man will wear his cockade in his own face; and the carnage on either side must be indiscriminate." Insurrections planned by Denmark Vesey and Nat Turner lent credibility to the notion that the South was a volcano ready to explode. Reports indicated that both these rebels planned to destroy the entire white community, as did the Boston free black David Walker, whose 1829 pamphlet spurred broad concern.[25]

The systematic defenses of slavery framed in the 1830s laboriously rebutted the South's supposed military weaknesses. A prominent theme of this so-called "Great Reaction" affirmed planters' ability to defend themselves without external assistance from a Union with free states. Proslavery ideologues tended to shift the focus from the natural rebelliousness of degraded slaves to the threat posed by "savage" blacks living apart from white masters. Depicting free people of color as the major threat allowed slaveholders to draw a new set of lessons from the Haitian revolution. John Drayton, for instance, argued, "there has been no instance of a successful insurrection of negro slaves" adding that "even at St. Domingo, the revolt commenced with the free mulattos, who had been educated and disciplined in France." Similar attempts were made to establish the image of the "loyal slave" as a historical fact and to depict the American Revolution as a period of harmony between blacks and whites. Slaves' devotion to their masters

[25] [Edwin Clifford Holland], *A Refutation of the Calumnies Circulated against the Southern and Western States* (Charleston: A.E. Miller, 1822), 86; Brougham's remarks (made in Vol. 1, Article 27 of *Edinburgh Review*) are quoted in Hugh Legaré, "Captain Hall's Travels," *SR* 8 (November 1829), 358; William Branch Giles in Richmond *Enquirer*, January 20, 1827 as quoted in his *Political Miscellanies* (unpaginated collection of writings published in 1830); Eugene Genovese, *From Rebellion to Revolution: Slave Revolts in the Making of the Modern World* (Baton Rouge: Louisiana State University Press, 1975).

during war had been noted during the Missouri debates, but it received far more extensive treatment in the fiction of William Gilmore Simms and Beverley Tucker, whose 1830s novels prominently featured black slaves defending the white community. By 1842, Samuel Cartwright mustered a series of examples of slave fidelity during national emergencies in order to conclude "the Ethiopian has, in his nature, a peculiar instinct, attaching him to his master" which had served as "proof against British intrigues, British power, and British abolitionism."[26]

The acid test of this new orthodoxy was whether slaves might be armed in defense of their republican masters, an idea that was broached by Henry Laurens during the Revolution and was then discussed with notable frankness by Deep South Congressmen in 1790. In his seminal proslavery essay of the 1835, Chancellor William Harper began to systematize what had been off-handed comments regarding the enlistment of black slaves as regular fighters. American slaves, he argued, were likely to follow the Spartan example in becoming soldiering "helots" if their masters were ever threatened from without. "We might use any strictness of discipline which would be necessary to render them effective, and from their habits of subordination already formed, this would be a task of less difficulty." Slaves' "physical strength" and their tendency to be "excitable by praise" would help them to "rush fearlessly and unquestioning upon any sort of danger." Under proper white supervision, "there are no troops in the world from whom there would be so little reason to apprehend insubordination or mutiny." If such arguments promoted countervailing objections to a racially mixed fighting force, they nonetheless indicate that pleas made late in the Civil War to arm Confederate slaves were far less novel than historians have often implied.[27]

The South Carolina politician James Henry Hammond showed that proslavery theory as often emerged from experience as from historical parallels. As he joined the nullifiers' mobilization for a possible civil war in 1833,

---

[26] Drayton, *The South Vindicated from the Treason and Fanaticism of the Northern Abolitionism* (Philadelphia: H. Manly, 1836), 298; Simms, *The Partisan* (New York, 1835); [N.B. Tucker], *The Partisan Leader: A Tale of the Future* (Washington, 1836); [Dr. Samuel Cartwright], "Canaan Identified with the Ethiopian," *SQR* 2 (October 1842), 356. Abolitionists never ceased to assume secession would spur a massive slave revolt, as is clear throughout Merton L. Dillon, *Slavery Attacked: Southern Slaves and their Allies* (Baton Rouge: Louisiana State University Press, 1990).

[27] Gregory D. Massey, "The Limits of Antislavery Thought in the Revolutionary Lower South: John Laurens and Henry Laurens," *JSH* 63 (August 1997), 495–530; William L. Smith in *DHFFC* 10: 753; William Harper, *Memoir on Slavery: Read Before the Society of the Advancement of Learning* (Charleston 1838), 38. J.L. Reynolds extended this consideration of ancient helotry in "Fidelity of Slaves," *DBR* 29 (November 1860), 569.

Hammond offered the services of his plantation's "efficient male force" to South Carolina officials. Yet he made clear that these should only be used in building fortifications and other menial labor and explicitly added that they should not be armed, since doing so would be "a dangerous policy" to be justified only by "the greatest extremities." A few years later, however, as his own innovations in plantation management proceeded, his most celebrated proslavery polemic bragged that nothing would "delight" southern slaves more than fighting against other blacks armed to defeat their masters. Remaining devoted to their owners, these slaves would "assist in stripping Cuffee of his regimentals to put him in the cotton-field, which would be the fate of most black invaders." Hammond did not linger on the question of military service, instead stressing how southern African-Americans might sustain agricultural production in the event of war. With slaves cultivating essential wartime supplies, all southern white men could join the war effort, thus giving the South the ability to "put forth more strength in such an emergency, at less sacrifice, than any other people of the same numbers." Such a stance became increasingly common by the late antebellum period and became a sort of orthodoxy for devoted Confederates.[28]

As proslavery theorists from the Atlantic coast speculated about their potential strength, frontier masters displayed southern military strength in a more direct fashion. The imposition of white violence by trans-Appalachian settlers not only swept away Indians and foreign interlopers but also seemed to forestall the sort of slave conspiracies that haunted the East. The military accomplishments of plantation masters like Andrew Jackson bred among southwestern slaveholders a confidence that they might brutally govern their slaves without provoking a violent response. The growing self-assertion of masters of the nascent cotton belt increased still further in 1835, in the aftermath of a rumored slave revolt that took place that summer. The frenzied mobilization, conducted largely at the neighborhood level, provided tangible evidence that white southerners' need not call on federal force to secure their safety. John Quitman (himself a New Yorker transplanted to Mississippi) noted how "every day's experience and observation" seemed to suggest that "our domestic institutions are based upon a more solid foundation than those of the non-slaveholding states." There thus existed "more real danger from the gradual and sapping tendencies of agrarian and

---

[28] Hammond to Robert Y. Hayne, February 7, 1833 in "Letters on the Nullification Movement in South Carolina, 1830–1834," *AHR* 7 (October 1901), 96; Hammond, *Two Letters On Slavery in the United States, addressed to Thomas Clarkson, Esq* (Columbia: Allen, McCarter, & Co., 1845), 11.

fanatical doctrines which, it is evident, are making way at the North" than in the South. That the "last retreat of freedom will be in the South" would be made possible by "our institution of domestic slavery," which was "in harmony with, and almost indispensable to, a constitutional republic."[29]

This show of white force in 1835 had long-lasting political implications, as General Felix Huston of Texas made clear fifteen years later, when he recalled the "Mississippi affair" before the Southern Convention meeting in Nashville. After addressing the "vast military strength of the State, and the promptitude with which the people armed," Huston singled out "the quiet submissive terror of the slaves" for consideration, which he saw as a direct result of having "every road and nearly every path in the country ... guarded as if by magic by armed men." Huston was explicit about the deeper meaning of this episode. "All in the Northern States, and some in the Southern States, believe that the existence of slavery amongst us impairs our military strength, and renders us comparatively weak." Such a misperception had "an intimate connection with, and considerable influence in, producing the wrongs and aggressions which are inflicted on us." Until widely held falsehoods were "exploded by actual experiment" (how this would work he did not explain), "the aggressions upon our rights, feelings, honor" would continue. After over a decade and a half of arguments to the contrary, those slaveholders who still doubted that they really were a "warlike and distinct people" were likely to choose degrading compromise over the risk of disunion and the attendant prospect of civil war.[30]

Jefferson Davis expressed this new sense of the South as more of a fortress than a flank in 1848, when he told fellow Congressmen that he had "no more dread of our slaves than I have of our cattle." As a military hero in his country's first foreign war, Davis helped to crystallize the image of the "martial South" more by his example than by his reasoning. The reputation of the South's militancy and of its violent assertiveness gained new credibility with the performance of southern troops in the war of invasion and conquest of Mexico. The display of heroism beyond southern borders

---

[29] Laurence Shore, "Making Mississippi Safe for Slavery: The Insurrectionary Panic of 1835" in *Class, Conflict, and Consensus: Antebellum Community Studies* (Westport, CT: Greenwood Press, 1982), 96–127; Quitman to his brother, October 17, 1835 in J.F. H. Claiborne, *Life and Correspondence of Jon A. Quitman* (New York, 1860), 138–9. See also Robert May, "John A. Quitman and His Slaves: Reconciling Slave Resistance with the Proslavery Defense," *JSH* 46 (November 1980), 551–70.

[30] *The Military Strength of the Southern States and the Effects of Slavery Therein, Addressed to the Southern Convention, by General Felix Huston.* (n.p, 1850), 2–3, 15–16.

A SOUTHERN PLANTER ARMING HIS SLAVES TO RESIST INVASION.

FIGURE 1.2. John Brown's failed "invasion" of 1859 inspired the Virginia artist David Hunter Strother to portray slaves' fidelity and to give visual expression to what had become a crucial aspect of proslavery orthodoxy. *From Harper's Weekly, November 19, 1859, used with permission of Dartmouth College Library.*

helped to remove doubts about vulnerability raised not only during the 1814 invasion of the Chesapeake but also by the "Runaway Scrape" of the Texas Revolution. With attention to southern military capacity came a growing reassessment of the master–slave relationship. On the eve of disunion, those African-Americans who thwarted John Brown's 1859 invasion at Harpers Ferry, Virginia, became a source of comfort for a great many southern whites (see Figure 1.2).[31]

Masters' confidence in managing slaves even during periods of armed conflict allowed them to dispense with what earlier generations had seen as the greatest benefit of unified American nationhood. Once combat on behalf of the Confederacy began, the earlier disputes could move policy in unexpected directions. In his controversial proposal late in the war to enlist slaves in Confederate armies, Jefferson Davis relied as much on his own experience as on his sectional posturing. While considering a program of black enlistment that was by any measure a revolutionary departure from earlier norms, Davis remembered when he had "led negroes against a lawless body of armed white men" near his isolated plantation at Davis Bend, Mississippi. This "experiment" was what gave Davis the "assurance" as

---

[31] Jefferson Davis, "Speech on Oregon Bill," in *PJD* 3: 315. John Hope Franklin, *The Militant South, 1800–1861* (Cambridge, MA: Harvard University Press, 1956).

commander-in-chief that slaves "might under the proper conditions, be relied on in battle."[32]

TEXIAN CALCULATIONS

Mississippi's proslavery mobilization of 1835 might have been even more widely known had Memucan Hunt, Jr. written the book he planned in its immediate wake. This young North Carolina slaveholder imagined how a tribute to planter militancy, if shrewdly written, might join the more bookish proslavery efforts produced a few years earlier by President Thomas Dew of William and Mary College and South Carolina governor George McDuffie. Though Hunt relinquished his book project and became a Brigadier General in the Texas army during the summer of 1836, he did not lose interest in defending slavery from outside enemies. Over the next decade, he became among the most important proslavery voices in the Texas republic, as he navigated a set of geopolitical alternatives with attention turned more to the future of New World bondage than to the interests of the breakaway fragment of Mexico's empire.[33]

Hunt's activities never gained him much fame during his own life (see Figure 1.3). In the years since, he has been neglected even by Texas historians. Such obscurity resulted from his early diplomatic failures and the tendency of other, more tactful voices, to drown out his few public addresses. The calculations made by Hunt and other proslavery ideologues deserve consideration, however, since they framed as a matter of experience, rather than of speculation, a question of growing importance to slavery's most dedicated supporters. As a global tide of emancipation spread from one Caribbean island across most of the western hemisphere, American masters wondered whether bondage would be more secure outside or within the federal Union governed by its 1787 Constitution. The events that unfolded during the decade of Texas independence framed an altogether unsurprising answer.

---

[32] *PJD*, 5: 123n; Davis, *The Rise and Fall of the Confederate Government* (Richmond: Garrett and Massie, 1938) 1: 442–3; Davis to Campbell Brown, June 14, 1886, in *HEH*.

[33] Memucan Hunt to Willie P. Magnum, December 2, 1834 and January 12, 1836 in Henry Thomas Shanks, ed., *The Papers of Willie Person Mangum* (Raleigh: State Department of Archives, 1952) 2: 226, 373–4. Hunt mentioned a coauthor of his planned book, who was likely James Pinckney Henderson, Hunt's friend from North Carolina, the future Texas ambassador to England and France, and the first governor of Texas after its 1845 annexation to the United States. For biographical information on Hunt, see *Gen. Hunt's Letter to Sam Houston* (n.p., 1849) and "Memucan Hunt, of Texas," *DBR* 13 (October 1852), 416–19.

FIGURE 1.3. Steel engraved portrait of Memucan Hunt, Jr. *From DeBow's Review, October 1853, used with permission of Dartmouth College Library.*

Hunt joined the Texas revolt as controversies over slavery in that territory emerged as a defining issue in U.S. politics. American interest in this
northeastern Mexican province dated from the Louisiana Purchase, which
some claimed pushed U.S. sovereignty past the Sabine River. After a lull in
expansionism under the cautious second term of James Monroe, John
Quincy Adams revived American proposals to add Texas to the Union by
working with the new Mexican federation that had recently established
its independence from Spain. In 1829, as a southwestern planter from
Tennessee assumed the presidency, an anonymous writer announced that

the time had finally come to make the Gulf of Mexico's western coast "a shield of defense impenetrable to the haughty Briton, the jealous Spaniard, and the predatory buccaneer."[34]

The same year that Andrew Jackson assumed the U.S. presidency, his Mexican counterpart, Vicente Guerrero, enacted a program of slave emancipation that fundamentally changed the Texas equation. When white settlers struck for their political independence from Mexico City a few years later, their previous resistance to this antislavery decree opened them to charges of returning "free soil" to the sway of bondage, an accusation that echoed the case made against Illinois masters in the 1810s and 1820s and against pro-slavery Kansas settlers in the 1850s. The Texas confluence of political independence and slavery restoration seemed to resist the tide of recent history, since between 1820 and 1835, not only had the United States banned slavery in most of what remained of territorial Louisiana, but Latin American republics had initiated a series of nationalist emancipations and the United Kingdom began the transition from slave to free labor across its Caribbean empire.[35]

There was never a secret slaveholders' plot to gain Texas independence, as some abolitionists would claim, though there certainly were ties between several early Texas partisans and plantation interests. The precise role of these proslavery influences in initiating the Texas Republic was less important, however, than the broadly shared conviction that this territory's future and the destiny of southern slavery were inextricably linked in a way that the Louisiana Purchase had never been. During his postpresidential political career, John Quincy Adams suspected Texas enthusiasts of working to "eternize" the institution. Such accusations found an echo in the South Carolinian William Gilmore Simms' giddy anticipation in 1847 that southwestern acquisitions might secure "the perpetuation of slavery for the next thousand years." Memucan Hunt focused on the same long-term implications in 1836 when he insisted to Mirabeau Lamar, another proslavery émigré, that adding Texas to the Union would "guarantee for future ages the existence of domestic slavery." He then explained stakes that were as high as any could imagine.

The fanaticism of the world is daily increasing upon the subject of domestic slavery, and believing as I do, that Almighty God intended, and by His divine wisdom

---

[34] "A Revolutionary Officer," *Considerations on the Propriety and Necessity of Annexing the Province of Texas to the United States* (New York: GF Hopkins, 1829).

[35] Lewis, *The American Union and the Problem of Neighborhood,* 193–5. Andres Resendez, *Changing National Identities on the Frontier: Texas and New Mexico, 1800–1850* (New Haven, CT: Yale University Press, 2005).

approves this domestic relation ... I am unwilling to survive the period at which it
ceases to be ... The omission to take such steps as are best calculated to keep up our
domestic relations, is, I conceive, a disregard of such actions and principles as are
best calculated to promote the best and happiest relations, and the purest system of
government which the wisdom of man has been enabled to devise.[36]

Hunt's proslavery enthusiasm assumed new relevance early in 1837, when
he became the chief Texas representative to the U.S. government. This job came
with a set of attractive perks, which allowed Hunt to share a celebratory glass
of wine with President Andrew Jackson, to commission a bust of himself from
Hiram Powers, and to secure the confidence of such powerful southern politicians as John C. Calhoun. Proof of his effectiveness came in his successful
appeal to the Mississippi state legislature which published, as if it were their
own, Hunt's praise of slavery as the "very palladium of [the state's] prosperity
and happiness." The future of this cherished institution, Hunt's ghostwritten
manifesto argued, required the addition of Texas to the Union and the corresponding return of the "equipoise of influence in the halls of Congress."[37]
Hunt's candor gained him more popularity in the Deep South than in Washington, where the Texas question soon proved more contentious than "the
attempt to restrict Missouri, nullification, and abolitionism all combined," as
another Texas diplomat reported. Hunt blamed the failure of annexation on
slaveholding "traitors" such as the American Secretary of State John Forsyth of
Georgia, who was unwilling to risk Democratic Party unity for the greater good
of black slavery. For the next several years, Hunt worked for the Texas Republic from his new home in Galveston, helping to establish the boundary with the
United States, heading the tiny Texas navy, and proclaiming his willingness to
protect the frontier against any renewed invasion from Mexico.[38]
During his time in Washington, Hunt briefly considered how slavery might
fare better as the nucleus of a new proslavery confederacy, which would be
reconstituted around an independent Texas republic. What he described as
the "annexation of the slave holding states" to Texas would bring his state

---

[36] Adams quoted in Merk, *Slavery and the Annexation of Texas* (New York: Knopf, 1972),
210; Simms to James Henry Hammond July 17, 1847, *LWGS* 2:332; Hunt to Lamar,
October 17, 1836 in *PMBL*.

[37] George Garrison, ed., "Diplomatic Correspondence of the Republic of Texas" in *Annual
Report of the American Historical Association for the Year 1907* (Washington, 1908) 1:
150 (wine); 1:229 (Powers' bust); Hunt to R.A. Irion, March 12, 1838, ibid 1: 317. Hunt
claims he shared authorship of the Mississippi report "with one other gentleman" in his
letter to R.A. Irion, July 11, 1837, ibid. 1:239; excerpts from the report itself are in Herbert
V. Ames, ed., *State Documents on Federal Relations* (New York: Da Capo, 1970), 225–6.

[38] William H. Wharton to Stephen Austin, December 11, 1836 and Hunt to Irion, August 11,
1837, "Diplomatic Correspondence," 1: 152, 256.

"incalculable benefits" since this alliance would "have the power to overrun all Mexico and make such a disposition of that country as it may be her interest to do until it could be peopled throughout with Anglo Americans." Texas and the slave states might form "the greatest nation on earth" from a population "united to us by the strongest ties of a common interest, a common origin, and a common history." Though Hunt's views were not shared within the Texas diplomatic corps, he captured an increasing openness among eastern planters to a destiny apart from the United States.[39]

Hunt's calculation of geopolitical alternatives can be usefully contrasted with those of Mirabeau Lamar, who served as Texas president from 1839 until 1841 and who was among a small group that was committed from the outset to building up an independent Republic free of any connection with the United States. Lamar's support for perpetual Texas independence grew from his earlier experience in proslavery politics, when he had served the Georgia governor George M. Troup in the 1820s and then lost a race for the U.S. Congress on a pronullification platform in 1832. Correspondents from the East intermittently warned him of the risk to slavery within a Union increasingly dominated by free state interests. Lamar adopted a similar view in his inaugural address, which proclaimed that Texans should be grateful that they would not suffer from the "long train of consequences of the most appalling character and magnitude" they would have endured upon incorporation within the United States. An earlier draft of his address provided a more candid assessment of the "safety of the very institution upon which [Texas's] own hopes of happiness are based." In this version, Lamar wondered why Texas should join a nation that was "known to be opposed to her peculiar and essential interests" and whose citizens were "daily sending forth their denunciations against her from the fire-side, the pulpit and the council chamber" in an attempt to cast slavery in the worst possible light.[40]

---

[39] Hunt to James Pinckney Henderson, April 15, 1837 in "Diplomatic Correspondence," 1:208–11; Irion replied that "visionary schemes of a glorious Republic are less calculated to advance the true interests of our Country than the practical common sense proposition to become a part of a great nation firmly established." Hunt recanted in a later letter, writing that "nothing can so much benefit my beloved and adopted country" as joining the Union that Hunt's forebears had helped to establish. "Diplomatic Correspondence," 1:254. For the marginal place of straight-out disunionism (rather than nullification) in the proslavery politics of the 1830s, see Freehling, *Road to Disunion*, 1: 337–8.

[40] Proslavery advice for Texas to remain independent, rather than seek admission to the Union, is conveyed in letters Lamar received from A.B. Longstreet [1837]; H.C. Phelps (January 21, 1838), T.J. Green (October 10, 1838), Henry Holcombe (October 22, 1838), and J.M White (June 1, 839), all in *PMBL* 2: 1–5, 26–27, 241–2, 257–63; 3: 10–11. "Inaugural Address," and "Notes" *ibid*, 2: 316–23, 324–7.

Lamar's insistence that Texas not reduce itself to an "unfelt fraction of a giant power" continued throughout his two-year presidency, during which he pursued an imperial agenda calculated to extend the Texas Republic to the Pacific. To prepare for this destiny, Lamar moved the Republic's capital from the center of its population to the frontier outpost of Austin, pursued the same program of Indian removal his Georgia mentor George M. Troup had counseled in the 1820s, and authorized the small navy under Memucan Hunt's command to blockade Mexican ports. His authorization of much less successful military campaigns into New Mexico proved to be a step too far. Besides destroying his presidency, this initiative brought a bitter attack from Hunt and nearly caused a duel between these former friends.[41]

Remaining outside the Union also exposed Texas slaveholders to troublesome international pressures. Like later Confederate diplomats, representatives of the Texas Republic grossly exaggerated their standing in the international community while minimizing global hostility toward any hint of proslavery propagandism. Hunt's friend James Pinckney Henderson initially insisted that any treaty with England contains a provision against the entry of black sailors into Texas ports; others argued for the right to import African workers directly from Cuba, if not from Africa itself. Yet the Texans' need for European support, whether in the form of recognition, economic backing, or military assistance in a possible war with Mexico, undermined all measures tarnished with proslavery associations. As real diplomatic efforts began, British determination to include Texas within its antislavery treaty making was far more important than the self-assured defiance of Texas planters. In 1840, Lamar was forced to subject himself to foreign views, as he personally assured Lord Russell that the link between Texas ambitions and the future of slavery had been grossly exaggerated by enemies of the new republic.[42]

---

[41] William C. Binkley, *The Expansionist Movement in Texas* (Berkeley, CA: University of California Press, 1925); *PMBL* 2: 346–69, 4:2, 28.

[42] Letters to Lamar from Wm. A. Thompson (October 28, 1836), Henderson (November 14, 1838), J.T. Lamar (June 10, 1839) in *PMBL*, 1: 480–1; 2: 290–1 3: 19–20; Lamar to Lord John Russell, October 12, 1840 in "Diplomatic Correspondence," 2: 903–4. Other proslavery Texans similarly complied with antislavery sensibilities, as can be seen in Hunt's cooperation with Secretary Forsyth on the slave trade in July, 1837 and in J. Pinckney Henderson's cautious interview with Viscount Palmerston, October 14, 1837 in "Diplomatic Correspondence," 1:248–51 and 2:812. Bernard Bee later feared (wrongly it turned out) that the British would seek to halt entry of American slaves to Texas since this was clearly "migration of slaves from one foreign jurisdiction to another." See Bee to Texas Secretary of State, July 14, 1841 "Diplomatic Correspondence," 1:509. The breadth and centrality of British efforts against the slave trade is concisely conveyed in Edward Keene, "A Case Study of the Construction of International Hierarchy: British Treaty – Making against the Slave Trade in the Early Nineteenth Century," *International Organization* 61 (2007), 311–39.

British interest in Texas escalated after 1841, just as the Texas presidency passed to Sam Houston, a leader with none of the deep proslavery convictions displayed by Lamar, Hunt, and their planter constituents. The political dynamics changed dramatically with the launching of English attempts to sponsor white immigration to Texas and to encourage the development of a free labor economy there. In 1844, John C. Calhoun used his position as the American Secretary of State to accuse England of attempting to extend emancipation from her own Caribbean colonies to free labor zones in Texas and Spanish Cuba, an apparently concerted effort to encircle the South with enemies, to undermine its cotton production, and to bring the Haitian revolution to its shores after a half-century hiatus. Calhoun's overt identification of slavery and annexation doomed the Senate treaty that was crafted to bring Texas as a full-fledged state into the American Union. Andrew Jackson came out of retirement to repair the damage, making the traditional argument for national security and throwing his support to James K. Polk's presidential bid, which would be waged with the tacit assurance that Texas annexation would be balanced by demands for American rights in Oregon. The admission of Texas to the Union was a precarious victory, achieved by only the slimmest of Congressional majorities. Free-state suspicions about this newest addition had enormous consequences, in setting an already divided country on course for war with Mexico and marking what the historian David Potter memorably termed the "ominous fulfillment" of American nationalism.[43]

Within Texas, the conniving between Sam Houston and British free-labor interests convinced proslavery ideologues that they faced their own "critical period" that was every bit as dangerous as that which had faced the Atlantic states during the 1780s. Once more, the geopolitics of mastery depended more than ever on the strength of a viable American Union. Hunt, who never seriously believed that independence was preferable to annexation, resumed ties in 1844 with American proslavery politicians like Calhoun while he took his case for joining the United States directly to his fellow Texans. In a widely noted address, Hunt recapitulated Calhoun's case against British abolitionism and explained how French wavering about bondage cast doubts on any prospective Texan-French cooperation. "Can we close our eyes to the important truth," he asked Texas voters, "that the Constitution

---

[43] Merk, *Slavery and the Annexation of Texas*; Freehling, *The Road to Disunion* 1: 353–452; David Brion Davis, *Slavery and Human Progress* (New York: Oxford University Press, 1984), 236–41; David Potter, *The Impending Crisis, 1848–1861* (New York: Harper and Row, 1976), 1. Joel Silbey, *Storm over Texas: The Annexation Controversy and the Road to Civil War* (New York: Oxford University Press, 2006).

of the American Union is at the moment the strongest bulwark, and almost the only protection against the growing power, the fanaticism, and the reckless violence of Abolitionism?" Then, with an ironic nod to Jefferson, he noted in closing how "the fate of unborn millions" rested on the willingness of Texas voters to affirm its political connection to the United States.[44]

After a Texas referendum assured the state's entry into the Union, Hunt shifted his attention from plantation slavery to the development of Texas railroads, a preoccupation that would consume his efforts until his death in 1856. Lamar kept the focus on the mixed prospects of southern slavery for a longer period of time. Finally admitting that the weakness of the Texas republic had imperiled "the best relation which has ever been established between the laboring and governing portion of mankind," Lamar roused Georgians by calling annexation "a thousand times more important to the South for the gigantic calamities which it will prevent, than for the immediate and positive blessings which it would bring, as great as they are." He based his case for union between "Texas and the South" on his belief that they were "two countries drawing their vitality from the same fountain; and therefore involved in a common destiny for good or ill." Like "the Siamese-twins," these were "bound together by a strong, natural ligament, which if severed, must bring death to both." To Texans, he made a slightly different case, insisting that only slavery had prevented the Republic from having "dwindled into pastoral ignorance and inefficiency." In accounting for why he relinquished his earlier well-known hostility to annexation, he explained "when I saw our government in collusion with England," he had "paused in my opinion and turned to seek for my country a shelter from the grasp of British cupidity beneath the only flag under which her institutions could be saved from the storms that threatened her."[45]

Back in 1839, Lamar had warned that annexation to the Union "once taken would produce a lasting regret, and ultimately prove as disastrous to liberty and hopes, as the triumphant sword of the enemy." Soon after Texas became a state in 1845, he saw these fears materialize and once more became convinced that antislavery forces in the North would imperil bondage within a newly expanded United States. Rejecting all talk of compromise over the

[44] Hunt to John C. Calhoun, October 2, 1844 and December 19, 1844 in *PJCC* 20: 20–22, 591–2; Hunt, *To the People of Galveston*, March 28, 1845 broadside held at BLY; David E. Narrett, "A Choice of Destiny: Immigration Policy, Slavery and the Annexation of Texas" *Southwestern Historical Quarterly* 100 (January 1997), 271–302.
[45] *Letter of Gen. Mirabeau B. Lamar, Ex-President of Texas, on the Subject of Annexation, Addressed to the Several Citizens of Macon, Georgia* (Savannah: Thomas Purse, 1844), 8, 15, 43; "To T.P. Anderson and Others, November 18, 1845" *PMBL* 4.1: 113.

territories acquired through war with Mexico, Lamar argued in 1850 that a
Union that "was intended to be a shield and bulwark to every section" had
"now assumed the aspect and character of a ferocious confederation of malignant powers for our utter ruin and desolation." Future generations, he
insisted, would have to fight for the only real option – complete and irreversible secession of all slave states from the federal Union.[46]

The secession crisis of 1850 both prompted Lamar to recur to positions
taken a decade earlier and caused him to address the issue of slave rebellion
for the first time in his public life. Like his former army comrade Felix Huston,
he believed that slaves were no more likely to revolt outside the Union than
within it, and he insisted that a race war, if it did occur, would not destroy
southern whites, as many masters feared. Yet Lamar was simultaneously
gloomier about future prospects and more avowedly "philanthropic" than
most frontier leaders in explaining the two most likely alternatives. If masters
formed a separate confederacy of slave states, a long and bloody war with the
rest of the Union would produce "border strifes – formidable invasions –
sudden incursions and bloody retaliations." Remaining in a Union beholden
to free state interests, however, would allow abolitionists to incite otherwise
innocent slaves to revolt, bringing about "the total butchery and destruction
of a race whose welfare and happiness every Southern man feels bound to
consult as well as his own." Given these choices, Lamar explained the proper
course of action in the guise of a paternalist:

if we are to be forced against our wishes into a great battle on this slavery question, it
is infinitely better that we should fight with the abolitionists, than with our own
slaves, – Let us not war with our friends, but our enemies – not against those who
serve us, but those who wrong us – not against the defenseless whom it were cruelty
to slay, but against those demons of disturbance, whose conduct will deserve every
blow we deal.[47]

Once Texas joined the United States, efforts to establish a separate proslavery confederacy required launching an unprecedented drive for secession
from the federal Union. Lamar realized how much more difficult this particular route had become, and after his failed attempt to lead Texas secession in
1850, he worked within the United States to influence how that government's
considerable power might best protect masters' interests. In what would be
his final calculation, Lamar accepted an appointment to serve as the
Buchanan administration's representative to Nicaragua, an area that in the

---

[46] "Inaugural Address;" *Gen. Mirabeau B. Lamar's Letter to the People of Georgia* (Mobile,
1850), 6–8.
[47] "To S.J. Ray and others" August 16, 1850 in *PMBL* 4.1: 271–2.

mid-1850s became the latest arena for determining slavery's New World destiny. His tough plea to Nicaraguan authorities in 1858 said less about bondage than about transit routes from the Atlantic to the Pacific. The clout he held in these negotiations was a marked contrast to the feeble attempts to extend a Texas empire over New Mexico a decade and a half earlier. The intervening years had taught Lamar about the realities of global power and allowed him to speak from experience in insisting how a treaty between an isolated republic and the United States secured mutual benefits. Such an alliance, he advised the Nicaraguans, would "not only bind the two nations in the bonds of perpetual friendship, harmony, and mutual interest" but would also allow them to realize the future by working to "lay the foundation of an instantaneous and glorious prosperity."[48]

CONTINENTAL EMPIRE AND THE FATE OF AMERICAN SLAVERY

In 1847, the Richmond *Enquirer* heard the same "fire bell at night" that had alarmed Thomas Jefferson during the Missouri crisis of 1820. This bell would keep ringing for the next thirteen years, until Abraham Lincoln's election on a free soil platform served as a fitting climax to what became the most divisive issue of nineteenth-century American politics. The sequence of events over this span has been detailed many times before. The controversy over territorial slavery was kindled by the Wilmot Proviso's attempt to ban slavery from the Mexican Cession even before any territory had been acquired. The crisis in 1850 over the admission of California set the stage for an even fiercer contest for Kansas, a territory that had been committed to free soil by the Missouri compromise of 1820. These battles coincided with efforts of slaveholders and their allies to acquire Spanish Cuba and to carry American slaves across the Caribbean, to Central America, and into the Amazon Valley of Brazil. A new vocabulary of an "irrepressible conflict," a "higher law," and of an "impending crisis" developed in these years, as territorial competition seemed to push rival sectional social systems towards all-out war.[49]

---

[48] Lamar to G. Juarez, March 20, 1858 in *PMBL* 4.2: 124–5.

[49] Richmond *Enquirer*, February 18, 1847. Among the most helpful interpretations of expansionism are Robert May, *The Southern Dream of a Caribbean Empire, 1854–1861* (Baton Rouge: Louisiana State University Press, 1973), William Freehling, "The Complex Career of Slaveholder Expansion," in *The Reintegration of American History: Slavery and the Civil War* (New York: Oxford, 1994), 158–75; and Michael A. Morrison, *Slavery and the American West: The Eclipse of Manifest Destiny and the Coming of the Civil War* (Chapel Hill, NC: University of North Carolina Press, 1997).

The debates over slavery in federal territories, in forming the main narrative of the American 1850s, are usually presented as a precursor to formal military conflict. Of course, this was true in many respects. Slaveholders themselves were acutely aware that the tensions over expansion threatened to spark civil war, and an increasing number welcomed such an outcome. But historians' fixation on the sectional "balance of power" has obscured masters' other geopolitical considerations and has directed attention away from slaveholders' speculation about other aspects of slavery's providential fate. As in earlier episodes, slaveholders used the territorial question to ponder the future of both their country and their mastery, combining old concerns with new perspectives. Senator Andrew Butler's invocation of another Jeffersonian phrase in 1847 typified this pattern. While he warned southerners that they had "the wolf by the ears" – and could neither hold it nor let it go – he did not share Jefferson's fears of the paralyzing effects of slaveholding. For him and other South Carolinians, the wolf represented not slavery, or even the North, but an American continental empire that threatened to transform itself from a guarantor of security to the agent of slaveholders' destruction.[50]

Southern masters looked to the newly expanded West more convinced than ever of their just claims to the region. Jeffersonians had resisted slavery restriction in 1820 by emphasizing their own role in securing the Mississippi Valley for the United States and by stressing the hostility New Englanders had earlier showed to western settlers. Masters in the late 1840s developed similar arguments but pushed them farther, placing a new emphasis on the South's participation in the Mexican War. Defenders of slavery were quick to note that nearly two-thirds of the invading armies had been raised in the slave states and that plantation society had provided heroes in the figures of Jefferson Davis, Zachary Taylor, John Quitman, and Alexander McClung. Denying Southerners "access" to territories that they had helped to win was especially unfair given who had done the fighting. Slaveholders' pleas for equitable treatment thus held far more appeal than the novel (and relatively abstruse) constitutional positions formulated by John C. Calhoun and the Southern Rights' theorists of the 1850s.[51]

---

[50] Butler, "Senate Speech of February 18, 1847," CG 29th Congress, 2nd session, 450; Ernest McPherson Lander, Jr., *Reluctant Imperialists: Calhoun, the South Carolinians, and the Mexican War* (Baton Rouge: Louisiana State University Press, 1980).

[51] "The Army in Mexico," *DBR* (October and November, 1848), 369; "A Virginian," [M.R.H. Garnett] *The Union, Past and Future: How it Works, and How to Save It* (Charleston: Walker and James, 1850), 6; [Calhoun], "The Address of Southern Delegates in Congress, to the Constituents," January 22, 1849, *PJCC* 26: 225–44; Elwood Fisher, *Lecture on the North and the South* (Portsmouth, VA: D.D. Fiske, 1849).

Territorial expansion of the late 1840s also subtly changed debate over the political "balance of power" between free and slave states, a notion first developed during the debates over Missouri and Texas and which had been extended by the paired admission of Michigan with Arkansas and of Iowa with Florida. When the even split between free and slave states ended with California's admission in 1850, the standard of measurement changed, and the important test became whether slaveholders could retain an effective veto of constitutional change by holding on to power in at least a fourth of the states of the Union. The sheer size of the continental empire led Muscoe Garnett to calculate that slavery's restriction would create a grand total of 66 free states, a tally that would swell to an even larger number in the likely event of additions from British Canada. The South's share of 15 slave states might dwindle too, given the tepidness about bondage evident in Delaware, and even at times in Virginia. For Edward Bryan, the threat posed by new free settlements in the West required masters to "review our position in this precarious game of putting new States on the chess-board, and calculate the chances of check-mate." Merely opening territories to slavery was not enough for Bryan, who insisted that only a resumption of the African slave trade could populate future slave states. Though there were formidable political difficulties with reversing the 1808 ban on slave imports (a signal Jeffersonian accomplishment), Bryan's calculation had a certain logic, which would entice even cautious Unionists such as Alexander Stephens of Georgia.[52]

There was clearly a deep sectional dynamic at work in expansionist proposals of the 1850s, most of which acknowledged how slavery's growth would offset the number of free states likely to be formed from the Mexican Cession. But pleas for a new round of southern expansionism also drew upon long-standing strategies of insulating American slavery from threatening foreign powers. International geopolitics were most evident in the campaign for Cuba, which in 1853 focused on threats of British-sponsored "Africanization" of the island and thus drew on the same vein of Anglophobia that John C. Calhoun had tapped in his 1844 warnings about British "meddling" in the case of Texas. In Central America, the international calculus involved national and racial predominance rather than slave rebellion. William Walker's plan to introduce slavery to Nicaragua gave a

---

[52] [Garnett], *The Union, Past and Future*, 8–9; Edward B. Bryan, *Letters to the Southern People Concerning ... the African Slave Trade* (Charleston: Walker and Evans, 1858), 41; Stephens "Farewell Address at Augusta, July 2, 1859," in Henry Cleveland, ed., *Alexander Stephens: Letters and Speeches* (Philadelphia: National Publishing Company, 1866), 646–7.

sectional twist to what had been his earlier emphasis on a national civilizing mission. In Walker's view, slavery was a quintessentially "American" means of subduing the wilderness through the use of bound labor.[53]

The projection of American power had already eliminated most foreign threats in areas directly adjacent to southern plantation zones. Demands for proslavery buffer areas within the Union thus tacitly admitted that it was free white settlers, not hostile foreigners, who posed a menace to the slaveholding regime. In demanding the introduction of slavery to Kansas, the Missouri Senator David Atchison concluded that by defying the 1850 Fugitive Slave Law, free neighbors would gradually siphon off his state's human property. Atchinson's failure to explain why Missouri's long border with Illinois had not had the same effect suggested that he was more interested in greater proslavery representation in Congress than in border safety. His similarly weak case that free state neighbors would be a prod to slave rebellion borrowed notions about threats once posed by Spanish, British, or Indian forces without acknowledging the important differences between these powers and white American citizens. The reality was less important than perceived antislavery intentions, however, which slaveholders publicized by pointing to the most inflammatory language they could find. They repeatedly invoked the threat issued by the Ohio Congressman Columbus Delano in 1847 to "establish a cordon of free states that shall surround" the slave South and to "light up the fires of liberty on every side until they melt your present chains and render all your people free." They also attributed to northern enemies threats to surround slavery like a scorpion, which would then sting itself to death or to extinguish slavery by surrounding it, just as one might kill a tree by girdling it.[54]

Each of these images lent credence to the growing conviction that slavery must either "expand or die." This new consensus would be adopted both by slaveholders and by leaders of the Republican Party and would achieve its most forceful expression in John Cairnes' *The Slave Power*, one of the most influential European considerations of the American Civil War. The conviction that the social formation of bound labor would expire if limited in its

---

[53] C. Stanley Urban, "The Africanization of Cuba Scare, 1853–1855," *Hispanic American Historical Review* 37 (February 1937), 29–45; *Speech of Lawrence M. Keitt at Orangeburg, SC* (np 1855); William Walker, *The War in Nicaragua* (Mobile: S.H. Goetzel, 1860).

[54] Columbus Delano in CG 29th Congress, Session 2, Appendix 281; responses began immediately (see Charleston *Mercury*, February 17, 1847) and continued through secession (see Robert Toombs' speech of November 13, 1860 in William Freehling and Craig M. Simpson, eds., *Secession Debated: The Georgia Showdown of 1860* (New York: Oxford, 1992), 40).

territorial extent marked a new stage in considering its westward future. As a slogan, the demand that slavery needed room for its very survival was effective, and it came to be as popular as the demand that territory won by southern blood should be open to southern settlement. But there was a mystical note struck in much of this writing that presented slavery as an organic entity, whose vitality depended on continual development toward ultimate perfection. Such a proposition resembled in many respects the shift in how issues of nationhood were then being understood. Social systems like slavery increasingly resembled those national entities that were part of a providential economy whose destiny would be determined less by human agency or by social forces like political economy than by higher powers whose ultimate intentions eluded human comprehension.[55]

The editor James De Bow was predisposed to understand slavery expansion in a more traditional fashion, accepting the same basic framework of political economy utilized by Jefferson and Madison as well as by those British writers who debated the "Mighty Experiment" of Caribbean free labor. For him, the economic and social consequences of relocating black workers depended on such variables as the relative density of population, the demand for products enslaved workers grew, and the vicissitudes of competition from other parts of a globalizing economy. De Bow never saw territorial expansion as an inherent principle of bound labor, and he advocated the future absorption of surplus labor in southern factory work rather than on far-flung western plantations.[56] Others who wrote for De Bow shifted discussion within the magazine from statistics to slogans, thereby making slavery's territorial future part of a cosmic unfolding of providential will. Beginning in the early 1850s, writers for *De Bow's* set aside the Jeffersonian understanding of "slavery diffusion" as an instance of political economy and instead took up how slaves might drain from the

---

[55] John Cairnes, *The Slave Power; Its Character, Career, and Probably Designs; Being an Attempt to Explain the Real Issues Involved in the American Contest* (New York: Carleton, 1862). One of the most intriguing attempts to connect an organically developing slave system to the rise of a distinctive nationality can be found in [James Chesnut, Jr.], "The Destinies of the South" *SQR* n.s. 7 (January 1853), 178–205. Providentialism was hardly a new perspective, of course, though its growing tendency to infuse discussions of slavery can be followed in Nicholas Guyatt, *Providence and the Invention of the United States, 1607–1876* (New York: Cambridge University Press, 2007), 214–58.

[56] De Bow, "The Origin, Progress, and Prospects of Slavery" *DBR* (July 1850), 9–20; idem, "Southern Population – Its Destiny," *DBR* 13 (July 1852), 18–19; Robert F. Durden, "J.D.B. De Bow: Convolutions of a Slavery Expansionist" *JSH* 17 (November 1961), 441–6. For the British application of political economy to emancipation, see Seymour Drescher, *The Mighty Experiment: Slavery versus Free Labor in the British Caribbean* (New York: Oxford University Press, 2002).

United States South toward their ultimate destiny in the tropics. Robert J. Walker had helped to make this southern dogma in an 1843 pamphlet urging Texas annexation. Others took it up and made it a tropical variant of manifest destiny, which might be applied toward slavery's spread into Cuba (as Dr. J.H. Van Evrie proposed) or toward the Amazon Valley (as the Virginia naval theorist Matthew Fontaine Maury argued). Imagining the massive movement of black workers toward tropical slavery thus formed a proslavery counterpart to the American Colonization Society's vision of developing free "civilization" along the coast of Africa.[57]

As some defenders of slavery widened their geographical perspective, others made bold new attempts to place slavery's growth in ever-broader chronological and conceptual frameworks. An anonymous essayist posed the deceptively simple question in his title, asking: "The Black Race in North America: Why was their Introduction Permitted?" His lengthy answer insisted that American slavery had been a pivotal force in modern history, since slave pioneers had settled the key issues of the Reformation by helping to make the North American wilderness into a Protestant bulwark against Roman Catholicism. The specifics of this intricate argument were less important than its emphasis on the universal significance of slavery's spread across the continent, a move that elevated shared understandings of national mission over the bloody turmoil then underway in Kansas. When slavery expansion was lifted out of this cosmic narrative it became merely "a bundle of riddles, a mass of anomalies, a chaos of contradictions." Once recognized as the "key to American history," proslavery expansion could be seen with "light and order" as "apparent discord" became "harmonized throughout."[58]

In building toward its sweeping formulations, this article intriguingly recast the connection between slaveholders' martial abilities and the South's "quasi-military constitution of society." The mastery of commanding whites over their conscripted black troops was nothing less than "the key of southern society and history, the solver of problems, the

---

[57] *Letter of Mr. Walker, of Mississippi, Relative to the Annexation of Texas* (Washington: Globe Office, 1844), 11–16; Dr. Van Evrie. "Slavery Extension" *DBR* 15 (July 1853), 1–13; M.F. Maury, "Direct Foreign Trade with the South," *DBR* 12 (February 1852), 126–48. Few seemed to be aware of earlier failures to introduce slavery to the Amazon, a point developed in Colin M. MacLachlan, "The African Slave Trade and Economic Development in Amazonia, 1700–1800," in Robert Brent Toplin, ed., *Slavery and Race Relations in Latin America* (Westport, CT: Greenwood Press, 1974), 112–45.

[58] "The Black Race in North America; Why was their Introduction Permitted?" *SLM* 21 (November, 1855), 641–84. *DBR* republished this article over the course of the following year, guaranteeing it an unusually large circulation and exposure.

reconciler of apparent contradictions, the revelation which explains all and enables us to stand up with open front and demand, not the charitable but the just verdict of the civilized world." An army that banded white officers and black workers against the common enemy of the American forest promised to give republican liberty a territorial empire of its own. Together, masters and slaves had already fought as "knights of the axe" in subduing the wilderness for Protestant freedom, leaving whites alone to take up the sword when human enemies tried to stop their American expansion across the continent. The completion of American supremacy, which coincided with the perceived doom of Catholicism in Europe, opened a new chapter, whose details were still to be determined. The ultimate disbanding of black fighters from this army of civilization might require the removal of manumitted slaves to Liberia, the Amazon Valley, or to Central America. White Americans' newest mission thus lay in pre-venting the African "exotic" (now changed from destroyer of forests to a plant), from acting to "strangle the trunk about which it has twined itself," and working instead to assure it would be "rooted up and transplanted to a more congenial soil."[59]

Similarly sweeping accounts proliferated during the Civil War, when Confederate nationalists framed slaveholders' global mission in similarly world-historical terms. Both antebellum and wartime visions of what expansion had meant emphasized slaveholders' relationship to a superintending Providence, a concern that minimized considerations of not just political economy but also those geopolitical dynamics that had transfixed earlier generations. There was a crucial difference between proslavery imperial visions put forth before and after secession, however, since prior to 1861, masters had little difficulty in trumpeting their quest for new territories as part of nationalist expansion. Slaveholders' power in U.S. politics underlay such assumptions, as can be seen in the breath-taking proposal made by the South Carolina promoter James Gadsden to Jefferson Davis in 1854. After having negotiated the purchase of the Gila River Valley from Mexico (bring-ing what would become southern Arizona into the Union), Gadsden set his sights on American stewardship of "a great federation of West Indian islands." Even Davis, who was at that moment using his position as Secre-tary of War to vindicate slaveholders' interests, might have been taken aback by Gadsden's suggestion that "the United States, true to her own interests" might "take the initiatory to protect the white race in St. Domingo, and give them the opportunity of recovering their power in that garden of Eden, from

[59] Ibid.

whence French incendiarism drove its Adams and Eves." Once Americans returned the cradle of black republicanism to a prelapsarian paradise of bondage, Gadsden predicted that "Hayti and Domingo would sing anthems to their deliverers from barbarism and her regeneration under the restoration of African slavery."[60]

Such bursts of rhetoric convey slaveholders' late antebellum exhilaration, even if they make it difficult to evaluate the exact relationship between building an American empire and rolling back the tide of emancipation. Giddiness should not obscure the corresponding anxieties that remained present at nearly every step of the process. Masters' governance of the American empire was widely understood to be a conditional state, dependent on the continued alliance with friendly partners in the free states. After 1854, masters' greatest fears concerned the rise of the Republican Party, and the threat that a free soil administration was poised for control of a federal government that had proved more powerful in shaping the North American continent than most would have expected. Late in 1860, when Republicans won the presidency, American imperialism entered a new phase that few slaveholders could ignore. Lincoln's opponents had pilloried him throughout his campaign for associating his free soil stance with Jeffersonian principles. A carefully crafted antebellum platform ultimately did not matter, since instead of being encircled and put on the road to "ultimate extinction," slavery was killed outright on the battlefield during the Union's war of invasion. Among the greatest factors that pushed Lincoln to embrace emancipation as a war measure was his own Jeffersonian conviction that the Mississippi Valley be held intact and that incursion from rival powers be prevented at all costs.

The day after Abraham Lincoln's election, Judah P. Benjamin expressed profound ambivalence about what American empire-making had ultimately accomplished. Achieving a continental domain led Americans away from their true constitutional principles, he argued, by convincing them that a Union meant to be federal in form was in fact an indestructible nation, whose continued existence was more important than the fate of any of its member states. In remarks delivered in California, the Louisiana Senator and future Confederate Secretary of State made the impolitic suggestion that the United States might have been better off had Thomas Jefferson refused the trans-Mississippi American domain that both speaker and his audience now called their home. The bizarre comments provided an appropriate epitaph for a Union that seemed likely thereafter to imperil the geopolitics

---

[60] James Gadsden to Davis, July 19, 1854 in *PJD* 5: 78.

of mastery. Slaveholders' experiment with national strength and international security in one federation was ending. On the horizon lay an altogether riskier step toward a new Confederate empire many masters would
work to make exclusively their own.[61]

---

[61] Judah Benjamin, *An Address upon the General Changes in the Practical Operation of our
Constitution Compared with its Theory, Delivered by Invitation of the Church of the
Advent, November 7, 1860* (San Francisco: Royal P. Locke, 1860), 16–17. Benjamin had
traveled to California on legal matters and would return to Washington in time for the
Senate to debate the Southern response to Lincoln's election.

2

The Compound Republic and the Cause of the South

Many of the same slaveholders who gloried in expanding their country's territorial borders congratulated themselves on keeping constitutional boundaries firmly in place. Their enthusiasm for wielding the power of the United States was thus offset by serious reservations about actions this same government might take at home. The vulnerability of slave society connected these seemingly opposing tendencies, shaping the aggressiveness of the "slave power" while nurturing that so-called "states' rights fetish" that persisted well after emancipation. The men and women who established these traditions considered their stances in more positive and expansive terms than such labels convey. White southerners understood their defense of a decentralized version of state sovereignty as a vital contribution to American liberty, just as they considered their march across the continent as achieving American grandeur.[1]

Proslavery constitutionalism has often been dismissed as an arid orthodoxy concerned primarily with the right of secession. Such associations have had less to do with antebellum constitutionalists than with the turgid postbellum apologies of Jefferson Davis, Alexander H. Stephens, and Albert Taylor Bledsoe. Antebellum practitioners were considerably more innovative than those who followed, being less intent on dissolving the Union than on defining the nature of a complicated federal Union and, broader still, on applying constitutional perspectives to an ongoing debate about American

---

[1] Arthur M. Schlesinger, "The State Rights Fetish," *New Viewpoints in American History* (New York: Macmillan, 1922); a searching critique of this tradition can be found in Orlando Patterson "The Unholy Trinity: Freedom, Slavery, and the American Constitution," *Social Research* 54 (Autumn 1987), 543–77.

nationhood. The historian David Potter shrewdly observed that the United States was perhaps "the only nation in history which for seven decades acted politically and culturally as a nation, and grew steadily stronger in its nationhood, before decisively answering the question of whether it was a nation at all." This debate over American nationhood rested not on theories of ethnic, cultural, or mythic origins that marked European political struggles of the same years. It turned instead on differing interpretations of the country's founding charter of 1787. Southerners were divided among themselves about the ultimate nature of the federal Union framed by a secret Philadelphia convention in the summer of that year. The state sovereignty arguments popularized by John Taylor and John C. Calhoun offered one version of events, which contested the nationalist positions articulated by John Marshall and Andrew Jackson. Looming over all these constitutional narratives were the indispensable formulations of the Virginia master James Madison.[2]

Historians have long appreciated Madison's centrality in framing the Constitution, assuring its ratification, and interpreting it over the course of the last forty years of his life. Few have noted how Madison's writings formed a touchstone in slaveholders' efforts to resolve the tensions between their own imperialism and the constitutional firewalls they built against majoritarian attempts to retard slavery's development. The "compound republic" that Madison set forth in the *Federalist Papers* proposed two realms of government that, in resisting any hostile encroachment from the other, could exemplify how "ambition must be made to counteract ambition." Jefferson Davis of Mississippi thought that such a system of intricately connecting parts and dual sovereignties, existing in multiple centers, was both "the best political organism which has ever existed among men" and "the most complicated in its machinery." Complexity assured that the nature of the Union would generate ongoing debate and contention, sparking political energies while providing direction and meaning concerning ultimate issues of identity and allegiance.[3]

---

[2] David Potter, *The Impending Crisis, 1848–1861* (New York: Harper and Row, 1976), 479.

[3] Lance Banning, *The Sacred Fire of Liberty: James Madison and the Founding of the Federal Republic* (Ithaca, NY: Cornell University Press, 1995); "Federalist 51" in Jacob E. Cooke, ed., *The Federalist* (Wesleyan University Press, 1961), 347–53; Jefferson Davis, "Address Before the Phi Sigma and Herman Societies," in *PJD* 4: 281. The interrelations of federative forms and overlapping political identities are thoughtfully addressed in Trish Loughran, *The Republic in Print: Print Culture in the Age of U.S. Nation Building, 1770–1880* (New York: Columbia University Press, 2007).

Slaveholders' most precarious interests were bound up with constitutional struggles throughout this process, though they were not always explicit about links between their constitutionalism and their mastery of human property. Planters won important initial victories in the framing of the federal government, where they achieved partial representation for their slaves, temporarily delayed a ban on the slave trade, and assured a means of claiming fugitives who crossed state lines in pursuit of freedom. Even more impressive victories followed, however, in determining the "grand boundary" between the state and the federal jurisdictions. What the historian William Wiecek has termed the "federal consensus" made slavery all but untouchable within those states where it existed, an advantage that was more important than any other in helping American slaveholders to resist the hemispheric trend of emancipation. In the end, many slaveholders came to see that the assurance of state control was insufficient, however, and they thus fashioned a new version of "Southern Rights" constitutionalism to meet new demands. These innovations did less to influence courts than to set the terms of the coming crisis by venturing a theory of sectional rights that might assure an equal, and perhaps even a predominate, share of national power. The key terms of American nationhood and state sovereignty persisted, though newer notions of Southern Rights and proslavery nationhood set the basis for the critical departure of 1860.[4]

VIRGINIA CONSTITUTIONALISTS AND THE NAMELESS NATION

In 1820, the Virginia planter John Taylor of Caroline warned against that "artificial phraseology" then producing "fine webs spun from the wombs of single words." Taylor had previously urged republicans to exercise agrarian virtue and to defend liberty by shedding blood, if necessary. He had nagged slaveholders to reform their agriculture and to support the colonization of free blacks beyond their borders. Near the end of his life, Taylor turned his attention from decisive action to the political language that governed the Union. "The tossing about of words," he warned, was the means by which freedom's

---

[4] William Wiecek, *The Sources of Antislavery Constitutionalism, 1760–1848* (Ithaca, NY: Cornell University Press, 1977); Earl M. Maltz, "Slavery, Federalism, and the Structure of the Constitution" *American Journal of Legal History* 36 (1992), 466–98; Mark E. Brandon, *Free in the World: American Slavery and Constitutional Failure* (Princeton, NJ: Princeton University Press, 1998). My understanding of the political dynamics of constitutional argumentation follows Keith E. Whittington, *Constitutional Construction: Divided Powers and Constitutional Meaning* (Cambridge, MA: Harvard University Press, 1999).

enemies were working "to resuscitate legions of those principles of despotism, which were intended to be suffocated by divisions and limitations of power."[5]

As Taylor realized, American constitutionalism departed from British precedents in being a matter of easily manipulated words rather than of inherited forms and more durable institutions. The meaning of specific terms had been part of the ratifying debate of the 1780s, when opponents scrutinized Constitutional terminology, and skeptically noted that document's omission of such basic words as "slavery" and "nation." After the new government acquired more "parchment protections" in the Bill of Rights, former anti-Federalists spoke out against such expansive phrases as the Preamble's "general welfare," or the First Article's "necessary and proper" clause. The most menacing word in this dissenting vocabulary however, was the notion of "consolidation," a term not present in the Constitutional text but which, from the 1780s through the Civil War, summed up the threat that centralizers posed in their quest to absorb supreme authority, to reduce the individual states to ciphers, and to impose a version of political serfdom on ordinary Americans. Taylor and his followers recognized an apocalyptic element of such "concentrated power," which they believed "destroys the counterpoise between freedom and restraint, and never fails to become the executioner of human happiness."[6]

Between 1815 and 1823, Taylor and other Virginian proponents of state sovereignty perceived that "consolidationism" that had been unsuccessfully attempted by the Federalist administrations of Washington and Adams was finding a new lease on life within the U.S. Supreme Court. The federal justices, led by Richmond's own John Marshall, appeared to be using new and dangerous notions of an "American people" and of a correspondingly menacing "national government" to bolster the power they had lost to the Jeffersonians in the other branches through the election of 1800. Virginians had been involved with the term "nation" as far back as the Philadelphia convention, when Edmund Randolph had introduced, and then withdrew, the plan for a "national government." Eliminating the term itself did not comfort Patrick Henry, who argued in the Virginia ratifying convention that by adopting the opening words "We the people" rather than "We the states," the framers had created "one great consolidated National

---

[5] John Taylor, *Construction Construed and Constitutions Vindicated* (Richmond, VA: Shepherd and Pollard, 1820), 200, 219.

[6] Saul Cornell, *The Other Founders: Anti-Federalists and the Dissenting Tradition in America, 1788–1828* (Chapel Hill: University of North Carolina Press, 1999); John Taylor, *New Views of the Constitution* (Washington, D.C.: Way and Gideon, 1823), 245.

government." Through the 1790s, Virginians sporadically took up the matter of whether the United States was truly a nation or not, witnessing the Supreme Court's effort to affirm nationhood in *Chisholm v. Georgia*, and applauding the reaction that took place with the ratification of the 11th amendment, and then in a "Revolution of 1800" that put advocates of "state rights" into power. Through this early period, conceptual confusion prevailed about the basic terms of nationhood in its constitutional bearings. Before 1820, John Taylor rarely used the term "nation" in a negative sense, distinguishing between the many virtuous "nations" of ordinary citizens and those "governments" that repeatedly encroached upon their popular rights.[7]

James Madison had staked out a middle ground on what would be a key issue when he identified the U.S. government as a "partly national, partly federal" form. In his influential discussion in *Federalist 39*, Madison applauded this new constitution's direct governance of citizens, and its ability to speak with one voice to the rest of the world, although he insisted that these qualities had not obliterated the important sovereign duties of the state. The compounded form of the new Union rested on the bold innovation of a divided sovereignty, in which the people would represent themselves as a national community in some duties and as members of their respective states in others. Madison's presidency saw American nationhood, in its cultural rather than in its constitutional sense, assume a more durable form as a result of its successful war against England. As new symbols, songs, and military heroes emerged, Madison appointed to the Supreme Court the Massachusetts Republican Joseph Story, who urged (using an image likely to raise hackles of his enemies): "Let us prevent the possibility of division, by creating great national interests which shall bind us in an indissoluble chain." Along with John Marshall, Story set this process in motion with a series of rulings, the most famous of which was *McCulloch v. Maryland*, a judgment that sharply curtailed the states' ability to resist federal programs and decisions.[8]

---

[7] The Massachusetts Senator Charles Sumner assembled a variety of early statements about U.S. "nationhood" in his polemical *Are We a Nation?* (Boston, MA: Wright and Potter, 1867). See also Doyle Mathis, "*Chisholm v. Georgia*: Background and Settlement" *JAH* 54 (June 1967), 19–29; and John Taylor, *An Inquiry into the Principles and Policies of the Government of the United States* (1814: 1950 reprint New Haven, CT, 1950), 33, 327, 394, 410.

[8] "Federalist 39" in Cooke, ed., *The Federalist*, 250–7; Story in 1815, quoted in Kenneth M. Stampp, "The Concept of a Perpetual Union," *JAH* 65 (June 1978), 24. For a modified view of Madison's analysis, which would have long-lasting influence among Virginians, see St. George Tucker, *Blackstone's Commentaries, With Notes of Reference* (Philadelphia, 1803) 1: 175–8.

Marshall demonstrated his renowned tactical skills in offering his most sweeping vision of nationhood in one of the least consequential of his decisions. He decided *Cohens v. Virginia*, a case involving a jurisdictional dispute over a Congressionally authorized lottery, in favor of state rights' antagonists like Judge Spencer Roane of Virginia, the son-in-law of anti-Federalist Patrick Henry. Yet Marshall won the larger point by affirming that the United States "form, for many, and for most important purposes, a single nation." It seemed self-evident to him that the country was fully united when engaged in war, when making peace, and even when setting common commercial regulations. He presented this process of nation-making as an ongoing act of collective will rather than as a final result of any conclusive deal-making of 1787. "America has chosen, in many respects, and to many purposes, a nation; and for all these purposes, her government is complete." States were thus "members of one great empire" and their governments acted for some purposes sovereign, for other purposes subordinate.[9]

Marshall's expansive vision pushed state sovereignty theorists from focusing energy on "consolidationism" to newfound vigilance in containing the federal government's pretense to "nationality." The appearance in 1821 of the "secret notes" of anti-Federalist Robert Yates of New York encouraged this shift by detailing how the clash between "nationalists" and "republicans" had provided the main dividing line in the drafting of the Constitution. Yates' account, which appeared two decades before the publication of Madison's own, more complete, notes of the Philadelphia convention, presented evidence of an attempted coup to dissolve the states entirely. This movement, Yates reported, had been fought back and finally defeated behind the convention's closed doors. Such shocking new evidence convinced states' rights theorists that nationhood was the work of a determined clique whose descendants were determined to resume their program, through the courts, the Congress, and perhaps, with the dispute over Missouri statehood still echoing, through a free state assault on the rights of slaveholders.[10]

---

[9] Marshall quoted in G. Edward White, *The Marshall Court and Cultural Change, 1815–1835* (New York: Oxford, 1991), 518. The larger contexts of Marshall's strategic battles with Virginia opponents are sketched in R. Kent Newmyer, "John Marshall and the Southern Constitutional Tradition," in Kermit L. Hall and James W. Ely, Jr., eds., *An Uncertain Tradition: Constitutionalism and the History of the South* (Athens: University of Georgia Press, 1989), 105–24 and Richard E. Ellis, *Aggressive Nationalism: McCulloch v. Maryland and the Foundation of Federal Authority in the Young Republic* (Oxford: Oxford University Press, 2007).

[10] *Secret Proceedings and Debates of the Convention Assembled at Philadelphia …* (Albany, NY: Websters and Skinners, 1821); Cornell, *The Other Founders*, 288–95.

In three books written between 1820 and 1824, John Taylor built on arguments in the newspaper war against the Marshall Court to form the basis of a new state rights' orthodoxy. His last and most influential work, *New Views of the Constitution*, drew upon Yates' notes in an effort to discredit the current Supreme Court, the authors of the *Federalist Papers*, and those nationalist initiatives recently undertaken by South Carolinians George McDuffie and John C. Calhoun.[11] Among the most intriguing of Taylor's arguments hinged on the failure of Philadelphia delegates in 1787 to give their creation a proper name. "The word America is used to designate a quarter of the globe in which the recited states were established," he explained, in a gloss of the Constitution's preamble. He concluded that the phrase "we the people of the United States of America" could not "designate a nation of Americans." "There are many states in America, but no state of America, nor any people of an American state." A writer in the *Richmond Enquirer* had earlier made a similar point, conceding that while poets and patriots might invoke "Fredonians, Columbians, or Americans," these terms were "appellations without authority." Three decades later, the exponents of state sovereignty appealed to the exact same logic as a rationale for the legitimacy of secession.[12]

Geographical names were not a trivial matter for "John Taylor, of Caroline," as he chose to appear in print. One might even say that territorial identity was Taylor's obsession, summed up by his conviction that "the geography of human nature sticks to a man like his skin, or travels with him like a shadow." Other Virginian constitutionalists adopted a similarly provincial perspective, which separated them from those slaveholders who cultivated wider perspectives in their migration to the West, or in their engagement with world markets, northern institutions, and international trends. Virginian's relative isolation drew its leading defender of states' rights toward a Jeffersonian notion of "a decentralized regime, an empire without a metropolis, a consensual union of free republics," to use Peter Onuf's apt

---

[11] McDuffie was known to be the author of the anonymous *National and State Rights Considered by "One of the People"* (Charleston, 1821), and his views were understood to be aligned with those of Calhoun at this stage.

[12] Taylor, *New Views*, 170–2; *Richmond Enquirer*, December 21, 1820. Sebastian de Grazie playfully explores this theme across a wider scope in *The Country with No Name: Tales from the Constitution* (New York: Vintage Books, 1997). For secession-era notices of American namelessness see William D. Porter, *State Sovereignty and the Doctrine of Coercion* (Charleston, SC: Evans and Cogeswell, 1860), 11; Benjamin Morgan Palmer, *A Vindication of Secession and the South* (Columbia, SC: Southern Guardian, 1861), 36, and Charles Sumner's rebuttal in *Are We a Nation?*, 46–50.

description.[13] This tradition conveyed only an intermittent interest in how state sovereignty protected slavery. More central to the early state-sovereignty theorists was Virginia's championing of civil liberties in the state resolutions against the Alien and Sedition Acts of 1798, and the benefits that federalism would bring to local development of literature and culture. As the Deep South took up their own constitutional theories in the late 1820s, a shift occurred, as Virginian masters like Abel Upshur and Beverley Tucker brought bondage closer to the center of their state's constitutional traditions.[14]

Opponents of Virginia constitutionalism registered disapproval of such a seemingly narrow championing of local identities. It was thus the Virginians' provincial stance, not their complicity with slavery, that laid these open to the same attacks recently launched against those who had planned New England's quasiseparatist Hartford convention during the war with England between 1812 and 1815. In denying American nationhood, Virginia theorists proved to be more than a bit out of touch with wider currents of nationalist patriotism. South Carolina Unionists registered some of the most skeptical remarks about overly ambitious state sovereignty claims, with one Charlestonian remarking that it was "a solecism to talk of sovereign and independent States that cannot levy a single battalion of armed men." Another noted that "the truth that the United States constitute one Nation and that the States are not Nations is found in various forms scattered all along the highway, which our country has been traveling since 1776." "It would be difficult to find historical evidence on any point more fully particular and various."[15]

Andrew Jackson, one of Tennessee's largest slaveholders, provided the most effective response to Virginians' skittish rejection of nationhood. His 1832 assault on nullification came in the wake of a frontier military career

---

[13] Peter Onuf, *Jefferson's Empire: The Language of American Nationhood* (Charlottesville: University of Virginia Press, 2001), 12. See also "Federalism, Republicanism and the Origins of American Sectionalism," in *All Over the Map: Rethinking American Regions,* eds., Edward Ayers et al. (Baltimore, MD: Johns Hopkins University Press, 1996), 11–37.

[14] Taylor, *Constitutions Constructed*; Thomas R. Dew, "On the Influence of the Federative Republican System of Government upon Literature and the Development of Character," *SLM* 2 (December, 1836), 261–82; Muscoe Garnett, *Address Delivered Before the Society of Alumni of the University of Virginia at Its Annual Meeting* (Charlottesville, VA: O.S. Allen, 1850); Abel Upshur, *The True Nature and Character of Our Federal Government* (Washington: Ruffin, 1840); N. Beverly Tucker, *A Series of Lectures on the Science of Government, Intended to Prepare the Student for the Study of the Constitution of the United States* (Philadelphia, PA: Carey and Hart, 1845).

[15] "Hamilton," *Review of the Late Pamphlet, under the Signature of "Brutus"* (Charleston, SC: James S. Burges, 1828), 38; *Argument of Thomas S. Grimke in the Case of the State Ex Relatione McCrady v. Hunt, April 1834* (Charleston, SC: J.S. Burges, 1834), 23.

and a victory as the "people's candidate" for president – two qualities that had already made him a potent advocate of American imperialism and democratic assertion. Yet if his own state rights' opposition to "consolidationist" policies had marked his earlier career, Jackson used the nullification showdown to express his hostility to what he considered the undemocratic "Virginia doctrines." He warned his fellow citizens to foreswear "eloquent appeals to your passions, to your State pride, to your native courage, to your sense of real injury" and charged that these had been "used to prepare you for the period when the mask which concealed the hideous features of disunion should be taken off." Before succumbing to the disorganizing theories of nullification, all true citizens should consider with horror the time when "this happy Union we will dissolve." "The protection of that glorious flag" would then be renounced, as would "the very name of Americans." Parrying constitutional theories with more visceral appeals, Jackson provided a *coup de grace* by stating that "to say that any State may at pleasure secede from the Union is to say that the United States are not a nation." This common-sense embrace of a shared American nationhood helped him reverse state sovereignty reasoning, which had reached constitutional conclusions by beginning with the absence of nationhood, and then moving toward a theory of the Union's divisibility.[16]

The Virginia distrust of national terminology persisted in the face of Jacksonian patriotic appeals and would become especially prevalent among those southern leaders of the 1850s who counseled secession. C. C. Clay of Alabama thus explained in 1858 how "the word National does not belong properly to the political vocabulary of this country." The case was usually more nuanced than Clay's, since national appeals, national legacies, and national futures still captivated slaveholders' imaginations. Compartmentalizing the issue provided one way out, as Jefferson Davis of Mississippi, another military hero, demonstrated. Not long after presenting himself "as an American, whose heart promptly responds to all which illustrates our national character, and adds new glory to our national name," Davis argued that it was a "heresy" to affirm that "ours is an [*sic*] union of people, the formation of a nation, and a supreme government charged with providing for the general welfare." Two years before leading a new nation at war with the United States, Davis tried to clarify his position by reducing his

---

[16] "Proclamation of Andrew Jackson, December 10, 1832," *in CMPP* 3: 1203–19; Jackson assaulted the "absurdity of the Virginia doctrine" in a letter to Van Buren, as quoted in Richard E. Ellis, *The Union at Risk: Jacksonian Democracy, States' Rights and the Nullification Crisis* (New York: Oxford University Press, 1987), 87.

convictions to a simple, and highly revealing, formulation. "We became a nation by the Constitution," he explained, quickly qualifying himself to announce, "whatever is national springs from the Constitution; and national and constitutional are convertible terms."[17]

STATE SOVEREIGNTY AND WHITE POWER

For many in the Deep South, the Virginians' tendency to spar over constitutional terminology was a tedious diversion from the real business at hand. Hugh Legaré of South Carolina sounded a typical complaint in 1828 when he observed that "no people was ever so much addicted to abstractions" as Americans were, and that "the University of Paris, in the hey-dey of scholastic divinity" could not match the country's "thorny, unprofitable, and unintelligible subtleties of dialectics." No less a nullifier than Maria Henrietta Pinckney admitted a few years later "the discussion of the elements of Government is dull, as is all abstract discussion." Yet she insisted, in a book appropriately titled *The Quintessence of Long Speeches*, that "if we undertake to talk politics, we must undertake to know about what we talk, and we cannot understand the nature of our Government, without referring to first principles."[18]

Despite their ingrained skepticism of Virginia abstractions, more and more Deep South masters adopted state sovereignty arguments over the course of the 1820s. They did so primarily because such doctrines became a useful tool in a new clash between peripheries and centers. The arrangement of powers over space had been a long-standing concern of Low Country slaveholders, who were acutely aware of their interest in pairing strong protection from outside threats with as much autonomy as possible in local matters. The exercise of slaveholders' rights against central authority had developed within a British constitutional order that was loose enough to assure that slave systems could freely be developed "beyond the line" of metropolitan legal guarantees.[19] The one notable

[17] C.C. Clay, *Speech on Slavery Issues at Huntsville Alabama* (np, 1859), 2; Davis to Malcolm D. Haynes, August 18, 1849 in *PJD* 4: 27; Jefferson Davis, October 11, 1858 in *JDC* 3: 327.
[18] Hugh Swinton Legaré, "Kent's Commentary" *SR* 2 (August 1828), 96; Pinckney "The Quintessence of Long Speeches" (1830) reprinted in Jon L. Wakelyn, ed., *Southern Pamphlets on Secession* (Chapel Hill: University of North Carolina Press, 1996), 8.
[19] Jonathan A. Bush, "The British Constitution and the Creation of American Slavery" in Paul Finkelman, ed., *Slavery and the Law* (Madison, 1997), Seymour Drescher, *Capitalism and Antislavery: British Mobilization in Comparative Perspective* (New York: Oxford University Press, 1987).

exception to this colonial "freedom to enslave" came from an attempt by British officials to restrict slavery in colonial Georgia during the mid-eighteenth century, an episode that ended after settlers successfully protested laws framed thousands of miles from where they would be enforced. The 1776 revolution against metropolitan authority clearly strengthened slaveholders' claim that local issues of race and slavery should be decided as close to home as possible. A long-standing distrust of central authority in these areas was evident in Deep South actions at the Federal Constitutional Convention and in Congress, though a similar dynamic was also at work in frontier masters' successful efforts to secure power for themselves in territorial Louisiana, and then in the territory of Missouri.[20]

Vindicating local power owed far less to the Madisonian conception of a "partly federal, partly national" government than to Madison's conceptual dividing line between state and federal jurisdictions. Deep South constitutionalists thus developed a particular fondness for *Federalist 45*'s lucid division of responsibilities into two broad categories. "The powers delegated by the proposed Constitution to the federal government are few and defined," Madison had written.

> Those which are to remain in the State governments are numerous and indefinite. The former will be exercised principally on external objects, as war, peace, negotiation, and foreign commerce; with which the last, the power of taxation will, for the most part, be connected. The powers reserved to the several states will extend to all the objects which in the ordinary course of affairs, concern the lives, liberties, and properties of the people, and the internal order, improvement and prosperity of the states.[21]

This formula of "internal" and "external" powers functioned as a beacon of proslavery maneuvering during the debates over Missouri statehood that raged between 1819 and 1821. Throughout this prolonged sectional crisis, slave state representatives witnessed the potential of a northern free soil majority to expand the national government's power over slavery as a state applied for admission to the Union. Yet however troubling this was as a political matter, an even greater danger seemed to come with the incursion on Missourians' constitutional

[20] James Oakes probes the Georgia case in "Slavery as an American Problem," in *The South as an American Problem* (Athens: University of Georgia Press, 1995); on territorial Louisiana and Missouri, see Dunbar Rowland, ed., *Claiborne Letter Books* (Jackson: Department of Archives and History, 1917), *passim*.
[21] "Federalist 45" in Cooke, ed., *The Federalist*, 292.

5 2   *Mastering America*

"right" to determine the status of slavery within their state's borders. In this sense, Missouri's ultimate admission revisited and reaffirmed the federal consensus that even more firmly placed slavery among those "domestic" concerns that lay under state control, even while it anticipated struggles of the coming decades by allowing the Congress to exercise its jurisdiction in the territories. The controversy in 1821 over Missouri's ban on free black emigrants was more complicated, and more fraught with trouble, since black citizenship in other states seemed worthy of constitutional protection under the constitution's "full faith and credit" clause.[22] In the wake of the Missouri settlement, the rights of free colored people continued to elude resolution, and this topic unexpectedly provided the occasion for the Deep South's first sustained defiance of federal authority. Low country planters hardly expected that their policing of nonwhites would stir conflict. As the South Carolinian Robert J. Turnbull put it, establishing the subordination of blacks and Indians had been "the principle subject of our policy and jurisprudence" from "time immemorial." The state's "Negro Seamen's Act" (which Turnbull had helped to craft after serving as a judge in the 1822 trial and execution of Denmark Vesey) revisited policies first adopted during the Haitian scare, when all visiting free black sailors had been lodged in Charleston jails. What began as a police measure precipitated an international and a constitutional crisis when a black Jamaican sailor named Henry Elkison brought a suit before Federal Justice William Johnson, who held that the newest law violated the 1815 commercial convention between the United States and England. Johnson's ruling coincided with a largely unrelated challenge mounted by white Georgians, who were then launching their own protest of federal diplomacy. Insisting that the U.S. government open lands it had promised to white settlers in an agreement reached in 1802, Georgians presented another case to test whether federal supremacy in making treaties could trump the exercise of white police powers over racial groups that threatened to

[22] Richard Brown, "The Missouri Crisis, Slavery, and the Politics of Jacksonianism," *South Atlantic Quarterly* 65 (1961); Robert P. Forbes, *The Missouri Compromise and Its Aftermath: Slavery and the Meaning of America* (Chapel Hill: University of North Carolina Press, 2006); Madison himself took part in the Missouri crisis, largely assuming the right of Missouri to frame a proslavery constitution, but venturing further in doubting Congressional power to legislate on the question in the territories. See Drew R. McCoy, *The Last of the Fathers: James Madison and the Republican Legacy* (New York: Cambridge University Press, 1989).

"infect" a slave population successfully insulated from other subversive forces.[23]

These two conflicts escalated as defiant Deep South officials warned how the exercise of federal power over "local" racial matters betrayed the Madisonian distinction between internal and external spheres. In 1823, Governor George Troup of Georgia lashed out at the Monroe administration, and rejected any plan that would allow Indians to remain in his state, where they would hold "a middle station between the Negro and the white man." A year later, he compared the federal protection of Indians within the state's borders with other "officious and impertinent intermeddlings with our domestic concerns." Troup expressed particular alarm with the American Colonization Society, which had recently proposed to use federal funds to send free blacks to Liberia. With a mounting bitterness, Troup declared that "soon, very soon," the federal government "discarding the mask, will openly lend itself to a combination of fanatics for the destruction of everything valuable in the southern country." He then insisted – in a vein that persisted over a decade of Indian debates still to come – that "the moment we cease to be masters, we shall be slaves."[24]

As Troup and other Georgians blustered, anxious white Charlestonians took a different tack, combining their blatant defiance of Justice Johnson's ruling with an ever-more sophisticated variant of state rights constitutionalism. The key figure in both these trends was Robert J. Turnbull, whose enthusiasm for detaining free black sailors coincided with his development of a Deep South constitutional case that rivaled the Virginia tradition of

---

[23] [Isaac E. Holmes and Robert J. Turnbull], *Caroliniensis on the Arrest of a British Seaman* (Charleston, 1823), 44, 50; Ulrich Phillips, *Georgia and State Rights: A Study of the Political History of Georgia from the Revolution to the Civil War, with Particular Regard to Federal Relations* (Washington, 1901). "Caroliniensis" added that "in every political condition in which she has ever been placed, whether as a colony of Great Britain, as one of the old Confederation, or as a member of the late Federal compact, [South Carolina] has invariably maintained, and adhered to this principle" of white regulation of racial inferiors. The manifold consequences of policing multiracial sailing crews can be following in George D. Terry, "South Carolina's First Negro Seamen Acts, 1793–803," *Proceedings of the South Carolina Historical Association* (1980), 78–93 and Alan January, "The First Nullification: The Negro Seamen Acts Controversy in South Carolina, 1822–60," (PhD thesis, University of Iowa, 1976).

[24] George Troup to John C. Calhoun, February 28, 1824 and "Special Message to the Legislature, May 23, 1825," both in Edward J. Harden, *The Life of George M. Troup* (Savannah, GA: E. J. Purse, 1859), 206, 298–9. See also "A Georgian," *An Appeal to the People of the United States* (np, 1824) and [William Drayton], "The Georgia Controversy," *SR* (November 1828), 551, both of which apply the internal/external division set forth in *Federalist* 45.

John Taylor. Of the two theorists, Turnbull had a far more cosmopolitan background, having lived as a child in British West Florida (where his father had failed miserably in planting colonial settlers), as a student in England, as a young man in Philadelphia (where he authored an idealistic tract on penitentiary reform and the injustices of slavery), and then in Charleston, where he studied law under anti-Federalist leader Rawlins Lowndes. Life as a Sea Island cotton planter taught Turnbull that the governance of slaves depended on brute force; his service as a judge in the Vesey prosecution deepened this conviction, as did his work in founding and leading the South Carolina Association, the shadowy organization responsible for enforcing the Negro Seaman laws through direct action. By the time he wrote *The Crisis* in 1827, Turnbull was convinced of the need for a radical reaction to outside threats. He even dreamed of the day when providence might erect an impassable range of mountains that would halt all communication between the free and slave states.[25]

Turnbull began *The Crisis* by invoking John Randolph's ridicule of the "abracadabra of the Constitution" and repeated his question: "When the scorpion's sting is probing us to the quick, shall we chop logic?" This was an odd beginning for a book that chopped logic with the best of the Virginia constitutionalists. Turnbull pulled out all stops in mustering a constitutional case against the "American System," filling page after page with quotations from Madison, Yates, and Taylor and their accounts of the inner workings of the Philadelphia convention in 1787. He developed his own insights about how the "general welfare" and "necessary and proper" clauses were intended to sharply limit, rather than to expand, the authority of the Congress, and offered a state sovereignty interpretation of the "concurrent powers" doctrine recently established by the Supreme Court. He even threaded his way through the intricacies of the "affirmative pregnant" and the "negatives pregnant," though these excursions did more to display his legal acumen than to reach a wide audience. He made sure as well to pay due

---

[25] James Hamilton, *An Eulogium on the Public Services and Character of Robert J. Turnbull, Esq., Delivered in St. Philip's Church, Charleston, on the November 22, 1833* (Charleston, SC: A.E. Miller, 1833); Robert J. Turnbull, *A Visit to the Philadelphia Prison* (Dublin, 1798); Turnbull quoted in [Edwin Clifford Holland], *A Refutation of the Calumnies Circulated against the Southern and Western State* (Charleston, SC: A.E. Miller, 1822), 55; "Brutus," [Robert J. Turnbull], *The Crisis: Or, Essays on the Usurpations of the Federal Government* (Charleston: A.E. Miller, 1827). A similar cosmopolitanism was evident in the state rights' constitutionalism formulated by President Thomas Cooper of South Carolina College, as I have developed in "Proslavery Calculations and the Value of Disunion," in Don Doyle, ed., *Secession as an International Phenomenon* (Athens: University of Georgia Press, forthcoming).

tribute to *Federalist 45*, extending the same legal strategy of differentiating between "internal" and "external" jurisdiction that he had framed in his defense of his state's Negro Seamen's Act.[26]

What set *The Crisis* apart and gained it a broad influence was its invocation of dangers "ten thousand times ten thousand" more important than nationalist economic policies. Turnbull at first spoke elliptically about "domestic institutions," lacing his references with coded nods to "dangerous topics," and "inflammatory" measures. This was not a sign of his embarrassment about slavery, as it might have been for some of the Virginia theorists. Instead, this strategy followed Turnbull's belief that the mere discussion of emancipation encouraged slave discontent, a conclusion supported by Denmark Vesey's supposed knowledge of Congressional debates over Missouri, and by the perceived effect of parliamentary debate on West Indian slavery. When *The Crisis* took aim at the American Colonization Society, perils were finally spelled out, leading Turnbull to warn: "The man who comes into my yard and preaches to my slaves . . . must not expect to go out with whole bones. So, also, if South Carolina desire domestic tranquility, she must separate from the Union if Congress insists upon the right to touch the subject of slavery, on the ground of it being an evil." Turnbull continued this same spirit of defiance in state papers prepared during the nullification crisis.[27]

Turnbull's verbal pyrotechnics may have rallied state action within South Carolina, but it was the national party system and, more particularly, the white supremacist appeals of Andrew Jackson's Democracy that dissipated the sense of crisis experienced in the late 1820s and early 1830s. In matters such as Indian policy, the Jackson administration was resolute in simultaneously applying federal might and state sovereignty to establish the white republic on the frontier. In other areas, including those of utmost concern to Carolinians, his administration deferred even more completely to local patterns, which were then implementing principles of racial exclusivity into state constitutions. Jackson's Attorney General endorsed the South Carolina's Negro Seamen's Act and tacitly encouraged similar measures in five other slave states. His party renounced the American System, and with it, any possibility of federal participation in African-American colonization. Newer threats were met

---

[26] [Turnbull], *The Crisis*; [*Idem.*], *Caroliniensis on the Arrest*, 49–50.
[27] [Turnbull], *The Crisis*; 137; *An Oration Delivered in the City of Charleston, Before the State Rights and Free Trade Party, . . . on the July 4, 1832, Being the 56th Anniversary of American Independence* (Charleston, SC: A.E. Miller, 1832).

with a similar decisiveness. During the 1836 controversies over abolitionist mailings, the Jacksonians favored local police power over the
federal delivery of the mail. The same year, Congressional Democrats
from both sections worked to ban antislavery petitioning through a series
of so-called "gag rules." Such mastery of a limited federal government
reassured slaveholders and discouraged them from following John C. Calhoun in significantly altering the role that the states played in the American
constitutional order.[28]

A decade of turmoil produced a corollary for the "federal consensus"
by giving slave states the full power to govern all their non-white inhabitants with the same full authority they held over their slaves. Marshall
himself took a step in this direction by ruling in *Barron v. Baltimore* that
the rights included in the first ten amendments were binding only on the
federal government, and not upon the states. Jackson protégé Roger B.
Taney completed the judicial revolution on behalf of white power. After
establishing a doctrine of local police power in the *Passenger* cases,
Taney moved in *Dred Scott v. Sandford* to eliminate the most basic
protections for African-Americans under the American constitution. At
first, a major beneficiary of such changes were southern Whigs, whose
activist program of roads, banks, and tariffs was largely inoculated from
charges of being an opening wedge to emancipationist "nationalization,"
as had been the case in the 1820s. The Republican Party's nationalist
doctrines after 1854 would be another matter, since these were
consciously yoked to the curtailment of slavery expansion, and to the
re-establishment of what Lincoln termed the institution's "course to ultimate extinction."[29]

The expansion of southern state-sovereignty claims after the 1830s
was especially impressive when compared with the fate of Caribbean
masters during the same years. The coexistence of local rights and imperial obligations in the West Indies had prompted colonial masters to

---

[28] January, "The First Nullification," 236–40; Leonard Richards, "The Jacksonians and
Slavery" in *Antislavery Reconsidered eds.*, Lewis Perry and Michael Fellman (Baton Rouge:
Louisiana State University Press, 1979); James Brewer Stewart, "The Rise of Racial Mod-
ernity and the Emergence of the Free White North, 1790–840," *JER* 18 (Summer 1998);
Lacy K. Ford, Jr. "Making the 'White Man's Country,' White: Race, Slavery, and State-
Building in the Jacksonian South," *JER* 19 (Winter 1999), 713–37.

[29] Wieneck "'Old Times There are Not Forgotten': The Distinctiveness of the Southern Con-
stitutional Experience," in Hall, ed., *An Uncertain Tradition*; Harold M. Hyman and
Wieneck, *Equal Justice Under Law: Constitutional Development, 1835–1875* (New
York: Harper and Row, 1982); "First Debate: Lincoln Reply," August 21, 1858, in
LSW, 514.

assert their own quasifederal rights that bore some resemblance to those expressed within the American South. During the French Revolution, planters in St. Domingue and the Windward Islands had even hinted at a right to secede from France, a position that French colonists in Martinique and Guadeloupe periodically offered until slavery was ended across the empire in 1848.[30] An even richer discussion of colonial prerogatives arose during the 1820s in Britain's "self-governing" colonies whose assemblies took the lead in resisting Parliamentary antislavery initiatives. The campaign to build on slave trade abolition and the "amelioration" of slavery in crown colonies was denounced as an unconstitutional dead letter by the representatives of Jamaica, Barbados, and other older colonies. Taking aim at Parliamentary supremacy was a difficult case, however, given the Declaratory Act passed during the imperial crisis of the 1770s. Proponents of centralized reform made their strongest and, ultimately, their most effective case, not by appealing to this precedent but by contrasting the narrow interests of white colonists with the exalted cause of imperially sponsored freedom. T. B. Macaulay sharply noted that if masters' claim to unchecked power was valid, "then is history a fable ... and the British constitution a name!" Anticipating the attacks made by Garrisonian abolitionists on the United States constitution in the late antebellum period, Macaulay cried out "let us break up the benches of the House of Commons for firewood, and cut Magna Charta into battle-dores!" sooner than allow masters to deform ancient British liberties.[31]

As early as 1823, when the British Parliament first endorsed comprehensive slavery reform as a prelude to emancipation, the *Charleston Mercury* realized that the West Indian disputes had "peculiar application to the situation of our Southern States." South Carolinians followed events in the British Caribbean carefully, reading West Indian newspapers, fretting about Caribbean insurrections, borrowing crucial aspects of their proslavery defenses, and, then, following the course of the

---

[30] David Geggus, " Racial Equality, Slavery, and Colonial Secession during the Constituent Assembly," *AHR* 94 (1989), 1290–308. Lawrence C. Jennings, *French Antislavery: The Movement for the Abolition of Slavery in France, 1802–1848* (New York: Cambridge University Press, 2000).

[31] Lowell Joseph Ragatz, *The Fall of the Planter Class in the British Caribbean, 1763–1833* (New York: The Century Company, 1928), 408–59; Macaulay's 1824 remarks were reprinted in "West Indian Slavery," *Quarterly Review* 32 (October 1825), 511, and later echoed in James Stephen, *England Enslaved By Her Colonies: An Address to the Electors and People of the United Kingdom* (London: R. Taylor, 1826).

"Mighty Experiment" that was instituted over planter protests during the 1830s.[32] American masters learned from this cautionary experience what it meant to wield the power of sovereign states within an intricately arranged federal Union. In *The Crisis*, Turnbull pitied the West Indians for having "no arm to lean on but that of an unnatural parent" and asked "what would not these colonists give, had they the means of resisting the mother country, which are so ample in our hands, for keeping Congress within the legitimate bounds of its authority?" Self-congratulation only went so far, since Turnbull also warned that without exerting their powers to the fullest, southern masters might find themselves facing down a hostile government intent on venturing beyond its legitimate bounds. From the explosion of the Haitian revolution to the worries about Cuban "Africanization" in the 1850s, southern slaveholders had looked to the Caribbean to imagine how their mastery might end with untold violence. The British experience taught that southern slavery might cease with far less chaos, if a strong government guided a transition toward a perfection of national consistency. In this example came a lesson that instilled its own sense of despair.[33]

THE METTERNICH OF THE MASTER CLASS

No one did more than the erstwhile nationalist John C. Calhoun to transfer the battle against abolitionism to the field of constitutional politics (see Figure 2.1). From his plunge into the tariff controversy in 1828 through his role as the key formulator of a Southern Rights platform two decades later, Calhoun sought to harmonize Virginians' state-rights distrust of "consolidationism" with the Deep South's embrace of proslavery power. In attempting to reconcile these two traditions into an integrated system, the South Carolinian surpassed even Madison as the single most sophisticated articulator of the compound republic's principles. Although Calhoun's work as a theorist was impressive, his signature innovations – from state interposition to the restorative power of the constitutional amending process to

---

[32] *Charleston Mercury*, December 10, 1823; Larry Tise, *Proslavery: A History of the Defense of Slavery in America, 1701–1840* (Athens: University of Georgia Press, 1987), 75–96; Seymour Drescher, *The Mighty Experiment: Free Labor versus Slavery in British Emancipation* (Oxford: New York, 2002); David Brion Davis, *Challenging the Boundaries of Slavery* (Cambridge, MA: Harvard University Press, 2003), 82–6; Edward Rugemer, "The Southern Response to British Abolitionism: The Maturation of Proslavery Apologetics," *JSH* 70 (May 2004), 221–48.

[33] Turnbull, *The Crisis*, 15, 64, 138.

FIGURE 2.1. John C. Calhoun of South Carolina. *From James Herring, National Portrait Gallery of Distinguished Americans (Philadelphia: Henry Perkins, 1835), used with permission of Dartmouth College Library.*

his posthumous plea for a sectionally-based dual executive – never garnered widespread support. As such, his achievement lay less in staking out advanced positions than in changing the course of the constitutional dialogue and recasting assumptions about the basis of America's constitutional order. His skill in explaining the compound republic as part of an integrated federal system proceeded in tandem with an equally impressive role as the indispensable architect of proslavery geopolitics. It was not in his arguments but in his actions to secure proslavery interests that he left his greatest stamp on what he termed America's "beautiful, complex, federative system of government." It was through an array of powerful positions within the federal government that he became both an heir to the American founders and a pioneer in a transatlantic project that presented a federative balancing of central and local powers as the best means of navigating between change and stability.[34]

Calhoun's constitutionalism was developed during the tariff controversy of the late 1820s, a fact that had significant long-term consequences for his theoretical writing. The sectional interests at the heart of this dispute lent it a far more recognizable geographical character than earlier "state sovereignty" objections to the Alien and Sedition Laws, or even to those controversies sparked by nationalizing initiatives in central banking or internal improvements, the key issues during Federalist and Jeffersonian administrations. Writers in the Deep South understood that the protective tariff of the 1820s was different in being "neither more nor less than an assumption by the government in power to regulate the distribution of labour and wealth throughout our country, and to apply the property of one portion of our citizens to encourage and reward the idle, or wasteful, or speculative projects of another." In this diagnosis, the campaign against the tariff was not merely a test run meant to forecast how the "real" issue of slavery might be faced when the time came. Like the threats posed by federally funded African colonization and the treaty protections of non-whites during this same decade, the "American System's" effort to shape the future course of national production both undermined the cotton belt's most vital economic interests and, more ominously, used what later generations would call "central planning" to "tamper" with the basis of its social order.[35]

Calhoun's "South Carolina Exposition" of 1828 said less about this threat to the "peculiar institution" (a euphemism that this document helped to popularize, and perhaps even to coin) than it did about the tariff's incompatibility with the 1787 federal Constitution. To indict the constitutional

---

[34] Calhoun, "Speech in Support of His Bill to Repeal the Force Act," April 9, 1834, *PJCC*, 12: 287. Among the many studies of Calhoun's constitutionalism, the most historically informed is Lacy K. Ford, Jr., "Inventing the Concurrent Majority: Madison, Calhoun, and the Problem of Majoritarianism in American Political Thought," *JSH* 60 (February 1994), 19–58. Wider perspectives on the post-Napoleonic rise of federative polities, and the challenges these faced after 1848 can be sampled in Robert C. Binkley, *Realism and Nationalism. 1852–1871* (New York: Harper & Brothers, 1935); Robert D. Bellinger, *Metternich and the German Question: States' Rights and Federal Duties, 1820–1834* (Newark, NJ: University of Delaware, 1991), Alan Sked, "The Metternich System, 1818–48, in *Europe's Balance of Power, 1815–1848* (London, 1979), 98–121; Timothy E. Anna, *Forging Mexico: 1821–1835* (Lincoln: University of Nebraska Press, 1998), and Daniel Ziblatt, *Structuring the State: The Formation of Italy and Germany and the Puzzle of Federalism* (Princeton, NJ: Princeton University Press, 2006).

[35] [Stephen Elliott], "Internal Improvements," *SR* 2 (November 1828), 472; William Freehling, *Prelude to Civil War: The Nullification Crisis in South Carolina* (New York, Harper and Row, 1966).

basis of nationalist duties on imports was a considerable challenge. Even Robert Turnbull admitted in *The Crisis* that the unambiguous power granted Congress to "levy taxes" and to "regulate commerce" made "the tariff laws, in their form, perfectly constitutional." Efforts to declare such measures impermissible were thus unlikely to succeed in even the friendliest courts, since judicial review focused primarily on whether there was a specific grant of textual authority that sanctioned a disputed policy. Calhoun's acute awareness of this difficulty pushed him toward an alternate set of constitutional mechanisms that made the people of the individual states – not courts, texts, or even an aroused public opinion – the proper tribunal for deciding whether a particular federal law passed constitutional muster. Sovereign bodies assembled to represent the "people" of the states thus became the authoritative voice in determining whether the "reserved powers" of sovereignty had been usurped. Such bodies could "look in the motives of legislators" entrusted with federal power, and thus move from "strict construction" to a realization that, as Calhoun put it, "the Constitution may be as grossly violated by acting against its meaning as against its letter." The efforts of Turnbull and others had already convinced most South Carolinians that a revenue measure meant to develop manufacturing was a violation of the Madisonian division of "internal" and "external" spheres. Calhoun pressed this point much farther, concluding that it was "a perversion of the high powers vested in the Federal Government for Federal purposes only." By equipping Carolinians with a means for asserting this position and moving toward a legal remedy that stood a chance of actually working, Calhoun reframed the terms of defiance and offered a way to restore the "proper" line between delegated and reserved sovereign powers short of secession or war. If states could interpose against the federal government (in a process popularly termed "nullification") what Calhoun termed as America's "system of governments" would prove to be truly self-regulating.[36]

Although Calhoun's turn toward new mechanisms and novel remedies came at a price to the reputation of his state and to his own personal ambitions on the national stage, these mechanisms and remedies eventually proved their worth by being transformed into a weapon against abolitionism. In 1833, South Carolina's nullification of the tariff seemed mostly

[36] Turnbull, *The Crisis*, 162; Taylor, *Tyranny Unmasked*, 132–8; "South Carolina Exposition," *PJCC* 10: 537; Calhoun to Sam Smith, July, 1828 *PJCC* 10: 403–4. The weakness of the constitutional case is exhaustively reviewed in Edward Stanwood, *American Tariff Controversies in the Nineteenth Century* (Boston, MA: Houghton, Mifflin and Co., 1903) 1: 291–348 and David P. Currie, *The Constitution in Congress: The Jeffersonians, 1801–1829* (Chicago, IL: University of Chicago Press, 2001).

counterproductive, in that it alienated allies across the rest of the slave South, fostered fierce division within its own borders, and, worst of all, elicited the so-called "Force Bill" from Andrew Jackson's Congressional allies, who were on the cusp of coordinating their own majoritarian version of white power. Calhoun considered the Force Act (which authorized the executive to compel obedience through the federal military) as "fetters forged and fitted to the limbs of the states" which would be "hung up to be used, as occasion may hereafter require." Attempts to end slavery in Washington, D.C. (a locale where Congressional jurisdiction over such "internal" matters was beyond any reasonable dispute) were immune from threats of nullification, since even South Carolinians could hardly hope to extend their state's authority all the way to the Potomac. Rather than revisit the idea of a state convention to meet this new threat, Calhoun took his case to his fellow Senators, urging that they evaluate emancipationist petitions according to "the motive and object intended." His case that the battle over Washington slavery was an initial step, to be followed by the regulation of the interstate slave trade and the curtailment of masters' rights within the states, drew the support of many of the same Senators who had scoffed at interposition during the tariff showdown. They agreed that to "pervert power to any other purpose inconsistent with the object of the grant" represented "a violation of the Constitution, not the less dangerous because not expressly forbidden."[37]

Calhoun believed that overreaching centralism – whether expressed in the form of the protective tariff of the 1820s or the abolitionism of the following decade – sprang from the constitutional "heresy" that the Union had created "one great national republic" that might legislate on any issue that the American people chose to address. The assertion of American nationality, which Jackson's Force Bill had done far more to legitimate than any jurisprudence of the toothless Marshall Court, thus appeared to Calhoun to be either "the source of that fanatical spirit which has raised this crusade against our institutions" or, at the very least, "the cause that had excited it into action." Continuing his preference for systems over texts, Calhoun offered the "antidote" for this error in popularizing a broader awareness

---

[37] "To M. Laborde, et al." March 27, 1833 *PJCC* 12: 152; "Address of Republicans," signed by Niles and Haynes," July 6, 1838, *PJCC* 14: 383. The consequences of nullification are set forth in Richard E. Ellis, *The Union at Risk: Jacksonian Democracy, State Rights, and the Nullification Crisis* (New York: Oxford University Press, 1987) while the constitutional maneuvering over the petitions can be followed in David P. Curry, *The Constitution in Congress: Descent into the Maelstrom, 1829–1861* (Chicago, IL: University of Chicago Press, 2005), 1–23.

that the Union was a "federate republic" where "State Rights would be found in this, as in all other cases of difficulty and danger, the only conservative principle in the system." Calhoun's appeal to such notions of state rights attracted broad support from across the Union and secured a truce with those proslavery Jacksonians who had been alienated by his advocacy of nullification. After the Senate adopted most of Calhoun's resolutions on the relationship between slavery and the constitution in 1838, these gained a positive hearing for an overtly proslavery version of state rights both in the national press and in the House of Representatives, which adopted a similar set of measures. In 1839, Calhoun took to the Senate floor with a sense of vindication, as he boasted of how the "states' rights creed" had proved itself as "the ark of our safety," in turning back "the greatest danger to which we have ever been exposed." Just as both houses of Congress rejected petitions against slavery in the federal district, so did leaders of each of the major political parties agree that abolition even in areas of clear federal jurisdiction was a *de facto* violation of state sovereignty. Heralding this extension of an earlier "federal consensus" about the validity of slavery legislation within state borders, Calhoun predicted that a restored balance in the constitution would be the first step toward "a great moral revolution in the tone of feeling and thinking in reference to the domestic institutions of the South."[38]

Calhoun's declaration of victory over political abolitionism within the United States allowed him to shift his attention during the early 1840s to foreign emancipationist threats, which he met by appealing to the law of nations rather than to constitutionalism. His assault on the United Kingdom's failure to return shipboard slave rebels who landed in the territorial waters of the Bahamas prepared him, when he became Secretary of State, to block the far more perilous British attempt to secure a sphere of influence in the independent Republic of Texas. In both these cases, Calhoun wielded the vigorous power of the federal government in "external" affairs with little concern for meeting the threshold of the "concurrent majorities" of both the slave and free states that he demanded of his antagonists. Considering the extremely close presidential election of 1844 as a conclusive referendum on the matter, Calhoun followed the same logic Jefferson had employed in the case of Louisiana, when the president had allowed southwestern security to trump constitutional scruples. As such, Calhoun gave his blessing to an

---

[38] "Remarks on his Resolutions on Abolition and the Union," December 28, 1837 *PJCC* 14: 37; "Remarks on Abolition," February 7, 1839 *PJCC*, 14: 548–9. Calhoun's 1839 remarks were in response to Henry Clay's antiabolitionist speech, which seemed to commit Southern Whigs to Calhoun's position.

enormous extension of the country's southwestern border with no more constitutional authority than a joint resolution barely passed by both houses of Congress.[39]

Calhoun's experiences in battling abolitionism made him more circumspect about how changes to the Union's geopolitical structures might alter the delicate balance of America's federal republic. In 1840, he anticipated the argument of Judah Benjamin by explaining how physical growth was "at once our glory and our danger." While expansion "increases our importance and elevates our pride, it swells, at the same time, the patronage of the government and strengthens its central tendency, which, if not resisted, must end in consolidation, by drawing the whole powers of the system to the centre." Six years later, Calhoun warned how expansionist military conflict would make matters even worse. "The influence of war will naturally be to obliterate the lines of distinction between the State and General Governments," he predicted. "We shall hear no more about State rights, but the Government will become in effect a consolidated republic. By our very success, it will give a military impulse to the national mind which can never be overcome." Calhoun still made claims upon U.S. power, as when he lent his enthusiastic support to a program of federal development of the Mississippi River between 1845 and 1846. As a residual sign of his own earlier nationalist tendencies, he was selective in assessing what forces might foster consolidationism and which would allow the separate states to achieve their full potential. The conduct of war and the partisan system of presidential elections stood out in his imagination as uniquely grave threats to the sort of "sound" federative principles that Americans should strive to perfect.[40]

Like other proslavery politicians who recalled the 1820 crisis over Missouri's admission, Calhoun believed that slaveholding influence in Washington depended on an equal representation of free and slave states in the Senate. Yet this feature was ultimately less important to Calhoun's constitutional vision than his understanding of the Union's amending power, which, as early as 1832, he termed the "pivot of the system" and

---

[39] "Motion in Regard to the Brig Enterprise," March 4, 1840,"Speech on the Case of the Brig Enterprise," March 13, 1840, *PJCC* 15: 129, 139–57; "Remarks on the Creole Affair," *PJCC* 16: 100–3. The best insight into Calhoun's acceptance of annexation via joint resolution comes from two secondhand sources: "Memorandum from Walker," December, 1844 *PJCC* 20: 433; and "Memorandum from Wharton," February 18, 1845 *PJCC* 21: 323.

[40] "Speech on the Distribution of Lands to the States," May 13, 1840, *PJCC* 15: 214; "Speech on the Abrogation of the Join Occupancy of Oregon," March 16, 1846, *PJCC* 22: 699.

one of the few indispensable features of a self-regulating compound republic. To blunt the charge that interposition was simply minority obstructionism, Calhoun had explained how three-quarters of the states (the ratio required for amending the constitution) assured that it would be "concurring majorities" – and not a single state – that ultimately bore responsibility for restoring original constitutional arrangements. Calhoun's constitution was not what judges said it was. It was not even what a supposedly sovereign state decreed it to be. His constitution was what three-quarters of the states imposed upon all members within the Union. His articulation of this position included an admission that the federation was likely to work differently depending on its size. "By diminishing or increasing the number of states necessary to amend the Constitution, the equilibrium between the reserved and delegated rights may be preserved, or destroyed at pleasure." The "balance of power" that mattered, then, was the ability of a fairly small group of states to block a simple "numerical majority" from imposing a sectional platform. At the time that he wrote, veto power rested with six of the Union's twenty-four states, a bloc that could be cobbled together by drawing the Gulf States together with Virginia and South Carolina. Even if the federation grew to thirty-two states (as it would by 1858), the requisite eight-state veto depended on adding the support of only Florida and Texas. Beyond this, the prospect seemed more daunting. In a transcontinental republic, blocking unfriendly (and irrevocable) constitutional changes would depend on the support of states like Tennessee, North Carolina, or Arkansas, where expansive notions of national sovereignty championed by Andrew Jackson had tended to hold sway.[41]

This calculus took on new relevance in 1847 when Calhoun emerged from self-proclaimed victories over American and British abolitionists to face the challenge posed by those territorial acquisitions he had fought hard to prevent. As American military forces occupied California and the Valley of Mexico, Calhoun was uncertain whether the compound republic could handle the addition of what seemed likely to result in a flood of new "free soil" states. In considering how to keep the Wilmot Proviso from shrinking the proslavery core to less than a quarter of the Union, Calhoun asked fellow Senators "Is there not a remedy in the Constitution?" At first, he turned once more to the principles of state sovereignty, making a plea that principles of "state equality" required that slaveholders and nonslaveholders be given

---

[41] "To James Hamilton, Jr." August 28, 1832, *PJCC* 11: 636–7. The intricacies of Calhoun's emphasis on the amending process is trenchantly laid out in Michael O'Brien, *Conjectures of Order: Intellectual Life in the American South, 1810–1860* (Chapel Hill: University of North Carolina Press, 2004), 829.

equal access to all territories gained through common military effort. This strained position, when embodied in resolutions, elicited far less support from fellow Senators than had Calhoun's 1837 motions against federal emancipation in Washington, D.C. Calhoun may never have intended to press the issue in Congress. By 1850, his Senate propositions had become the basis of a series of resolutions passed by slave state legislatures, which would rally the cause of constitutional "equality" in the territories, spur a new Southern Rights movement, and even establish a newspaper devoted to these principles in Washington, D.C.[42]

Early in this campaign, Calhoun showed a clear reluctance to shift his ground from state sovereignty to arguments based on "Southern" rights. At times, he appeared to so minimize links to his native region that he termed the slave states as merely that "portion" of the federal Union "where Providence has cast my lot." This disinclination to base his proslavery territorial program as a sectional prerogative had a strategic component, since appeals for a "balance of power" between the North and South were likely to cost Calhoun the sort of national influence that he had cultivated as the country's chief diplomat in the mid-1840s. Yet such a stance also resulted from the fact that his vision of the constitutional order had seldom focused on sectional mechanisms and had instead built its logic around states, a single federal government capable of energetic action on the world stage, and a "concurrent majority" represented in the amending process held by three-quarters of the Union. Until the late 1840s, Calhoun considered constitutional "equilibrium" mainly in terms of the balance that existed between the reserved powers of the states and those delegated to the federal government.[43]

An alternate view of equilibrium, rooted in the rough parity between free and slave states, would only appear in the systematic overview of the

---

[42] "Speech and Resolutions on the Restriction of Slavery from the Territories," February 19, 1847; Currie, *Constitution in Congress*; *Descent*, 141–3; Manisha Sinha, *The Counterrevolution of Slavery: Politics and Ideology in Antebellum South Carolina* (Chapel Hill: University of North Carolina Press, 2000). Calhoun no doubt expected the Senate to table these resolutions, since the body had already defeated his similar attempt, back in 1837, to link state equality to a failure to annex Texas.

[43] "Speech and Resolutions," 169; "To T.G. Clemson," November 6, 1846 *PJCC* 23: 526; "To A.M. Clemson, December 27, 1846," *PJCC*, 43–4. Duff Green to Calhoun, February 22, 1846, *PJCC* 22: 614–16. Calhoun's reluctance to make a constitutional case for southern rights made him no less enthusiastic to deploy the politics of southern loyalty and to attack dissenting southern representatives as traitors to their region. For a concession that southern unity was more useful than state rights in meeting abolition, see his letter to A. Burt, August 7, 1844 *PJCC* 19: 526.

Constitution that Calhoun undertook in the mid-1840s, and completed shortly before his death in 1850. Significantly, these writings presented sectionalism either as an aberration (resulting from hostile actions of the "nationalist" abolitionists) or as little more than an accident (resulting from the natural tendency of parties to coalesce in "contiguous" areas where easy communication and commerce facilitated interstate ties). Calhoun's conceptual universe thus had difficulty in embracing the slave South as a meaningful actor in its own right, worthy of a systematic defense of a single defining interest or of a unified position within the constitutional order of things. When he set his mind to constitutional arguments (rather than the political means of assembling coalitions and unifying his electoral base), Calhoun was less likely to consider the "South" as the crucible of a stable political identity or a platform for appeals to fair treatment. It was more often a vague place on the map that he would do his best to defend. Though he frequently expressed pride in defending the slave states as a unit, his position in 1847 shared something of the skepticism expressed that same year by the Austrian prince Klaus Metternich. Calhoun's "South" no less than Metternich's "Italy," was at root more of a "geographical expression" and "useful shorthand" than an entity whose "political significance" required addressing it as part of a functioning geopolitical system.[44]

Over the last three years of his life, Calhoun moved from a constitutionalism based on federalism to one that was concerned primarily with asserting the duties and responsibilities exercised by northern and southern sectional units. This shift had less to do with any rethinking of his "Southern" allegiances than with a growing sense of how ill-suited state sovereignty arguments were to the deepening crisis over slavery in the territories. After a series of fits and starts, Calhoun in 1849 broadcast his conceptual breakthrough in his "Southern Address" which, after it drew the support of forty proslavery Congressmen, received wide circulation. The sturdiest groundwork for Southern Rights as a constitutional matter came in Calhoun's ten-paragraph explication of Article V's fugitive slave clause. Though the issue of personal liberty laws had acquired new salience in his correspondence between 1847 and 1849, Calhoun's lengthy consideration of this topic in the Southern Address was largely tactical, in that it allowed him to direct attention toward those pledges that the free states had made to southern masters at the Philadelphia convention. From this basis, Calhoun returned to his main concern about the territories, building an argument that

---

[44] "Disquisition" in *PJCC* 28: 182–3, 219–21; Metternich quoted in Denis Mack Smith, *Mazzini* (New Haven, CT: Yale University Press, 1994), 51.

renounced as illegitimate any attempt by the Congress "to distinguish between the domestic institutions of one State, or section, and another, in order to favor the one and discourage the other."[45]

Calhoun lived only long enough to hint at the implications of this new position. In 1850, his defiant opposition to California's admission came with a warning – that the North would soon be called "to provide for the insertion of a provision in the constitution" that would reestablish that "equilibrium between the sections" that had been "destroyed by the action of the government." When the *Discourse on the Constitution of the United States* appeared in 1851, these veiled challenges became a set of concrete suggestions. Turning his attention to the dangers that a "weaker section" faced in sinking to a state of "dependence and subjection," Calhoun made the genuinely stunning proposal of a dual presidency, which he considered the only remaining hope that the slave states would continue to exercise the sort of executive power that would direct the American future. Over the many pages that it took him to reach this bottom line, two qualities stood out, both of which showed for a final time his consummate gift for argumentative maneuver. The first was his ability to discuss the opposing interests of slave and free states as if these had been built into the structure of American politics from time immemorial. The second was even more daring – his presentation of one of the most sweeping visions of a remodeled Union in terms of a simple plea for the restoration of a lost Republic.[46]

SOUTHERN RIGHTS AND SECTIONAL REMEDIES

In the ten years that followed California's admission as a free state, disputes about territorial slavery escalated, the contours of American politics shifted, and sectional debates came to dominate all other business undertaken by the U.S. Congress. As attention turned from New Mexico and Utah to Kansas and the Caribbean tropics, a cadre of proslavery constitutionalists evaluated the compound republic according to a single criteria – its ability to protect what they termed Southern Rights. These innovators undertook a more ambitious project than had been ventured by slaveholding constitutionalists like Taylor or Calhoun, both of whom had beaten back nationalist

---

[45] [Calhoun], "The Address of Southern Delegates in Congress, to their Constituents," January 22, 1849, *PJCC* 26: 225–44; for Calhoun's growing concern about northern compliance in returning fugitive slaves, see "Letter to Charles James Faulkner, August 1, 1847," and "Address," October 23, 1847, *PJCC* 24: 480, 617, and "Address," April 4, 1848 *PJCC* 25: 292.

[46] The *Discourse* has recently been republished in *PJCC*, vol. 27.

encroachments by restoring the supposedly pristine federative principles of 1787. The political battles of the mid-century fostered the suspicion that slaveholders' real problem lay not in deviations from the founding but in the fact that Philadelphia had been the scene of a bad bargain. New circumstances showed that hemming in federal power – whether through appeals to the text, or by the Calhounian extrapolations of state sovereignty principles – meant little in a world where masters' most vital interests required their active implementation of national power.[47]

At the core of the Southern Rights program lay a reassessment of the 1787 "meeting of Sages and Heroes" that American civic culture had regularly showered with praise. In 1860, the iconoclastic George Bagby of the *Southern Literary Messenger* insisted that the Philadelphia Convention had been a "scene of a violent and discordant struggle for power," where "sharp politicians" had "decided a contest whose stake was empire." While Bagby paid homage to anti-federalist heroes like George Mason and Patrick Henry, the logic of his position rested on words first voiced by none other than James Madison. On June 30, 1787, at what was a critical moment for the Convention, this "father of the Constitution" had asserted that the main division in the Union resulted "partly from climate, but principally from the effects of [states] having, or not having slaves." Madison followed this striking observation – which was not made public until 1840 – with the claim that "if any defensive power were necessary, it ought to be mutually given to these two interests." To round out his comments, he then articulated the quintessentially Madisonian principle that "wherever there is power of attack, there ought to be given a constitutional power of defense." In the context of the mid-1850s, such a frank acknowledgment, coming as it did from the perceived architect of the compound republic, provided bracing evidence that "the sectional line between North and South was almost as deeply drawn in 1787" as it was in debates over the future of Kansas.[48]

---

[47] Arthur Bestor, "State Sovereignty and Slavery: A Reinterpretation of Proslavery Constitutional Doctrine, 1846–1860," *Journal of the Illinois State Historical Society* 54 (Summer 1961), 117–80; idem, "The American Civil War as a Constitutional Crisis," *AHR* 69 (January 1964), 327–52.

[48] [George Bagby], "Notice of New Works," *SLM* 31 (September 1860), 238. "Barbarossa," [John Scott], *The Lost Principle; or, the Sectional Equilibrium: How it Was Created – How Destroyed – How it May Be Restored* (Richmond, VA: James Woodhouse and Co., 1860), 15. Madison's comments were part of his private notes from the Philadelphia Convention, which were made public in H.D. Gilpin, ed., *The Papers of James Madison* (Washington D.C., 1840). In 1823, John Taylor had pointed to a watered-down version of this speech that Robert Yates had included in his 1821 *Secret Proceedings*; see *New Views of the Constitution*, 56, 249.

As early as 1847, John Archibald Campbell of Alabama recognized the potential importance of Madison's piece of "concentrated wisdom." During a visit to the free states that summer, the Mobile lawyer had come across Wendell Phillip's indictment of Madison's "proslavery constitution," and immediately realized how masters might "circulate to great advantage, excluding a few paragraphs" the same evidence to make their own case for rights imperiled by expansion, war, and a gathering sentiment favorable to emancipation within the remaining French slave colonies. After four further years of consideration, Campbell excerpted Madison's words in a pamphlet of his own, using this authority to bolster the grassroots Southern Rights Associations then opposing the Compromise of 1850. Campbell was perhaps the first defender of slavery to insist that Madison's 1787 speech, along with the series of replies it drew forth, embodied the "principles which should constitute the cornerstone of the Constitution." The compound republic's failure to implement Madison's advice, and to incorporate a sectional remedy into the country's organic charter convinced him that the masters had faced "almost insurmountable embarrassments" from the outset of American nationhood. Subsequent events at home and abroad caused him to warn that "slavery cannot exist in this Union, under the existing state of public opinion, and experiencing from its government assaults of the most inveterate and obstinate character." He even warned, in an echo of Calhoun, that continued union depended on the willingness of the northern representatives to alter the constitutional mechanism by agreeing to explicitly proslavery amendments. Without such measures, slaveholders would be forced to "seek their safety and happiness" through "a new constitution and a different confederation."[49]

Campbell's pairing of the Madisonian commentary with disunionist ultimatums resulted from his deep anxieties about the American empire. Though in 1846 he had predicted that a growing population density would end slavery within decades, the territorial acquisitions from Mexico seemed likely to "produce the most disastrous consequences to the Southern States" even more quickly. Such alarm caused Campbell to develop a set of insistent demands that the U.S. government commit the entirety of its power and

[49] Campbell to Calhoun, November 20, 1847 *PJCC* 14: 669; [Campbell], "The Rights of the Slave States," *SQR* n.s. 3 (January 1851), 104, 142, 145. See also *Substance of Remarks of John A. Campbell, at the Organization of Southern Rights Association* (Mobile: Dade, Thompson, 1850) and Campbell, *Address upon the Life and Public Services of John C. Calhoun* (Mobile, 1851). Campbell's career is detailed in Saunders, *John Archibald Campbell, Southern Moderate, 1811–1889* (Baton Rouge: Louisiana State University Press, 1997).

influence to protect slavery across the Mexican Cession's enormous expanse. "The government can perform no passive neutral part" in guaranteeing an interest already subjected to ceaseless attacks; indeed, both the Congress and the executive had "received powers to fulfill duties" and thus, had "obligations to those who have reposed trust and delegated authority." In addition to developing this position in private correspondence and in proslavery periodicals, Campbell joined William C. Yancey in committing the Alabama Democratic Party to support only a presidential candidate pledged to a territorial slave code. The Party's national convention of 1848 ignored this demand when it supported Lewis Cass and his version of "popular sovereignty" (a formula that shifted decisions about western slavery from the Congress to the territorial authorities). Intent on pushing Congress to act on slavery's behalf, Campbell then authored a set of resolutions adopted by the Southern Convention assembled in Nashville during the summer of 1850. Over the course of the following year, he became a leading proslavery critic of "noninterference," predicting that any failure to act positively on slavery's behalf would "overturn all legal and constitutional barriers against abolition."[50]

There was more of the attorney than the master in Campbell's call to "produce a law or custom which sanctions slavery operative in the territory where the slave is." Lingering echoes from his days as a West Point cadet could also be heard in his insistence that each master needed "an army or navy to guard his frontiers or coasts, and to punish the enemy who harbours his property." Yet what most distinguished Campbell's positions in the late 1840s and early 1850s was his unusually cosmopolitan understanding of the perils that American masters faced both within and beyond U.S. borders. Campbell paired his close readings of William Channing and of the Garrisonians (the former was to him a far greater threat than the latter) with a series of weighty considerations of current European scholarship on ancient and modern bondage and with warnings about how rapidly slaveholders' rights in the British Caribbean had eroded upon Parliamentary intervention there. He hoped that his sober scholarly forays might "direct the attention of our people, in a broad and liberal spirit of inquiry to a thorough investigation of the nature of our institutions" and might even nudge fellow masters to consider "the

[50] Campbell to Calhoun, March 1, 1848, *PJCC* 25: 213–17. The range of constitutional positions is set forth in Robert R. Russel, "Constitutional Doctrines with Regard to Slavery in Territories," *JSH* 32 (November 1966), 466–86 and Donald E. Fehrenbacher, *The Dred Scott Case: Its Importance in American Law and Politics* (New York: Oxford, 1978).

melioration of this institution in whatever manner experience has shown it to be practicable." In asserting the institution's flexibility, Campbell hoped to convince masters to provide legal barriers against the separation of slave families through sale, a move he hinted might be the first step toward a docile black labor force that was nominally free. European experience had, after all, shown that it was not opponents of slavery, or even slaves themselves, but masters who had been "the first to discover the evils of slavery, when it becomes an evil, and to seek an escape from the constraints it imposes."[51]

If Campbell risked being branded a Deep South heretic in speculating about a transition from slavery to free labor, he remained firm that masters themselves must control any modification of their social order. Along with other early leaders of the Southern Rights movement, he insisted that bondage was more than simply a regional property interest. Here lay an indispensable part of what made the "South" a distinctive society and a meaningful political entity in the first place. Slavery, Campbell noted, had been understood at least since the time of the Constitution as "the central point about which Southern Society is formed" and had thus become the region's chief identifying feature. Other writers went still further, offering pleas for the "rights of the South" that made region a proxy for slaveholders' class interests. In 1851, the pamphleteer Peter Della Torre demonstrated the rhetorical power of such metonymy when he argued (again in the context of sectional "rights" to the territories) "you cannot speak, you cannot think of the South without slavery. It is included in her idea." On the eve of secession, the Rev. James Henley Thornwell conveyed with particular transparency how "the Southern man, politically, is the slaveholder." Lamenting how the election of Lincoln would strip the South of all its claims, Thornwell stipulated that "the rights of the South are the rights of the South as slaveholding."[52]

---

[51] Campbell to Calhoun, March 1, 1848; "Rights of the Slave States," 123; "Slavery Throughout the World," *SQR* n.s. 3 (April 1851) 317; "Slavery in the United States," *SQR* 12 (July 1847), 114. See also "The Tariff," *SQR* 9 (January 1846), 114–49; "Slavery Among the Romans," *SQR* 14 (October 1848), "The British West Indian Islands," *SQR* 16 (January 1850) and, for a survey of all these, Justine M. Mann, "The Political Thought of John Archibald Campbell, 1847–1851," *Alabama Law Review* 22 (1969–70).

[52] [Peter Della Torre], "Is Southern Civilization Worth Preserving?" *SQR* n.s. 3 (January 1851), 206; James Henley Thornwell, *The State of the Country: An Article Republished from the Southern Presbyterian Review* (Columbia: Southern Guardian Steam-Power Press, 1861), 20. John Minor Botts (the only Virginia Congressman to support slavery's restriction) provided a withering indictment of such logic in *Speech at Dinner at Powhatan Court House* ([Richmond], n.p.), 5.

Using regional appeals to advance the interests of slaveholders worked well enough as prescriptive rhetoric. But this technique furnished a weak basis for reasoned arguments before a court, a fact that accounts for Campbell's reluctance to transfer his argument for slavery's positive protection in the territories out of the political system and into those judicial arenas that demanded greater constitutional rigor and precision. His qualms about vindicating masters' rights through a ruling of the Supreme Court persisted even after he was made an associate justice of that body in 1853. Once his fellow justices agreed (against Campbell's advice) to take up the case of the Missouri slave Dred Scott, he issued a notably restrained concurring opinion. He did join the majority in agreeing that federal restriction of territorial slavery was impermissible, though he did so by taking a narrow view of the territorial clause, which he concluded "confers no power upon Congress to dissolve the relations of the master and slave on the domain of the United States, either within or without any of the States." Significantly, he declined to join Chief Justice Roger Taney's bolder suggestion that for Congress to ban slavery in the territories would constitute a violation of masters' Fifth Amendment claims to due process. He even intimated that Lewis Cass' position on popular sovereignty was constitutionally sound, conceding that "how much municipal power may be exercised by the people of the Territory, before their admission to the Union, the courts of justice cannot decide." Such a question "must depend, for the most part, on political considerations, which cannot enter into the determination of a case of law or equity." Backing away from demands for forceful government protection of masters' rights in the West was not an indication of weakening resolve on Campbell's part. It revealed instead his appreciation that what should have been done at the Philadelphia convention in 1787 was a different question than what had actually transpired there.[53]

As Campbell no doubt realized, advanced proslavery constitutionalism of the 1850s could be effective even if it did not change the way judges or even Congressmen interpreted the compound republic. The Southern Rights Associations that spread after the admission of a free soil California, and which were resurrected in 1860, sought to mobilize resentment about the South's "unequal" access to a burgeoning American empire and to center Southern politics on an aggressive identification with slavery. The fruits of these efforts could be seen in a newly popular vocabulary of Southern

[53] In "Rights of the Slave State," Campbell had attacked the "vicious principles" of the Clayton Compromise, which had sought to push the territorial issue toward the courts. The larger context of his opinion is provided in Fehrenbacher, *The Dred Scott Case.*

Rights, a term that had been invoked only sporadically, and with little consistency prior to 1848.[54]

The strength of the newer, more effective appeals to "Southern" rights depended on their ability to yoke a growing sense of sectional distinctiveness (a trend that coincided with the canonization of proslavery polemics) with Jacksonian notions of "equality." In condemning what proponents considered an invidious distinction between freeborn white men, Southern Rights orators and pamphleteers drew upon mainstream republican commitments. A South Carolinian helpfully framed the issue by asserting how the equality "of rights and privileges between citizen and citizen, pursuit and pursuit, and one portion of the country and another" constituted the "deep and solid foundation of our political fabric." The second major aspect of Southern Rights claims – the demand that free states enforce the 1850 Fugitive Slave Law – similarly drew out the sectional dimensions of the constitutional regime of obligations and rights. This issue implied that it was the free North and the slave South that formed the key parties to the Constitution, and that further union depended on white Americans' mutual recognition of one another's equality. These two elements of late antebellum politics – the territorial issue and the fugitive slave controversy – took on an importance that neither could have produced on its own. The electrifying appearance of Harry Macarthy's most successful Confederate song showed how a decade of complaints had readied countless Confederate soldiers to march off to battle in 1861, singing:

> Hurrah! Hurrah!
> For Southern Rights Hurrah!
> Hurrah for the Bonnie Blue flag
> That bears the single star![55]

---

[54] Edwin Holland anticipated the Southern Rights position in *A Refutation of the Calumnies Circulated Against the Southern and Western States*, writing (at 8) "it must be conceded that the people of the South and West have certain established constitutional rights and privileges contradistinguished by their peculiar situation, from those of the North and East, the surrender of which would be worse than the wildest insanity." Conway Robinson even used the phrase, though with no more precision, in "Slavery and the Constitution: Rights of the Slave-Holding States, and of the Owners of Slave Property, Under the Constitution of the United States," *SLM* 6 (January 1840), 89–106.

[55] J.C. Oswald, *Address Delivered at Walterboro Before the Colleton Rifle-Corps, on the Fourth of July, 1848* (Charleston, 1848), 7; Harry Macarthy, *The Bonnie Blue Flag*. J. Mills Thornton provides the single best explication of Southern Rights principles of equality, though in a way that minimizes its proslavery intentions, in *Politics and Power in a Slave Society, Alabama, 1800–1860* (Baton Rouge: Louisiana State University Press, 1978), esp. 204–27, 442–61. The possibilities of extragovernmental popular constitutionalism are a primary theme of James Vernon, ed., *Re-Reading the Constitution: New Narratives in the Political History of England's Long Nineteenth Century* (Cambridge: Cambridge University Press, 1996).

The seemingly empty emotionalism of Southern Rights sloganeering struck many observers as superficial. The proslavery unionist John Pendleton Kennedy of Maryland summed up this case in 1861 when he asked "What are Southern rights? Everybody speaks of them, nobody defines them. So vague, so misty, so variable, they escape every attempt to define them." Kennedy, who was a leading Whig lawyer and an influential plantation novelist, was too keen a student of the sectional conflict to underestimate the effectiveness of such vague claims, however. Unable to wish away a program that brought disparate regional complaints under a single rubric of "equality or independence," Kennedy nonetheless scored points in noting how disunion was likely to do far more harm than good to slavery's territorial expansion or to attempts to claim fugitive slaves that reached free soil. In previous writings, Kennedy had indicated he was aware of the book-length effort that had in fact systematized (and thus defined) what Southern Rights constitutionalism was all about. The dubious credit of moving this program from an ill-defined battle cry to a sweeping "new theory of the Constitution" belonged to John Scott of Virginia. On the eve of the fateful 1860 presidential election, he presented American readers with something genuinely new in American constitutional discourse – offering up what he termed *The Lost Principle; or the Sectional Equilibrium: How it Was Created – How Destroyed – How it May be Restored.*[56]

John Scott spent most of the 1850s sharpening his polemical skills as a proslavery journalist and commanding a cavalry company that would in 1860 oversee John Brown's execution. In 1858, the prolonged struggle to establish slavery in Kansas inspired him to draw upon an earlier legal training, which had been fostered by his father (a prominent Fauquier County judge) and capped by graduation from the law department of the University of Virginia and his admission to the state bar in 1841. *The Lost Principle* was less a legal argument than a historical detective story, however, since it sought to establish the true basis of the Constitution's

---

[56] John P. Kennedy, *The Great Drama: An Appeal to Maryland* (Baltimore: John D. Toy, 1861), 8; idem, *The Border States: Their Power and Duty in the Present Disordered Condition of the Country* (Philadelphia: Lippincott's, 1861), 7. The ubiquitous slogan "equality or independence" was introduced by "A Virginian," [M.R.H. Garnett] *The Union, Past and Future: How it Works, and How to Save It* (Charleston: Walker and James, 1850), a pamphlet that drew attention throughout the 1850s. Scott's contribution, by contrast became most influential only after 1865, as can be seen in Albert Taylor Bledsoe in "The North and the South at the Convention of 1787," *Southern Review* 2 (October 1867), 358–88.

"three-fifths compromise," the ratio by which 60 percent of the slave population was included in each state's Congressional representation. Scott set Madison's 1787 commentary about the division of free and slave states alongside a string of related commentaries and actions to reveal a hitherto "lost principle" that an "equilibrium" between the North and South had in fact been intended by the founders, even if not implemented in a particularly open way. In the maneuverings over the basis of political power between the free and slave states, he thus located "the groundwork of the political edifice, with reference to which every other part was made." Scott devoted little effort to the question whether the 1787 assembly had created a nation, or simply a compact among coequal states. His contribution shifted the debate altogether by asserting that this document represented "a Great Treaty between two nations of opposite civilizations, and, in many respects, opposite interests." Here, he grandly exclaimed, lay a discovery that revealed that the founders' compound republic was "even more complex than it has been generally supposed to be."[57]

Scott repeatedly noted the relevance of his theory of sectional equilibrium to the political demands of the 1850s. Unlike Calhoun and Campbell (who sensed the shortcomings of proslavery federalism, but clung to state rights argument for lack of a better alternative) Scott openly admitted how "the exercise of State sovereignty within State jurisdiction" could not "move an inch beyond those consecrated limits." To project power into the territories through a federally sponsored slave code, or to reach into the free states in pursuit of fugitives required a doctrine capable of uniting all the slave states into a single unit. So much the better, he believed, that the founders' own constitutional principles tended to "obliterate, wherever their common civilization is threatened, State lines, and to resolve the Southern States into one community." Scott hoped that this principle might, in establishing new proslavery claims, empower the U.S. government to restore the sectional political equilibrium that framers such as Madison had intended. Yet he also acknowledged that "in case of a dissolution of the Union," slave states that recognized their hitherto "hidden" constitutional history would be

---

[57] Appleton's *Cyclopedia of American Biography*, 7: 243. Perspectives on Scott's varied activities from the 1850s can be sampled in "Modern Chivalry of Virginia," *New York Times*, June 26, 1857; "The African Slave Trade," *National Era*, October 21, 1858, and "John Brown and His Companions," *Spirit of the Times*, January 14, 1860 while his later military exploits are discussed in his *Partisan Life with Col. John S. Mosby* (New York: Harper & Brothers, 1867) and his "Scout Life with the Black Horse," *Philadelphia Weekly Times*, May 24, 1879.

"held together by a common bond, and would be led to frame, under better auspices, a common government."[58]

Unlike his proslavery predecessors, Scott explained that territorial exclusion and the workings of the tariff played only a minor role in the South's marginal status within the Union. The North's usurpation of the Union and the subsequent decline of sectional equilibrium resulted instead from the federal government's assault on the slave trade, commenced in 1808. Along with other advocates for importing more human cargo from Africa, Scott believed that reversing the South's minority status within the Union was impossible as long as current immigration trends continued. What made his argument novel was his insistence that the original constitutional agreement over "importation and migration" had intended to coordinate government action on immigration policy so as to sustain an equal population in both the sections. According to this view, the founders had sought to link the importing of slaves and the migration of white immigrants from Europe, so that a ban of one would trigger a similar restriction on the other. If such a theory had little basis in the historical record, it allowed Scott to make sectional parity the predominant theme of proslavery constitutionalism, and by extension, the end point of a thoroughly sectionalized vision of American destiny.[59]

If Scott followed Calhoun in fashioning an overtly proslavery vision of constitutionalism, his embrace of sectionalism as the compound republic's chief distinguishing feature offered a glimpse of the future. Oddly enough, his treatise returned in its conclusion to a set of specifically Virginia positions that offered the sort of federalist remedies that one might have expected from John Taylor or Spencer Roane rather than from the Deep South theorists of positive power. The longest chapter of the *Lost Principle* moved readers from the plains of Kansas and the halls of Philadelphia to the tragedy that postrevolutionary Virginia had experienced in the late 1780s. Scott wistfully imagined how Virginia might have saved itself had it rejected the federal constitution and continued the glorious career commenced under the Articles of Confederation. "By mixed fraud and violence" the state had been "dragged handcuffed into the new Union," while the "rash innovators" who "erected this mighty despotism in its place" pulled George

---

[58] [John Scott], *The Lost Principle*, v–viii. During the Kansas debates in Congress in 1858, Scott had written a series of essays on sectional equality for the *Richmond South*, edited by Roger Pryor. He reworked much of this material for his book, adding his thoughts on Madison and the 3/5's clause he had developed in the interim.

[59] *Ibid*, 193, 207–15.

Washington away from the Chesapeake to New York, and installed him there as the first American president. The loss of Washington to the new federal project was a grievous injury to Virginia, in that it "arrested forever his useful career" in building a transportation system that would have made the oldest American commonwealth an empire unto itself. With such thoughts in mind, Scott quixotically dropped his concern for defending the use of federal power in the territories, and instead advocated a return to the loose structure of the Articles government. Doing so was an effective reversal of Calhoun's equally desperate turn, late in his life. Rather than follow Calhoun's dual executive plan – which used a sectional program to check centralization and restore federalism – Scott considered how a renewed federalism might eventually, by bolstering internal state development, restore a sectional balance that had become by the 1850s only a distant memory.[60]

Such inventive remedies, whether proposed by Calhoun, Scott, or other Southern Rights theorists, prepared the way for an upsurge in geopolitical inquiry over the course of secession winter. Considerations of how principles of federalism, sectionalism, and nationalism might be reconfigured in the aftermath of the Republican party's presidential victory were nearly as rich as those that had been broached during the 1780s founding. A good many slaveholders built upon late antebellum proposals to tinker with inherited forms. Scott and others instead welcomed the chance to erect a new slaveholding Union, and to insist that this new Confederate republic include only states devoted to the institution of slavery. In this new polity, questions would remain about exactly how government structures would manage the challenges of independence, war, and diplomacy. But what increasingly mattered were not the details of the system but the results that it might secure. As with those who undertook the American Revolution, secessionists insisted that inherited political forms were important, but only insofar as they could muster the strength necessary to preserve even more important inherited rights.

[60] Ibid, 103, 223, 66, 221–2; for another plea that a return to the Articles of Confederation would solve the crisis over slavery, see [William Monroe McCarty], *A Glance at State Rights* (Richmond: James Woodhouse and Company, 1860).

PART TWO

THE CONTOURS OF PROSLAVERY AMERICANISM

S lavery is sectional in its character, but national in its relations – local in its situation, but worldwide in its influences. Its strength is not in written constitutions. Its might is not in armed force. Its power is in the manufactures which it supports – the industry which it employs – the sentiments which it nurtures – the civilization which it upholds.

"Works of Calhoun,"
Southern Literary Messenger, June 1854

That providence of God, by which so large a number of the States of this Union have been supplied with a population who cannot be absorbed by the body politic, but must exist among us, and for so long a time, in a distinct and menial position, provided the means of safety to the whole Union in the coming conflict which is already awakening the fears of the country. If we do not greatly mistake the signs of the times, it is to these States that all eyes and all hopes will be turned as the great bulwarks of American liberty. The African race in these States will give them this advantage of position.

Rev. William A. Smith
Lectures on the Philosophy and Practice of Slavery, 1856

3

Republican Masters and American Mission

In late March of 1790, Pennsylvania Representative Thomas Scott closed a week of bitter debate by asserting that "what is said, and more particularly what is finally done in Congress at this time will in some degree form the political character of America on the subject of slavery." Like most in his audience, Scott realized that launching the compound republic would not simply equip Americans with the means to express their national will. An invigorated Union would foster a more precise articulation of national purpose and values as well. A series of questions remained. Would new Constitutional forms furnish a "solid foundation" for "exploding the principles of negro slavery," as Scott's fellow Pennsylvanian Tench Coxe had predicted a year and a half earlier? Would the House follow the advice of Benjamin Franklin and other antislavery petitioners who sought to approach "the very verge" of congressional powers to remove "*this Inconsistency from the Character of the American people*"? Was it possible to honor the Constitution's twenty-year protection of the slave trade and still testify to what James Madison called "the sense of America" that this trade was an affront to humanity? Or would U.S. leaders cede the mantel of humanitarianism to the British, who the previous year had bolstered their claims of national virtue with a grassroots petition campaign against slaving?[1]

---

[1] Scott, Coxe, Franklin petition, and Madison quotations from John P. Kaminski, ed., *A Necessary Evil?: Slavery and the Debate Over the Constitution* (Madison, WI: Madison House Publishers, 1995), 226, 255–6, 119, 212, 207. This debate is discussed in Richard S. Newman, "Prelude to the Gag Rule: Southern Reaction to Antislavery Petitions in the First Federal Congress," *JER* 16 (Winter 1996), 571–99 and Joseph C. Burke, "The Pro-Slavery Argument in the First Federal Congress," *Duquesne Review* 16 (Spring 1969). Christopher Leslie Brown situates the 1788 British petitioning in the context of transatlantic rivalries in *Moral Capital: The Foundations of British Antislavery* (Chapel Hill: University of North Carolina Press, 2006), 446–50.

Representatives from South Carolina and Georgia helped to answer such questions by unleashing a vigorous attack on what James Jackson of Savannah derisively termed the antislavery "fashion of the day." While securing for their constituents the full benefits of the African slave trade (which would peak between 1803 and a ban imposed in 1807), Jackson, Thomas Tudor, and William Loughton Smith broadcast a remarkably broad defense of bondage to their fellow members of the first House of Representatives. This trio's lengthy considerations demonstrated their adeptness at using republican principles to legitimate a system of slavery that had developed within the context of monarchical empire. They lavished attention on economic and geopolitical necessity and warned in dire tones about the racial mixture likely to follow emancipation. They considered the slave societies of the Old and New Testaments (quoting extensively by chapter and verse) while also attending to the ancient slaveholding republics of Greece and Rome. They set these examples beside extensive reflections from the Scottish writer John Millar, British naval accounts of the Caribbean, and the racist speculations ventured in Thomas Jefferson's *Notes on the State of Virginia*. Yet having made the sort of wide-ranging case usually associated with the late antebellum period, these American pioneers of proslavery polemics neither refined nor systematized their arguments nor committed them to durable form. Subsequent defenders of slavery would be nearly entirely ignorant of the exhaustive proslavery efforts taken at the very outset of the American political nation.[2]

James Jackson and his colleagues dropped their efforts in part because they considered their arguments in instrumental terms – to be used in the pursuit of a particular objective rather than to be valued in their own right. As they were acutely aware, an overtly proslavery message could cause as much harm as good. The taunting laughter of their Congressional opponents anticipated the savage satire of Benjamin Franklin, who in May of 1790 memorably compared Jackson's labored pleas to the rationalization of white slavery made by the Algerines a hundred years earlier. Franklin associated the very sophistication of proslavery arguments with slaveholders' diabolical corruption. Rather than convert

---

[2] Jackson in Kaminksi, ed., *A Necessary Evil*, 206. Materials later published in *Annals* cannot convey the full breadth of proslavery polemics during these sessions, which are more evident in contemporary newspaper coverage contained in *DCFFC* vol. 12. Unlike abolitionist writers, who regularly invoked this episode, James D.B. De Bow skirted it in his otherwise comprehensive "Early Congressional Discussions of Slavery," *DBR* (July 1857), 35–47.

listeners to their point of view, Congressional appeals inspired the same sense of befuddled astonishment displayed by those twentieth-century historians who have dismissed the South's "feudal dream" and marveled at its "fantastically imaginative" attempt to cultivate a "weirdly beautiful flower, the black orchid of antebellum Southern intellectual culture." From the vantage point of 1790, Scott similarly remarked how "an advocate for slavery, in its fullest latitude, at this age of the world, and on the floor of American Congress too" was nothing less than "a phenomenon in politics."[3]

It would be several decades before proslavery advocates would be ready to offer a secular vindication of republican slavery to pair with the religious defense (whose distinct trajectory and implications requires consideration in a separate chapter). The polemics that came to be known as the "proslavery argument" were a set of interrelated political and cultural interventions shaped by sectional, national, and international dynamics. By the 1850s, the particular exigencies that inspired such efforts had been largely obscured, and slaveholding nationalists systematized what had been haphazard arguments into something approaching a distinctive world view. All New World slaveholders were, by virtue of their sizeable investment in human property, attuned to the geopolitics of mastery. What made the U.S. case different – and what lent it a distinctively American character – was the expectation that national legitimacy might ultimately rest less on the constitutional maneuvering and partisan alliances than on the worth of abstract ideas and the depth of intellectual convictions. The proslavery defenses of the late

---

[3] For laughter, see Lloyd's Notes "March 17, 1790" in *DCFFC*, 12: 738; [Franklin], "Sidi Mehemet Ibrahim on the Slave Trade," in J. A. Leo Lemay, ed., *Benjamin Franklin: Writings* (New York: Library of America, 1987), 1157–60; Louis Hartz, *The Liberal Tradition in America: An Interpretation of American Political Thought Since the Revolution* (New York, 1955); Joel Williamson, *A Rage for Order: Black-White Relationships in the American South Since Reconstruction* (New York: Oxford, 1986), 15; Scott in Kaminksi, ed., *A Necessary Evil*, 226. Franklin's use of parody to undermine proslavery had precedent, as explained in Lester B. Scherer, "A New Look at 'Personal Slavery Established,'" *WMQ* 30 (October 1973), 645–52. The general rhetorical context is addressed in Peter A. Dorsey, "To 'Corroborate our Own Claims": Public Positions and the Slavery Metaphor in Revolutionary America," *American Quarterly* 55 (September 2003), 353 while an important analysis of the dependence of antebellum slavery "debates" on a mutual regard of an opponent's worth and integrity appears in Betram Wyatt-Brown's curiously underappreciated "Proslavery and Antislavery Intellectuals: Class Concepts and Polemical Struggle," in Lewis Perry and Michael Fellman, eds., *Antislavery Reconsidered: New Perspectives on the Abolitionists* (Baton Rouge: Louisiana State University Press, 1979), 308–36.

antebellum period faced a considerable challenge in decreeing that bondage would rise or fall not simply on matters of interest or authority.
These invited outsiders to consider the institution's compatibility with
broadly shared notions of American values and visions of a globally
redeeming national mission.[4]

BOISTEROUS PASSIONS AND
NATIONAL VIRTUES

Twenty-three years before offering President Thomas Jefferson 530 million acres west of the Mississippi, the French minister Francois Barbé-
Marbois set in motion another transaction that would have similarly
momentous consequences for American slavery. Through a prolonged
series of drafts and revisions, Governor Jefferson transformed a list of
queries sent by Marbois into the only book he ever published. The chapter
on "Manners" that he included in *Notes on the State of Virginia* encap-
sulated better than any other text the founders' primal anxieties about
slaveholding's tendency to corrupt republican character. "The whole
commerce between master and slave is a perpetual exercise of the most
boisterous passions, the most unremitting despotism on the one part and
degrading submission on the other," Jefferson wrote. The worst result of
this archetypal brutality concerned the "rising generation" of American
republicans.

Other children see this, and learn to imitate it ... The parent storms, the child
looks on, catches the lineaments of wrath, puts on the same airs in the circle of

---

[4] Larry Tise, *Proslavery: A History of the Defense of Slavery in America, 1701–1840*
(University of Georgia Press, 1987) usefully challenges the prevailing conflation of American
proslavery with Southern sectionalism, though nonetheless obscures the distinctiveness of
antebellum polemics. The particularly American nature of proslavery can be tracked in
James Oakes, "Slavery as an American Problem," in Larry Griffin, ed., *The South as an
American Problem* (University of Georgia Press, 1995); David Brion Davis, *Slavery and
Human Progress* (New York: Oxford, 1984) and, in comparative terms, in Peter Kolchin,
"In Defense of Servitude: American Proslavery and Russian Proserfdom Arguments, 1760–
1860," *AHR* 85 (October 1980), 809–27 and Barbara Weinstein, "Slavery, Citizenship,
and National Identity in Brazil and the U.S. South," in Don Doyle and Marco Antonio
Pamplona, eds., *Nationalism in the New World* (Athens: University of Georgia Press,
2006) 248–71. My interest lies in tracking the process by which this world-view manifested
itself, not with asserting its integrity and coherence, a project pursued in Eugene Genovese,
*The Slaveholders' Dilemma: Freedom and Progress in Southern Conservative Thought,
1820–1860* (Columbia: University of South Carolina Press, 1992) and in Elizabeth Fox-
Genovese and Eugene D. Genovese, *The Mind of the Master Class: History and Faith in
the Southern Slaveholders' Worldview* (New York: Cambridge University Press, 2005).

smaller slaves, gives a loose to his worst of passion, and thus nursed, educated, and daily exercised in tyranny, cannot but be stamped by it with odious peculiarities ... [In] permitting one half the citizens thus to trample on the rights of the other, [slavery] transforms those into despots, and these into enemies, destroys the morals of one part, and the *amor patriae* of the other. For if a slave can have a country in this world, it must be any other in preference to that in which he is born to live and labour for another.[5]

This extended critique drew upon fairly conventional understandings, popularized by Montesquieu, Franklin, and a host of other writers who linked slavery to underdevelopment, both in its retarding effect on colonial economics and its sapping of moral capacities. Yet Jefferson's words, appearing as they did as a semiofficial position after the Revolution, formed a uniquely powerful expression of the challenges American masters faced in restructuring their society upon a republican basis. The image of the dissolute planter and his overworked, alienated slave spoke as much to the uncertain future of internal development as to the geopolitical insecurities that made plantations vulnerable to military invasion. The diagnosis that Jefferson provided thus proved remarkably long-lasting, persisting as the central text of a republican antislavery canon long after the Union had proven its ability to survive in a hostile world. The precise words from "Manners," repeated so often as to become formulaic, thus furnished a baseline nationalist critique of slavery that appealed to colonizationists, immediatists, and free soil advocates, especially once the passage circulated among the new country's foreign critics.[6]

---

[5] Jefferson, *Notes on the State of Virginia* (Boston: Lilly and Wait, 1832), 169–70; Douglas L. Wilson, "The Evolution of Jefferson's *Notes on the State of Virginia*," *VMHB* 112 (2004), 98–133.

[6] St. George Tucker, *Blackstone Commentaries* (Philadelphia, 1803) vol. 2 appendix, 69–70; Charles Rich, *Annals* 16th Congress, 1st session (February, 1820), 1399; Daniel J. McInerney, *The Fortunate Heirs of Freedom: Abolition and Republican Thought* (Lincoln, NE: 1994), 85, 186; Daniel R. Goodloe, *The Southern Platform: or, Manual of Southern Sentiment on the Subject of Slavery* (Boston, MA: J.P. Jewett, 1858). British writers excerpted "Manners" from its reprinting in Jedidiah Morse's 1789 *Geography* and thus lent this passage a crucial role in the transatlantic understanding of Virginia. See William Winterbotham, *An Historical, Geographical, Commercial, and Philosophical View of the United States of America* (1796), 207; John Payne, *A New and Complete System of Universal Geography* (New York: John Low, 1799), 211; John Adams, *View of Universal History from the Creation to the Present Time* (London: G. Kearsley, 1795), 18; John Harriott, *Struggles Through Life: Exemplified in the Various Travels and Adventures in Europe, Asia, Africa, and America* (London J. Scriven, 1808), 240; Francis Maseres, *Occasional Essays on Various Subjects Chiefly Political and Historical* (London: Robert Wilks, 1809), 302.

Defenders of slavery had little choice but to respond to the national and transnational critics who circulated Jefferson's searing indictment. Some neutralized his analysis by insisting that he had not really meant what he had said. In 1818, John Taylor of Caroline speculated that his friend and regular correspondent had suffered from the "moral fermentation" and "temporary effervescence" associated with a "war for liberty." Observations made during more tranquil periods convinced Taylor that he and Jefferson agreed that slaves were "too far below, and too much in the power of the master, to inspire furious passions" and were thus "more frequently the objects of benevolence than rage." Since "children from their nature are inclined to soothe, and hardly ever suffered to tyrannize over them," it seemed more accurate to say that enslaved blacks "open instead of shut the sluices of benevolence in tender minds." In 1820, Senator William Smith of South Carolina took this same case back onto the floor of Congress, reversing Jefferson's terms by insisting that "the whole commerce between master and slave is patriarchal." He added that southern slaves had become "so domesticated, or so kindly treated by their masters and their situations so improved" that their enslavement had ceased to be a source of discontent.[7]

Another approach was to offer up an antidote to Jefferson's memorable passage on "Manners," a strategy anticipated by those in the first Congress who appealed to the discussion of black racial inferiority contained in a chapter from *Notes* titled "Laws." Using Jefferson against himself involved a knotty rhetorical problem, however, since the succinct clarity of Jefferson's antislavery tableau was far better suited to distillation and circulation than was his comparatively labored exploration of the "real distinctions nature has made" between black slaves and their white masters. As many have noted, Jefferson's testimony about the "unfortunate difference of color" (which he discussed in terms of "the reticular membrane" and of the "scarf skin" and the "color of the bile") were a chilling anticipation of modern biological racism. Yet Jefferson's animus toward the capacities of black men and women would only be adequately appreciated by those who immersed themselves in this vile text long enough to experience its cumulative effect.

---

[7] John Taylor, *Arator: Being a Series of Agricultural Essays; Practical and Political* (Baltimore, MD: J. Robinson, 1817), 44–5; William Smith, *Annals* 16th Congress, 1st session (January 1820), 267–70. See also Thomas R. Dew, "Abolition of Negro Slavery" *AQR* 12 (September 1832), 250–1; J.L. Reynolds "Fidelity of Slaves," *DBR* 29 (November 1860), 570. In 1850, Edward Bryan implied that Jefferson's words were of northern origin; see *The Rightful Remedy. Addressed to the Slaveholders of the South* (Charleston, SC: Walker and James, 1850), 71.

No single phrase or image matched the currency of his "boisterous passions" passage; the most quotable lines were those concerned not with perpetuating slavery but with removing black freedmen from the white republic.[8]

Observations made by Edmund Burke in 1775 thus became almost by default the favored means of neutralizing Jefferson's assault on bondage. In the midst of his defense of the colonies, Burke had noted that the "vast multitude of slaves" were a central aspect of those "circumstances attending the southern colonies which makes the spirit of liberty still more high and haughty than in those to the northward." He then explained:

Where [widespread enslavement] is the case, in any part of the world, those who are free are by far the most proud and jealous of their freedom. Freedom is to them not only an enjoyment, but a kind of rank and privilege. Not seeing there, that freedom, as in countries where it is a common blessing, and as broad and general as the air, that it may be united with much abject toil, with great misery, with all the exterior of servitude, liberty looks among them like something more noble and liberal . . . . [With] all masters of slaves who are not slaves themselves . . . the haughtiness of domination combines with the spirit of freedom, fortifies, and renders it invincible.[9]

Burke's words became epigrammatic over the first half of the nineteenth-century, as proslavery writers invoked his authority as the consummate explanation of how domination bred an inherent love of liberty. A passage quoted by John Taylor in the 1810s, and introduced by Nathaniel Macon in a Congressional debate of 1820 would be incorporated into the still more influential proslavery polemics of George McDuffie, Thomas

[8] Recourse to the racialism of *Notes* during the 1790 Congressional debates is documented in Kaminski, *A Necessary Evil?*, 214, 217, 220. Bruce Dain, *The Hideous Monster of the Mind: American Race Theory in the Early Republic* (Cambridge, MA: Harvard University Press, 2002) situates Jefferson's racialism, while later antiabolitionist invocations of these passages include John Campbell, *Negro-Mania: Being an Examination of the Falsely Assumed Equality of the Various Races of Men* (Philadelphia, PA: Campbell & Power, 1852), 434–43 and John H. Van Evrie, *Subgenation: The Theory of the Normal Relation of the Races* (New York, John Bradburn, 1864), 39–41.
[9] Edmund Burke, "Speech on American Conciliation, March 22, 1775," in *Edmund Burke on the American Revolution: Selected Speeches and Letters* (New York: Harper and Row, 1966), 85. An early and influential proslavery use of this speech appeared in Bryan Edwards, *The History, Civil and Commercial, of the British Colonies in the West Indies* (Dublin: L. White, 1793), 206. For a contention that Burke's words were quoted by proslavery writers more frequently than any other text, see William Sumner Jenkins, *Pro-Slavery Thought in the Old South* (Chapel Hill: University of North Carolina Press, 1935), 290.

Dew, Beverley Tucker, and William Harper.[10] As claims about slaveholders' "high and haughty" sense of liberty became more familiar, Burke's testimony was extended ever more broadly. By 1858, Dr. J. G. M. Ramsey was ready to explain how slaveholders' "great jealousy of liberty" not only influenced "the master spirits of the Revolution South" but could also be seen in "their truest allies and compeers North – Hancock, Warren, Otis, Adams, and others." All of these men, Ramsey insisted (albeit inaccurately) had personally "held the Negro in bondage." In 1854, B. F. Stringfellow applied Burke's observation to all white southerners, asserting that in a republic based on racial slavery, the institution "elevates the character not only of the master, the actual owner of slaves, but of all who wear the colour of freeman." The spirit of racial aristocracy, which diffused outward from masters to the rest of free society, could alone assure "the preservation of our Republic, in all its purity."[11]

There were several incongruities in slaveholders' seeming preference for Burke over Jefferson. That Burke's observations were unsubstantiated by personal experience should have mattered to men like William Gilmore Simms, who regularly insisted that only southern whites be allowed to enter "the discussion of institutions which lie so far below the surface as ours." And Burke was not just any foreigner, but a prominent opponent of the Atlantic slave trade who had warned since 1765 that the political capacities of white American masters had been sapped by their "unlimited right over the lives and liberties of others."[12] Yet

[10] Taylor, *Arator*, 123–4; Nathaniel Macon, *Annals* (January 1820), 228; McDuffie, "Message as Governor" *Journal of the General Assembly of the State of South Carolina for the Year 1835* (1835), 8; Dew, "Abolition of Negro Slavery," 253; [Beverly Tucker], "Note to Blackstone's Commentary, Being the Substance of Remarks on the Subject of Domestic Slavery, Delivered to the Law Class of William and Mary College, December 2, 1834" *SLM* 1 (January 1835), 230; William Harper, *Anniversary Oration; Delivered . . . in the Representative Hall, Columbia, S.C. December 9, 1835* (Washington, D.C.: Duff Green, 1835), 11–12.

[11] J.G.M. Ramsey to Leonidas Spratt, April 23, 1858, in William B. Hesseltine, ed., *Autobiography and Letters of J.G.M. Ramsey* (Nashville, TN: Tennessee Historical Commission, 1954), 93; B.F. Stringfellow, *Negro-Slavery, No Evil; or The North and the South* (St. Louis: M. Niedner & Co, 1854), 29. See also Robert Toombs *An Oration Delivered before the Few and Phi Gamma Societies of Emory College, at Oxford, Ga., July 1853* (Augusta, GA: Steam Power Press of Chronicle and Sentinel, 1853), 21; Robert Hunter, *Observations on the History of Virginia* (Richmond, VA: Clemmit and Fore, 1855), 33; George Sawyer, *Southern Institutes* (Philadelphia, PA: J.B. Lippincott, 1858), 373–5; "The Philosophy of Secession," *SLM* 34 (September and October 1862), 550.

[12] Simms, "Miss Trollope and the Americans," *AQR* 7 (1832), 231; Simms further claimed that slave institutions "may not be seen, and can only be judged of and known by those who feel them." [Burke], "History of Europe," *The Annual Register . . . for 1765* (London: J. Dodsley, 1766), 33–7. Burke's antislavery passage is a good deal less pointed that is implied by Conor Cruise O'Brien, *The Great Melody: A Thematic Biography and Commented Anthology of Edmund Burke* (Chicago, IL: University of Chicago Press, 1992), 92.

perhaps the greatest irony in his canonization by proslavery ideologues was the fact that Burke's words were much closer to Jefferson's than most admitted, or may have even realized. Testifying to slaveholders' "stubborn spirit" and their attachment to the "haughtiness of domination" was not meant as praise, nor were the comparisons he made between colonial masters, England's own "Gothic ancestors," and the modern-day Polish gentry. Burke himself was specific on this point. In an aside that proslavery writers often omitted, he clarified that "I do not mean, sir, to commend the superior morality of this [liberty-loving] sentiment, which has, at least, as much pride as virtue in it." Pride hardly numbered among those civic traits likely to sustain popular government. Slaveholders' selfish "spirit of liberty" could easily be made into a threat to harmony and public spirit, a point that Burke's antagonist Josiah Tucker established when he used this formulation to cast doubts upon republicanism itself.[13]

Such distinctions mattered less and less as the geopolitical uncertainties of the post-Revolutionary period receded. It was no coincidence, then, that the proslavery vogue for Burke coincided with a shift from a politics of virtuous restraint toward a partisan polarity that made masculine individualism and self-assertion into a Jacksonian ideal. The gendered aspect of this ideal was central to its logic. The sanctioning of male pursuit of private ends (especially in economic terms) was accompanied by a broad cultural consensus that American womanhood was the true repository of national virtue and that American mothers were the primary guarantors of future national development. The proslavery writer Thomas Dew of Virginia exemplified this understanding of female development (which he insisted was historically intertwined with the institution of slavery), and did so by blending older eighteenth-century notions of stadial theory with new national imperatives. Taking up a question that Jefferson had never addressed, Dew insisted that "the advantages resulting from the ameliorated condition of woman" and her "immense

[13] Josiah Tucker, *A Letter to Edmund Burke, Esq* (Glocester, RI: R. Raikes, 1775), 23–4. Congressman Ezra Gross of New York captured this point in noting that "in order to raise our happiness to perfect ecstasy ... [Burke] assures us that we resemble the ancient Goths (I wonder he did not say Vandals) and modern Poles ... I hope ... to the end of time, it may be a slander upon our character to compare us with the barbarians of ancient or modern Europe." *Annals* (February 1820), 1248. Antislavery forces in the British Parliament were on guard against attempts to yoke Burke's legacy to colonial slavery, as James J. Sack explains in *From Jacobite to Conservative: Reaction and Orthodoxy in Britain, 1760–1832* (New York: Cambridge University Press, 1993), 171.

influence on the destiny of our race" was "acknowledged by all."
Woman's importance, Dew continued, lay in "the duty of rearing into manhood a creature, in its infancy the frailest and feeblest which Heaven has
made – of forming the plastic mind – of training the ignorance and imbecility
of infancy into virtue and efficiency." As such there was "no moral power,
the magnitude of which swells so far beyond the grasp of calculation, as the
influence of the female character on the virtues and happiness of mankind."[14]

Dew's comments implied that slavery's influence on women within slaveholding households should matter at least as much to the republican future
as the effect of "boisterous passions" on the master, the slave, or on the male
children of plantations.

Two of the most influential pieces of British travel writing of the 1830s
agreed, and these helped to seal the link between slaveholding routines
and national destiny. Frances Trollope cast fresh light on Jefferson's
own Monticello by revisiting the relationship between the President and
his black slave Sally Hemings (who, as Trollope did not note, had been
the half sister of his own dead wife). Moving beyond James Callender's
1800 attack on Jefferson, Trollope embroidered her account by following
the mulatto daughter of Hemings and Jefferson through the American
slave markets, thereby establishing a theme that would percolate through
Anglo-American culture until it culminated in William Wells Brown's
antislavery novel *Clotelle; Or, the President's Daughter.*[15] A somewhat

---

[14] Thomas R. Dew, *Review of the Debate in the Virginia Legislature of 1831 and 1832*
(Richmond, VA: T.W. White, 1832), 38; Rosemary Zagarrie, "Morals, Manners, and
the Republican Mother," *American Quarterly* 44 (June 1992), 192–215; Ruth H.
Bloch, "The Gendered Meanings of Virtue in Revolutionary America," *Signs: Journal
of Women in Culture and Society* 13 (Autumn 1987), 37–58; Jan Lewis, "The Problem
of Slavery in Southern Political Discourse," *Devising Liberty: Preserving and Creating
Freedom in the New American Republic* (Stanford: Stanford University Press, 1995),
265–300.

[15] Sidney P. Moss and Carolyn Moss, "The Jefferson Miscegenation Legend in British Travel
Books," *JER* 7 (Autumn 1987), 253–74 establishes a lull of transatlantic interest in Jefferson's relationship with Sally Hemings between the relatively ineffectual attacks made by
Federalist enemies and Trollope's 1832 book. More recent work suggests the same chro-
nology applies to this episode's salience in American public life and letters. Besides the
several pertinent essays in Jan Lewis, Peter Onuf, eds., *Sally Hemings and Thomas Jefferson: History, Memory, and Civic Culture* (Charlottesville: University of Virginia Press,
1999) see Elise Virginia Lemire, *"Miscegenation": Making Race in America*, (Philadelphia:
University of Pennsylvania Press, 2002), 11–34, which suggests the limited success of
Federalist attacks on Jefferson.

more mixed evaluation of plantation life came from Harriet Martineau's influential discussion of the "Morals of Slavery," which appeared just five years after Trollope's book. Somewhat surprisingly, Martineau began her consideration with a series of tributes to the mercy, generosity, and purity of those individual masters who she had met firsthand. She thus concluded (in a spirit that found both Jefferson and his critics half-right) that "every slaveholder's temper is subjected to a discipline which must either ruin or perfect it." The bulk of Martineau's critique concerned slavery's effect on female members of the household, a problem that led her to the volatile issue of masters' sexual exploitation of their slaves. "Every man who resides on his plantation may have his harem," Martineau lamented, before she added that "those who, notwithstanding, keep their homes undefiled may be considered of incorruptible purity."[16]

The sexual temptations of plantation life had transfixed metropolitan observers for decades, and the critique took on a sectional and partisan dynamic in the Federalist attacks upon so-called "Virginia Luxuries" during the first party system. Yet, lampooning the hypocrisy of Virginia Republicans never achieved the same cultural potency as indictments of the 1830s, which presented southern "harems" as a uniquely grave threat to American character. Abolitionists, clearly influenced by contemporary British outrage about the "indecent" lashing of female slaves in the West Indies, expended an enormous amount of attention on what the Charleston-born abolitionist Angelina Grimké termed slaveholders' "brutal lust." More damning still was the commentary of eminently respectable moralists such as the Rev. Francis Wayland of Rhode Island and the Rev. William Ellery Channing of Massachusetts. When Channing declared in 1835 that "a slave-country reeks with licentiousness," both southerners and their northern allies expressed shock at what was termed a "terrible passage" which "for the extent of its vituperation and the essence of uncharitableness has no parallel in the English language." Channing's conclusion that the southern states were "tainted with a deadlier pestilence than the plague" was lent credence by those mixed race children who provided *prima facie* evidence of sex across the color line. This sort of "practical amalgamation" was subjected to public scrutiny by the noisy political contention of the 1836 presidential election, which raised questions about the slave mistress

---

[16] Harriet Martineau, *Society in America* (New York: Saunders and Otley, 1837), 316, 320.

and mulatto children of the future Vice-President Richard Johnson of Kentucky.[17]

As interracial sexuality became a matter of national discussion, frank admissions about slaveholders' indiscretions were tucked within the pro-slavery canon. In his celebrated review of Martineau, William Gilmore Simms acknowledged that there were grounds for complaint about the "illicit and foul conduct of many among us, who make their slaves the victims and the instruments alike of the most licentious passions." Simms argued that the sexual excesses of masters should not be singled out, however, since "the negro and the colored girl in the south supply the place, which, at the north, is usually filled with factory girls." He even considered, in a passage he would omit in later versions, how creating a "mulatto" class would gradually eliminate the "moral difference" between the races. The very same year, William Harper agreed that southern inter-racial sex was not a particularly serious social evil, since it neither degraded the already degenerate black women nor removed them from any useful part in society (as he claimed was the case with white prostitutes in large free cities). Such liaisons might even do more harm than good, since these taught young white males that there was "something of degra-dation in the act" of intercourse outside of matrimony. Six years later, James Henry Hammond assumed a more typical defensive mode in his insistence that the slave States not be offered up "as a holocaust on the altar of immaculateness, to atone for the abuse of natural instinct of all mankind." Concealing the sordid tangle of intergenerational fornication then underway within his own household, Hammond insisted that such "intercourse is regarded in our society as highly disreputable." If masters' sexual predations were "carried on habitually," it "seriously affects a

---

[17] Michal J. Rozbicki, "The Curse of Provincialism: Negative Perceptions of Colonial American Plantation Gentry," *JSH* 63 (November 1997), 727–52; Brown, *Moral Capital*; Ronald G. Walters, "The Erotic South: Civilization and Sexuality in American Abolitionism," *American Quarterly* (May 1973), 177–201; Diana Paton, "Decency, Dependence, and the Lash: Gender and the British Debate over Slave Emancipation, 1830–1834," *Slavery and Abolition* 17 (1996), 162–84; Rev. George Bourne, *Slavery Illustrated in its Effect upon Woman and Domestic Society* (Boston, MA: Isaac Knapp, 1837); Sarah M. Grimke, *Letters on the Equality of the Sexes* (Boston, MA: Isaac Knapp, 1838); Channing, *Slavery* (Boston, MA: James Munroe, and Co., 1835), 95; James Trecothick Austin, *Reply to the Reviewer of the Remarks on Dr. Channing's Slavery* (Boston, MA: John H. Eastburn, 1836), 13; Fletcher, *Studies on Slavery In Easy Lessons* (Natchez, MS: Jackson Warner, 1852), 207–11; Thomas Brown, "The Miscegenation of Richard Mentor Johnson as an Issue in the National Election Campaign of 1835–1836," *CWH* 39 (March 1993), 5–30.

man's standing," he reported, even as he knew that in his own case this was not at all true.[18]

The disrepute of interracial sexuality extended beyond the case of specific individuals to rekindle a sectional dialogue about southern self-control. An overly defiant tone could embarrass masters in the same way that James Jackson's wide-ranging defense of slavery in 1790 had done. Thomas Morris of Ohio broadcast Harper's admissions of plantation sexuality from the floor of the Senate in 1839, treating his concession as proof that the South really did "reek with licentious-ness." A growing evangelical presence raised concerns about dissolution and moral laxity within the South in these same years, so that by the 1850s, unpre-cedented efforts would be taken to police black-white sexuality in urban areas such as Richmond, Virginia. That similar campaigns were never effectively imposed upon plantation communities does little to obscure a more general trans-formation in proslavery self-understanding. On the eve of disunion, those who vindicated bondage deflected attention from the temptations available to white masters and instead followed Dew's discussion of slavery's supposedly uplifting effect on free white women. They also paid increasing attention to the ennobling presence that an elderly "uncle" or "aunt" had on southern youth. This image of the aged black "mammy" was especially potent, in that it effectively "displaced sexuality into nurture and transformed potential hostility into sustenance and love," as the historian Elizabeth Fox-Genovese has deftly summarized.[19]

[18] Simms, "Miss Martineau on Slavery," *SLM* 3 (November 1837), 647; Harper, *Memoir on Slavery: Read Before the Society for the Advancement of Learning of South Carolina* (Char-leston, SC: James S. Burges, 1838), 25–9. Simms recognized his possible transgression in ending his discussion of mulattos with the quick command to "turn from this unpleasant subject." A later reprint of his piece dropped the suggestion, even as he remained "willing to acknowledge our guilt in the South" as long as the region was judged "not as slaveholders" but as fallen humans motivated by the universal carnal drives. See *The Proslavery Argument* (Charleston, SC: Walker, Richards and Company, 1852), 230. For information on the slave woman and her daughter that Hammond and his own son both took as mistresses see Drew Gilpin Faust, *James Henry Hammond and the Old South: A Design for Mastery* (Baton Rouge: Louisiana State University Press, 1982), 86–8. It was not these tangles, but actions that compromised the chastity of his white nieces that caused Hammond to be ostracized from Carolina society.

[19] Joshua D. Rothman, *Notorious in the Neighborhood: Sex and Families across the Color Line in Virginia, 1787–1861* (Chapel Hill: University of North Carolina Press, 2003); Elizabeth Fox-Genovese, *Within the Plantation Household: Black and White Women of the Old South* (Chapel Hill: University of North Carolina Press, 1988), 292. For discus-sions of the effect of slavery on white women, see "Northern and Southern Slavery," *SLM* 7 (April 1841), 314 and Marcus Bell, *Message of Love: South Side View of Cotton is King and The Philosophy of African Slavery* (Atlanta, GA: Daily Locomotive, 1860). The perspective expressed in proslavery tracts differed from the fiction of the 1850s, which, as William Taylor has noted, popularized the repressively patriarchal character of the plantation; see *Cavalier and Yankee: The Old South and American National Character* (New York: G. Braziller, 1961) 145–76.

Plantation idylls of caring servants and adoring white children came relatively late, culminating not in the antebellum proslavery argument but in the wartime and postbellum imaginings of Confederate households under Yankee assault. As late as 1843, Nathaniel Beverley Tucker could still complain that the "relation between the white child and his negro nurse, or that between the half-grown boy and the gray-headed family servant" had inspired no significant literary reflection. Tucker believed that on the level of lived experience such interactions provided members of the master class "some of our best, as well as earliest lessons of feeling and of manners." He was concerned however that "our school-books" provided nothing that would help southern youth "to cherish and per-petuate the holy affections engendered in this relation" and thus "check the growth of pride, arrogance, and selfishness, by keeping alive this sympathy between the highest and the lowest." Having already explained at some length "the moral relation between the African servant and the Caucasian master," Tucker shared Jefferson's focus on what it meant to be raised amidst relations that had "come down from generation to gen-eration" through intergenerational patterns of bondage. What troubled him was not the risk of corruption, but the scant attention directed toward those Christian virtues instilled within slaveholding house-holds.[20]

Within a decade of Tucker's 1843 lament, nostalgic plantation scenes had become a fixture of transatlantic culture. The sensational effect of Stephen Foster's music and of the minstrel-like elements of the *Uncle Tom's Cabin* phenomenon broadcast images of "Old Folks at Home" far more effectively than Tucker might have thought possible (see Figure 3.1). The politics of Foster's music and of "Uncle Tom Mania" was an unstable blend of racial sentimentalism and an affirmation of black humanity. As such, most slaveholders looked on both these phenomenon with considerable suspicion. What they no doubt appreciated, however, was how the debate over republican slavery had moved from the character of the master or the child in isolation to address the entire ensemble within southern households. In announcing "the Southern States are an aggregate, in fact, of communities, not of individuals," John C. Calhoun's oft-quoted proslavery Senate speech of 1838 captured an emerging orthodoxy. Most white Americans were willing to accept the view of the plantation as a

[20] [N.B. Tucker], "Constructions of the Constitution," *SQR* 3 (April 1843), 449–52. See also Tucker, "An Essay on the Moral and Political Effect of the Political Relation between the Caucasian Master and the African Slave," *SLM* 10 (June, August 1844), 329–39, 470–80.

FIGURE 3.1. As a mature expression of proslavery domesticity, this detail from Edward Williams Clay's 1841 lithograph stresses the multigenerational character of the plantation community. Clay visually suggests how a "humanized" bondage need not corrupt plantation-reared white children, while he uses a caption to convey the planter's pledge to nurture his "poor creatures" who had been a "sacred legacy from my ancestors." *"America," Courtesy of Library of Congress.*

stable unit, though disagreements continued whether southern households were dins of iniquity and zones of conflict or, as Calhoun would put it, they were "little communities" pervaded by harmony and humane reciprocity.[21]

---

[21] Eric Lott, *Love and Theft: Blackface Minstrelsy and the American Working Class* (New York: Oxford University Press, 1995); Sarah Meer, *Uncle Tom Mania: Slavery, Minstrelsy, and the Transatlantic Culture of the 1850s* (Athens: University of Georgia Press, 2005); Calhoun "Further Remarks in Debate on his Fifth Resolution," (January 10, 1838), *PJCC* 14: 80–6.

"A PERFECT ARMORY OF ARGUMENT"

In 1835 – two years before Ralph Waldo Emerson called "The American
Scholar" to throw off the "courtly muses of Europe" – Chancellor
William Harper offered an unusually dark formulation of national self-
assertion. "We should not learn in a servile spirit," Harper instructed his
audience in Columbia, South Carolina. Nor should white Carolinians
"receive unquestioned every dogma which the master may communicate."
The tyrant in question was a foreign public opinion that took form
through "the censures of a foreign tourist or an [sic] European periodical
print." Merely to dismiss such transatlantic assaults – which had grown in
intensity since the Anglo-American war of 1812 – was no longer sufficient.
The ominous national and international dimensions of antislavery challenged masters like Harper to "thoroughly understand" an institution that
"mixes itself with all the habits and relations of society" and "determines
whatever is peculiar in the character of our people and our government."
The murky fate of nullification and the recent move toward apprenticeship
in the British West Indies indicated that state sovereignty was not the
bulwark some expected it to be. With larger shifts underway, and with
the tide of global opinion seeming to change, Harper believed "moral
resources" were "of greatest efficacy," not least because "the consciousness of a good cause gives double strength to the combatant."[22]

By the end of 1837, Harper had followed his own advice, as had William
Gilmore Simms, another South Carolina contributor to the American canon
of proslavery writing. The sense of common purpose in these two men's
essays assumed new dimensions sixteen years later when, in the spring of
1853, Charleston and Philadelphia publishers reprinted them alongside the
1845 letters written by James Henry Hammond to the English abolitionist
Thomas Clarkson and an expanded version of Thomas R. Dew's "Abolition
of Negro Slavery," which had first appeared in the *American Quarterly
Review* of 1832. The Charleston *Courier* welcomed *The Pro-Slavery
Argument: As Maintained by the Leading Writers of the South* as a "*the-
saurus* of facts and arguments to those who wish to know slavery as it is,
and the adamantine reasoning by which the institution is supported." The
Southern Quarterly Review hailed the volume as "a perfect armory of
argument, exhausting all the facts and philosophies in behalf of the morals

[22] Emerson, quoted in Kenneth S. Sacks, *Understanding Emerson: The "American Scholar
and His Struggle for Self-Reliance* (Princeton: Princeton University Press, 2003); Harper,
Anniversary Oration, 6.

of Slavery, and placing the institution, as it exists among us, on an unassailable foundation."[23]

In contrast to Emerson's Transcendentalism, Manhattan's "Young America," or any other expression of nationalist ferment, South Carolina's "Great Reaction" launched on behalf of slavery typically boiled its arguments down to the orthodoxy of accepted truth before declaring that further inquiry was unnecessary.[24] Such a tendency was evident even before the anthologies of the 1850s systematized Harper's unyielding excursion into the "naked, abstract question whether it is better that the institution of praedial and domestic slavery should, or should not, exist in civilized society." In 1845, the *Southern Quarterly Review* greeted the publication of Hammond's *Letters* and the correspondence between the Baptist clergymen Richard Fuller and Francis Wayland with a report that there was "nothing more to be added." "We are entitled to consider the slave question as a closed one," this journal explained, "and the institution as vindicated in a manner the most triumphant." Entering a global debate only to curtail discussion was among the distinctive features of proslavery writing as a genre. This quality suggests something important – if often overlooked – about the ecology of proslavery polemics and about their unusually complicated stance toward "public opinion." In contrast to the Deep South Congressmen who railed against the "fashion" of antislavery in the 1790s, antebellum defenders of bondage appreciated the seemingly omnipotent power of widely diffused sentiments. In "public opinion" lay what Simms termed "the aggregate of small truths, and the experience of successive days and years." These,

---

[23] Harper, *Memoir on Slavery*; Simms, "Miss Martineau on Slavery"; *The Proslavery Argument*; Hammond, *Two Letters On Slavery in the United States, addressed to Thomas Clarkson, Esq.* (Columbia: Allen, McCarter, & Co., 1845); [Dew], "Abolition of Negro Slavery," *AQR* 12 (September 1832), 189–265; *Charleston Courier*, May 26, 1853; "Critical Notices," *SQR* n.s. 8 (October 1853), 548–9. For some earlier American responses to the British campaign against colonial slavery, see George Tucker, "Negro Slavery," *AQR* 2 (September 1827), 237–67; and Whitemarsh Seabrook, *Review of the Critical Situation* (Charleston, 1827). Edward Rugemer usefully traces a series of *Mercury* articles on this same theme in "The Southern Response to British Abolitionism: The Maturation of Proslavery Apologetics," *JSH* 70 (May 2004), 221–48.

[24] William Frederick Poole applied the phrase "great reaction" to this period in *Antislavery Opinions Before the Year 1800: Read Before the Cincinnati Literary Club, November 16, 1872* (Cincinnati, OH: Robert Clarke, 1873), 72. Most modern scholars borrow the terminology from William Freehling, *Prelude to Civil War: The Nullification Controversy in South Carolina, 1816–1836* (New York: Oxford University Press, 1965).

when "heaped together, form a general principle, which is of final conviction in every bosom."[25]

As was the case with many aspects of proslavery polemics, it was the antislavery movement that established how the nineteenth century's "march of mind" brought bondage before the "bar of public opinion." Daring to defend slavery before such a global tribunal required considerable circumspection. In his 1828 consideration of the American Colonization Society, William Harper confided that the Denmark Vesey conspiracy and the uprising in British Demerara had each been initiated by a circuit of information that had "constantly reminded [slaves] that there are those in the world who think them the victims of injustice, and who have the power to protect and relieve them." Over the course of 1835, an ambitious postal campaign in the United States, a broadly publicized attack on apprenticeship by evangelical Britons, and a flurry of antislavery petitions to the U.S. Congress showed Senator William C. Preston how easily "public sentiment" on both sides of the Atlantic could be "lashed into excitement." As efforts were taken to monitor the mails and criminalize the possession of antislavery material, the staunchly proslavery writer Edmund Ruffin cautioned readers of his magazine to cease all deliberations at once. The nullifying editors of the *Columbia Telescope* resolved that any who publicly broached the topic of emancipation should have "his tongue ... cut out and cast upon the dunghill."[26]

Late in the fall of 1835, as Harper troubled over the "dark and uncertain rumors" that produced widespread "distrust and alarm" among whites, his former law student James Henry Hammond attempted to suppress the antislavery petitions then flooding into Congress. While Hammond sensed that the time had come to "roll back the misdirected tide of public sentiment," he was uncertain about which forum might "cover us best both behind and before and make the triumph as bloodless as possible." Only after the so-called "gag rule" that Hammond had helped to impose was lifted in 1845

---

[25] Harper, *Memoir*, 15; "Fuller and Wayland and Hammond's Slavery Correspondence," *SQR* 8 (July 1845), 253; Simms, "Miss Martineau" 648. Caribbean planters were even more anxious about discussion, in part because several newspapers in Jamaica were edited by free blacks; see Andrew Lewis, "'An Incendiary Press': British West Indian Newspapers During the Struggle for Abolition," *Slavery & Abolition* 16 (1995), 346–60.

[26] Seymour Drescher, "Public Opinion and the Destruction of Colonial Slavery," in James Walvin, ed., *Slavery and British Society, 1776–1846* (London: Macmillan, 1982) and Davis, *The Problem of Slavery in the Age of Revolution*. [William Harper], "Colonization Society," *SR* 1 (February 1828), 219–34; William C. Preston, "Speech of March 1, 1836," *CG, Appendix* (24th Congress), 221; [Ruffin], "Movement of the Abolition Societies," *Farmers' Register* 3 (September 1835), 287–9; *Columbia Telescope* quoted in E.S. Abdy, *Journal of a Residence and Tour of the United States* (London: John Murray, 1835), 381.

would he move to his own public defense of bondage. After entering the fray, Hammond's earlier squeamishness soon passed. Through the 1850s, he would brag, with a confidence increasingly shared by other proslavery writers, how "firmly convinced" he was that "the more [slavery] is discussed, the stronger we shall become everywhere."[27]

Qualms about discussing slavery were often rooted in proslavery writers' acute sense that their slaves followed public contention, and were thus likely to discern any division among whites. Harper's stance was no doubt shaped even more profoundly by the experiences of his British-born father, the Rev. John Harper, who had traveled as a Wesleyan itinerant through the Caribbean and New England in the 1790s before establishing himself in South Carolina. The Rev. Harper's move from Antigua (where both of his two sons were born) did not inoculate him from the paranoia bred by the Haitian Revolution. In 1803, as the "black republicanism" of Haiti seemed likely to spread to the mainland, a mob of Charleston whites suspected that Rev. Harper (who had opened a bookstore as well as begun plans to build a church) might possess Methodist literature critical of slavery. When this vigilante group failed to locate Harper, they dragged one of his colleagues to a water pump and might have drowned the unfortunate man had not a sympathetic onlooker used the end of her gown to disable the pump. Harper quickly made assurances in print about his soundness and that of his church (doing so indirectly, lest the topic of antislavery enter into public dialogue in any way). His professions ended the affair with no apparent damage to the reputation of his oldest son, who, the next year, befriended children of the planter elite by enrolling as a student at the newly formed South Carolina College.[28]

William Harper remained in Columbia upon graduation and married into the Coalter family, establishing kin ties with the Virginia Tuckers and the South Carolina Prestons, two of the South's most intellectually inclined families and future collaborators in the slavery polemics of the mid-

[27] Harper, *Anniversary Oration*, 7; Hammond quoted in Drew Faust, *James Henry Hammond*, 162, 279. For Hammond's central role in the gag rule dispute, see William Freehling, *The Road to Disunion Vol. 1: Secessionists at Bay, 1776–1854*, (New York: Oxford, 1990) 287–350 and William Lee Miller, *Arguing about Slavery: The Great Battle in the United States Congress* (New York: Knopf, 1996).

[28] *Charleston Courier*, November 2, 1847; Elsa Goia, *Slave Society in the Leeward Islands at the End of the Eighteenth Century* (Yale University Press, 1965), 292. For more on the 1803 episode, see Cynthia Lynn Lyerly, *Methodism and the Southern Mind* (New York: Oxford, 1998), pp. 127–8 and A.M. Chreitzberg, *Early Methodism in the Carolinas* (Nashville, TN: MEC South Publishing, 1897), 78, 278 (which notes that after relocating to the upcountry, the Harpers befriended another Methodist, Elijah Hammond, whose son James Henry Hammond was born in 1807).

1830s. His meteoric ascent in politics and law then introduced him to still more sites of slavery-induced conflict. He joined Nathaniel Beverley Tucker and William C. Preston in Missouri shortly before the U.S. House debated the restriction of slavery there, and quickly assumed the highest judicial post in that state. Then, upon returning to South Carolina on the brink of that state's bitter tariff dispute, he was appointed to a brief term as a U.S. Senator and then elected Speaker of the South Carolina House. By the age of forty, he assumed the first of several distinguished judicial positions in South Carolina, even as he continued to court political controversy in his staunch advocacy of free trade and of nullification. His defense of the nullifier's Test Oath (a measure ruled unconstitutional by his fellow justices) made him one of the most divisive figures in the state. By 1834, Harper had demonstrated both a propensity for conflict and support for those compulsions that ordered slave society against all dissenters.[29]

Harper's internalization of a judicious tone tempered his message and caused him to offer sweeping statements of principle rather than divulge the personal dimensions of his loyalties. He spoke less for himself than for the class of slaveholders when he noted that some "among ourselves, instead of attending to what passes before their own eyes, and under their own observation" were "content to take up their opinion, ready-made from the haphazard speculations and vehement invectives" of outsiders. He asked wavering Carolinians to consider how "most or all of the schemes which have been proposed for the abolition of slavery, or the mitigation of its evils, are useless or impracticable, or dangerous, and likely to do infinitely more harm than good." Though he hinted he might pursue this question more deeply in the future, the chance would not come in the *Southern Review*, which lacked the enthusiasm for slavery controversy displayed by later southern periodicals. Hugh Legaré, the journal's most frequent contributor and its guiding spirit, summed up a collective sentiment by blithely noting "whether slavery is, or is not reconcilable with what is called by philosophers the law of nature, we really do not know." Legaré then dismissively remarked that while slavery's morality would be "no doubt, a very good theme for young casuists to discuss in a college moot-club," it was hardly suited for a serious-minded journal.[30]

[29] John Belton O'Neall, *Biographical Sketches of the Bench and Bar of South Carolina* (Charleston, SC: SG Courtenay, 1959) 1: 270–4; *Charleston Courier*, June 24, 1834.
[30] [Harper], "Colonization Society," [Hugh Legare], "Hall's Travels in North America," *SR* (4 November, 1829) 321–69; and Michael O'Brien, *A Character of Hugh Legare* (Knoxville: University of Tennessee Press, 1985). Cf. William C. Preston's 1836 argument that slavery discussion was inappropriate in the U.S. Senate because that body was "neither a college nor a club, but a constitutional assembly"; "Speech of March 1, 1836," 222.

In 1837, Harper pushed forward, affirming that bondage was "deeply founded in the nature of man and in the exigencies of human society." Following the mode of philosophical inquiry associated with the high-toned quarterlies, his *Memoir on Slavery* blended British sources (especially Edward Gibbon Wakefield's recent essay on colonial political economy), with American writers like Dew, Tucker, and James Kirke Paulding. His most innovative arguments betrayed the influence of fellow nullifier and controversial deist Thomas Cooper, whose "infidel" principles had recently cast a cloud over his leadership of South Carolina College. Harper's edgy assertion that "it is as much in the order of nature, that men should enslave each other, as that other animals should prey upon each other" thus went beyond Thomas Dew's comparison of human and animal "domestication" to echo Cooper's starker 1835 position that "inferiority of animal caste is the great and universal basis and defense of subjugation." Harper's dismissive attitude toward the "unmeaning verbiage of natural equality and inalienable rights" (which he believed formed the "ornament" rather than the "substance" of Jefferson's Declaration of Independence) similarly extended Cooper's objection that Americans "talk a great deal of nonsense" in assuming that "every man is born free, and equal to every other man." Harper even borrowed sparingly from Cooper's materialist racism, in noting how the "anatomist and physiologist" had demonstrated beyond question that "the races differ in every bone and muscle, and in the proportion of brain and nerve."[31]

Harper's *Memoir* became the pivot of the proslavery canon less because of the force of its argument than because of its repeated republication. When Harper's work appeared, T.R. Dew's far more reserved "Review of the Debate in Virginia" had already begun its migration from the pages of Robert Walsh's Philadelphia *American Quarterly Review* (where it had been balanced by his fellow Virginian Jesse Burton Harrison's plea for emancipation and African colonization) through three much lengthier pamphlets (appearing in 1832, 1833, and 1849), and finally into both the 1852 *Proslavery Argument* and the *De Bow's Review* series of proslavery

---

[31] Harper, *Memoir*, 5, 8–9, 11, 37; Dew, *Review of the Debates*, 29–30; [Thomas Cooper], "Slavery," *SLJ* 1 (November 1835), 188–94; Michael O'Brien notes the novelty of Harper's attack on the Declaration and of Cooper's racism in *Conjectures of Order: Intellectual Life in the American South, 1810–1860* (Chapel Hill: University of North Carolina Press, 2004), 948, while David Brion Davis explores the larger importance of linking slavery to the subordination (and domestication) of animals in "At the Heart of Slavery," *In the Image of God: Religion, Moral Values, and Our Heritage of Slavery* (New Haven, CT: Yale University Press, 2001), 123–35.

"classics" that ran from 1849 through 1856. Harper's essay was even more intricately knit into the program of southern magazine publishing that emerged in the late 1830s and 1840s. Daniel K. Whitaker, who would go on to found the influential *Southern Quarterly Review*, first committed Harper's spoken address to print, using four consecutive issues of the *Southern Literary Journal* to place its arguments before the public. After this appearance and an ensuing pamphlet publication, the *Memoir* was featured as the lead article in T. H. White's Richmond *Southern Literary Messenger*, which had recently published Simms's essay on Martineau.[32] Political journalists like Duff Green, who along with T. H. White was among the first to expand Dew's article into a much longer pamphlet, saw the virtues of such publicity, and intermittently proposed a program of proslavery publishing in Washington, D.C. Little more came of these plans than the weekly *Southern Press*, which languished between 1850 and 1852 without notable impact on either the substance or distribution of proslavery polemics. This would be the closest the antebellum South would come to establishing a proslavery analogue to the lobbying and publishing work done by the evangelical abolitionist and Liberty Party founder Joshua Leavitt. As a result, there would be no American counterpart to the sort of metropolitan proslavery pamphleteering commissioned and financed by the British West Indian lobby in the late eighteenth and early nineteenth centuries. By rooting their work in the literary, commercial, agricultural, and religious press aimed primarily at slaveholding audiences, U.S. proslavery writers thus distanced their enterprise (without separating it completely) from an association with mere political maneuvering.[33]

Proslavery editors proved as important as authors in seeking to "combine everything shedding light on our institutions" in volumes that could be

[32] [Jesse Burton Harrison], "Slavery Question in Virginia," *AQR* 12 (December 1832) 379–426; Thomas R. Dew, *Review of the Debate*; idem, *Abolition of Slavery: A Review of the Debate in the Virginia Legislature, 1831–32* (Washington: Duff Green, 1833); idem, *An Essay on Slavery*, 2nd edition (Richmond,VA: J.W. Randolph, 1849); "Professor Dew's Essays on Slavery," *DBR* 10 (June 1851) 658–64; "Slavery in the Virginia Legislature of 1831–2," *DBR* 20 (January 1856), 118–40; "Judge Harper's Memoir on Slavery," *SLJ* 3 (January 1838–April 1838); "Memoir on Slavery," *SLM* 4 (October 1838), 609–36; "Memoir on Slavery," *DBR*8 (March 1850), 232–43.

[33] W. Stephen Belko, *The Invincible Duff Green: Whig of the West* (Columbia: University of Missouri Press, 2006), 284–5; *United States Telegraph*, November 20, 1835; Howard C. Perkins, "A Neglected Phase of the Movement for Southern Unity," *JSH* 12 (May 1946), 153–203; James M. McPherson, "The Fight Against the Gag Rule: Joshua Leavitt and Antislavery Insurgency in the Whig Party, 1839–1842," *Journal of Negro History* 3 (July 1963), 177–95; B.W. Higham, "The West India 'Interest' in Parliament, 1807–1833," *Historical Studies* 13 (1967), 1–19.

bound and placed on library shelves alongside the most eminent British quarterlies. James D. B. De Bow ventured a particularly systematic attempt to provide southwestern as well as eastern masters with "all the standard treatises" that had allowed "the South" to "know the 'reason' of her 'faith.'" The *Southern Literary Messenger* of Richmond was committed to sponsoring new material of all sorts through the 1850s, and, at times, it objected to being characterized as a journal defined by the narrowly sectional defense of slavery. But in 1858, as the magazine entered its third decade, John R. Thompson accurately noted that the "argument in support of the 'peculiar institution' has been stated over and over again" in its pages. The topic had been "viewed in all possible lights" had been "turned this way and that" and "considered from the beginning to the conclusion and from the conclusion to the beginning." "Upon the abstract proposition of slavery, its justice, its humanity, its happy social consequences," Thompson accurately insisted that there was "nothing to be said that cannot be found in the volumes of the *Messenger*."[34]

As the stream of proslavery writings increased, so did formulaic proclamations of intellectual triumph. Facing the specter of the Wilmot Proviso in 1848, Judge Joseph Henry Lumpkin of Georgia reasoned how "the violent assaults of these fiends have compelled us in self defense to investigate this momentous subject in all of its bearings" and had thus developed within the South "a firm and settled conviction that duty to the slave as well as the master forbids that the relation should be disturbed." Lumpkin further testified that "his mind was never more at ease than at present upon this subject." A decade later, Edward Bryan of South Carolina reminded listeners that "the formidable crusade against Southern civilization" remained "essentially one of opinion," and warned them "when public opinion acquires a velocity, it is not to be tampered with." The proper solution was not withdrawal but engagement, since "opinion must be met by counter opinion, just as sword must be met by sword and fact by fact." In such resolve lay the basis for what George Fitzhugh called "slavery aggressions" and the efforts undertaken by late antebellum and Confederate publicists to justify southern bondage upon the world stage.[35]

---

[34] "Negro Slavery at the South," *DBR* 7 (October 1849), 289; "Memoir on Slavery," *DBR* 10 (March 1851), 232; "Northern Views of a Southern Journal," *SLM* 22 (January 1845), 61–2; [Thompson], "Editors Table" *SLM* 26 (May 1858), 392.

[35] Lumpkin to Howell Cobb, January 21, 1848 in *TSC Corr.*, 94–5; E.B. Bryan, "Speech at the Knoxville Commercial Convention," in *Richmond South*, August 20, 1857; Fitzhugh, "Slavery Aggressions," *DBR* 28 (February 1860), 132–9.

A shifting awareness of global audiences was apparent in the compressed evolution of William Harper's own writings. In his 1835 call for self-assertion, Harper had insisted that Carolinians were not only "republicans and lovers of freedom" but were among the few modern societies who could "afford to be republicans" without endangering social order. His 1837 *Memoir* by contrast said hardly anything about republicanism and instead insisted that "civilization" was the proper criteria for judging the South's system of bound black labor. If this transformation revealed an important reactionary streak in proslavery polemics, it also heralded the efforts taken by Harper's successors to appeal beyond American borders. In 1859, a note of greater optimism would be sounded by the Rev. Stephen Elliott Jr. whose father's *Southern Review* had three decades earlier offered "fellow citizens" a journal "which they may read without finding themselves the objects of perpetual sarcasm, or of affected commiseration." Even if attacks upon the slave South had escalated, the younger Elliott remained convinced that "the time has passed when a people might wrap itself in the consciousness of its integrity, and brave the world." If "in former days, each nation stood apart, and when it was separated by distance from another, cared but little for its opinion," the forces of commerce and rapid communication assured that the world's "judgment" was henceforth able to "be concentrated upon any people with fearful rapidity and terrible power." Greater interconnectedness might pose special perils to American slaveholders, he admitted, but there was little to be done about it. It was with a note of fatalism rather than alarm that Elliott thus concluded that he and other masters were "in the world and of the world" whether they chose to be or not.[36]

COTTON, NEGROES, AND THE FATE OF CIVILIZATION

Near the end of his *Memoir*, William Harper moved from his survey of bondage as the "sole cause" of all past civilizations to consider how the South's "great staple" had "contributed more than anything else of later times" to the civilization of the nineteenth century. By "enabling the poor to obtain cheap clothing," slave-grown cotton had both "inspired a taste for comfort, the first stimulus to civilization" and provided employment to those whose sustenance (no less than the shirts on their backs) depended

[36] Harper, *Anniversary Oration*; Harper, *Memoir*; SR prospectus quoted in O'Brien, *A Character of Hugh Legare*, 52; Rev. Stephen Elliott Jr. *Annual Address Before the Clarisophic and Euphradian Societies of the South Carolina College* (Charleston, SC: Walker and Evans, 1860), 11–12.

on a textile industry that flourished on both sides of the Atlantic. For slave-holders to vindicate bondage was not simply to deliver themselves from attack. It was to protect "millions of human beings, who are far removed from us, from the most intense suffering, if not from being struck out of human existence."[37]

Fourteen years later, with Harper in the grave, the American cotton crop doubled in size, and nearly a million more slaves toiling across an expanding Union, William Gilmore Simms' *Southern Quarterly Review* featured another Columbia writer, who elaborated at even greater length how "negro emancipation would be inevitably the deathblow of our civilization." Louisa McCord clarified how the cause of slavery extended beyond the interest of her state, her section, or even of "this whole great empire, this young giant" of America, "whose infant strength startles its European forefathers with its newborn might." Two interrelated phenomena bolstered her conviction that "our civilization of this world of the nineteenth century – must fall with negro emancipation." First was her belief, developed through personal experiences in managing cotton plantations of her own, that "Negro emancipation is the emancipation of brute force" and that black liberation would produce "a barbarism tenfold worse than Gothic or Vandal." McCord imagined the possible "extinction of the cotton crop" in only slightly less apocalyptic terms, insisting that such a disaster would bring "certain and uncontrollable as fate – the extinction of civilization" across the entire globe.[38]

The similarities between Harper's and McCord's diagnosis resulted in part from their membership in the same Columbia, South Carolina, intellectual circles. In the case of McCord, a combination of personal experiences, temperament, and timing inspired her to develop aspects of Harper's argument that were tangential to his *Memoir on Slavery* as a whole. She thus came as close as any other proslavery writer to pushing Thomas Cooper's "infidel" mixture of political economy and racial science to its logical conclusion. The roots of McCord's interests in both these topics extended

---

[37] Harper *Memoir*, 57.
[38] McCord, "Negro and White Slavery – Wherein Do they Differ?" *SQR* n.s. 4 (July 1851), 129. She made a similar point in "British Philanthropy and American Slavery," *DBR* 14 (March 1853), 277. These and McCord's other proslavery essays have been assembled in Richard S. Lounsbury, *Louisa S. McCord: Political and Social Essays* (Charlottesville: University Press of Virginia, 1995). Cf. Hammond's 1845 prediction that "the sudden loss of two million of bales of cotton" would "shake down castles, palaces, and even thrones," in a crisis stretching "from the deserts of Africa to the Siberian wilds – from Greenland to the Chinese wall" in *Two Letters*, 34.

back to her childhood in Philadelphia, where she had first been exposed to a rousing public debate over free black "indolence" and to the program of nationalist development overseen by her father, Langdon Cheves, who served as the president of the Second Bank of the United States. In marrying Thomas Cooper's protégé David McCord in 1840, she solidified her position in the more intellectually inclined community of South Carolina College, where conventional academic assumptions about the inefficiencies of slave labor and the limited importance of racial differences had come under fire beginning in the 1820s. If Harper offered his consideration of slavery in the guise of an oracle, hoping to end discussion with the air of authority, McCord did so as a relentless advocate, who sought to convert wavering opponents to her point of view. The urgency of her appeal, like that of her contemporary George Fitzhugh, resulted from her expectation that the passing of old orthodoxies brought new opportunities. She was contemptuous of Fitzhugh's flirtation with socialism and of his coy avowal that a color-blind system of quasi-slavery lay on the horizon. McCord set before herself an easier task. She wanted experts deluded by outmoded notions to ratify what much of the world had already come instinctively to realize – that cotton grown by black slaves had through a mysterious process become the fulcrum of human happiness.[39]

The shifting assessment of slave and free labor during the 1850s indicated that the dim reputation of the South's economic order might soon be rehabilitated. Up through the late 1840s, even political economists working within the South followed Adam Smith and David Ricardo in accepting the superiority of free labor as a basic axiom.[40] Such a consensus produced two different sorts of proslavery responses. Most intriguing was the attempt of John C. Calhoun and Nathaniel Beverley Tucker to pair an admission of slavery's economic lag with boasts about the South's social stability, which

[39] Despite the appearance of Leigh Fought, *Southern Womanhood and Slavery: A Biography of Louisa S. McCord, 1810–1879* (Columbia: University of Missouri Press, 2003), the most incisive overview of McCord's biography appears in the afterword of Lounsbury, *Louisa McCord*. The McCord's marriage also introduced Louisa to the Columbia legal establishment, a point intriguingly developed in Alfred L. Brophy, "'A Revolution Which Seeks to Abolish Law, Must End Necessarily in Despotism': Louisa McCord and Antebellum Southern Legal Thought," *Cardozo Women's Law Journal* 5 (1998), 33–77. Cooper's explained in his 1835 essay on "Slavery" how his own view of black inferiority was based on his four-decade-long interaction with free African-Americans in Philadelphia.
[40] Seymour Drescher, *The Mighty Experiment: Free Labor versus Slavery in British Emancipation* (New York: Oxford, 2002); Jay R. Carlander and W. Elliot Brownlee, "Antebellum Southern Political Economists and the Problem of Slavery," *American Nineteenth Century History* 7 (September 2006), 389–416.

they linked to slavery's unique ability to "harmonize" the otherwise antagonistic forces of labor and capital. Thomas Cooper and Dew took another
path by building on the French economist Jean-Baptiste Say's admission that
there were a number of limited cases in which free labor did not achieve the
optimal economic results that slavery offered. The mutually reinforcing
tendency of proslavery polemics and ever-greater refinements in the empiri-
cal basis of the "science" of political economy increased the number of such
"exceptions" to free labor superiority. By the late 1840s, leading theorists
had concluded that slavery was the most efficient (if not the most moral)
system under frontier conditions (where it prevented the dispersion of population), in tropical climates (where workers' acquisitive urges were dissipated), and, perhaps even in those instances where the racial characteristics
of the labor force required the violence of bondage to motivate a human
class of "drones."[41]

Both of these leading attempts to rebut the antislavery assumptions of
classical political economy deployed racial arguments, and thus followed the
same turn to "hard" racialism seen in American law, science, politics, and
culture during the late antebellum years. By 1852, the South Carolina Congressman Lawrence Keitt followed the familiar argument that republicanism
required eliminating "distinctions of class" with a more novel insistence that
"there must be a difference of races" in any stable system of popular government. Such a proposition allowed him to conclude that "the destruction of
African slavery would be the destruction of republicanism." A slightly different approach involved dire predictions about the disastrous economic
consequences of free black labor. Such a conclusion was familiar enough
within the slave South, where writers had routinely pointed to the "failures"
of black industry in Haiti, in northern cities, in Liberia, and in southern free
black communities. What was distinctive about the 1850s was the

---

[41] Calhoun, "Further Remarks," 80–86; Tucker, "An Essay on the Moral and Political
Effect," 470–1; Cooper, "Slavery," 192; Dew, *Review of the Debate, passim.* The efforts
of Calhoun and Tucker are best understood as part of the "republican" quest to achieve a
harmonious economic order, in light of Ricardo's vision of increasing class conflict. Another
dimension of this effort can be seen in the intensifying Anglo-American disputes over "white
slavery" that dated to the late eighteenth century. For more on these complicated developments, see Jeffrey Sklansky, *The Soul's Economy: Market Society and Selfhood in American Thought, 1820–1920* (Chapel Hill: University of North Carolina Press, 2002), 77–80;
Marcus Cunliffe, *Chattel Slavery and Wage Slavery: The Anglo-American Context,
1830–60* (Athens: University of Georgia Press, 1979); Martin J. Burke *The Conundrum
of Class: Public Discourse on the Social Order in America* (Chicago, IL: University of
Chicago Press, 1995) and Tise, *Proslavery* (which demonstrates an early disposition to
contrast the ease of American plantation work with European forms of agricultural labor).

newfound willingness of European observers to venture racial explanations in assessing the troublesome case of the postemancipation Caribbean. A series of labor crises, and the turn to various forms of coolie and indentured labor there, pushed even liberal political economists to conclude that the "mighty experiment" of black free labor was far less successful than its enthusiasts had predicted. The ridicule that Negrophobes like Thomas Carlyle heaped on the idle "Quashee" lent racism increasing respectability within British culture. This process both undermined the humanitarian strain of early British anthropology and cleared the way for that "hard racism" destined to be a key ingredient of late Victorian imperialism.[42]

Louisa McCord's earliest investigations of political economy focused neither on the relative merits of slave and free labor nor on the salience of race. Her debut concerned a French polemicist who had not challenged the general European disapproval of bound labor. For McCord and her husband, the appeal of Claude-Frédéric Bastiat and his *Journal des Economistes* lay primarily in the slashing attacks he launched against protectionist policies and the statist reforms proposed by the European left. Bastiat attained prominence at a crucial moment for the program of free trade political economy, when a movement against protectionism had completed its successful mass campaign against the British Corn Laws only to find itself facing a tougher adversary in the socialism invigorated by the 1848 revolution in France.[43] The antislavery proclivities of Bastiat (who was often termed the "French Cobden") were thus less important to the McCords and their free trade allies than his talent for attacking recognizable enemies in a "heroic vein, a highly rhetorical manner" and "with general adroitness of argument and felicity of diction." David McCord was so struck by Bastiat's wit that he urged Charlestonians to subscribe to his *Journal* and to read it regularly. Louisa McCord likewise announced in the aftermath of the 1848 revolutions that the Frenchman's example could help Americans to overcome those

---

[42] Keitt quoted in *Southern Quarterly Review* n.s. 5 (April 1852) 538; Michael A. Morrison and James Brewer Stewart, *Race and the Early Republic: Racial Consciousness and Nation Building in the Early Republic* (Roman & Littlefield, 2002); Drescher, *The Mighty Experiment*; Christine Bolt, *Victorian Attitudes Towards Race* (London: Routledge, 1971); O'Brien, *Conjectures of Order*.

[43] Robert M. Hendrick, "Frédéric Bastiat, Forgotten Liberal: Spokesman for an Ideology in Crisis" (New York University PhD Dissertation, 1987) provides a helpful overview, while Bastiat's rhetorical and political skills furnish the main theme of Margaret A. Ray, "The Lighter Side of the Dismal Science: The Humor of Economics," *Social Science Journal* 28 (1991), 227–42; and Alain Béraud and François Etner "Bastiat et les Liberaux: Exist-t-il Une Ecole Optimiste en Economie?" *Politique Revue d'Economie Politique* 103 (1993), 287–304.

"fantastic visions of fraternity" that "domineer in each brain-sick fancy which struts upon the stage its little hour of rule."[44]

If McCord, like Harper, made civilization rather than republicanism her primary point of reference, she conveyed a distinctly popular dimension of her crusade to make political economy "the science of the crowd." This science "alone, with its great and simple truths, seems to hold forth some hope of a real regeneration" she wrote, adding that "those who are ahead in the race of knowledge" should "give to those who need" and "guide those who stumble in the dark." A similar popularizing imperative marked her efforts to broadcast the scientific "facts" of racial hierarchy. In Simms' *Southern Quarterly Review*, she explained how the anatomical basis of black inferiority had become "sacred to the learned" but "like all other similar questions" needed a set of popularizers before it could "become vulgarized to common opinion." Developments in the Caribbean, which Thomas Carlyle's notorious attack on the "Negro Question" drew into sharp focus, lay the groundwork for racist anthologies comparable to the emerging proslavery canon. Early in 1851, McCord speculated that if the subject of race was "fairly brought before the white man, and investigated as a great philosophic question deserves to be investigated," the world would "arm in defence of our institutions."[45] Just a few months later, she greeted the compendious *Negro-Mania*, which the Philadelphia printer (and former Chartist) John Campbell assembled in just the sort of form McCord had desired. Both she and her husband thereafter publicized black inferiority with the same zeal they had devoted to the free-trade cause. Each of them was careful to sidestep the fevered religious debates that pitted polygenists such as Josiah Nott (who rejected the Biblical account of a single creation) against the proslavery clergy whose defenses of bondage were rooted firmly in scriptural literalism.[46]

---

44 "Political Economists" *American Whig Review* 6 (October 1850), 378; [David McCord], "Henry Clay and the American System," *SQR* 10 (July 1846), 197; [Louisa McCord], "Justice and Fraternity," *SQR* 15 (July 1848), 370. David McCord indicated in his piece how he became acquainted with Bastiat through the free-trade, antislavery *Westminster Review*; he later took credit for urging his wife to translate the work from the French, see McCord to John C. Calhoun, May 24, 1848, *PJCC* 25: 431.

45 [Louisa McCord], "The Right to Labor," *SQR* 16 (October 1849), 139; idem, "Diversity of the Races – its Bearings upon Negro Slavery," *SQR* n.s. 3 (April 1851), 408.

46 "Negro Mania," *DBR* 12 (May 1852), 507–24; Campbell, *Negro-mania: Being an Examination of the Falsely Assumed Equality of the Various Races of Men* (Philadelphia, 1851); David James McCord "Life of a Negro Slave," *SQR* n.s. 7 (January 1853), 206–27; idem, "Africans at Home," *SQR* n.s. 10 (July 1854), 70–96; "Practical Effects of Emancipation," *DBR* 18 (April and May 1855), 474–96, 591–602.

McCord's attention to the "sciences" of race and political economy gave
way during the early 1850s to a series of attacks upon feminism that would
define her as a public figure. After skewering the female suffrage arguments
set forth in the *Westminster Review* (whose bad behavior put this erstwhile
free-trade ally beyond the pale), McCord then engaged in the transatlantic
controversies spurred by Harriet Beecher Stowe's *Uncle Tom's Cabin*.[47]
Soon, enough, however, she realized that proslavery Anglophobia endangered the economic system best suited to the cotton South's continued prosperity. In an angry written exchange with the tariff advocate Henry Carey,
McCord insisted that England, for all her faults and dubious antislavery
proclivities, remained "the pioneer of progress." America, she added, was
destined to be considered by other countries as "her noblest offset." What
she termed "English machinations" would only increase if Carey's protectionism prevailed; what was needed was that "freedom of exchange" and
economic interdependence that could alone provide "some security from
[Britain's] intermeddling with our institutions."[48]

McCord concluded her writing career by returning to the topics of slavery
and political economy, two fields of inquiry that had normally been the preserve of men. She rebutted the notion that "man of every race" was "equally to
be clinched down by the universal laws of Mr. Carey's universal system of
'social science.'" In 1856, with her husband dead, her father suffering from
dementia, and with her own eyesight fading, McCord scolded with even more
vigor the proslavery writer George Frederick Holmes, who had ventured a
willingness to dispense with political economy in favor of a new "science of
society." "It is sheer madness to throw away our armor at the very moment
when we should be girding it on to the defense," McCord complained, explaining that the problem lay not in the field of inquiry, but in the cumulative effect
of biased practitioners, and especially in the stubborn refusal of Europeans to
understand the central importance of race. "Men and prejudices have gone
against us; but science cannot be swayed by prejudice or outcry," she wrote.

[47] "Enfranchisement of Woman," *SQR* n.s. 5 (April 1852), 322–4; "Woman and Her Needs,"
DBR 13 (1852), 267–91; "Uncle Tom's Cabin," *SQR*, n.s. 8 (January 1853), 81–120;
"British Philanthropy and American Slavery," *DBR* 14 (March 1853), 258–80; "A Letter
to the Duchess of Sutherland, from a Lady of South Carolina," *Charleston Mercury*, August
10, 1853. These writings – which have helped to establish McCord's notoriety among recent
scholars – are usefully analyzed and placed in context by Manisha Sinha, "Louisa Susanna
McCord: Spokeswoman of the Master Class in Antebellum South Carolina," in Susan
Ostrov Weisser and Jennifer Fleischner eds., *Feminist Nightmares Women at Odds: Feminism and the Problem of Sisterhood* (New York University Press, 1994), 62–87. A far
more sympathetic approach is taken in Fox-Genovese, *Within the Plantation Household*.
[48] "Carey on the Slave Trade," *SQR* n.s. 9 (January 1854), 153.

"All that is now needed for the defense of United States negro slavery and its entire exoneration from reproach, is a thorough investigation of fact, an investigation which will force sight into eyes that now will not see, and hearing into ears that now will not hear."[49]

McCord based her confidence less on the intellectual power of white men and women than on the economic might of those white cotton bolls she termed "the great peace-maker of the world, the destined civilizer of unexplored realms, the link of nations." Her own cotton-mania matched that of America as a whole during the 1850s, as enthusiasts of the crop moved well beyond this product's "national benefit" that Governor Stephen Miller had praised in an early proslavery address of 1824. As millions of bales were shipped from southern ports, one enthusiast decreed that "the universe is but a cotton mill, elaborating the necessities of men." The combination of great riches and widely-dispersed comforts fixed the association of cotton with human amelioration, thus setting it apart from sugar, tobacco, or even rice, each of which had bred images of luxury and dissipation that had made earlier antislavery boycotts a mark of personal integrity. Cotton, by contrast, could easily be hailed for having "exerted its influence upon the subjective or intellectual as well as upon the outward or objective domain of the creation." In the view of both McCord and James Henry Hammond, this commodity assured that the South would enjoy global clout if secession and war ever became necessary. The residual effect of this antebellum cotton-mania remained a key element of the Confederacy's missionary appeal even after European diplomats rebuffed threats of a cotton embargo. The same cotton boll that drew a poetic tribute from Henry Timrod in 1861 inspired the Rev. John T. Wightman to speculate how God had chosen the South's "inexhaustible agricultural treasures" as his favored mechanism for enriching Anglo-Saxons and thus keeping "the Bible and the press under the control of Protestantism."[50]

[49] "Carey on the Slave Trade," 137; "Slavery and Political Economy," *DBR* 21 (October and November 1856), 337, 444–445. The latter essay was a pointed response to George Frederick Holmes, "Slavery and Freedom," *SQR* (April 1856) 62–95. McCord's tribulations are described in Fought, *Southern Womanhood and Slavery*.

[50] McCord, "Charity Which Does not Begin at Home," *SLM* 19 (April 1853), 194; Miller quoted in Freehling, *Prelude to Civil War*, 81–2; D. D. Deming, "The Power of Cotton," *DBR* 22 (May 1857), 543; Wilson, "Cotton, Steam and Machinery," in *SLM* 27 (September 1858), 173; Hammond, "Speech Before the U.S. Senate, March 4, 1858," in *CG* 35th Congress, First Session, Appendix, 68–71; Henry Timrod, "The Cotton Boll" in Simms, ed., *War Poetry of the South* (New York: Richardson & Co., 1867), 313–15; Wightman, *The Glory of God the Defense of the South* (Charleston, SC: Evans and Cogswell, 1861). Another notable case of Confederate cotton-mania can be seen in *The Providential Aspect and Salutary Tendency of the Existing Crisis* (New Orleans, 1861).

As these examples suggest, carefully reasoned explanations of economic behavior held less political and cultural import than catch-phrases capable of distilling intricate positions into everyday language. David Christy, the Ohio advocate of tariffs and African colonization, was thus chosen to lead off the second major compendium of proslavery writing largely because he, like Bastiat, had a knack for memorable terminology. Lending the title of his own book *Cotton is King* to Mississippi editor Ebenezer Newton Elliott, Christy replaced Harper as the opening voice in this final collective attempt to establish the legitimacy of bondage. The classic essays of Harper and Hammond were republished just as they had appeared in *The Proslavery Argument* of 1852. Those of Dew and Simms were replaced by a selection of Samuel Cartwright's "niggerology," an ethical treatise by Virginian Albert Taylor Bledsoe, and a "scriptural argument" by the Rev. Thornton Stringfellow. The national basis of proslavery defense was conveyed by Christy's long opening work (which had drawn its sharpest critiques from Southerners), by two articles provided by Princeton theologian Charles Hodge, and by Chief Justice Roger B. Taney's opinion in the Dred Scott decision. When war commenced in 1861, both of the volume's northern contributors would join Taney (a Marylander) in steadfast support of the Federal Union. As the political differences of the *Cotton is King* contributors suggested, notions of proslavery mission had by 1860 moved well beyond the initial orbit of haughty Carolinians.[51]

Southerners who joined the McCords in the free-trade camp helped to elaborate a distinct vision of proslavery nationhood. Their basic skepticism about linking national projects to government actions provided an economic counterpart to the distrust Virginian constitutionalists had bred about that "nameless nation" that was framed in 1787. Yet the economic critique of government coexisted with a deeper appreciation for what McCord called "this giant power" of America "whose yet undeveloped strength is appointed to stamp with its world-waking spirit the destinies of human nature." The global vision she helped to systematize drew as much from the language of American empire as from an incipient southern nation. McCord's warnings against premature disruption of current economic and

---

[51] Prof. E.N. Elliott, *Cotton is King; and Proslavery Arguments* (Augusta, GA: Pritchard, Abbott & Loomis, 1860). Among the harshest indictments of Christy's politics came in Marcus A. Bell, *South-Side Version of Cotton is King*, an extended tribute to cotton and slavery that self-consciously addressed itself to "American women." Hodge's early warnings about the consequences of perpetuating slavery indefinitely do not appear, as noted in Peter Wallace, "The Bond of Union: The Old School Presbyterian Church and the American Nation, 1837–1861,"(PhD Dissertation, University of Notre Dame, 2004), 407–8.

political ties were balanced by her admission that the time might come when all the slaveholding states would be driven to radical action. Regardless of the South's geopolitical future, McCord reserved her greatest praise for "the wonderful development of this western continent" by black slaves under the care of determined masters. The crude racial invective that she made her stock in trade did not prevent her from acknowledging how Africans had been "transplanted at the same time with ourselves" to the New World, and had thus become "a vital organ" to the "young giant of America."[52]

Though McCord regularly maintained that black slavery fulfilled a divine decree, her personal religious convictions were notably weak. Those who formulated an evangelical strain of proslavery nationalism would have been as puzzled by her inattentiveness to the Bible as she was perplexed by the neglect shown by most political economists to the "realities" of race and of cotton. Holy Writ, after all, provided a seemingly unassailable basis for slaveholding stewardship, for Protestant mission, and even, in the story of Ham's curse, for distinctive racial destinies. Relating these religious authorities to the circumstances of Southern masters would be the task of another set of nationalists, whose work proceeded within the context of America's Protestant traditions.[53]

---

[52] McCord, "Separate Secession," *SQR* n.s. 8 (October 1851), 298–317. McCord's stance during the secession crisis of 1850–1 followed that of her father, a leading advocate of cooperation among all the Southern states.

[53] See Fought, *Southern Womanhood and Slavery*, for a consideration of the McCords' religious laxity.

4

Reformed Slaveholders and the Gospel of Nationhood

In 1787, at the very moment when Deep South delegates to the Philadelphia Convention worked to shield slavery from outside assaults, the Rev. Henry Pattillo of North Carolina imagined how faithful Christians might build up proslavery unity from within. His suggestions were framed by a seemingly simple question. Was it "really true, what many assert, That the slaves are the occasion of more guilt to our country, than any, or all other sources of evil?" The issue of morality in a slave society was no idle concern for Pattillo, or for the ideal "Plain Planter" that he addressed. As a master himself and as one of his state's leading Presbyterian clergymen, Pattillo knew all too well the corruptions bred by absolute power over another human soul. In a distinctly Jeffersonian vein, he noted the trials of governing those enslaved against their will and acknowledged how the "vicious part of our countrymen may storm, and rage, and act the incarnate fury; and then blame the Negroes as the cause of their wickedness." Then with a flourish more Calvinist than republican, he announced that "God, the judge of all, will form a very different estimate, and find the cause of [masters'] vices in their own depraved natures, and ungoverned passions."[1]

---

[1] Rev. Henry Pattillo, *The Plain Planter's Family Assistant: Containing an Address to Husbands and Wives, Children and Servants* (Wilmington, 1787), 7–10. See also Douglas Ambrose, "Of Stations and Relations: Proslavery Christianity in Early National Virginia," in John R. McKivigan and Mitchell Snay, eds., *Religion and the Antebellum Debate over Slavery* (Athens: University of Georgia Press, 1998); *idem*, "Sowing Sentiment: Shaping the Southern Presbyterian Household", *Georgetown Law Journal* (November 2001), and, for a selection from the text and a helpful introduction, Jeffrey Robert Young, *Proslavery and Sectional Thought in the Early South, 1740–1829: An Anthology* (Columbia: University of South Carolina Press, 2006).

Like most post-Revolutionary masters troubled by republican slavery, the Rev. Pattillo was concerned not just with present inconsistencies or universal human shortcomings but with a future in which vice might triumph over perishable virtue. He took solace in the "increases in humanity" among those republican masters who supposedly meted out fairer punishments and provided greater sustenance than they had during the colonial period. He was similarly cheered by the tendency of most of his fellow slaveholders to feel "a kind of brotherly or parental affection" for dependents of both races. Such evidence nearly convinced him that human bondage might not destroy what he thereafter termed America's "terrestrial paradise." Yet anxieties accompanied Pattillo's exuberance when it came to "the omission of this duty of religious instruction to the slaves." Neglecting the spiritual welfare of bound workers represented a "great national evil, and the source of numerous others to society." This shortcoming posed a particular threat to white American children, whose "language... manners and ... ideas" were receiving "a tincture from being bred up with so many pagans." A first step toward remedying the current irreligion of slaves – and the accompanying degeneration of white southern youth – came in the fifty questions of Pattillo's "The Negroe's Catechism," which he attached to the end of his pamphlet. Here was not just instruction, but a tool capable of extending the principles of gospel truth to each and every member of the extended plantation household.[2]

The history of proslavery Christianity over the following seventy-five years was in large part an attempt to make Pattillo's vision into a functioning reality. In hoping to ameliorate the institution of bondage through the inculcation of Christian principles, Pattillo, like those who followed his example, ceded the ultimate destiny of the institution to the mysterious workings of providence. Despite this seeming fatalism, there was a utopian aspect to his proslavery evangelism that lent it a fundamentally different character than those secular polemics that turned to scriptural authority without any real intention of offering a personal witness of Christian faith.

---

[2] Pattillo, *The Plain Planter's Family Assistant*; idem, *Sermons* (Wilmington: James Adams, 1788), 67–70; *A Geographical Catechism* (Halifax: Abraham Hodge, 1796), 51–2 (for "terrestrial paradise"). A starkly different picture of white discipline and African-American religiosity in Pattillo's Granville County neighborhood emerges from Jeffrey J. Crow, "Slave Rebelliousness and Social Conflict in North Carolina, 1775–1802," *WMQ* 37 (January 1980), 79–102 while the broader complex of Deep South yearnings to "humanize" slavery is explored in Joyce Chaplin, "Slavery and the Principle of Humanity: A Modern Idea in the Early Lower South," *Journal of Social History* 24 (Winter 1990), 299–315.

The force of evangelicalism went beyond Bible argument, even if a knowledge of God's word was an indispensable part of this vision of organic order. As a cultural and nationalist movement no less than a religious one, slaveholders' evangelicalism sought to elaborate a world where hierarchies were leavened by self-control and stewardship, where the gospel would be lived by all members of society, and where friendly support from abroad might allow a nation of masters to display their Godliness to the rest of the world.[3]

Far greater numbers of white southerners would be swept up in nineteenth-century evangelicalism than would ever be involved in elaborating secular proslavery arguments. Teasing out the aspects of southern Christianity most relevant to proslavery nationalism requires keeping a fairly sharp focus on those self-conscious descendents of a Reformed tradition who extended their influence from a post-Revolutionary base in the Atlantic states across an ever more expansive slaveholding South. Something of the southern clergy's aspirations can be seen in two enclaves that began as early as the 1790s to reconcile American bondage and republican freedom within the context of an inherited Protestant tradition. In Lexington, Virginia, the Liberty Hall students of the Rev. William Graham were taught to vindicate bondage according to doctrines contained in the Westminster Confession; the graduates of this institution would become among the first American-educated clergy to carry the Reformed message to the farthest reaches of the slaveholding South. A similarly important hearth of proslavery religiosity was located in Liberty County, Georgia, where a community of transplanted New England Congregationalists fostered a powerful mix of Calvinist principles and profit-maximizing plantation agriculture. To probe how proslavery Christianity emerged from these and similar locales of "liberty" helps to explain how southern whites reconciled slavery with both republican and Protestant traditions. Redeeming an institution from its own corruptions could be understood in these settings as a means of doing God's work and of

---

[3] Pattillo, *The Plain Planter's Family Assistant*; Erskine Clarke set forth the Utopian dimensions of this Reformed vision in *Our Southern Zion: A History of Calvinism in the South Carolina Low Country, 1690–1990* (Tuscaloosa, AL: University of Alabama Press, 1996), *Wrestlin' Jacob: A Portrait of Religion in Antebellum Georgia and the Carolina Low Country* (1979: reprint, University of Alabama Press, 2000); and *Dwelling Place: A Plantation Epic* (New Haven, CT: Yale University Press, 2006). Thomas Cooper, *Two Essays on the Constitution* (Columbia, 1826), 41 demonstrates how even proslavery deists could not resist quoting scripture.

establishing a reformed slaveholding ethic as the quintessence of American Christianity.[4]

CHRISTIANIZING AMERICAN PLANTATIONS

Missionary campaigns to Christianize New World slaves commenced with the rise of the Brazilian slave system during the seventeenth century, extended to far-flung plantation zones in practically every corner of the Atlantic world, and then culminated late in the nineteenth century, when evangelicals battled colonial administrators over the terms of freedom in Africa. Across this enormous chronological and geographical expanse, masters, missionaries, and government officials routinely disagreed with one another. Among the few points of consensus was the shared perception that religion was second only to law in setting the boundaries of plantation authority. Masters consistently fought to keep the upper hand, though there were occasions when they actively encouraged the evangelization of men and women they presumed to hold as human chattels.[5] From this broad perspective, the cohesion that would prevail among the free white population in the American South between 1840 and 1860 stands out as truly remarkable. Unlike any other program of African-American evangelization, the southern "mission to the slaves" would simultaneously

[4] Paul Conkin, *The Uneasy Center: Reformed Christianity in Antebellum America* (Chapel Hill, NC: University of North Carolina Press, 1995). For Liberty Hall and William Graham, see Ambrose, "Of Stations and Relations" and Young, *Proslavery and Sectional Thought*, 167–72; for Liberty County, Georgia, see Erskine Clarke, *Wrestlin' Jacob* and *Dwelling Place, passim*.

[5] The early stages of this process are authoritatively explained in David Brion Davis, *The Problem of Slavery in Western Culture* (New York: Oxford University Press, 1966), 165–222. Among the most useful recent works are James H. Sweet, *Recreating Africa: Culture, Kinship, and Religion in the African-Portuguese World, 1441–1770* (Chapel Hill, NC: University of North Carolina Press, 2003); Robert C. H. Shell, *Children of Bondage: A Social History of the Slave Society at the Cape of Good Hope, 1652–1838* (Hanover, NH: University Press of New England, 1994); Jon F. Sensbach, *A Separate Canaan: The Making of an Afro-Moravian World in North Carolina, 1763–1840* (Chapel Hill, 1998); Christopher Leslie Brown, *Moral Capital: Foundations of British Abolitionism* (Chapel Hill: University of North Carolina Press, 2006); Mary Turner, *Slaves and Missionaries: The Disintegration of Slave Society, 1787–1834* (Urbana: University of Illinois Press, 1982); Armando Lampe, *Mission or Submission? : Moravian and Catholic Missionaries in the Dutch Caribbean During the 19th Century* (Gottingen: Vandenhoeck & Ruprecht, 2001); Keith Hunte, "Protestantism and Slavery in the British Caribbean," in Armando Lampe, ed., *Christianity in the Caribbean: Essays on Church History* (University of the West Indies Press, 2001); Laennec Hurbon, "The Church and Afro-American Slavery," in Enrique Dussel, *The Church in Latin America* (Tunbridge Wells, 1982) 363–74, and Martin A. Klein, *Slavery and Colonial Rule in French West Africa* (Cambridge: Cambridge University Press, 1998).

recast (but hardly control) life in the slave quarters while it provided masters with a central element of nationalist self-understanding.[6]

American plantation missions prior to 1820 largely failed in their objectives, though these disappointments resulted not from any lack of effort or from any sustained clerical hostility to bondage. The British evangelicals who worked from the late seventeenth century through the American Revolution to extend the gospel to rice and tobacco workers on the mainland worked diligently to reconcile human bondage with a political culture devoted to rights and freedom. Yet even as the Rev. Thomas Bacon encouraged Chesapeake slaves to honor their masters as "God's overseers," most plantation owners shielded their human property from missionary influences. Low Country planters expressed a particular skepticism about outside authorities, realizing that any effort to brunt colonial slavery's brutality raised troublesome questions of who was ultimately in charge.[7]

The republican reconfiguration of religious authority brought new opportunities, as did the emergence of a native-born slaveholding clergy over the first third of the nineteenth century. Presbyterians such as John Holt Rice and Charles C. Jones joined Low Country Baptists Richard Furman and Basil Manly and Methodists like William Capers to counter any lingering associations of white southern Protestantism with antislavery.[8]

---

[6] Milton C. Sernett, *Black Religion and American Evangelicalism: White Protestants, Plantation Missions, and the Flowering of Negro Christianity, 1787–1865* (Metuchen, NJ: Scarecrow Press, 1975); Janet Duitsman Cornelius, *Slave Missions and the Black Church in the Antebellum South* (Columbia: University of South Carolina Press, 1999); Margaret Creel Washington, *A Peculiar People: Slave Religion and Community Culture among the Gullahs* (New York: New York University Press, 1987); Jack P. Maddex, Jr., "A Paradox of Christian Amelioration: Proslavery Ideology and Church Ministries to Slaves," in *The Southern Enigma: Essays on Race, Class, and Folk Culture*, Walter J. Fraser Jr. and Winifred B. Moore Jr. eds., (Westport, CT: Greenwood Press, 1983), 105–18.

[7] Davis, *The Problem of Slavery in Western Culture*, 197–222; Jon Butler, *Awash in a Sea of Faith: Christianizing the American People* (Cambridge, MA: Harvard University Press, 1991), 129–63; Jeffrey Robert Young, *Domesticating Slavery: The Master Class in Georgia and South Carolina, 1670–1837* (Chapel Hill: University of North Carolina Press, 1999); Leland J. Bellot, "Evangelicals and the Defense of Slavery in Britain's Old Colonial Empire," *JSH* 37 (February 1971).

[8] Sylvia Frey, *Water from the Rock: Black Resistance in a Revolutionary Age* (Princeton: Princeton University Press, 1991); Robert Calhoon, *Evangelicals and Conservatives in the Early South, 1740–1861* (Columbia: University of South Carolina Press, 1988); Donald G. Mathews, *Religion in the Old South* (Chicago: University of Chicago Press, 1977); Christine Leigh Heyrman, *Southern Cross: the Beginnings of the Bible Belt* (New York: Knopf, 1997); Anne C. Loveland, *Southern Evangelicals and the Social Order, 1800–1860* (Baton Rouge: Louisiana State University Press, 1980).

These men's sense of mission was kindled by regular contact with their own slaves, interactions with other masters, and by sporadic attempts to foster communion with fellow evangelicals beyond southern borders. A trip to England in the 1820s exposed William Capers to metropolitan skepticism about plantation–zone spirituality, while correspondence with fellow Presbyterian Thomas Chalmers of Scotland caused John Holt Rice to broaden his view of America's place in the world. Charles C. Jones launched his missionary efforts after struggling with the dilemmas of slavery while a student at Andover and Princeton seminaries. John Adger extended this pattern twenty years later, when he began a mission to black Charlestonians immediately upon his return from an extended stay in Syria. While a mixture of motives operated in each of these cases, a recurrent factor was the desire to justify the moral capacity of one's home and to prove that godliness was possible even in areas where the enslaved majority lacked meaningful rights before the law.[9]

Most masters remained skeptical about missionary influences through the first third of the nineteenth century. Whitemarsh Seabrook's 1834 conclusion summed up a wider suspicion that there was not "a contrivance better calculated in time to separate us from our property" than introducing the Bible to American slaves. Some secular critics knew scripture well enough to appreciate the potential explosiveness of the Exodus story, or of the Minor Prophets. Most such anxieties resulted from the perceived connection between evangelical proselytizing and a series of slave rebellions that Seabrook and others in positions of power followed with some care. In 1822, the Rev. Edwin Holland of Charleston lashed out at the "swarm of MISSIONARIES, white and black" who were implicated in the Denmark Vesey conspiracy. Holland reflected "how blasphemously the word of God was tortured" by slaves who had fallen under the influence of "apostolic vagabonds" and their "religious magazines, newspaper paragraphs, and insulated texts of scripture." His warnings gained new relevance later that same year, when Rev. John Smith of the London Missionary Society was accused by Caribbean planters and the Anglican establishment of instigating a bloody slave revolt in Demerara. In Jamaica, the slaveholding Rev. George Bridges similarly

---

[9] William May Wightman, *Life of William Capers, D.D., One of the Bishops of the Methodist Episcopal Church, South; Including an Autobiography* (Nashville, TN: Southern Methodist, 1858); Clarke, *Wrestling Jacob*, 10–5; John B. Adger, *My Life and Times, 1810–1899* (Richmond, VA: Presbyterian Committee of Publication, 1899).

participated in the backlash against dissenting missionaries (which included black as well as white evangelists). The Colonial Union that Bridges helped to lead even set the torch to biracial evangelical chapels after the so-called "Baptist War" of 1831.[10]

Proslavery clergy in the United States met concerns about slave religiosity in more subtle ways than Caribbean masters did, insisting that their evangelizing efforts would be more effective than brute force in quelling the rebellious spirit of enslaved African-Americans. In 1825, John Holt Rice of Virginia predicted that an educated white clergy conveying oral instruction would prevent "some crisp-haired prophet, some pretender to inspiration" from "feigning communications from heaven" and thus working to "rouse the fanaticism of his brethren" and prepare them "for any work however desolating and murderous." Aware of a burgeoning Afro-Christianity that lay beyond white control, the Georgia Methodist James O. Andrew accurately noted that American slaves would have "religion of some sort" regardless of master's efforts to insulate them from the Christian Gospel. "If the pure stream of the water of life flows not to [to the slave], he will drink at the foul stream of a lawless and destructive superstition," Andrew warned, shortly before the black preacher and visionary Nat Turner launched his insurrection. For Andrew, the alternatives were simple. "The owner has only to choose whether [his slave] shall imbibe the doctrines of a pure and blessed godliness, which will make him better, happier, and more useful; or the principles of a half pagan superstition, which

---

[10] [Edwin Holland], *A Refutation of the Calumnies, Circulated Against the Southern and Western States, Respecting the Institutions and Existence of Slavery Among Them* (Charleston, SC: A.E. Miller, 1822), 11–12; Whitemarsh Seabrook, *An Essay on the Management of Slaves, and especially, on their Religious Instruction* (Charleston, 1834); Michael Craton argues that the antimissionary paranoia of West Indian whites resulted not only from the actual increase in evangelicalism but also from the decline of other explanations for slave restiveness, such as African importations (which ceased in 1807), or from the imperial rivalries and natural rights ideologies of the French Revolutionary era. See *Testing the Chains: Resistance to Slavery in the British West Indies* (Ithaca, NY: Cornell University Press, 1982), 241 and "Christianity and Slavery in the British West Indies, 1750–1865" *Historical Reflections/ Reflexions Historique* 5 (1978), 141–59. For the crucial transnational and interimperial contexts of early-nineteenth-century slave missions, see Sylvia Frey and Betty Wood, *Come Shouting to Zion: African American Protestantism in the American South and British Caribbean to 1830* (Chapel Hill, NC: University of North Carolina Press, 1998) and Catherine Hall, *Civilizing Subjects: Metropole and Colony in the English Imagination, 1830–1867* (Chicago, IL: University of Chicago Press, 2002).

sanctifies the vilest practices and indulges the foulest passions and lusts of a fallen heart."[11]

Perhaps with the turmoil of Caribbean slavery in mind, South Carolina's masters orchestrated a campaign to co-opt rather than resist plantation evangelization. In 1829, Charles Cotesworth Pinckney displayed a typical array of motives in assuring fellow rice planters that spreading "true religion" through a carefully monitored program of oral instruction would not only dissuade slave rebelliousness, but also "counteract their reluctance to labor." No less important was his prediction that "our national character would be relieved from its only real opprobrium" if planters took the lead in spreading the Gospel to their slaves. By 1845, the Christian indoctrination of plantation workers had become a statewide movement, ratified by the assemblage of clergy and politicians who traveled to Charleston in May of that year. The sixty-one planter testimonials that this group published said far less about the threat of insurrection than they did about the positive influence of religious discipline on labor productivity. Worship services conducted within the secured confines of the plantation quarters seemed as likely as improvements in health and diet to transform Christianized workplaces into models of economic efficiency.[12]

Though maximizing profitability was important, so too was a respect for republican sensibilities, which distinguished the mature phase of Christianization from earlier appeals that had compared evangelical household rulers to kings or invoked "the salutary terrors of religion" as the proper response to unruly workers. Experience with the comparatively stable slave population of coastal South Carolina encouraged the leading theorists of antebellum slave conversion to draw attention to those internal mechanisms that seemed capable of coexisting with cruder forms of coercion. Much was made of St. Paul's instruction for servants to obey "not with eye-service

---

[11] John Holt Rice, "The Injury Done to Religion by Ignorant Preachers. A Sermon Delivered Before an Education Society in Sept., 1825," *Virginia Evangelical and Literary Magazine* 8 (November 1825), 604; James O. Andrew, "The Southern Slave Population," *Methodist Magazine and Quarterly Review* 13 (July 1831), 318. Such perceptions and their relevance to the "experiential" dimensions of proslavery evangelicalism are the topic of Charles F. Irons, *The Origins of Proslavery Christianity: White and Black Evangelicals in Colonial and Antebellum Virginia* (Chapel Hill: University of North Carolina Press, 2008), a superb book that appeared too late for me to incorporate it more fully in this chapter's argument.

[12] Pinckney, *An Address Delivered in Charleston, Before the Agricultural Society of South Carolina* (Charleston: A.E. Miller, 1829); *Proceedings of the Meeting in Charleston, S.C. May 13–15, 1845, on the Religious Instruction of the Negroes, Together with the Report of the Committee and the Address to the Public* (Charleston, VA: B. Jenkins, 1845).

as men pleasers, but as servants of Christ." It was in this same spirit that the Rev. James Henley Thornwell argued in 1847 that "the Gospel is our mightiest safeguard; for it governs in secret as well as in public; it cultivates the conscience" and thus established "a more vigilant watch over individual conduct" than the world's best police forces.[13]

Clergy often warned that conversion of slaves required masters to share in the expression of Christian piety. As the Rev. Thomas Clay of Georgia warned, "to make this system [of evangelical faith] truly and permanently beneficial upon plantations, the entire discipline and economy of the plantation must be established and regulated in harmony with it." Owners, in short, were unlikely to enjoy the full benefits of a docile work force unless they governed slaves "according to those very principles he wishes them to govern themselves." Evangelical expectations discouraged any simple equation of Godliness with a profitable business venture. For masters to experience their own "new birth" was part of a larger set of assurances about how the faithful might discover to their own satisfaction how holy texts sanctified slavery. The Rev. James Smylie of Mississippi, who himself was a major cotton planter, explained what it was like to discover the righteousness of slaveholding. "Instead of hanging down his head, moping and brooding over his condition, as formerly, without action," the Christian master of slaves "raises his head, and moves on cheerfully, in the plain path of duty." "Instead of viewing the word of God, as formerly, come with whips and scorpions to chastise him into paradise, he feels that its 'ways are ways of pleasantness and its paths peace.'"[14]

---

[13] Portsmouth Baptist Association of 1800 quoted in Douglas Ambrose, "Of Stations and Relations: Proslavery in Early Virginia," 52; Louis-Phillip Gallot de Lormerie to Madison February 24, 1802 Robert J. Brugger, et al. eds., *The Papers of James Madison: Secretary of State Series* (Charlottesville: University Press of Virginia, 1986) 2: 486–7; [Thornwell], "Religions Instruction of the Black Population," *SPR* 1 (December 1847), 110. Among the pleas for servants to exceed "eye service as men-pleasers" (a formulation seen in both Ephesians and 1 Colossians) were Charles C. Jones, *A Catechism of Scripture, Doctrine, and Practice: For Families and Sabbath Schools, Designed Also for the Oral Instruction of Colored Persons* (Savannah: T. Purse, 1845), 129–31; William Capers, *Catechism for the Use of the Methodist Missions* (Richmond: John Early, 1852), 14, 22; Robert Ryland, *The Scripture Catechism, for Coloured People* (Richmond, VA: Harrold & Murray, 1848). Edwin T. Winkler, *Notes and Questions for the Oral Instruction of Colored People* (Charleston, SC: Southern Baptist Publication Society, 1857) proved an exception, in emphasizing the Ten Commandments rather than Pauline instructions.

[14] Thomas Clay, *Letter in Proceedings of the Meeting in Charleston*, 58; James Smylie, *A Review of a Letter from the Presbytery of Chillicothe, to the Presbytery of Mississippi, on the Subject of Slavery* (Woodville, MI: Wm. A. Norris, 1836), 4.

Smylie and other proslavery clergy saw the conversion of masters as a step toward a broader melding of Christian rights and Christian duties within an idealized evangelical household. As such, the mission to the slaves moved easily into a mission to convert the master class as a whole. The Presbyterian evangelist I.S.K. Axson lectured Georgia planters in the early 1830s that they incurred obligations every time they went "to the Bible for proof that the institution of slavery in itself is not sinful nor is to be condemned." He insisted on his own corresponding right to visit "the same treasure-house of authority" to offer "a few directions for the purpose of showing, what, in order to meet the same will of God you must do with [slaves] when in your possession, and how as spiritual beings you must treat them." What southern ministers brought out from this Biblical "treasure-house of authority" was a mode of family governance that had long been a fixture of the Protestant tradition. What was new about proslavery evangelism of the nineteenth century was its conviction – borne of hope as well as anxiety – that the certainties of daily household routines would provide an antidote to what seemed to be an increasingly disruptive set of social and political upheavals.[15]

The Rev. A.B. Van Zandt of Virginia clarified the Bible's potential to structure everyday southern life when he admitted that while scripture furnished neither "a detailed system of philosophy" nor "a treatise on political economy," it remained "a grand system of truth, in which are revealed all the principles which are necessary to regulate all the diversified relations and duties of mankind." The message of the Bible had less to do with the Gospels or even with theology than with those parts of Paul's epistles that detailed the relations between husbands and wives, parents and children, and masters and servants. The Reverend Ebenezer Boyden of Virginia displayed unusual directness in reasoning that the "divine legislative acts" contained in the New Testament "constitute a slave code, just as distinctly and broadly as the laws of any Southern State of this Union." Leaders of the Deep South bar agreed with such comparisons. While serving as a justice of the U.S. Supreme Court, John Archibald Campbell explained how Christianity, by supplying "the constituent principle of the family," became the "central point" of slave society and its "attractive principle of social union that collects and combines its members and constitutes its order." Christopher Memminger of South Carolina provided an evangelical

---

[15] I.S.K. Axson, *Individual Responsibility: An Address Before the Association for the Religious Instruction of the Negroes, in Liberty County, Georgia* (Savannah, GA: Thomas Purse, 1843), 36–7.

antidote to Jefferson's depiction of "boisterous passions" as a threat to the national future. "Each planter in fact is a Patriarch," Memminger explained.

> His position compels him to be a ruler in his household. From early youth, his children and servants look up to him as the head, and obedience and subordination become important elements of education. Where so many duties depend upon his will, society assumes the Hebrew form. Domestic relations become those which are most prized – each family recognizes its duty – and its members feel a responsibility for its discharge. The fifth commandment becomes the foundation of the society. The state is looked to only as the ultimate head in external relations while all internal duties ... are left to domestic regulation. In consequence of this, it has followed that the South has ever been more steady and conservative than the North. The leveling ultraisms of the day have never found here a congenial soil.[16]

The goal of evangelizing households implied that missionary efforts marked a transitional phase, which might cease once Godly patriarchs took full responsibility for the spiritual welfare of their dependents (see Figure 4.1). This vision was still in the distant future during the 1850s, however, as invigorated southern denominationalism prodded each branch of proslavery Protestantism to follow the lead of Southern Methodists, who alone increased their annual missionary expenditures from $46,765 in 1850 to $138,545 ten years later. Southern boasts that nearly a half of a million African-Americans had become full-fledged members of Protestant churches was tempered by the sense that there were "special obligations" that required "a scheme of missionary effort, coextensive with the entire limits of this population." To reach the three million additional slaves who were supposedly unchurched involved the daunting task of moving beyond those eastern enclaves where evangelical efforts had enjoyed the broadest planter support, and tackling the notoriously Godless reaches of the Mississippi Valley and the frontier cotton belt. The agenda inspired both organized denominational outreach to the southwest and the efforts of individual planters, who purchased tracts, catechisms, and other material

---

[16] A.B. Van Zandt, *God's Voice to the Nation: A Sermon Occasioned by the Death of Zachary Taylor, President of the United States* (Petersburg: JA Gray, 1850), 9–10. Ebenezer Boyden, *The Epidemic of the Nineteenth Century* (Richmond, VA: Chas H. Wynne, 1860), 7; John A. Campbell, *The Institutions, Duties and Relations of Alabama, An Oration Before the Erosophic and Philomathic Societies of the University of Alabama, July 12, 1859* (Tuscaloosa, 1859), 20; Christopher Memminger, *Lecture Before Young Men's Library Association of Augusta, Georgia, April 10th, 1851, Showing American Slavery to be Consistent with Moral and Physical Progress of a Nation* (Augusta, GA: W.S. Jones, 1851), 14–15.

Dec. 5, 1863   THE ILLUSTRATED LONDON NEWS·   561

FAMILY WORSHIP IN A PLANTATION IN SOUTH CAROLINA.—SEE PAGE 574

FIGURE 4.1. In one of his many sympathetic portrayals of plantation life, the British artist Frank Vizetelly featured a white planter family and their slaves being led in worship by a black preacher. *Illustrated London News, December 5, 1863, used with permission of Dartmouth College Library.*

produced by a rapidly expanding program of proslavery evangelical publishing.[17]

As the missionary enterprise entered its final decade, concern for individual souls – and for Christianized households – gave way to the still more stirring realization that "the Christian people of the South *are the South*," as the Rev. Abner A. Porter put it in 1850. James Henley Thornwell lauded this sense of corporate purpose in what historians recognize as the most accomplished expression of an evangelical proslavery ethos. By extending

---

[17] Methodist statistics appear in Sernett, *Black Religion and American Evangelicalism*, 290; William Brownlow's rough approximation of 465,000 "total colored membership" of Southern churches would be misleadingly repeated as authoritative by *Southern Cultivator* 16 (December 1858), 378; "The Churches and Slavery," *DBR* 26 (January, 1859), 118; and, with particular flourishes, in William J. Sasnett, *Progress: Considered with Particular Reference to the Methodist Episcopal Church, South*, (Nashville, TN: Southern Methodist Publishing, 1856), 214; and David Christy, *Pulpit Politics: or Ecclesiastical Legislation on Slavery* (Cincinnati: Faran & McLean, 1862).

the Gospel to slaves, masters were "consolidating the elements of your social fabric, so firmly and compactly, that it shall defy the storms of fanaticism," Thornwell explained in his 1850 *tour de force*. He then assured fellow slaveholders that by making an internal enemy into a religious ally, the basis for social harmony would be laid. "The spectacle you will exhibit of union, sympathy, and confidence among the different orders of the community, will be a standing refutation of all their accusations against us."[18]

It is important to avoid hasty conclusions about the solidarities forged by these well-publicized missionary efforts. Thornwell's notion that plantation harmony would usher from that "Christian knowledge" that "softens and subdues" was proved a lie by the actions of slaves, especially during their wartime quest for liberation. Christianity of the sort that emerged in the 1850s thus acted mainly as a cohesive force among whites. Stephanie McCurry and others have persuasively argued that evangelical family order did foster a cross-class identification of male patriarchs, whose prerogatives of household mastery included those whose family dependents included a wife and children but no slaves. Within the largest plantations, however, this same sense of household purpose and stewardship included slaveholding women, and the missionary skills of unofficial female evangelists were lauded by several testimonials submitted to the 1845 Charleston convention. The blurring of class and gender divisions in this evangelical ideal was perhaps less remarkable than the interdenominational nature of the movement. The 1845 collaboration was a moment of Deep South ecumenical cooperation that would not be equaled until the wartime evangelization of Confederate soldiers a decade and a half later.[19]

A few clergy hinted that plantation missions might provide a platform for proslavery separatism, though they were generally not disposed to present Christianization as a predecessor to an independent slaveholding nation. The Virginia Baptist Rev. Thornton Stringfellow suggestively noted in his discussion of the Abrahamic covenant how bondage had been "incorporated in the only national constitution emanating from God." But, through the late 1850s, it was the U.S. Constitution of 1787, not an imagined new charter

[18] [A.A. Porter] "North and South," *SPR* 3 (January 1850), 377; Thornwell, *The Rights and Duties of Masters: A Sermon Preached at the Dedication of a Church Erected in Charleston, S.C. for the Benefit and Instruction of the Colored Population* (Charleston, SC: Walker and James, 1850), 50–1.

[19] Thornwell, *Rights and Duties*, 49; Stephanie McCurry, *Masters of Small Worlds: Yeoman Households, Gender Relations, and the Political Culture of the Antebellum South Carolina Low Country* (New York: Oxford University Press, 1995); *Proceedings of the Meeting in Charleston*, 5, 21, 36, 37 39, 42, 56, 62, 63, 64.

of southern nationhood, that seemed to best embody divine decrees regarding slavery. Like the bulk of the proslavery clergy, Stringfellow combined a commitment to sectional interests with a stubborn Unionism borne of his desire for social order. The depth of such clerical Unionism had many sources, but chief among them were a series of intricate efforts to create networks of Christian fellowship extending well beyond the world of southern plantations.[20]

PLANS OF UNION AND THE CONTAINMENT OF SECTIONALISM

Late in 1822, in the wake of Denmark Vesey's conspiracy and trial, the Rev. Richard Furman cautioned white Charlestonians to rethink their state's prevailing inward turn. Furman, who was then the Deep South's leading Baptist, relinquished his earlier commitment to black evangelization, a program that would not be revisited in the city for another quarter century. He instead called for a day of thanksgiving and humiliation that would make clear that "publicity, rather than secrecy" marked "the true policy to be pursued." A public day of gratitude, if sanctioned by the governor and observed widely throughout the state, would not simply register divine dependence. It would broadcast the ties that existed between the Deep South whites and the rest of the federal Union. "The Negroes should know, that however numerous they are in some parts of these Southern States," they were badly overmatched within the American republic as a whole. Furman argued that public worship might thereby remind slaves that even Northerners with qualms about slavery's immorality would unite with fellow whites if they ever witnessed "slaves in our Country, in arms, wading through blood and carnage" to launch an insurrection.[21]

Associating the extended Union with the security of slave society came naturally to Furman, who simultaneously affirmed proslavery principles within his state and enthusiastically supported those denominational "spiritual economies" that were then redrawing the boundaries of American religious practice. Furman had already shown his skill in pushing through Baptist "associational" initiatives in education, ministry, and, beginning in

---

[20] Stringfellow, *Brief Examination of Scripture Testimony on the Institution of Slavery* (Washington: Congressional Globe Office, 1850), 7; idem, *Slavery: Its Origin, Nature, and History, Considered in the Light of Bible Teachings, Moral Justice, and Political Wisdom* (New York: John F. Trow, 1861), 53–4.

[21] Richard Furman, *Rev. Dr. Furman's Exposition of the Views of the Baptists, Relative to the Colored Population in the United States in a Communication to the Governor of South Carolina* (Charleston, 1822).

the 1810s, in foreign aid missions. Differences on the topic of slavery seemed to matter little in the creation of a powerful axis between Rhode Island and Furman's Low Country base of operations. Most Carolinians would have appreciated the early fruits of this collaboration, which had led to the appointment in 1807 of the Rhode Island Baptist Rev. Jonathan Maxcy as the first president of South Carolina College, the election in 1814 of another Brown University alumnus, David Rogerson Williams, as South Carolina's first evangelical governor, and the continuing stream of young Carolinians like Basil Manly Jr., William Bullein Johnson, and Edwin T. Winkler toward theological training in Providence.[22]

If Furman took pride in the results of this expansive Baptist network, he had already begun by the 1810s to consider ways to foster even greater nationalization of his fledgling denomination. Upon becoming the first president of the Baptist's Triennial convention in 1814, he threw his full support behind the establishment of Columbian College in Washington, D.C., an effort that would be the chief concern of the Philadelphia *Columbian Star and Christian Index*, edited by Low Country Baptist William T. Brantley. Evangelizing the young republic through such educational initiatives remained a potent source of inspiration well after Furman's death in 1825. The early faculty of new Baptist colleges like Furman, Wake Forest, and the University of Richmond strove toward this goal, as did leading Carolinians like Brantley and Johnson. Alongside such missionary and educational work, Baptists in the slave states simultaneously sensed the need to use state-level initiatives to foster religious publishing closer to home. Here there was a relative lag, as the subscription list kept for the Furman Theological Institute for 1830 made clear. Of the nine religious weeklies furnished for the school's reading room that year, four came from Boston, two (including Brantley's *Christian Index*) came from Philadelphia, one from New York, while only two Charleston papers (the Presbyterian *Southern Watchman* and the Catholic *Intelligencer*) were published within the slave states.[23]

[22] James A. Rogers, *Richard Furman: Life and Legacy* (Macon, GA: Mercer University Press, 1985); Butler, *Awash in a Sea of Faith*, 257–88; M. L. Bradbury, "Structures of Nationalism," in Ronald Hoffman and Peter J. Albert, *Religion in a Revolutionary Age* (Charlottesville: University Press of Virginia, 1994). Furman's efforts within the state are assessed in Sylvia Frey, *Water from a Rock* and Rachel Klein, *The Unification of a Slave State: The Rise of the Planter Class in the South Carolina Backcountry, 1760–1808* (Chapel Hill: University of North Carolina Press, 1990). There has of yet been no adequate account of such ties between Baptists of Rhode Island and of the Deep South.

[23] Henry Smith Stroupe, *The Religious Press of the South Atlantic States, 1802–1865* (Durham: Duke University Press, 1956), 13.

The dependence on outside publishing might have been cause for concern under any circumstance. It assumed crisis proportions, however, in the overheated atmosphere of 1835–6, the year that South Carolina Baptists finally launched their own weekly paper under the editorship of William Henry Brisbane. The cause of this distress was the postal campaign undertaken by northern abolitionists the previous summer, which injected discord into denominations no less than it did into political parties. Angry responses across the white South cast new suspicions about journals originating from the North. The appearance of antislavery British Baptists at the 1835 Triennial Convention in Richmond deepened the slave South's sense of isolation. Free-state Baptists, for their part, were suddenly presented a new model for interaction, in being given the opportunity to relinquish their American ties so that they might bask in the heroic accomplishments of such English co-religionists as the Rev. William Knibb, who had followed a successful campaign against Jamaican slavery with an onslaught against the system of apprenticeship instituted there.[24]

Slaveholding Baptists initially responded to these developments by assuming a defensive posture within new journals such as the Richmond *Religious Herald*, the *Christian Index* (which in 1834 relocated from Philadelphia to Georgia), and the *South Carolina Baptist*. By the early 1840s, these proslavery brethren had regained enough self-assurance to commence a series of correspondence that abolitionists would circulate on both sides of the Atlantic. Proslavery Baptists took a risk in rebutting antislavery evangelicalism with compendia of proslavery scripture, an approach that drew charges of pharisaical Biblicism. Thornton Stringfellow, the author of the most thorough such collection, impressed New Englanders mainly for his "matchless impudence." The *Baptist Magazine* of London reported that Stringfellow's efforts worked primarily to "lower the southern churches in the estimation of our countrymen." A series of similarly acrimonious and demeaning exchanges bore heavily on Beaufort planter and clergyman Richard Fuller. Late in 1844, Fuller eagerly began a more amenable set of written exchanges on slavery's morality with President Francis Wayland of Brown University. Though Wayland had condemned slavery in his widely regarded treatises on political economy and moral philosophy, he and Fuller went out of their way to find what common

---

[24] William Wright Barnes, *The Southern Baptist Convention, 1845–1953* (Nashville: Broadman Press, 1954); Thomas F. Harwood, "British Evangelical Abolitionism and American Churches in the 1830s," *JSH* 28 (August 1962), 287–306; Hall, *Civilizing Subjects*, 107–20. In 1832, Brantley's coverage of Jamaica in the *Christian Index* drew attention to the religious intolerance of Anglicans rather than the slave unrest that had prompted attacks against the Baptists. See issues from April 14, April 21, May 5, and June 16, 1832.

ground they could. The civility of their interchange assured that comity would prevail between Baptists across the United States even after the southern faithful adopted an explicitly sectional organization in 1845.[25]

There was already a conflicted set of tendencies at work, then, when a tangled controversy over slaveholding missionaries led to the creation of the Southern Baptist Convention (SBC), a body destined to become the largest of all American denominations. Mainly the work of delegates from Georgia (fully 90 percent of whom were slaveholders) and from South Carolina, the Augusta meeting that created the SBC effectively exchanged the Deep South's long-standing institutional ties to New England for an even closer association with those Virginia representatives who attended the meeting. The fruits of this effort lay less in the institutionalization of proslavery sectionalism, however, than in a long-delayed consolidation of evangelical operations into one centralized organization, a goal that Furman had set decades earlier. Despite the wishes of some who took part at Augusta, there remained a great many areas for future cooperation of the SBC with such national associations as the American Sunday School Union of Philadelphia. In the period between 1845 and 1860, the Convention stirred far more controversy in its "modernizing" imperative than it did by any effort on behalf of bondage. The most heated Baptist polemics of the late antebellum years concerned the fierce battle over a "Landmark" movement, whose strength was based among those trans-Appalachian churches that had long distrusted foreign missionary work. On the eve of the Civil War, Baptists

---

[25] The inaugural issue of the *Baptist Antislavery Correspondent* 1 (February 1841) expressed its desire to "embody the Correspondence between the [Baptist Antislavery] Convention and Southern Baptists, on the subject of Slavery, as connected with the church" and then reprinted the exchange between Elon Galusha and Richard Fuller that inspired Thornton Stringfellow's first publication on behalf of slavery. This was Stringfellow, *A Brief Examination of Scripture Testimony on the Institution of Slavery* (Richmond: Religious Herald, 1841) which was attacked both in "Thornton Stringfellow on Slavery," *Christian Reflector* April 26, 1843 and "Vindication of Slavery," London *Baptist Magazine* (April 1841), 185–6. Fuller, who was already a prominent participant in maneuvers over slavery within the church, saw his profile rise markedly with his interchange with Galusha, with a series of letters to the *Christian Reflector*, and, most of all, with *Domestic Slavery Considered as a Scriptural Institution: in a Correspondence between the Rev. Richard Fuller and the Rev. Francis Wayland* (New York: Lewis Colby, 1847). For Wayland's role as sectional mediator, a bane of abolitionists, and eventual supporter of Lincoln, see John R. McKivigan, "The Sectional Division of the Methodist and Baptist Denominations as Measures of Northern Antislavery Sentiment," and Deborah Bingham Van Broekhoven, "Suffering with Slaveholders: The Limits of Francis Wayland's Antislavery Witness" both in Snay and McKivigan, *Religion and the Antislavery Debate*.

had all but relinquished their interest in pursuing Deep South Christianization along recognizably nationalist lines.[26]

Both observers at the time and historians since have extracted the
1845 formation of SBC from this messy and conflicted denominational
history and paired its splintering from the free states with the nearly
simultaneous division of the Methodist Church into sectional wings.[27]
Grouping these two events is, to be sure, a helpful reminder of the schis-
matic potential of the slavery controversy. Yet such an approach, which
has worked its way deep into the historiography, risks overstating the
consequences of the Baptist reorganization while simultaneously obscuring the enormous bitterness sown by the "Great Secession" that disrupted
American Methodism over the course of 1844 and 1845. The structural
rigidity of the Methodist order – a feature apparent in its hierarchy as
well as in its liturgy – made it much more difficult for leaders to finesse the
issue of slavery's morality. The same interplay of antislavery British
evangelical efforts, of internal activism from American abolitionists,
and of proslavery counterattacks that had produced the SBC set the stage
for a far more toxic Methodist dispute over slaveholders' ability to serve
at the highest level of the church. The lingering effects of the Methodist
schism were made still more contentious by its centralized control of
valuable church properties, local newspapers, educational institutions, and,
most important of all, of a publishing empire whose fate would only be decided
by the U.S. Supreme Court in 1854. Friction between northern and southern
Methodists only increased with the angry polemics of Augustus Baldwin

---

[26] Mary Burnham Putnam, *The Baptists and Slavery, 1840–1845* (Ann Arbor, MI, 1913);
Willie Grier Todd, "The Slavery Issue and the Organization of a Southern Baptist Convention," (PhD Thesis, University of North Carolina at Chapel Hill, 1964). Robert
G. Gardner, *A Decade of Debate and Division: Georgia Baptists and the Formation of
the Southern Baptist Convention* (Macon, GA: Mercer University Press, 1995), follows
slaveholding for each of the delegates. Southern Baptist cooperation with the American
Sunday School Union is noted in John W. Kuykendall, *Southern Enterprize: The Work
of National Evangelical Societies in the Antebellum South* (Westport, CT: Greenwood
Press, 1982), 124.

[27] For explicit connections between these two schisms, and the impending secession of southern states from the United States, see John C. Calhoun, "Speech on the Slavery Question,"
March 4, 1850, *PJCC* 27: 199–200; C. C. Goen, *Broken Churches, Broken Nation:
Denominational Schisms and the Coming of the Civil War* (Macon, GA: Mercer Univer-
sity Press, 1985); and Mitchell Snay, *Gospel of Disunion: Religion and Separatism in the
Antebellum South* (New York: Cambridge University Press, 1993). Attempts to broaden
the focus can be found in [William J. Grayson], *Letter to His Excellency Whitemarsh
B. Seabrook, Governor of the State of South Carolina, on the Dissolution of the Union*
(Charleston, 1850), 19 and several excellent essays, from Snay, *Religion and the
Antebellum Debate over Slavery.*

Longstreet and Henry Bascom, whose distrust of coreligionists in the free states blurred into a condemnation of free society as a whole.[28]

If the Methodist schism provided the clearest case of how slavery in the churches escalated antebellum sectionalism, the impact of this division was offset by the denomination's comparative neglect of nationalizing imperatives, however. As a dissenting tradition focused mainly on the piety of individual believers, Methodism lacked the same political sense of corporate purpose that prevailed within those groups descended from once-established Churches. Following in the footsteps of John Wesley (whose dissenting ambivalence was compounded by a tepid Loyalism during the American Revolution) meant something quite different than hearkening back to such Reformation-era figures as John Knox, Jean Calvin, or the authors of the Westminster Confession. One can scarcely imagine a Methodist counterpart to the Rev. Thomas Smyth's bold attempt to trace both the Declaration of Independence and the American Constitution to Presbyterian sources. Nor would it have meant as much for a Wesleyan to have joined the Rev. Thomas V. Moore in explaining how "the Reformation of the sixteenth century was in a plenary and potential sense, the source of our American liberty."[29]

An awareness of Reformation-era lineages helps to explain how American Presbyterians like Smyth and Moore effectively replaced Furman's

---

[28] Donald Matthews, *Slavery and Methodism: A Chapter in American Morality, 1780–1845* (Princeton: Princeton University Press, 1965); Richard Carwardine, "Trauma in Methodism: Property, Church Schism, and Sectional Polarization in Antebellum America," in Mark A. Noll, ed., *God and Mammon: Protestants, Money and the Market, 1790–1860* (New York: Oxford University Press, 2002). Augustus Baldwin Longstreet, *A Voice from the South: Comprising Letters from Georgia to Massachusetts, and to the Southern States, with an Appendix* (Baltimore, MD: Western Continent Press, 1847); Henry Biddleman Bascom, *Methodism and Slavery; with other Matters of Controversy Between the North and South* (Frankfurt, KY: Hodges, Todd & Pruett, 1845).

[29] Fred J. Hood, *Reformed America: the Middle and Southern States, 1783–1837* (University, AL: University of Alabama Press, 1980); Thomas Smyth, *Ecclesiastical Republicanism; or the Republicanism, Liberality, and Catholicity of Presbytery, in Contrast to Prelacy and Popery* (Boston, 1844); idem, "Presbyterianism, The Revolution, The Declaration of Independence, and the Constitution," *SPR* 1 (March 1848), 34–78; Rev. Thomas V. Moore, *The Reformation the Source of American Liberty. An Address Delivered Before the Union Society of Hamden Sydney College, June 9, 1852* (Richmond, VA: Chas. H. Wynne, 1852), 6. Anticipating a position taken by some Reformed clergy during the Confederacy, Smyth affirmed in 1848 that "every government, therefore, as it regards the foundations and obligations of authority, is a theocracy, derived immediately from God, and enforced and adjudged by God" (and distinguished this position from the notion of an established state church). See "Relations of Christianity to Civil Polity," in *Complete Works* (Columbia, SC: R.L. Bryan, 1910), 10: 488.

Baptists as the most zealous exponents of evangelical nationalism within the slave South after 1830. The Reformed churches that were allied under the banner of Presbyterianism had pursued public influence during the early nineteenth century with such intensity that many suspected them of theocratic aspirations. Clergy had responded to such accusations by detailing their "republican" ecclesiology, and arguing how well suited they were to providing a common bond between North and South. This same nationalist outlook worked to overcome the sectional differences over slavery that split the Baptists and Methodists in 1845. On a more limited scale, a similar pattern emerged among American Episcopalians, another church whose cultural power far exceeded its relatively modest size. As recent historians have shown, the cultural importance of these two groups of clergy lay not simply in the wealth and standing of their communicants. Their enthusiasm for cosmopolitan intellectual endeavor and their mastery of the grammar of nationhood were at least as important in establishing their increasing ability to speak on behalf of the southern master class.[30]

Particular class, ethnic, and geographical alignments assured that Presbyterians and Episcopalians would present their variants of proslavery Americanism in distinctive ways. The center of gravity for Episcopalians was among the elite segments of the Atlantic states. Its clergy would, until late in the antebellum period, be more influenced by British evangelical trends (especially the Oxford movement) than by the challenge of evangelizing the American frontier. The basic axis of Presbyterianism reached back to the mid-eighteenth century, when a series of ties first developed between Pennsylvania, the College of New Jersey, and the Scotch-Irish settlers of the Shenandoah Valley in Virginia. In 1801, this core both expanded, with a Plan of Union that allowed missionary cooperation with the New England Congregationalists, and splintered, with the departure of southwestern clergy who founded the Cumberland Presbyterian Church. In the Deep South, Calvinist groups with ties to New England and to Europe would be haphazardly incorporated into the national General Assembly between 1800 and 1839. To further complicate these patterns, American Presbyterians maintained important connections with coreligionists in Scotland. They

---

[30] Eugene Genovese, "Religion and the Collapse of the American Union," and *idem, A Consuming Fire: The Fall of the Confederacy in the Mind of the White Christian South* (Athens: University of Georgia Press, 1998); Michael O'Brien, *Conjectures of Order: Intellectual Life in the American South* (Chapel Hill, NC, 2004), 1098–1157; Jack P. Maddex, Jr. "The 'Southern Apostasy' Revisited: The Significance of Proslavery Christianity," *Marxist Perspectives* 7 (1979), 132–41.

were especially drawn to the paternalist efforts of Edinburgh's Thomas
Chalmers and to the political debates elicited by the Free Church movement
of the 1830s and 1840s. [31]

Sectional strains among Episcopalians never pushed the Church
toward schism, despite the tensions that existed between the training
and ordaining of black clergy such as Alexander Crummell and the proslavery stances taken by many prominent northern clergy up through the
Civil War.[32] By contrast, slavery emerged as a disruptive force within
American Presbyterianism as early as the 1790s, when antislavery clergy
first tried to commit the Church to emancipation. In 1815, amidst a flurry
of postwar patriotism, the English emigrant George Bourne pushed slavery
back into the center of the Presbyterian General Assembly's agenda.
Rebuffed in his proposal to deny communion to "manstealers" (whom
he had already banned from his own Virginia congregation), Bourne
angrily insisted that "a man who says that he is a Christian and a Republican and has any connection with slavery only exposes himself to ridicule
for he is so simple that he can not [sic] discern right from wrong, or so
deceitful that he professes honesty while he is a THIEF." The personal
nature of this assault – and Bourne's insistence that the failings of slaveholders implicated the entire nation – led to a series of charges, counter-
charges, and finally, to Bourne's expulsion by the General Assembly. The
1818 meeting of that body, which included hardly any Deep South representation, unanimously agreed to pair its rejection of Bourne's appeal with
a public denunciation of the "gross violation" of bondage and an appeal to
"speedily ... efface this blot on our holy religion" through "complete
abolition of slavery throughout Christendom." The means of doing so
would be provided by the American Colonization Society, which had

[31] Conkin, *The Uneasy Center*, 147–8; Ernest Trice Thompson, *Presbyterians in the South, Volume I, 1607–1861* (Richmond, VA: John Knox Press, 1963); Clarke, *Our Southern Zion*; Peter J. Wallace, "The Bond of Union: The Old School Presbyterian Church and the American Nation, 1837–1861," (PhD thesis, University of Notre Dame, 2004); Andrew E. Murray, *Presbyterians and the Negro: A History* (Philadelphia: Presbyterian Historical Society, 1966); Rev. John Robinson, *The Testimony and Practice of the Presbyterian Church in Reference to American Slavery* (Cincinnati, OH: John D. Thorpe, 1852).

[32] Carl Stockton, "Conflict Among Evangelical Brothers: Anglo-American Churchmen and the Slavery Controversy, 1848–1853," *Anglican and Episcopal History* 62 (December 1993), 499–513; Seabury, *American Slavery, Distinguished from the Slavery of English Theorists* (New York: Mason Brothers, 1861). For the revealing pro-Confederate tendencies of Bishops in the Church of England, see Richard Blackett, *Divided Hearts: Britain and the American Civil War* (Baton Rouge, LA: Louisiana State University Press, 2001).

been organized two years earlier by the Presbyterian minister Robert Finley.[33]

Nearly two decades after this 1818 accord on slavery had been reached, the "Old School" and "New School" factions separated. Even specialized studies differ about the exact role abolitionism played in this 1837 schism. Beyond contention is the fact that after a prolonged struggle, a combination of theological conservatives and southern antiabolitionists repealed the 1801 Act of Union, expelled four synods in New York and Ohio, and reconfigured the remnant "Old School" as the inheritor of Church traditions and its powerful, Princeton-based theological apparatus. A few Old School partisans like William S. Plumer of Richmond subsequently tried to identify the New School with abolitionism, a weak charge considering the staunchly proslavery sentiments expressed by founders of that branch's "United Synod of the South." The Old School itself never took explicitly proslavery ground (a result of the fact that representation of the slave states in that body only increased from 30 percent of all General Assembly churches in 1837 to 43 percent two years later). The geographical issues that were at play operated less in terms of North and South than in delivering a vital core, stretching from the Hudson through the Mississippi Valley, from what Benjamin Morgan Palmer later termed New England's "dangerous theological speculations" and from the Northwest's "motley assemblage" of Yankee-influenced synods, where "every hue and colour of the ecclesiastical prism" seemed to prevail. A renewed alliance between the established Southeast and a Mid-Atlantic region dominated by Princeton grew stronger through the efforts of Charles Hodge. As an avowed nationalist and an orthodox Presbyterian, Hodge had become even more deeply troubled than the Baptist Francis Wayland had about the divisive possibilities of abolition. In 1835, Hodge warned how antislavery, if left

---

[33] Bourne's campaign commenced in the wake of two wartime thanksgiving sermons delivered on days of national humiliation; afterward he attacked slaveholding as a national sin as well as a grave personal transgression. A full account of this episode, which had significant impact on later Garrisonians, is laid out in John W. Christie and Dwight L. Dumond, *George Bourne and The Book and Slavery Irreconcilable* (Wilmington, NC: Historical Society of Delaware, 1969), 39 (for quote), 100, 201–2; *Extracts from the Minutes of the General Assembly of the Presbyterian Church in the United States of America* A.D. *1818* (Philadelphia: Thomas and William Bradford, 1818), 28–33. These minutes indicate that the only Deep South minister to attend the 1818 Assembly was Massachusetts-born Aaron Leland; overall, only 21 of the 134 delegates represented states south of the Potomac. For an admittedly biased account of the centrality of Presbyterians in African colonization, see Archibald Alexander, *A History of Colonization on the Western Coast of Africa* (Philadelphia: William S. Martien, 1846).

unchecked, could make Americans "two nations in feeling, which must soon render us two nations in fact."[34]

The ability of proslavery Unionism to thrive in both Old and New School Presbyterianism can be clarified by taking a closer look at two prominent anti-abolitionists who combated sectionalism until 1861, when each pursued fiercely competing understandings of wartime patriotism. George Junkin, who was born into a flinty Pennsylvania family with more faith than resources, may never have met Joseph Clay Stiles, the son of a wealthy rice planter and nephew of one of that legion of Baptist planters whom Richard Furman had recruited to the pulpit. From such starkly dissimilar backgrounds, both Junkin and Stiles were each pushed by inexplicable tragedy toward ministerial careers. Junkin attended college only upon the insistence of his mentor Andrew Carothers, a crippled former artisan who had given up his trade after the family's white maid had poisoned him with arsenic. Junkin's subsequent initiation into Calvinism at a New York City seminary instilled in him a commitment to doctrinal purity that was intense even by Presbyterian standards. After work on behalf of a manual labor school, he used his terms as president of three different colleges to implement his guiding principle that "every good school is a monarchy, but of a patriarchal character." His reputation within the Presbyterian General Assembly was shaped primarily by his vigorous 1835 prosecution of Albert Barnes for heresy, a key event in the escalation of the "Old School" campaign against the "New England Theology."[35]

The 1840s found Junkin courting controversies that were increasingly tinged with the politics of slavery and abolition. He ran afoul of those who hired him as president of Miami College when he attacked antislavery clergy as pawns of the

[34] Statistics based on *Minutes of the General Assembly of the Presbyterian Church* (Philadelphia: Lydia R. Bailey, 1837 and 1839), 626–30 (for 1837) and 271–4 (for 1839). Benjamin Morgan Palmer, *The Life and Letters of James Henley Thornwell* (Richmond, VA: Whittet and Shepperson, 1875), 193; Hodge, "Slavery," *Biblical Repertory* 8 (April 1835), 301; Robert J. Breckeridge, "Alleged Hostility to the Congregational Church, and to the People of New England," *Baltimore Literary and Religious Magazine* 5 (March 1839). Wallace, "Bond of Union" lays out the major positions and provides a meticulous analysis of shifting positions, thus moving beyond the classic accounts of C. Bruce Staiger, "Abolitionism and the Presbyterian Schism of 1837–1838," *Mississippi Valley Historical Review* 36 (December 1949), 391–414; Elwyn A. Smith, "The Role of the South in the Presbyterian Schism of 1837–38," *Church History* 29 (March 1960), 44–63; Earl R. MacCormac, "Missions and the Presbyterian Schism of 1837," *Church History* 32 (March 1963), 32–45 and James H. Moorehead, "The 'Restless Spirit of Radicalism': Old School Fears and the Schism of 1837," *Journal of Presbyterian History* 78 (Spring 2000), 19–33.
[35] D. X. Junkin, *The Rev. George Junkin: A Historical Biography* (Philadelphia: J.B. Lippincott and Co., 1871); Junkin, *Two Addresses delivered at Oxford, Ohio* (Cincinnati, OH: Western Church Press, 1841), 26; Earl A. Pope, *New England Calvinism and the Disruption of the Presbyterian Church* (New York: Garland, 1987), 262–94.

British and insisted that a program of African colonization alone could "save this fair land from being deluged in the blood of its inhabitants, and this free nation from the chains of servitude to European despots." However divisive Junkin's antiabolitionism was in Ohio, it did not bar his election as the Moderator of the 1844 Old School General Assembly, where he tempered his skepticism of foreign influence by praising a delegation from the Free Church of Scotland (which would by the following year be mired in controversy surrounding its solicitation of funds from American slaveholders). In 1845, Junkin used his position on the Assembly's Standing Committee on Bills and Overtures to push a plan (most closely associated with James Henley Thornwell of South Carolina) that distanced the Church from any imputation of slaveholding's sinfulness. If this stance never went so far as to repeal the Assembly's 1818 denunciation of slavery as a social evil, the resolve to avoid the "ruin and unnecessary schism between brethren" enhanced the antiabolitionist inclinations of the Old School's northern wing. In 1848, Junkin moved into the South itself, accepting the presidency of Washington College, the successor of William Graham's Revolutionary-era Liberty Hall academy. For the next twelve years, Junkin helped the college to move past the uproar created by his predecessor, the Virginia native William Henry Ruffner, who, in 1847, had proposed to ban slavery west of the Blue Ridge Mountains. In navigating through the sectional controversies of the 1850s, Junkin combined steady support for African colonization with growing ties to Virginia Presbyterianism. Besides penning a series of sharp newspaper critiques of *Uncle Tom's Cabin*, he blessed his daughters' marriages to Thomas J. Jackson and to William Preston, Washington College faculty who would later serve as generals in the Confederate Army.[36]

The evangelism of Joseph Clay Stiles was driven more by the heart than by the head and involved efforts to widen rather than narrow the terms of Christian fellowship. His conversion came when he was in his late twenties, when the death of his nineteen-year-old wife caused a broken Stiles to relinquish his law practice and his Georgia slaves in favor of Andover Seminary, which offered a variant of the same Congregationalist Calvinism that he had been

---

[36] Junkin, *The Integrity of our National Union vs. Abolitionism; An Argument from the Bible* (Cincinnati: R.P. Donough, 1843), 78; *A Review of the Rev. Dr. Junkin's Synodical Speech, in Defence of American Slavery* (Cincinnati: Daily Atlas, 1844); Junkin, *The Rev. George Junkin*, 436–60; *Minutes of the General Assembly of the Presbyterian Church in the United States of America* (Philadelphia: W.S. Martien, 1845), 8–22; Ruffner, *Appeal to the Citizens of West Virginia* (Louisville: Examiner Office, 1847); "Departure of Lexington Emigrants for Liberia," *The African Repository* 26 (April 1850), 110–12. For Junkin's authorship of the "Theophilus" essays that the *Richmond Watchman and Observer* published in *Uncle Tom's Cabin*, see Wallace, "Bond of Union."

taught while an undergraduate at Yale College. After earning a divinity degree from Andover, Stiles spent several years as an evangelist in Georgia and in Kentucky, where he showed a flair for polemical writing and for fierce confrontation, two qualities that later informed his sharp-edged plea for political Union. After a series of battles on behalf of the "New School" in Kentucky, Stiles assumed a pulpit in Richmond between 1844 and 1848 and then relocated to New York, a move that allowed William Plumer and other Richmond stalwarts to complete the Old School's domination of Virginia Presbyterianism. The Stiles family moved north only after assurances were made that his new congregation would accept his wife's ownership of slaves. Such was the first indication that a program of sectional reconciliation based on mutual white understanding would become his primary concern. Not long after speaking out against abolitionism at the New School Assembly in Detroit, Stiles became the primary southern agent of the American Bible Society. He then showed the same talent for interregional enterprise by taking a leading role at the Southern Aid Society, an effort that made national harmony among whites into an evangelical goal. The Society, financed by northern opponents of abolition, promised to "radiate kindness into the spirit of the North and thus abate its severity" while simultaneously trying to "breathe confidence into the heart of the South and thus open it to imbibe the mental and moral wealth of the North, while she freely imparted her own in return." Stiles pursued a similar objective in his critical examination of *Modern Reform*, which supporters noted had been "written by a Southern man long living at the North" who had "enjoyed ample opportunity to judge of the institution in the one section of our country, and of the Abolition spirit in the other."[37]

The slaveholder-friendly conservatism preached by Junkin and Stiles held fast throughout most of the 1850s. Signs of trouble arose in Junkin's

---

[37] "Joseph Clay Stiles," in Rev. James Stacy, *A History of the Presbyterian Church in Georgia* (Atlanta: Westminster, 1912), 296–300; Rev. Robert Davidson, *History of the Presbyterian Church in the State of Kentucky* (New York: Robert Carter, 1847), 346–68; John L. Mason to Stiles, May 20, 1848, Joseph Clay Stiles Papers, HEH; Stiles, *Speech on the Slavery Resolutions, Delivered in the General Assembly* (New York: Mark Newman, 1850); Peter J. Wosh, *Spreading the Word: The Bible Business in Nineteenth-Century America* (Ithaca, NY: Cornell University Press, 1994), 200–5; Gerard Hallock, *History of the South Congregational Church, New Haven, from its Origins in 1852 till January 1, 1865* (New Haven, 1865), 19–59; *First Report of the Southern Aid Society* (New York: D. Fanshaw, 1854), 22; Stiles, *Modern Reform Examined: Or, the Union of North and South on the Subject of Slavery* (Philadelphia: Lippincott and Co., 1857); testimony of November, 1858 written by Gardiner Spring and others in Stiles Papers, HEH. For the broader context of slavery and missions in the 1850s, see Victor B. Howard, *Conscience and Slavery: The Evangelistic Calvinist Domestic Missions, 1837–1861* (Kent: Kent State University Press, 1990), 121–31 and Kuykendall, *Southern Enterprize*.

household late in 1859, when reports circulated that he and his family had been poisoned by a household slave (though the dose of arsenic that she used was so large it acted "as an emetic" and thus resulted in no fatalities). The real moment of truth came two years later, when President Junkin insisted that the U.S. flag continue to fly over Washington College in the wake of Lincoln's election. This stance provoked the college's greatest crisis since the Ruffner pamphlet controversy of 1847. Junkin fled to Philadelphia without his daughter (who would become one of the Confederacy's leading poets) and there set about writing his final book, *Political Fallacies*, with the aim of rooting out the heresies of secession. He even sent a copy of the work to his son-in-law "Stonewall" Jackson, whose Presbyterian religiosity was then making him an international phenomenon as the South's own "Cromwell in Gray."[38]

Stiles had already traveled in the opposite direction as Junkin returned to the North. Soon after divisions over slavery caused the New School to split along sectional lines in 1857, Stiles was called to a theological post in Virginia, which he declined in favor of another assignment as an evangelist across the Deep South. After his secession-winter appeal on behalf of constitutional compromises, Stiles became one of the leading preachers in Stonewall Jackson's brigade, choosing loyalty to his birthplace with no less fervor than Junkin had displayed. Most of his attention during the 1850s had focused on northern shortcomings rather than on southern ones, and in his book-length response to Lincoln's election, Stiles insisted that "Christianity will be national healer" primarily by helping to "reconcile the temper of the North to slavery" and serving to correct "the judgment, conscience and aims of Yankees who were violating both their faith and the national Constitution." His prediction that war would "make the North and the South mutually respect each other" would be proved wrong by 1862, when he observed that "if ever a people were calmly, deeply, bitterly despised on earth, the North is by the South." His new mission involved warning Confederates against the "many national evils" they had "brought with us when we swarmed out of the great American hive."[39]

Stiles' newfound stature helped him to play a central role in the 1862 "Plan of Union" that joined the southern remnants of the Old and New School within

---

[38] Richmond *Dispatch* quoted in *Liberator*, July 8, 1859; Junkin, *Political Fallacies: An Examination of the False Assumptions, and Refutation of the Sophistical Reasonings which have Brought on this Civil War* (New York: Scribner, 1863); Junkin, *George Junkin*.

[39] Stiles, *The National Controversy: Or, the Voice of the Fathers upon the State of the Country* (New York: Rudd and Carleton, 1861), 72; Stiles to "Dear Wife," December 11, 1862, Stiles Papers, HEH; Stiles, *National Rectitude the Only True Basis of National Prosperity: An Appeal to the Confederate States* (Petersburg: Evangelical Tract Society, 1863), 32.

a single Confederate denomination. With this success, the organizational efforts began more than a half-century earlier became nearly complete. The division of the Presbyterian Church along strictly sectional lines was finalized in 1869, when the northern Old and New School similarly reunited. Sectionalism would thus finally be triumphant within American Presbyterianism after political reunion had taken hold. By that time, however, the desire to form a national consensus on slavery had become little more than a distant memory.[40]

PUBLIC WORSHIP AND CLERICAL PROPHECY

Most lay evangelicals rooted their faith not in denominational structures, educational initiatives, publishing projects, or even plantation missions, but in the familiar routines of private devotion and regular church services. It was in worship and in the proceedings of local congregations that biracial Christian communities grappled directly with the morality of slavery as a set of concrete dilemmas involving actual masters and their slaves. The affairs of individual churches were better suited to addressing the intricacies of these troublesome relationships than in fostering particularly meaningful perspectives on either sectionalism or proslavery American nationhood. Even religious masters were hesitant to blur the line between faith and secular power, lest they betray their own understanding of Protestant religious liberties and desecrate the pulpit as wantonly as they accused abolitionists of doing. In urging white Southerners to render political power unto Ceasar, proslavery writers agreed both with Edmund Burke's assertion that "no sound ought to be heard in the church but the healing voice of Christian charity" and with his belief that the religious sanctuary was a "place where a one day's truce ought to be allowed to the dissensions and animosities of mankind."[41]

---

[40] Harold M. Parker Jr., *The United Synod of the South: The Southern New School Presbyterian Church* (Westport: Greenwood Press, 1988); Lewis G. Vander Velde, *The Presbyterian Churches and the Federal Union, 1861–1869* (Cambridge: Harvard University Press, 1932). Northern consolidation in the Baptist church was delayed much longer, so that a northern counterpart to the Southern Baptist Convention was only established in 1907, with Charles Evans Hughes as President.

[41] Attempts to mobilize Burke's words (expressed in *Reflections on the Revolution in France*) as a critique of Northern antislavery include Robert Young Hayne, "Speech of January 25, 1830," *Register of Debates in Congress* (Washington, D.C.: Gales and Seaton, 1830), 53; T.R. Dew in *Proslavery Argument*, 459; Drayton, *The South Vindicated from the Treason and Fanaticism of the Northern Abolitionists* (Philadelphia: 1836), 303; L. Keitt, "Patriotic Services of North and South," *DBR* 21 (November 1856), 508; and "American Slavery in 1857," *SLM* 25 (August 1857), 88. See also George D. Armstrong, *Politics and the Pulpit: Discourse Preached in the Presbyterian Church, Norfolk, on Thursday, November 27, 1856* (Norfolk, VA, 1856); Loveland, *Southern Evangelicals and the Social Order* and Richard Carwardine, *Evangelicals and Politics in Antebellum America* (New Haven: Yale University Press, 1993).

The proslavery clergy understood how this pervasive distrust of "political preaching" conditioned their own comparatively limited participation in public affairs. Yet despite the widespread skepticism, those who had faithfully defended slavery as a divine institution managed to reframe the boundaries between religious observance and nationalist development over the course of the 1850s. In 1859, the Rev. Thomas Smyth conveyed a new consensus in arguing that "to convert the pulpit into an instrument of political agitation is most certainly to invade its sacredness . . . But to make it the means of instructing Christians in the Christianity of their political relations is simply to accomplish one of the ends for which it was intended." A species of nationalist preaching became acceptable in large part through the observation of official days of thanksgiving and fasting, which evangelical politicians sanctioned on a state-by-state basis in the 1840s and 1850s. By the time of secession crisis, such occasions had helped to make Christian ministers a fixture in public life across the slave South, thus laying the basis for the still more important role they would play as architects of Confederate nationhood.[42]

Few devoted as much attention to the possibilities of everyday pulpit ministry as the Rev. Benjamin Morgan Palmer, whose antebellum fame depended not on his considerable ecclesiastical and theological work nor on any meaningful defense of slavery, but on his reputation as one of America's most dazzling preachers. Palmer had cultivated his status as an oracle from the mid-1840s, when he first appeared before congregations "in some sort as the prophet of God." In the years that followed, he would regularly instruct fellow clergy how to similarly become a "certain great somebody, with superhuman qualifications," as one of his many admirers paraphrased his instructions. Church ministry for Palmer was not simply a platform for electrifying performances, however, but a means of assuring that Christians came "together in the mass, where they may feel a brotherhood of nature and of race, – where the artificial distinctions of wealth, position, education, and rank, shall for the moment be obliterated, in and of themselves." His ideal of worship included the expectation that sermons would be as intellectually rigorous as they were

---

[42] Thomas Smyth, "National Righteousness" *SPR* 12 (April 1859), 25. The geographic and chronological scope of days fasting and thanksgiving can be seen in the bibliography compiled in Snay, *Gospel of Disunion*, 226–36, in Charleston *Courier*, October 30, 1847 (conveying Thanksgiving proclamation of Florida's first governor); and in Benjamin Franklin Morris, *Christian Life and Character of the Civil Institutions of the United States: Developed in the Official and Historical Annals of the Republic* (Philadelphia, George W. Childs, 1864), 598–600, which helpfully reprints Thanksgiving proclamations issued by the governors of Georgia, North Carolina, South Carolina, Florida, Tennessee, and Mississippi in 1858.

emotionally riveting. The explication of Calvinist doctrine should "form
the staple of all preaching" he steadfastly insisted, warning that the
clergy's growing penchant for mere "exhortation" risked becoming
"frothy declamation." Achieving Christian sanctification was possible
only if conducted by a clergy who understood that "exhortation is only
the edge of the sword, of which doctrine must be the blade." [43]

The nationalist implications of religious worship assumed increasing
importance for Palmer over the late antebellum period, both in his conduct
of Thanksgiving services in New Orleans (where he relocated from South
Carolina late in 1856) and in his shifting understanding of the role that
nations played in a mysterious providential economy. In an 1850 review,
Palmer worked to limit the significance of collective worship, reasoning that
"the State, in its corporate capacity as State" neither "has a soul – is immortal" nor "can fall from holiness." By this logic, "when the chief magistrate
recommends a public fast, or public thanksgiving, he does not, as the High
Priest of the nation, offer a national worship" but acted simply "as the
representative of a Christian people, and merely as their voice." By the late
1850s, Palmer had shifted his attention away from the nature of the state as
an aggregate of individuals, conditioned by environment to display certain
common traits, to explore how "historic nations" had appeared as important actors at every stage of human history. Borrowing from the German
romantic writer Friedrich von Schlegel, Palmer began to devote his attention
to how a nation "often has a character as well defined and intense as an
individual" and to explain how human progress depended on the willingness
of a "historical people" to recognize and then to perfect the distinctive
mission God entrusted them to fulfill.[44]

[43] Thomas Cary Johnson, *The Life and Letters of Benjamin Morgan Palmer* (Richmond, VA: Presbyterian Committee of Publication, 1906), 88–9, 136; B.M. Palmer, *The Warrant and Nature of Public Worship* (Columbia: I.C. Morgan, 1853); *idem*, "A Plea for Doctrine as the Instrument of Sanctification," *SPR* 3 (July 1849) 52. Palmer's vision of Christian unity during worship contrasted with his distaste for secular attempts to "merge all political and religious associations into one, and to make the State one great commune, in which men shall rather herd than live together." In his mind, "the well-being of society is best promoted, not by consolidating all interests and confounding all distinctions, but by an accurate division of labor and responsi-bility." See "Church and State," *SPR* 3 (April, 1850), 590.

[44] Palmer's move to New Orleans and his immediate adoption of Thanksgiving services are documented in B.M. Palmer Papers, Presbyterian Historical Society, Montreat, North Car-olina; Palmer, "Church and State," 582; *idem, The Influence of Religious Belief Upon National Character: Delivered Before the Demosthenian and Phi Kappa Societies* (Athens: Banner Office, 1845), 30; *idem, Our Historic Mission: An Address Delivered Before the Eunomian and Phi-Mu Societies of La Grange Synodical College, July 7, 1858* (New Orleans, 1859), 3.

By the time of his extraordinary Thanksgiving sermon of 1860, Palmer had already explored the nature of Americans' distinctive mission, which he associated with the spread of republicanism, the vindication of religious freedom, and, most important, the harmonizing of "labor and capital" through the institution of domestic slavery. His understanding of nationality rested on a potent blend of philosophical perspectives and a deeply – rooted religious sensibility. As a Confederate nationalist, he would continue to denounce that "shallow nominalism which would make such a word as 'nation' a dead abstraction, signifying only the aggregation of individuals." His gospel of nationhood persisted over the course of a Confederate career during which he regularly explained how his own Godly nation represented "an incorporate society" that "possesses a unity of life resembling the individuality of a single being."[45]

Palmer never reflected on how and why he had shifted his emphasis from the artificiality of the state to the transcendent nature of certain "historical" national collectivities. His transformation combined personal experiences – foremost his reliance on Schlegel while teaching a seminary course on Church history and his relocation to New Orleans during the late 1850s – with a confluence of political, cultural, and theological shifts within Deep South Calvinism as a whole. Palmer's home state of South Carolina had already demonstrated the inherently political nature of state-sponsored prayer, a factor that caused a tone of apology from those Presbyterians who observed such occasions. In 1833, nullifiers had learned the unintended consequences of practices when a number of Unionist clergy (especially those within the Unitarian and Presbyterian fellowships) responded to an invitation for fasting by printing pleas for calm, order, and (in a clear rebuke of nullification) of respect for federal supremacy. Late in 1850, Southern Rights radicals issued another proclamation on the eve of a state convention called to consider secession from the Union. Several urban-based ministers

---

[45] Palmer, "The South: Her Peril and Her Duty" as reprinted in Jon Wakelyn ed., *Southern Pamphlets on Secession* (Chapel Hill: University of North Carolina Press, 1996), 66; *National Responsibility Before God: A Discourse on the Day of Fasting, Humiliation and Prayer* (New Orleans, 1861), 4, 15. Precisely the same formulation about rejecting "shallow nominalism" appears, with only the change of "nation" to "state" in later Palmer's later address *A Discourse Before the General Assembly of South Carolina, On December 10, 1863, Appointed by the Legislature as a Day of Fasting, Humiliation, and Prayer* (Columbia, 1864) 3. Perhaps following Calhoun, Palmer often used "state" as interchangeable with a specific political society, rather than its government per se. For a probing exploration of how Palmer's theological inquiries addressed matters of race as well as nation, see Stephen R. Haynes, *Noah's Curse: The Biblical Justification of American Slavery* (New York: Oxford University Press, 2002).

used the occasion to place defenses of slavery alongside carefully crafted explanations of state sovereignty. The Rev. A.A. Porter of Charleston came out with an especially fiery call to separate from the North and thus to acknowledge that there were "two nations in the womb" of the American Union. The apparent religious sanction given to secession encouraged radicals to distribute Methodist Whitefoord Smith's more restrained effort in a sizeable print-run of 25,000 copies.[46]

In contrast to this sprinkling of secessionist sermonizing, the state's most celebrated evangelicals remained staunch Unionists throughout the lengthy crisis of 1850–2. Palmer's mentor, James Henley Thornwell, conveyed an especially fervent set of Unionist pleas, doing so less in his capacity as a minister than as a citizen, a professor, and as the president of South Carolina College. In 1850, Thornwell affirmed that "the dissolution of this Union – as a political question – is the most momentous which can be proposed in the present condition of the world." Americans were asked to "determine the political condition of the race, for ages yet to come," he insisted, explaining that disunion would assure that "all our schemes of Christian benevolence and duty – our efforts to convert the world – to spread the knowledge of Christianity among all people, and to translate the Bible into all languages, must be suddenly and violently interrupted." A year later, having already seen the vast majority of Presbyterian ministers follow his Unionist lead, Thornwell intensified his position by declaring that an undivided United States was "commissioned from the skies, as the Apostle of civilization, liberty and Christianity to all the races of man." "Ours will be no common

---

[46] *State Papers on Nullification* (Boston, MA: Dutton and Wentworth 1834), 319; S.G. Bulfinch, *The Benefits and Dangers Belonging to Seasons of Public Excitement* (Charleston: J.S. Burges, 1833); Richard P. Cater, *A Discourse Delivered in the Presbyterian Church* (Pendleton, OR: Messenger Office, 1833); Thomas Goulding, *A Fast Day Sermon* (Printed at the Telescope Office, 1833). For the 1850 appeal, see Henry D. Capers, *The Life and Times of C.G. Memminger* (Richmond: Everett Waddy, 1893), 199–200; Rev. Whitefoord Smith, *God, The Refuge of His People A Sermon Delivered Before the General Assembly of South Carolina, on Friday, December 6, 1850 Being a Day of Fasting, Humiliation and Prayer* (Columbia, 1850); A.A. Porter, *Our Danger and Our Duty: A Discourse Delivered in the Glebe-Street Presbyterian Church, on Friday, December 6th, 1850* (Charleston, 1850); Ferdinand Jacobs, *The Committing of Our Cause to God: A Sermon in the Second Presbyterian Church on the Day of Fasting, Humiliation, and Prayer* ; William H. Barnwell, *Views upon the Present Crisis: A Discourse Delivered in Saint Peter's Church, on the 6th of December, the Day of Fasting, Humiliation and Prayer Appointed by the Legislature of South Carolina* (Charleston, SC: E.C. Councell, 1850); T.O. Summers, *Christian Patriotism, a Sermon Preached in Cumberland Street, ME Church, Charleston, SC* (Charleston, 1850).

punishment, as it will be no common sin, if instead of obeying the command which requires us to be a blessing to the world, we exhaust our resources and waste our advantages in biting and devouring each other." He concluded that if the United States ceased to exist, "our tears shall bedew its grave; and our hopes for liberty and man be buried with it."[47]

The outspoken Unionism of Thornwell and other evangelical leaders sparked a broader discussion of the relationship among revealed religion, the protection of slavery, and the political destiny of the South. Late in 1851, during a brief lull in political activity, the most thorough scriptural case for disunion came not from a minister but from the newspaper writings of Edward McCrady, an Episcopal layman and prominent Charleston lawyer. McCrady began by condemning both Thornwell and the Methodist Bishop William Capers for allowing a "preconceived opinion of one's own, to assume the form and force of an inexorable law, binding and fettering the Almighty arm." He then gave a religious slant to the views of his nephew William Henry Trescot, who had recently presented the Union as a provisional form that, having completed the first stage of American's global mission, was destined to be superseded by a series of multiple republics, each with a more definite sense of its providential calling. McCrady located a Biblical parallel for this vision of progressive dissolution in the destruction of the tower of Babel, drawing a connection between the building of a "universal" temple and the growth within the United States of "a mob of States" that would soon "prove but little better than a mob of individuals." Pleading with Carolinians to embrace a "more distinctive mission" than mere republican stability and territorial growth across the continent, McCrady closed on a relatively subdued note, proposing the possibility that God might "dissolve the present Union, not in frustration, but in furtherance of our great mission."[48]

Benjamin Morgan Palmer staked out a middle ground between Thornwell's patriotic insistence on Union and McCrady's stark presentation of a Divine mandate for secession. In a series of asides rather than in one substantial

---

[47] Thornwell, *Thoughts Suited to the Present Crisis A Sermon on the Occasion of the Death of John C. Calhoun, Preached in the Chapel of the South Carolina College, April 21, 1850* (Columbia: A.S. Johnson, 1850), 7; [Thornwell], "Critical Notice," *SPR* 4 (April 1851), 447–8. See also Carwardine, *Evangelicals and Politics*.

[48] [Edward McCrady], *Our Mission: Is It to be Accomplished by the Perpetuation of our Present Union? The Questions Considered by the Light of Revealed Religion, in a Review of the Political Positions of Some of Our Clergy* (Charleston, SC: Walker and James, 1851). Trescot, *The Position and Course of the South* (Charleston, SC: Walker and James, 1850).

piece, Palmer would during the early 1850s consider how the Hebrews had shown the ability simultaneously to achieve cohesion and expansion through their inherent "elasticity" as a people. He admitted he could hardly be "indifferent" about the Union's post-Mexican War expansion to the Pacific, which had subjected "the elasticity of our government" to "severer tests than its framers ever dreamed." If the Union "shall succeed, by its immense moral power, in moulding and casting to its own shape and form that stubborn civilization of past centuries" (as he labeled the societies of Asia), it would "discover a life which the government of four thousand years denies every other government – and republicanism will come forth amidst the acclamations of the world, to receive the chaplet of triumph, which shall forever adorn her brow." The triumph of Palmer's hopes over his fears seems to have been sealed by his move to New Orleans a short time later. By 1858, he was boasting that "the broad bird which bears our escutcheon in his beak, flaunts it over one quarter of the globe." While "poising upon the highest peak of the Rocky range," this eagle "dips one wing in the Atlantic, and the other in the Pacific across the breadth of a continent." The election of Lincoln thus presented a moment of personal reckoning for Palmer, forcing him to reject the notion that a single republic could "span the breadth of a hemisphere, and bathe its feet at once in the waters of the Gulf and of the Lakes." The course of subsequent events convinced him that "the future historian will look back upon this movement of secession as the movement which rescued the whole country just as it was slipping into empire – an empire to be shattered at last, after the manner of all the empires of the earth – and least of all to be endured on this continent."[49]

Other clergy articulated the same nationalist idioms and themes that Palmer set forth, even if few replicated his idiosyncratic mix of Biblical insight, Romantic philosophy and spread-eagle imperialism. Repeatedly, proslavery observations of national Thanksgivings included affirmations of American mission. An 1848 ceremony in Georgia provided the occasion for the Rev. Samuel K. Talmage to explain how Scripture, in conveying the saga of the Israelites, "often address men in their congregated character, as families, as cities, as churches, as states, as nations." For Talmage, the Hebrew example offered proof that there was "a national, as well as an individual character in this world" and that there were "national virtues, national crimes . . . national blessings, national judgments." At a Tennessee

---

[49] "The Intellectual and Moral Character of the Jews," *SPR* 1 (Dec. 1847) 30–55; "Import of Hebrew History," *SPR* 9 (April 1856), 582–610; "Mormonism," *SPR* 6 (April 1853), 559–90; *Our Mission*, 14; *A Vindication of Secession and the South from the Strictures of Rev. R.J. Breckinridge, in the Danville Quarterly Review* (Columbia, 1861), 46.

service in 1854, the Rev. Ira Morey showed that even Thanksgiving observations that had been called forth on behalf of the welfare of an individual
state bred nationalist perspectives. After listing notable events from across the
Union, Morey was left to conclude that "in our own peaceful inland state
there has been little remarkable during the year." There was nothing new in
emphasizing the role that secular nations played in a divine order. The same
understanding had been a key force in the popular Protestant nationalism of
the early modern period. As recent scholars have noted, a growing body of
Reformed Bible-readers identified with the chosen nation of Israel, thus placing their political communities within a sacred cosmology. The same tendency
would be at work in the early American republic, even after the revolutionary
disestablishment of churches shifted responsibility for national holiness to the
Christian people and away from a state-supported clergy.[50]

Facing the secession crisis late in 1860, Palmer excised earlier references
to Schlegel and distinguished his own efforts from that of the "dainty
philosopher, coolly discoursing of the forces of nature and her uniform
laws." He realized that the same Scripture that delineated duties with precision provided few certainties about how nations would be guided by a
providential will. In such circumstances, he returned to his role as a prophet,
open to divine inspiration, and determined to "ascertain the nature of the
trust providentially committed to us." It was also as a prophet, striving to
discern the designs of the Almighty, that he concluded that slaveholders had
been called "to conserve and perpetuate the institution of domestic slavery
as now existing with the right, unchallenged by man, to go and root itself
wherever Providence and nature may carry it." In contrast to his earlier
emphasis on American themes of republicanism and religious freedom,
Palmer in 1860 declared that southern masters, in forming a new Confederacy, would make a national covenant as Christian masters, and this "particular trust assigned to such [a historic] people" would become "the pledge
of the divine protection." In articulating masters' particular destiny during
the crisis, Palmer thus transformed a secular dialogue about the ameliorative
effects of slavery into the language of providential duty.[51]

---

[50] Talmage, *Reasons for Public Thanksgiving: A Discourse Delivered Before the Legislature
of Georgia, in the Representative Chamber, on Thanksgiving Day, November 29, 1849*
(Milledgeville, 1849), 7; Morey, *A Thanksgiving Sermon Preached in the Presbyterian
Church, Greeneville, Tenn., Thursday, November 30th, 1854* (Knoxville, 1855), 21.
Adrian Hastings, *The Construction of Nationhood: Ethnicity, Religion, and Nationalism*
(New York: Cambridge University Press, 1997); Anthony D. Smith, *Chosen Peoples:
Sacred Sources of National Identity* (New York: Oxford University Press, 2003).
[51] Palmer, "The South: Her Peril and Her Duty," 67.

At the threshold of the Confederate war, proslavery Protestants such as Palmer had grown accustomed to their role as committed nationalists. Just as importantly, they were showing a willingness to make the discussion of national destiny a staple of their pulpit oratory. In doing so, they had introduced a range of powerful metaphors that distinguished the federal polity of the United States from the national mission that might best be completed under the tutelage of a new government. In the 1840s, Palmer had explained how the Hebrew "nation" was "the mere shell or rind" of the church, "thrown around it for temporary protection, afterward to be thrown off by its development." In 1851, McCrady made a similar point about a Union that might one day be regarded as little more than "the shed casket of the chrysalis which had preserved the humbler thing only to prepare and usher it into a more beauteous form and more active and joyous life." The government situated in Washington was "a mere outward form or vesture, which having served its purpose, now worn with age and rent by the expanding life it had shielded from external injury, was at length about to be changed for another and a better." Palmer's Thanksgiving sermon of 1860 demanded a more Biblical cadence, which he provided in his charge to the audience: "if we cannot save the Union, we may save the blessings it enshrines ... if we cannot preserve the vase, we will preserve the precious liquor it contains."[52]

As could be seen in other aspects of proslavery Americanism, the notions of national mission and destiny that would equip Confederates with their most powerful themes were initially the creations of Unionists such as Palmer. The fast-day sermons delivered by the Confederate clergy during the war would be among the most intense expressions of national purpose. Their relevance would only increase with the unexpectedly grave sacrifices of war. Yet such practices, which rested on theological understandings of divinely sanctioned nationhood, left certain issues unresolved. Prophesying about the future might have the sanction of Scripture, but it was likely to be done in the spirit of conjecture rather than of definitive command. Pursuing a historical nation's divinely appointed mission could be an all-encompassing venture, but it still implied that even the Godliest nature was subject to larger designs. Both before and after 1860, a providential view of the world thus meant that nationhood was a means to important ends, but it could never simply be an end in itself.

[52] "The Intellectual and Moral Character of the Jews," 40; McCrady, *Our Mission*, 8; Palmer, "The South: Her Peril and Her Duty."

5

Fragments from the Past, Histories for the Future

Members of the Georgia Historical Society might have expected a poetic flourish from the speaker they invited to their 1845 annual meeting. What they got, in the oration of South Carolinian William Gilmore Simms, came remarkably close to a call to collective worship. "A national history, preserved by a national poet, becomes, in fact, a national religion" Simms urged his Savannah audience, explaining to them that it was humans – not a divine God – who established a nation's claims upon posterity. Past events that were "endowed with vitality by the song of the poet" transformed a "sacred" locale into "a shrine for far-seeking pilgrims."[1] As one of the slaveholding South's chief historical priests, Simms keenly appreciated how historical romances, biographies, articles, and poems could dramatize the South Atlantic states' sagas of discovery, settlement, and warfare. His own work sought to imaginatively reconstruct emotionally satisfying historical events and circumstances and thus to make him into the sort of nationalist oracle who "gives shape to the unhewn fact, ... yields relation to the scattered fragments ... unites the parts in coherent dependence, and endows, with life and action, the otherwise motionless automata of history." In Simms's mind such efforts to revisit the past were ultimately what made "nations live."

During the late antebellum years, the same masters who cheered expansion, embraced slavery, and adopted evangelical religion, followed Simms in

---

[1] William Gilmore Simms, "History for the Purposes of Art," in *Views and Reviews* (New York, 1845), 24–5. Simms' notion was praised by a future enemy in [William Tecumseh Sherman], "Views and Reviews" *SLM* 13 (April 1847), 250–1; his breadth of activities are conveyed in Sean R. Busick, *A Sober Desire for History: William Gilmore Simms as Historian* (Columbia: University of South Carolina Press, 2005).

acquiring a durable tradition of traditions. Casting their gaze backward in time set them apart from American masters of the colonial period, who had displayed a notable indifference toward their local inheritances.[2] Across a range of activities and institutions, and in a variety of political settings, a body of written history emerged between 1830 and 1860, accompanied by a culture of historically informed celebrations, societies, annual addresses, and monuments. In these, slaveholders developed a crucial aspect of proslavery nationalism, which led them to debate the nature of the revolutionary legacy, the location of their emotional allegiances, and the possibility that the current sectional hostilities had deep colonial roots. Those who created a separate proslavery republic in 1861 would reshape these powerful antebellum themes and synchronize them with a new collective future outside the United States.

While slaveholders' view of the American past generated internal debates, it also developed in tension with an even more vibrant tradition of New England historical culture, which was increasingly swept up in the political struggles over American slavery. The success of narratives focused on the Puritans, the Boston Tea Party, and Bunker Hill challenged men like Simms to play catch-up and to offer claims capable not simply of fostering local attachments but of elaborating an alternative version of the American story as a whole. In the end, their venture in this regard was marked by more failures than successes. As slaveholders entered the final crisis of the Union, the fragments of a supposed "Southern" past lacked an overriding vision capable of situating the region as a whole within a meaningful historical framework. Only with the Confederate war would the possibilities for a distinct southern history emerge, in the heroic military saga that brought slavery to a dramatic close.

REVOLUTION IN SOUTH CAROLINA

William Gilmore Simms achieved his greatest success in his historical and fictional work portraying South Carolina's Revolutionary upheavals. This was to be expected, since his entire state seemed transfixed by a period

---

[2] T.H. Breen addresses the colonial and revolutionary gentry's inattention to history in "Of Time and Nature: A Study in Persistent Values in Colonial Virginia" in *Puritans and Adventurers: Change and Persistence in Early America* (New York: Oxford University Press, 1980), while the transatlantic aspects of antebellum southern historicism are charted by Michael O'Brien, *Conjectures of Order: Intellectual Life in the American South, 1810–1860* (Chapel Hill University of North Carolina Press, 2004) and Elizabeth Fox-Genovese and Eugene Genovese, *The Mind of the Master Class: History and Faith in the Southern Slaveholders' Worldview* (New York: Cambridge University Press, 2005).

marked by tremendous internal disruption, partisan warfare, plantation disorders, and prolonged military occupation. Indeed, for the first fifty years of independence, official remembrances paradoxically turned such profound dislocations into a basis of civic union. A set of unifying patriotic practices lent a popular dimension to the first-rate Revolutionary histories produced by the Charleston writer David Ramsay and to the patriotic memoirs of General William Moultrie. By the early 1830s, something of the earlier discord returned, however, as different versions of a heroic past became weapons in a state verging toward a civil war within its borders. Disputes among white Carolinians would be as much about the present as the past, as they raised fundamental questions about the nature of a Revolutionary inheritance and the bounds of patriotic dissent.[3]

That the fight over Carolina's wartime past coincided with the semicentennial of the Revolution was the responsibility of those nullifiers who mobilized support by calling for a new era of defiant rebellion. As the state became increasingly politicized, young leaders like Robert Barnwell Smith set aside the technical details of Calhounite constitutionalism and instead popularized the association between nullification and "the abstract, isolated principle of liberty" that included the "glorious inalienable right" to overthrow oppression by force. This fire-eating identification with "the spirit of '76" drew a series of sharp retorts from those who valued the substance of past patriotic accomplishments rather than the spirit that had produced these. No one better dramatized this Unionist commitment to a historic inheritance than an unnamed Revolutionary veteran who, in 1832, stood on his crutches to attack Barnwell Smith as being a traitor, and to insist that the Revolutionary War's most precious legacy was an undivided United States. An intact federal Union, this aged soldier argued, alone could transmit Revolutionary gains to future generations of South Carolinians.[4]

The nullification-era clashes over the meaning of the American Revolution both seared the state and set patterns that would influence the entire slaveholding South over the succeeding generation. At the outset, neither the

---

[3] William Taylor, *Cavalier and Yankee: The Old South and American National Character* (New York: G. Braziller, 1961), 261–98; John Hope Franklin, "The North, the South, and the American Revolution," *JAH* 62 (June 1975), 5–23; David Waldstreicher, *In the Midst of Perpetual Fetes: The Making of American Nationalism, 1776–1820* (Chapel Hill: University of North Carolina Press, 1997); Paul D. H. Quigley, "'That History is Truly the Life of Nations': History and Southern Nationalism in Antebellum South Carolina," *South Carolina Historical Magazine* 106 (January 2005), 7–33.

[4] Rhett quoted and soldier described in Laura White, *Robert Barnwell Rhett: Father of Secession* (New York: Century, 1931), 19.

fire-eaters nor the Unionists made an explicitly local appeal, or invoked details from local historical episodes. They instead drew from those national idioms that had been nurtured in the early republic's partisan contests. Nullifiers made their boldest appeals on the Fourth of July when they typically invoked a Democratic–Republican pantheon made up of such figures as Sam Adams, Thomas Jefferson, and Patrick Henry, three radicals whose conviction had led them to break the comfortable, but ultimately degrading, ties of empire. Inspired by the global context of this "age of revolution," nullifiers also crossed national borders to find non-American heroes, and went so far as to praise the Jacobins of the French (if not the Haitian) Revolution. Pride of place in radicals' historical imagination went to the Declaration of Independence, which became a central aspect of their argument that enduring tyranny without resistance made heirs unfit carriers of a sacred inheritance.[5]

The fire-eaters' embrace of Jefferson's Declaration coincided with the rejection by the proslavery "Great Reaction" of that document's commitment to human equality. Nullifiers made a crucial distinction, which would last through the Confederate experience, by rejecting Jefferson's "glittering generalities" and going straight to his insistence that a "long train of abuses and usurpations, pursuing the same object" required patriots "to throw off such government, and to provide new guards for their future security." Most of the slaves present at the defiant Independence Day celebrations of the early 1830s would have grasped the inconsistency of slave masters appealing to universal human rights. But the fact that the fiery appeals did not spark greater slave resistance may demonstrate radicals' success in recasting the day as a tribute to their own power rather than to abstract ideology. Linking a past history of revolt with a determination to meet new threats affirmed that masters' absolute authority could face down outside forces. Robert Barnwell Smith and his followers linked independence and rights to the security of the southern order, knowing all too well, as Smith put it in 1834, that "a slaveholding people must be mad, or worse than mad, who do not hold their destiny in their own hands."[6]

---

[5] [Robert J. Turnbull], *The Crisis: Or, Essays on the Usurpations of the Federal Government* (Charleston, SC: A.E. Miller, 1827), 121; Turnbull, *An Oration Delivered in the City of Charleston . . . . on the 4th of July, 1832, Being the 56th Anniversary of American Independence* (Charleston, SC: A.E. Miller, 1832), 3; Smith in *Charleston Mercury*, October 19, 1830; *Speech of the Hon. George McDuffie at a Public Dinner Given to Him by the Citizens of Charleston, May 19, 1831* (Charleston, SC, 1831), 28–9.

[6] "The Grahamville Celebration: Speech of Hon. R. Barnwell Rhett," *Charleston Courier*, July 6, 1859; [David F. Jamison], "The National Anniversary," *SQR* n.s. 2 (September 1850), 171. David Armitage documents the wider context for considering the Declaration through the lens of sovereign power rather than idealistic principle in *The Declaration of Independence: A Global History* (Cambridge: Harvard University Press, 2007).

Smith's own involvement in radical politics connected his plea for the masters' undisputed authority with an opposition to federal Union. In 1837, he renamed himself R.B. Rhett, adopting the last name of a distant colonial ancestor to replace that of a father who had been an actual veteran of the Revolutionary war. For the next quarter-century, he continued to invoke the abstract ideas of the Revolution and the adoption of independence as a model for dissolving the American federation, but expanded the range of concrete references as he became particularly fond of the Massachusetts examples of Lexington, Concord, and the Boston Tea Party. This recasting of the patriots' movement as a platform for secession was a powerful tonic for a younger generation, who made Rhett's tributes to the Revolutionary past a prevailing theme across the state. In 1855, after explaining in a lengthy article that "It is not the Precept of Our Revolutionary Tradition to Preserve the Union," the radical editor Leonidas Spratt apologized for "having said but little that has not occurred to all our readers, and which could not but have been better said by many of them." The version of the Revolution associated with proslavery radicals traveled beyond Carolina borders, with even staunch Jacksonians such as Alexander Meek of Alabama proclaiming how "the Fourth of July gave birth to something better than a nation. It gave birth to an idea, to liberty – to principles never before recognized, without which all nationhood would be tyranny."[7]

Carolina Unionists rejected the connections between winning American independence and radical efforts to dissolve the federal Union by force. They appealed to a different set of themes that circulated among an even more influential segment of the master class between the 1830s and the secession crisis of 1860. In broad terms, proslavery Unionists believed that the spirit of the Revolution was less important than its various embodied legacies. This sense of preserving an inheritance could be seen in the Unionists' emphasis on the figure of George Washington (whose warnings against sectionalism assumed increasing importance), on the Constitution (whose role in creating

---

[7] Leonidas Spratt, *A Series of Articles on the Value of the Union to the South, Lately Published in the Charleston Standard* (Charleston: James, Williams, and Gitsinger, 1855), 24–5; A.B. Meek, *National Welcome to the Soldiers Returning from the Mexican War* (Mobile, 1848), 5. Other Carolinian assertions of Revolutionary principles include W. Allston Pringle, *An Oration Delivered Before the Fourth of July Association at the Hibernian Hall* (Charleston, SC: Walker and James, 1850); Lewis Malone Ayer, *Southern Rights and the Cuban Question: An Address Delivered At Whippy Swamp on the Fourth of July, 1855* (Charleston, SC: Walker and James, 1855), 3; and, especially, William R. Taber, *The Harmony of Power and Law, the Basis of Republicanism: An Address Delivered Before the Moultrie and Palmetto Guards, June 28, 1856 in Hibernian Hall* (Charleston, SC: A.J. Burke, 1856).

a stable Union seemed more important than its affirmation of rights), and, most effectively of all, on those veterans whose earlier sacrifices required later generations to overcome their differences through compromise. In the early 1830s, Charleston Unionists enlisted as many living patriots of the Revolution as they could find to write letters and drink toasts at their own Independence Day gatherings, which they carefully orchestrated to temper the radicals' celebration. One of these "citizen soldiers of '76," typically hailed "the real Patriots of the present day" who were "emulating their illustrious sires of old in perpetuating the blessings bequeathed the American family, and nobly sustaining their existing government." In the upcountry, the site of the war's fiercest conflicts, Benjamin Franklin Perry, the son of a Massachusetts infantryman, condemned nullification as an act of "sacrilegious parricide." Perry appealed to a generational divide in issuing a pointed challenge: "Show us ten revolutionary soldiers, and we will warrant that nine of them" opposed the radical program.[8]

Perry's distrust of abstract principles pushed him, along with Simms and other Unionists, to develop South Carolina's own history, and these men became the primary force in re-orienting Carolina's national perspective toward a more local understanding of the Revolutionary past. Efforts to record and popularize the state's wartime history had begun with David Ramsay's work in the early 1800s and continued with Alexander Garden's 1822 *Anecdotes of the War for Independence,* whose folkloric heroes made it the Carolina equivalent of Parson Weems' *Life of Washington.* At the same time, however, the bitterness of nullification produced a hiatus in "Palmetto Day," which had been one of the few efforts during the early republic to celebrate local (as opposed to national) history. Observations of this anniversary of Fort Moultrie's defense on June 28, 1776, were suspended in the late 1820s lest they become platforms for political strife.[9] Unionists tried to recapture some of these traditions while initiating new ones, as Perry did in traveling to the Battlefield of Cowpens in 1834 to remind Carolinians of the heroic sacrifices made there. Perry also began publishing veterans' reminiscences in William Yancey's *Greenville Mountaineer* and in William Gilmore Simms' *Southern Magnolia.* This was no anomaly, since the Unionists were

[8] William Drayton, *An Oration ... To Which IS Added an Account of the Celebration of the 55th Anniversary of American Independence by the Union and State Rights Party* (Charleston, 1831); B.F. Perry, "Fourth of July Oration Delivered at the Baptist Church at Greensville, South Carolina, on the Fourth of July, 1831," in *Biographical Sketches of Eminent American Statesmen With Speeches, Addresses and Letters by Ex-Governor B.F. Perry of Greenville, S.C.* (Philadelphia, 1887), 47–64. Lillian Adele Kibler, *Benjamin F. Perry: South Carolina Unionist* (Duke: Duke University Press, 1946), 104.
[9] Rogers, "Southern Carolina Federalists", *SCHM* (1970), 17–32.

responsible for the most important efforts after 1835 to record and to analyze the state's Revolutionary history. This trend was evident in the chronicles of Judge John Belton O'Neall (who had invalidated the nullifier's test oath before taking up state history), and in the schoolbooks of B.R. Carroll and Simms (who were among the most outspoken Charleston Unionists).[10]

Simms' career provided a helpful perspective of how themes that divided the state in the early 1830s converged in intriguing and important ways thereafter. By 1833, Simms was moving away from the typical Unionist appeal to order, compromise, and respect for the past to attack fire-eaters' own tyrannical impulses. It was the despotism shown by his state's government, not that of Andrew Jackson, that most disturbed Simms. He was particularly upset about nullifiers' requirement that militia members swear primary allegiance to the state, a measure he considered an "odious ordinance of that petty dictatorship" which had made South Carolina a "damnably defiled scene of brutal persecution." He confided in 1832 to a northern friend that South Carolinians "have learned in the last two years to hate one another with a religious zeal – to long for the blood of those whose pulses have once thrilled under the cordial and friendly pressure of those hands, which, in a moral sense, are now, like the claws and fangs of the wolf." He then sadly concluded that "nothing but blood and free draughts of it too, can quench [sic] the exasperated and burning though half smothered fire, chafing with lava, fervor and fury in every bosom."[11]

---

[10] Len Travers, "The Paradox of 'Nationalist' Festivals: The Case of Palmetto Day in Antebellum Charleston," in William Pencak, Matthew Dennis, and Simon P. Newman, eds., *Riot and Revelry in Early America* (University Park: Pennsylvania State University Press, 2002), 273–95. *The Mountaineer*, edited by William Yancey, published Perry's 26 articles on "Revolutionary Incidents" between November 22, 1834, and August 22, 1835; in 1842, the series resumed in *The Magnolia*, edited by Simms. See Kibler, *Perry*, 205. Perry's later works on the revolution included "The Revolutionary History of South Carolina" *SQR* 11 (April 1847), 468–85, and his postwar *Biographical Sketches of Eminent American Statesmen* (1884). O'Neall published both *The Annals of Newberry* and *The Bench and Bar of South Carolina* in 1859, but he was at work on gathering historical materials for these works much earlier. In an 1842 letter to Perry, Simms wrote that "between yourself and Judge O'Neall our mountain districts ought to be well gleaned of their traditionary resources." *LWGS* 1: 312. B.R. Carroll, a Unionist and one of Simms' closest Charleston associates, published his *Historical Collections of South Carolina* (New York, 1836) prior to his editorship of the *Southern Literary Journal* in 1838. The Unionist thrust of local history was evident as well in the popularity of William Cullen Bryants' "Song of Marion's Men" during the 1850s.

[11] Simms to James Lawson, November 25, 1832, and January 19, 1833 *LWGS* 1: 46–51. See also Perry, "An Address at the Celebration of the Fifty-Fourth Anniversary of the Battle of the Cowpens, on the Battle-Ground, in Spartanburg District, South Carolina, 1835," in *Biographical Sketches*, 65–83.

Since childhood, Simms had idolized the heroes of the Revolutionary War, who were the subjects of his first poems and who became the central inspirational figures in his tribute to the French revolution of 1830. Yet his disillusionment with the nullifiers' test oath made him newly aware that popular uprisings against authority had costs as well as glories. His first two Revolutionary novels, *The Partisan: A Tale of the Revolution* and *Mellichampe*, combined historical research with a willingness to "paint the disasters of the country, where they arose from the obvious error of her sons, in the strongest possible colours." In dramatizing the dark consequences of coercing loyalty, both books drew unmistakable parallels with the contemporary dilemmas of Unionists like himself. *The Partisan* presented a fictionalized version of Isaac Hayne, who was executed by the British in 1780 for violating the terms of an unwilling profession of obedience to the crown. *Mellichampe* showed patriot retribution against "one of the most malignant and vicious of the Southern loyalists," and demonstrated, as Simms later explained, that "the ebullitions of popular justice, shown in the movements of revolution, are of most terrible effect, and of most imposing consequence." One lesson of revolution, he warned, was that "the excesses of patriotism, when attaining power, have been but too frequently productive of a tyranny more dangerous than its exercise, and more lasting in its effects, than the despotism which it was invoked to overthrow."[12]

Simms turned to other historical themes as his career developed, and he produced romances set in the colonial period and on the cotton frontier and completed a state history that would have been adopted for the state's public schools had not nullifiers objected to its Unionist politics. But he never lost sight of the Revolution or ceased to puzzle through the meaning of South Carolina's experience during these years. As he expanded his stock of historical knowledge, Simms immersed himself in considerable controversy over Carolina's internal divisions. In 1846, he initiated a bitter dispute with the Cunninghams, a set of Loyalist descendents who would take a leading part in the campaign to purchase Mount Vernon in the 1850s. He then entered an intensifying conflict between the Revolutionary claims of Massachusetts and those of South Carolina, shifting from what in his novels had been a critical stance toward his state's actions toward a full-fledged defense

---

[12] Simms, "Introduction," *The Partisan: A Tale of the Revolution*, revised edition, 1853, v–viii and "Introduction," *Mellichampe: A Legend of the Santee*, revised edition, 1853, 1–6. See also C. Hugh Holman "William Gilmore Simms' Picture of the Revolution as a Civil Conflict," *JSH* 15 (November 1949), 442–62.

of her patriotic claims. In 1848, he took sharp issue with Lorenzo Sabine's unflattering contrast between New England's relative solidarity and the sharp division that divided both Carolina's Tories and Whigs and the state's masters and slaves.[13]

As Simms' consideration of the Revolution took on an increasingly sectional aspect, he was drawn into the controversy over the South's capacity to defend itself. What Lorenzo Sabine termed the "military weakness of the South" existed "only in the imagination of the abolitionists," Simms insisted, though his own documentary record provided a murkier picture than his novels' portrayal of the "loyal slave." Senator Charles Sumner drew from Simms's work in his insistence that it was the state's "shameful imbecility from slavery" that had tarnished its Revolutionary record; this aside would be part of what incensed Preston Brooks and drove him to cane Sumner during the late spring of 1856. In the wake of this sensational outbreak of Congressional violence, Simms undertook a controversial speaking tour of the free states, denouncing "the small traffic of politics, in the hands of hireling politicians" as "an outrage upon sacred histories." It was not simply pride that mattered in considering past accomplishments, he insisted. "To tear away from the hearts of men their loving faith in the virtues of their sires" was to "slay the very hopes of a [*sic*] people" and to "deprive them of all the most noble stimulants which goad a people to great performance." Assaults on reputation were far more insidious than those taken by the "incendiary who should penetrate your sanctuaries and burn your archives." His thinly veiled attacks on Sumner (whose physical state remained precarious) drew a sour response from Simms' northern audiences.[14]

Simms' defense of slaveholders' wartime heroism furnished useful material to the next generation of fire-eaters like Lawrence Keitt, who was more likely to discuss southern patriotism than the Boston Tea Party (an event that Rhett and other older radicals continued to favor). This was not an

---

[13] Simms, "The Civil Warfare in the Carolinas and Georgia during the Revolution," *SLM* 12 (May, June, and July 1846), 257–65, 321–36, 385–400; *idem,* "Biographical Sketch of the Career of Major William Cunningham, of South Carolina," *SLM* 12 (September and October 1846), 513–24, 577–86; "South Carolina in the Revolution," *SQR* 14 (July 1848), 470–501. David Moltke-Hansen provides a shrewd analysis in "Why History Mattered: The Background of Ann Pamela Cunningham's Interest in the Preservation of Mount Vernon," *Furman Studies* 26 (December 1980), 34–42.

[14] "South Carolina in the Revolution"; "South Carolina in the Revolution: A Lecture," in *LWGS* 3: 521; Miriam J. Shillingsburg, "Simms's Failed Lecture Tour of 1856: The Mind of the North," *Long Years of Neglect: The Work and Reputation of William Gilmore Simms,* ed., John C. Guilds (Fayetteville: University of Arkansas Press, 1988), 183–201.

altogether unintended consequence of Simms' project, since in the early 1840s he had begun to direct his attention to how pride in the past could promote "unanimity among our citizens" that might assure that an "invasion will never again set hostile foot on the shores of our country." If his understanding of the Revolution was malleable enough to produce a wide range of reflections, Simms' career demonstrated that by the mid-nineteenth century the articulation of identity and difference had replaced a critique of power as the model for resistance to government. The particular had itself become revolutionary. The North Carolinian William Holden summed up this broad shift in 1855, saying that "as the great idea of the eighteenth century was that of *union against tyrants*, so is that of the nineteenth century, *the independence of nationalities*." To the dismay of some Unionists who had sought stability in past unities, romantic nationalism had made an incarnated past as threatening to the status quo as abstract principles had once been.[15]

As the details of local history took on revolutionary connotations, celebrations of distinctively state events tapped into the same political energy that Carolinians had displayed during their nullification-era July Fourth observances. Before 1850, radical Charlestonians had paid scant attention to the June 28th anniversary of the Battle of Fort Moultrie, but as a new campaign for separate state secession evolved, they rapidly deployed local history for overtly political uses. The observation of "Palmetto Day" had not completely lapsed; after it ceased to be a civic holiday, several militia companies had taken up the date for their annual meetings. City newspapers of the 1840s had also begun to mark the occasion by printing B.R. Carroll's account of the battle, which had successfully repulsed the British navy in 1776. Yet it was the impending admission of California by Congress, not any disinterested respect for the past that motivated William Martin to weave themes from this battle through his Palmetto Day Address of 1850. He began "The South, Its Dangers and its Resources" on an understated note, thanking historians like Carroll (most of whom remained staunch Unionists) without whose efforts "the engagement at Fort Moultrie would be regarded an inconsiderable affair." He then moved to

---

[15] Simms, *The History of South Carolina, From its First European Discovery to its Erection into a Republic* (Charleston: S. Babcock, 1840), 214–15, 237, 323; Simms, *The Sources of American Independence . . . . Delivered at Aiken S.C.* (Aiken: Burges and James, 1844), 25; Holden, *Oration Delivered in the City of Raleigh, July 4, 1856* (Raleigh, 1856), 7. David Brion Davis notes the "confusion between democratic revolutions and wars for national liberation" in *Revolutions: Reflections on American Equality and Foreign Liberations* (Cambridge: Harvard University Press, 1990), 74.

enlist Revolutionary veterans in the Southern Rights' movement, knowing that few survivors would confront and embarrass him, as they had done to nullifiers two decades earlier. "If their shades could respond to the question," they would counsel "determined resistance," Martin insisted. "If the leaders of that immortal struggle were alive to tell us of all their difficulties," they would testify that the "supineness of friends" was far worse than "the hardships of the camp and the horrors of the battlefield." While recognizing the "terrible" nature of Carolina's "partizan" revolutionary war, Martin still concluded, in a more traditionally radical fashion, that "the highest veneration we can pay to [the fathers'] memories is to preserve, untarnished, the liberties they died to bequeath to us."[16]

Martin's Southern Rights' appeal to Carolina's Revolutionary past outraged the U.S. soldiers stationed in Fort Moultrie, the site of this quasi-secessionist celebration. The following year, as radical South Carolinians continued to promote disunion, the fort's commanding general refused to allow the militias to use the grounds to stage a similarly fire-eating performance. The *Charleston Mercury* bristled at a ban that forbade patriots from assembling on "the ancient battlefields on which their fathers encountered a foreign foe." It warned readers that "an enemy is in possession" of that hallowed spot which was "as dangerous to the peace of our city as the British fleet we repulsed." The leaders of the local militias resolved that "they could appreciate the insult and resent it" and thereby marched on the scheduled morning from Charleston to Sullivan's Island, where the original "Palmetto Fort" had been situated. A correspondent of the *Charleston Mercury* signed "Seventy-Six" emphasized that the truly sacred ground lay outside the current fortification; there, the spilling of patriot blood made this locale "more hallowed by heroic recollections in the hearts of the people than any other." The rival editor, John Cunningham, elevated the anniversary as the defining event in the state's history, claiming that this 1776 episode "gave us pride, as a people, sovereignty as a body politic" and even "independence as a separate nationality." Referring to the Palmetto flag (which itself recalled the colonial fort built from a local variant of the palm tree), Cunningham explained that "our emblems derived from [the

---

[16] William E. Martin, *The South, Its Dangers and Its Resources An Address, Delivered at the Celebration of the Battle of Fort Moultrie, June 28* (Charleston, SC: Edward C. Councell, 1850), 5, 30. Compare this to the innocuous J.J. Pope, *Oration Delivered in The Fort at Moultrieville, on the Twenty-Eighth of June, 1849* (Charleston, SC: James S. Burgess, 1849). Across the state, Independence Day was still far more important than Palmetto Day, as John Barnwell conveys in *Love of Order: South Carolina's First Secession Crisis* (Chapel Hill: University of North Carolina Press, 1982), 108–9.

battle] are our own; let us, henceforth, have no other; least of all, those of the oppressor," by which, of course, he meant the Stars and Stripes floating over Fort Moultrie and the more distant Fort Sumter. True to the spirit of romantic nationalism, such gestures lashed out against a despotic government less for what it did than for what it represented as a contaminating and fundamentally illegitimate foreign presence.[17]

The *Mercury* continued throughout the summer of 1851 to refer to federal troops as "The Army of Occupation" and stirred even more anxiety by suggesting that Fort Sumter, a spit of land in the center of the harbor, would no longer host the Charleston citizens who had grown accustomed to day trips to the site. In October of that year, as the election for a state secession convention approached, the paper ominously noted the arrival of one hundred additional troops and warned that this represented as grave a threat to Carolinians as the Redcoats had posed to Boston after the Tea Party. What had begun as a local controversy became a matter of serious concern across the South, with the influential *Richmond Enquirer* condemning the commanding officers' "impolitic effort" that had "furnished new fuel for the inflammatory outbursts of the disunionists." The *Savannah Georgian* predicted that "the general Government has caused the popular mind throughout [South Carolina's] limits to thrill with indignation." Union strength in the Carolina upcountry was likely to be curbed by these historic echoes, making secession in the view of this Georgia paper "decidedly probable."[18]

A popular vote against separate state secession resolved this crisis, though not before the image of federal tyranny in Charleston Harbor had been taken up and circulated as the newest weapon within the fire-eaters' rhetorical arsenal. In 1851, Robert Barnwell Rhett had remarked that "if he had been invited to storm the fort, instead of speaking under its shadow, he should most cheerfully have obeyed the call." He dramatized this same preference in his unsuccessful plea that Governor John Means use state troops to drive the U.S. armies from the harbor. By 1855, Lewis Ayer acknowledged that fire-eaters had made a strategic mistake in not escalating

---

[17] "Fort Moultrie," and "Anniversary of the Battle of Fort Moultrie," in *Charleston Mercury*, June 26, 1851; July 2, 1851. Benjamin Perry continued to make ties between his Unionism and the Revolutionary past, and after some radicals welcomed ties with Great Britain, he asked, "How can any one utter such sentiment with the revolutionary history of South Carolina fresh in his reading?" *Speech of B.F. Perry of Greenville District Delivered in the House of Representatives of South Carolina, on the 11th of December, 1850* (Charleston, SC: J.B. Nixon, 1851), 35.

[18] *Richmond Enquirer*, July 1, 1851; Savannah Georgian quoted in *Richmond Enquirer*, July 23, 1851.

the crisis on the day that the fort had been closed to patriotic observation. An attack timed to draw parallels would have usefully connected the past and the future. June 28 should have been "the time we Secessionists should have struck," since "one drop of blood shed in the good cause that day, would, "long ere this, have redeemed, regenerated and disenthralled" the South and might even have initiated a second war for Independence.[19]

In the end, the anniversary of June 28, 1776 would matter less than the aura that awareness of that date lent to the patriotic associations of Charleston Harbor. In 1861, when Fort Sumter became the last vestige of federal authority within the state of South Carolina, *De Bow's Review* hearkened to the Revolutionary-era history of the Palmetto fort and then urged readers: "erase 1776 from the record and substitute 1860, and history need not be written anew." Throughout the slaveholding South as a whole, the forts that surrounded Carolina's largest and oldest city had become something more than a crossroads of federal and state authority. They had been re-remembered as the site of earlier heroic deeds that called for a dramatic reenactment. With a bombardment looming, Revolutionary echoes became, as the *Charleston Mercury* had predicted they would, not "merely a memory of the past, but a type of the future."[20]

STATE HISTORY AND A VIRGINIA GEORGE WASHINGTON

As Charlestonians observed Palmetto Day in 1860, the recently formed South Carolina Historical Society took a break from the military drilling, religious exercises, and patriotic display to gather in Hibernian Hall, assembling in the same building where northern and southern wings of the Democratic Party had splintered just a few weeks earlier. This group, which had been formed to address issues "peculiarly dear to Carolinians," turned its attention away from current politics to hear Thomas Hanckel's plea for the relevance of the distant past:

We must make ourselves masters of our State history, we must fill our minds with the knowledge of its details, we must become deeply imbued with its spirit of independent responsibility and self-reliant strength ... Our State history [must] be the strength of our State life, and the bond of its citizenship. It is an inheritance which has come down to us, either to squander or neglect, or to cherish and preserve.

---

[19] *Charleston Mercury*, July 2, 1851; White, *Rhett*; Ayer, *Southern Rights and the Cuban Question*, 9.
[20] "Editorial Notices" *DBR* 30 (February 1861), 251; "The 28th of June," *Mercury*, June 28, 1851. See also William Gilmore Simms, "Now Wave the Green Palmetto" Newberry (SC) *Rising Sun*, February 6, 1861.

If it is of any worth to us, we must accept it heartily and understand it thoroughly.[21]

Internal disputes over Americans' Revolutionary inheritance had delayed the formation of a South Carolina Historical Society. When its founders did assemble, their determination to "master state history" took on a sharper and more defiant edge than was typical of organizations established in Virginia, Alabama, North Carolina, and ten other southern states before the Civil War. These groups, along with their counterparts in most of the free states, helped to make the late antebellum period the high point of state-oriented historical activities. The flurry of state histories, celebrations, myths, legends, and monuments offset the sectional and national trends in politics that marked this period and reinforced the emotional attachment that bound citizens to each of the distinct polities within the federal Union.[22]

Founders of state historical societies typically justified their efforts as a way to bolster unity within the states and to overcome the fierce partisanship that was as prevalent in state capitals as it was in Washington, D.C. Unlike the patriotic revivals then underway within European "small nations," such organizations hardly ever articulated a well-defined oppositional program, and most were intent on showing how local heroes had contributed toward the collective American enterprise. Groups in the Atlantic states focused their attention on how their ancestors had laid the groundwork for national political independence and had then defended American rights through the sacrifices of war. Historical activities in the Gulf and frontier states lent

---

[21] F.A. Porcher, *Address Pronounced at the Inauguration of the South Carolina Historical Society, June 28, 1857* (Charleston, 1857); Thomas Hanckel, *Oration Delivered on the Fifth Anniversary of the South Carolina Historical Society, at Hibernian Hall, in Charleston, on Wednesday Evening, May 23, 1860* (Charleston, 1860), 32–3. For other South Carolina associations of historical memory and state patriotism, see Lewis Malone Ayer, *Patriotism and State Sovereignty an Oration Delivered before the Two Societies of the South Carolina College* (Charleston: A.J. Burke, 1859); William Henry Trescot, "Oration Delivered Before the South Carolina Historical Society, Thursday, May 19, 1859," *Russell's Magazine* (July 1859), 289–307; and William Dennison Porter, *State Pride: An Oration before Callipoean and Polytechnic Societies of the State Military School, at Charleston* (Charleston, SC: Walker, Evans, and Co., 1860).

[22] Among those who appealed to history as a unifying source, see "President Cushing's Address," in *Collections of the Virginia Historical and Philosophical Society* 1 (Richmond, VA, 1833), 9–13; "Virginia Historical and Philosophical Society," *SLM* 1 (February 1835), 257; Judge Bowie's Address," *Transactions of the Alabama Historical Society, at Its First Annual Meeting, Held at the University of Alabama, July 14, 1851* (Tuskaloosa [sic], 1852), 12; and "Georgia Historical Society," *SQR* 3 (January 1843) 41–2, which discussed the sudden upsurge in state-based histories. A convincing account of the achievements of antebellum historians can be found in Eileen Ka-May Cheng, *The Plain and Noble Garb of Truth: Nationalism and Impartiality in American Historical Writing, 1784–1860* (Athens: University of Georgia Press, 2008).

themselves toward the more diffuse theme of a white civilization advancing across their territories. When interstate rivalries did emerge, these tended to pit the slave states against one another rather than against the free states. One of the most volatile flash points concerned the lingering attempt of North Carolinians to promote the Mecklenburg Declaration of Independence as a source for Thomas Jefferson's document of July 4, 1776.[23]

William Cabell Rives' address to the Virginia Historical Society in 1847 offered a typical understanding of how best to harmonize local, state, and national memories. Competing claims could be federalized in the realm of history, just as conflicts could be displaced in the compound republic, as long as both state and national allegiances were seen as extensions of an even more fundamental commitment of citizens to the domestic sphere. "All our public affections take their origin in the small, but magic circle, which defines our home, and thence spread, by successive expansions, 'till they embrace and repose upon our entire country," Rives explained, charting a republican filial piety that was expansive and cumulative rather than exclusive and jarring. In visiting a stock theme for proponent of local history across the Union, he then concluded that "the more intensely [historical attachments] glow at the centre, the warmer will their radiations be felt upon the circumference." "The more we love our State, the more we shall love the Union of which it forms a constituent and honored part."[24]

The harmony between the state and the nation was as fraught with many of the same difficulties as the larger structures of the compound republic on which it was modeled, however. Paying homage to the past would thus increasingly involve the same tensions that troubled a polity that was by turns national, federal, and sectional. Rives himself visited the problems Virginians faced in having long been drawn to "the false glare of national honors," which he called to be set aside so that they could set about "returning, with gifts and honors to their paternal altars." Proponents of the state rights' constitutionalism of the 1820s were likely to frame the issue in even sharper terms, of course, and they increasingly did so by adding a historical

---

[23] Miroslav Hroch, *Social Preconditions of National Revival in Europe: A Comparative Analysis of the Social Composition of Patriotic Groups among the Smaller European Nations* (Cambridge: Cambridge University Press, 1985); Abigail Green, *Fatherlands: State-Building and Nationhood in Nineteenth Century Germany* (New York: Cambridge University Press, 2001). Michael O'Brien provides a helpful overview of historical societies and a brief account of the Mecklenburg controversy, which represented an important historical variant of North Carolina's antebellum defensiveness, in *Conjectures of Order*, 623–53.

[24] "Mr. Rives's Address," *The Virginia Historical Register and Literary Advertiser* 1 (January 1848), 2–8.

dimension to the notion of "state nationalities" developed by John Taylor and Spencer Roane. By the 1830s, Beverly Tucker had moved beyond the negative argument about the federal Union's "namelessness," and began to explore how Virginians might connect on an emotional level to the details of a past that was too glorious to be neglected. He and his followers at the College of William and Mary moved more rapidly than the Carolina fire-eaters to substitute a series of state holidays for national ones, to conjure up a set of inspiring state symbols and heroes, and to nurture the affective ties between the "Old Dominion's" past, present, and future. Tucker struck out from the official historical societies in his insistence that the local did not shine warmth on the national, but was a means of keeping dangerously nationalizing tendencies at bay.[25]

Attempts to harmonize competing claims upon the past were even more complicated by the mounting controversies over slavery. These ensured that white Americans from the free and slave states would reach different understandings of the interconnections between homes, states, and the American nation at large. The image of the timeworn ancestral plantation would raise the question in the starkest terms, and become the main impediment to making domesticity the basis of national community. Was the reliance of the nation on stable homes threatened primarily by the intrusion of slave dealers, a theme developed by abolitionists and then, with enormous influence, by Harriet Beecher Stowe? Or were abolitionists the main culprits in introducing domestic discord and by compromising the familial nature of an increasingly Christianized form of bondage, as proslavery writers were likely to argue? As a struggle mounted whether the country's "divided house" would be united on a basis of freedom or slavery, imagined homes of the present became fraught with political significance, but so too did the ancestral estates of those slaveholding Virginians of the American Revolution.[26]

The federal and sectional divides that emerged within the historical arena led slaveholders during the late antebellum period to expend an enormous amount of cultural energy on the figure of George Washington. As the case of nullification-era South Carolina showed, southern Unionists had long

[25] Tucker, "Political Science; A Discourse on the Questions, 'What is the Seat of Sovereignty in the United States, and What the Relation of the People of Those States to the Federal and State Governments, Respectively,'" *SLM* 5 (August 1839), 559–66. Brugger, *Beverley Tucker: Head over Heart in the Old South*, 128, 243.
[26] For a different view, which emphasizes the "regressive" politics of the domestic idea and of plantation life, see George Forgie, *Patricide in the House Divided: A Psychological Interpretation of Lincoln and His Age* (New York: Oxford University Press, 1979).

nurtured Washington's legacy, recurring to his plea for sectional amity in his 1796 Farewell Address, making him a centerpiece of an embodied national history, and associating him with the federal government seated in the city that bore his name. State rights' forces tried to resist the Unionist associations of the national patriarch, with Beverley Tucker typically asking Virginians in 1838 whether they would "share your portion in Washington with the French of Louisiana, and the Dutch of New York, and the renegades from every corner of the earth, who swarm their great commercial cities, and call themselves your countrymen and HIS!" In 1850, during his last address to the Congress, John C. Calhoun claimed Washington for the entire slaveholding region, insisting that this "illustrious southerner" should be recognized as the country's most famous slaveholder. The Virginian James P. Holcombe, who would later serve in the Confederate Congress, followed Calhoun's lead in 1853 by lashing out against the "diligent effort" antislavery historians were making "to rob us of our interest in the great fame of Washington by representing him as a man of Northern character."[27]

Such concerns to lay claim to Washington's legacies were manifest in southern slaveholders' two collective attempts during the 1850s to provide an alternative to the massive obelisk on the banks of the Potomac River that was planned as a federal tribute to Washington. On Independence Day of 1848, the country's political establishment gathered a short distance from the capitol to hear the Massachusetts Whig Robert Winthrop explain how this towering structure, which was expected to triple the height of the Bunker Hill monument, would be an "all-sufficient centripetal power, which shall hold the thick clustering stars of our confederacy in one glorious constellation forever!" This Unionist plea echoed earlier efforts to transfer Washington's body to the federal capitol, a plan that in the 1830s had prompted Virginians to propose the interment of the corpse in Richmond

---

[27] Tucker, "A Discourse on the Genius of the Federative System of the United States," *SLM* 4 (December 1838), 769; Calhoun, "Final Remarks on the Compromise," *PJCC* 27, 230–1; James P. Holcombe, *An Address Before the Society of Alumni of the University of Virginia, at Its Annual Meeting, Held in the Public Hall* (Charlottesville, VA, 1853), 38–42. The well-known provision in Washington's will to free his slaves (after his wife's death) was undercut by the subsequent sale of Mount Vernon slaves in the late 1810s and by P.T. Barnum's exhibition of an elderly black women who claimed to be Washington's nurse. Washington's legacy as a master is explored in Henry Wiencek, *An Imperfect God: George Washington, his Slaves, and the Creation of America* (New York: Farrar, Straus and Giroux, 2003); Benjamin Reiss, *The Showman and the Slave: Race, Death, and Memory in Barnum's America* (Cambridge, MA: Harvard University Press, 2001); Russ Castronovo, *Fathering the Nation: American Genealogies of Slavery and Freedom* (Berkeley, CA: University of California Press, 1995); and Francois Furstenberg, *In the Name of the Father: Washington's Legacy, Slavery, and the Making of a Nation* (New York: Penguin, 2006).

instead. While the matter was settled by the Washington's family's decision to maintain the Mount Vernon tomb, rival claims to his legacy continued after this initial mobilization. The effort to enlist Washington as a proud Virginian continued in the 1850s, most popularly in the construction of an equestrian monument raised to honor him in Richmond. During these same years, "southern ladies" worked with even more publicity to preserve the Mount Vernon home, tomb, gardens, and plantation as a national shrine.[28]

These efforts, which stretched over much of the 1850s, intentionally broadened the debate over Washington's status by enlisting thousands of citizens as donors, volunteers, and spectators. Some shared the skepticism of the fire-eating *Charleston Mercury*, which predicted that "before [the national monument's] completion, the Union will no longer exist, or will only exist as a consolidated despotism, built upon the rights abstracted from the states." Yet, a larger number of slaveholders believed that there was more to be gained in shaping the image of Washington than in simply scoffing at prevailing patriotic trends. Leaders of southern historical societies were among the first to send blocks from each of their states to be set within the obelisk, a gesture than both registered a collective devotion to the first president and affirmed the integral position of the states within the Union. A steady stream of Washington-related developments continued, and these were featured during the 1850s by Whiggish editors who recognized them as a new opportunity to inculcate Unionist patriotism.[29]

Even before the officials of the Virginia Historical Society sent a state block for the national obelisk, they initiated plans for their own tribute to be planted beside the state capitol building in Richmond. Leading this effort was the Richmond attorney Conway Robinson, who was an early theoretician of Southern Rights, a Unionist Whig, and an outspoken enthusiast of documenting Virginia's colonial history. While neither Robinson nor the other monument officials detailed how they selected Thomas Crawford's design from among the dozens of entries, commentary by the Richmond press suggests some of their leading considerations. There was a generally positive (though not unanimous) reaction to the militancy of this equestrian Washington, which at the time of the commission in 1850 represented a

---

[28] Kirk Savage, "The Self-Made Monument: George Washington and the Fight to Erect a National Monument," *Winterhur Portfolio* 22 (Winter 1987), 225–42. Frederick F. Harvey, *The History of the National Washington Monument* (Washington, 1903).

[29] *Charleston Mercury*, April 12, 1851. Washington memorial activity of the 1850s was followed with particular regularity in the pages of the *Washington National Intelligencer, Knoxville Whig, Montgomery Advertiser, Charleston Courier, Augusta Southern Field and Fireside*, and *Natchez Whig*.

relatively unusual portrayal of Washington in the heat of battle. Even more important was Crawford's proposal to surround Washington on horseback with a pantheon of Virginia heroes. What most distinguished the monument, in fact, was not its representation of Washington but its inclusion of six statues that would stand around the perimeter of the first president. Hovering above a set of iconic statesmen, Washington was not only brought within Virginia borders but was situated in the context of distinctive state heroes (see Figure 5.1). As the *Richmond Enquirer* stagily noted at the time, here would be a creation that "even in the ruined condition in which it may appear in far-off ages," might be "taken, fragment for fragment, and by the Anti-quary's skill be brought to light as the Virginia Washington Monument."[30]

Which six Virginians should be assembled to pay homage to Washington spurred an ongoing series of political maneuvers, which Crawford, who was himself a New Yorker, wisely delegated to local decision-makers. Only two heroes – Patrick Henry and Thomas Jefferson – were considered indispen-sable, and when their twelve-foot likenesses arrived in 1855, with accom-panying shields for "Revolution" and "Independence," the identity of the remaining four were still in doubt. The Unionist *Richmond Whig* recog-nized the "delicacy and difficulty" of the pending decision and lobbied hard, and ultimately with success, to retain John Marshall and "Justice" among the group. Westerners interested in the project likewise hailed the inclusion of their region in the person of Meriwether Lewis and his shield of "Colonial Times." Presidents Madison and Monroe seemed to be appropriate choices for the remaining two spots, but Governor Henry Wise, whose administra-tion emphasized state self-sufficiency, chose the pairing of George Mason with "the Bill of Rights" and Thomas Nelson with "Finance" to express his own distrust of federal glory, economic dependence, and the nationalizing heritage of the "Virginia Dynasty."[31]

The size, scale, and artistic merit of Crawford's work drew considerable outside notice, and with this attention came intentionally provocative remarks about Virginia's role in the current slavery controversy. A writer

---

[30] *Richmond Enquirer*, February 15, 1850; Lauretta Dimmick "'An Altar Erected to Heroic Virtue Itself': Thomas Crawford and his Virginia Washington Monument," *The American Art Journal* 23 (1991), 52–8; *Historical Account of the Washington Monument in the Capitol Square, Richmond VA* (Richmond, 1869).

[31] *Richmond Enquirer*, February 12, 1850; *Richmond Whig* carried the greatest number of negative articles about Crawford's design in the weeks following its adoption. For arrival of the Henry and Jefferson statues, see *Richmond Enquirer*, August 18, 1855 (where Henry's likeness is described as a mix of Henry Wise and John Calhoun) and *Richmond Whig*, February 22, 1856.

FIGURE 5.1. This image appeared a week before Thomas Crawford's Richmond Equestrian Monument was unveiled. It inaccurately featured a complete set of "Virginia heroes" surrounding the pedestal, showing a grouping that would not in fact be complete until after the Civil War. *Harper's Weekly, February 20, 1858. Used with permission of Dartmouth College Library.*

in the *New York Tribune* argued in 1856 that the bronze masterpiece "should stand where the whole country could see it, and not be hidden in a corner frequented only by negroes and negro-drivers." He then noted that Washington and other Revolutionary Virginians might be lynched if they could return to life and speak as frankly about slavery in the late 1850s as they had while founding the nation upon principles of universal freedom. Debates in the local press suggested that there was a sensitivity to such matters among white Virginians. There had been concern in 1850 that black Richmonders might read more than was intended in the shift from white marble (the typical material of Washington sculptures at that point) to the darker shade of bronze, though this material was nonetheless chosen as the noblest form. Subsequently, there was a sharp local reaction to the mistaken assumption of a Philadelphia writer that a slave had become one of the figures being discussed for inclusion in the Virginia grouping. This was of course not the case, though black slaves did play a critical role in the monument's erection after several of them were purchased outright by the Association as laborers.[32]

On February 22 and 23, 1858, sporadic press coverage gave way to inaugural ceremonies that drew the enormous crowd of 50,000. As the largest patriotic assembly in the city's history, this electrifying moment was generally believed to have surpassed even the mythic visit to Richmond made by General Lafayette during his 1824 tour. The current debate over slavery in Kansas heightened the political tensions, as did a simultaneous Mount Vernon fundraiser that brought both the Alabama fire-eater William Yancey and the Massachusetts Whig Edward Everett to take part in the activities. In unveiling the statue, Senator Robert Hunter discussed the need to follow Washington's prudence, noting: "He saw that the right of an individual to manage his own affairs in his own way, if they concerned only himself, implied a corresponding obligation on him not to intervene in the affairs of others where they alone are interested." Governor Henry Wise, obliquely referred to the need for a Democratic party consensus over slavery in Kansas, exclaiming: "If none other under Heaven can draw us to each other, that talisman can touch the chords of unison, and clasp us hand to hand, and bind us heart to heart, in the kindred heirship of one Patriot Father!"[33]

As speeches gave way to a ritual of verbal interchanges among leading participants, it became clear that this homage to Washington would feature more division than comity. Senator James Mason, whose grandfather George Mason was slated as the next addition to the monument, sounded a common theme of the state rights' contingent when he announced that "Virginia has brought Washington back to Virginia." William Yancey meanwhile made a Calhounite plea for Washington's soundness on slavery, a move that goaded

---

[32] *New York Tribune*, July 10, 1856; Dimmick "'An Altar Erected to Heroic Virtue Itself'"; Thomas Crawford to Louisa Ward Crawford, February 10, 1850, quoted in Robert L. Gale, "Thomas Crawford, Dear Lou, and the Horse," *VMHB* 66 (1958), 177. Both the *Richmond Enquirer*, August 28, 1855, and the *Richmond Whig*, September 1, 1855, corrected the Philadelphia *North American* writer who had misinterpreted the *Enquirer*'s suggested that the servant/soldier Peter Francisco (who was white and free rather than enslaved) be included as a tribute to non-elite heroes. Evidence for the association's expenditure of $1800 on slave laborers is provided in Thomas B. Brumbaugh, "The Evolution of Crawford's 'Washington'" *VMHB* 70 (1962), 3–29.

[33] Hunter, "Oration on the 22nd February, 1858," *SLM* 26 (March 1858), 167–84; "Hon. Henry A. Wise's Speech on the 22 February, 1858," *SLM* 26 (April 1858), 241–4.

William Cabell Rives and Edward Everett to link Washington's traditional Unionist associations to Crawford's militant image. They implied that, if alive, the Mount Vernon hero would rally the country to suppress disunion by force. James Barron Hope, a protégé of Beverly Tucker, also had conflict in mind, but one that would defend rights rather than preserve the Union. His inaugural ode noted visitors from across the Union but expressed particular hospitality to those from "summer-wedded lands" who were devoted to "spreading our faith and social system wide," presumably on the Kansas plains. Hope warned his listeners that "smooth Calvins" were apt to "preach wrong and Murder" with their "Vindictive eulogies on servile crime" and in a pointed question to the statue asked: "while this bronze remains/ Shall this great people prove a race of Cains?" His poem concluded on a surprisingly bleak note that affirmed:

> ... if our rights shall ever be denied,
> I call upon you, by your race's pride,
> ... to unfurl
> Our banner where the mountain vapors curl;
> Lowland and valley then will swell the cry,
> He left us free: thus will we live, or – die![34]

During the crisis of 1860–1, Virginians were likely to focus on Charleston Harbor than on their own Washington Monument, whose varying national, state, and sectional connotations seemed too conflicted for immediate use. The monument had become part of the landscape, however, and no doubt lent itself to provoking unrecorded reflections of those who passed it by on the way to the secession convention that winter. In 1858, Roger Pryor had imagined the lingering effect of earlier festivities:

The people of Virginia, as they gathered around the base of her great son's monument, saw "Revolution," the "Henry," and "Independence," the "Jefferson," and gazing upon their heroic images looked forward with resolute hearts and determined minds to the future, ready to "pay the price of eternal vigilance," for their liberties; nay more, to offer up their lives in such a cause. This was the national feeling throbbing in all southern hearts around the monument on the February 22, 1858, which has just faded into the past, leaving, however, its thoughts, feelings, and emotions to burn eternally in the bosoms of all men worthy to bear the name of our noble Commonwealth.[35]

---

[34] *Richmond Enquirer*, February 23, 24, 1858. Hope chose not to submit his poem to the press, instead publishing it for the first time in *Poems of James Barron Hope* (Richmond, VA, 1859), 13–42.

[35] "The 22nd of February – The Moral Significance of the Inauguration," *Richmond South*, semiweekly edition, February 28, 1858.

Once Richmond was selected as the Confederate capital, the nationalist implications of Crawford's equestrian figure would be recast, furnishing a prototype for the Confederate government's seal, which was adopted in 1863. President Jefferson Davis did more than anyone to claim this icon for the Confederacy, which he did by making it the main prop of his Washington's birthday inaugural of 1862. This was a deeply ironic association, since while Davis had had played no role in Crawford Richmond's commission, he had directly prevented the same sculptor from placing a "liberty cap" on the representation of Liberty that would top the new U.S. capitol building. That federal commission, which was granted during Davis' term as President Franklin Pierce's Secretary of War, would be erected in 1864, at a time when the U.S. government had moved past worrying about the symbolism of emancipation and had entered into the process of implementing its substance.[36]

Early Richmond advocates of a Virginia Washington monument promised that a work of bronze could fix a sense of the past, since it "tells but one story; it has no false readings or perversions; it cannot lie; it speaks only of honor and true glory." Nothing could have been further from the truth, as was demonstrated by the tangled history of Crawford's sculpture – and of the competing state, sectional, Unionist, and Confederate nationalist claims it called forth. Like the patriotic holidays, symbols, songs, and stories then in circulation, this monument would convey no intrinsic, stable meaning. Such fluidity allowed Senator Clement Clay to make a remarkable claim in 1863, when he introduced legislation that placed the figure of a mounted Washington on the Confederate seal. Rather than connecting the Confederacy to the first American president, Clay hoped it might represent a deep-rooted southern type. Confederates were a "nation of horseman," he explained, who were defined more for their mastery of inferior beings than for their framing of republics. The "cavalier" tradition, older even than Washington, was worthy of inclusion on the seal of state primarily because of its unique ability to "indicate the origin of Southern society."[37]

---

[36] William C. Davis, *Jefferson Davis: The Man and His Hour: A Biography* (New York: Harper Collins, 1991), 237, 394. An indirect link between Jefferson Davis and the earlier Washington festivities came with William Yancey's presentation of Washington's cane once Davis became Confederate president. Yancey had been given this heirloom in Richmond during the monument's unveiling. See Eric Walther, *The Fire-Eaters* (Baton Rouge, LA: Louisiana State University Press, 1992), 81.

[37] "Notes from Meeting of Board of Alderman, February 14, 1842," in Washington Monument Mss., LV; *SIN*, March 12, 1863; see also Robert E. Bonner, *Colors and Blood: Flag Passions of the Confederate South* (Princeton: Princeton University Press, 2002), 109–15.

COLONIAL HISTORY AND SOUTHERN DISTINCTIVENESS

Senator Clay's bold attempt in 1863 to transform George Washington from a Unionist founder to a slaveholding colonial cavalier was not entirely unprecedented. Three years earlier, in the wake of John Brown's raid at Harpers Ferry, Virginia Congressman Thomas Bocock had dedicated a Washington statue in the District of Columbia by hailing the first president as a "our great forest-born cavalier." Such gestures reflected more than an attempt to root an avowedly nationalist figure in a distinctively southern past. They showed how attention to colonial history might be able to mobilize southern unity in ways that Revolutionary remembrances simply could not. Histories of European colonial ventures and the growth of colonial societies reminded Americans of how varied the social, economic, and political character of the early colonies had been. Making Washington a culmination of a "cavalier" tradition, however, also signaled the absence of an exemplary southern colonial founder, and the attendant failure of the southern regional imagination to find an alternative to New England's Plymouth Pilgrims or to Massachusetts' John Winthrop.[38]

Most antebellum attention to southern colonial history placed the romantic stories of Jamestown's Pocahontas, or Florida's Ponce De Leon within the same nationalist frame that southern historical societies employed while hailing the Revolution. Until quite late, distinctiveness was less important than chronological preeminence, whether it came to Floridians' pride in having the Union's oldest city (in St. Augustine), or North Carolinians' attempt to broadcast how Raleigh's first English incursion had been made within their borders. Virginians best realized the power of being first, though they took little satisfaction in having to remind outsiders that it was Jamestown, rather than Plymouth, that had nurtured the first permanent English settlement in what would become the United States. It was with a sense of distinct frustration that they insisted that the Chesapeake experience had not only produced a deep vein of Revolutionary leadership but had anticipated social norms and political principles which would later flower within the American republic.[39]

---

[38] Thomas Bocock, "Oration Delivered on the Occasion of the Inauguration of Mills' Equestrian Statue of Washington," in *National Intelligencer*, February 23, 1860.

[39] Ann Uhry Abrams, *The Pilgrims and Pocahontas: Rival Myths of American Origin* (Westview, 1999); *The Early History of Florida: An Introductory Lecture Delivered by George R. Fairbanks, Esq., Before the Florida Historical Society* (St. Augustine, FL, 1857), 14; John Marshall, *The Life of George Washington* (1804); George Tucker, *The History of the United States* (1856).

Boosters of Virginia history were clearly jealous of enormous success enjoyed by New Englanders in presenting their own colonial history as the most compelling prelude to the formation of the United States. The rich and complicated tradition of New England filial piety developed rapidly after the 1820s, when the region's leadership sought to compensate for their wavering political influence by developing a regional mode of cultural memory.[40] The conviction that America was primarily a projection of New England settlement and ideas spread beyond the northeast and was regularly taken up by southern slaveholders themselves. Pilgrim tributes might have been expected from the New England Societies of Charleston and New Orleans, but they were also heard in Natchez, Mississippi, where, in 1843, William Mason Giles claimed, with little apparent fear of controversy, that "the light of freedom first dawned on our shores when the Mayflower landed at Plymouth." Members of New Orleans' First Presbyterian Church similarly heard the Rev. Robert L. Stanton praise the "Puritan spirit" and counsel that "as long as the Pilgrim spirit lives" they "need not despair of the Republic." Even Texans found themselves identifying, even before joining the Union, with "those who brought to old Plymouth's rock the race we love to own." Such trends caused Frederick Porcher to ask fellow South Carolinians in 1857: "what child has not been taught to believe religiously, that all that is good, all that is noble, all that is venerable in our country is derived from the Puritan who landed on the rock of Plymouth? And that whatever we enjoy of Christianity and civilization, is but the force of that great wave which receives its central impetus from that respectable piece of granite?"[41]

There was a full arsenal of anti-Puritan themes to debunk what was becoming an increasingly popular national legend. Yet casting aspersions on the New England past and shining light on its darker aspects was much

---

[40] John D. Seelye, *Memory's Nation: The Place of Plymouth Rock* (Chapel Hill: University of North Carolina Press, 1998); Laurence Buell, *New England Literary Culture: From Revolution through Renaissance* (Cambridge: Cambridge University Press, 1986); Harlow Sheidley, *Sectional Nationalism: Massachusetts Conservative Leaders and the Transformation of America, 1815–1836* (Boston, MA: Northeastern University Press, 1998).

[41] William Mason Giles, *An Oration Delivered in the City of Natchez on the Fourth of July, Before the Citizens and the Corps of the Natchez Fencibles* (Natchez, 1843), 9; Robert L. Stanton, *Ungodly Nations Doomed: A Discourse Preached on the Occasion of the Annual Thanksgiving, November 29, 1849* (New Orleans, 1849) 20; Henry Thompson, *Oration on the Anniversary of Independence* (Houston: National Intelligencer Office, 1839), 7; F.A. Porcher, "Address Pronounced at the Inauguration of the South Carolina Historical Society," 15. See also Job Tyson, *Discourse Before the Historical Society of Pennsylvania, February 21, 1842 on the Colonial History of the Eastern and Some of the Southern States* (Philadelphia, 1842).

easier than erecting a meaningful alternative. Slaveholders who did attempt to frame a rival understanding of the country's deepest historical roots paid homage to a different set of heroic individuals who either initiated their own idealistic colonial ventures or anticipated republican freedom by vindicating local rights. Marylanders celebrated Lord Baltimore's proclamation of religious liberty in 1643, and boasted how this regime "presented to the government of the United States the best example of republican simplicity in its form and action of government." Georgians hailed James Oglethorpe as a man "fired with benevolence" who was "determined to devote the best years of his manhood to the foundation of a new colony." Prototypical colonial republicans also received their due, with some Virginians looking to Nathaniel Bacon's revolt in 1676 as a step toward eventual independence, and Louisiana histories stressing how the 1768 revolt of New Orleans merchants marked a turning point in New World resistance to foreign tyranny.[42]

The Virginia settlement at Jamestown was the most important alternative to the Pilgrim founding, since it alone had the mythic characters capable of taking on epic proportions. Yet despite their best efforts, Virginian attempts to emulate the Plymouth celebrations by sponsoring periodic commemorations at Jamestown were judged as failures even by their strongest supporters. Attempts in 1857 to mark the 250th anniversary of this first colonial settlement drew out an especially notable series of laments. Those who made the trek to the site of the ancient settlement might have reflected more on their inheritance had they not complained so bitterly about a local wheat farmer, who had insisted that their celebration be kept clear of the area that the landing party supposedly stepped ashore, lest the crop he planted there be damaged. A call the following year to establish a monument to John Smith on the site generated even less attention than the celebration had.[43]

Virginian's own comparative neglect of Jamestown was exacerbated by the increasingly negative emphasis placed upon the first introduction of

---

[42] Joseph Chandler, *Civil and Religious Equality: An Oration Delivered at the Fourth Commemoration of the Landing of the Pilgrims of Maryland* (Philadelphia, 1855), 48–9; Stephen Elliott Jr., *A High Civilization the Duty of Georgians: A Discourse Delivered Before the Georgia Historical Society, on the Occasion of its Fifth Anniversary* (Savannah, 1844) 3, 8; John E. Ward, *Address Before the Georgia Historical Society* (Savannah, 1858), 30; Charles Campbell, *A History of the Colony and Ancient Dominion of Virginia* (Philadelphia, PA: J.B. Lippincott, 1860), 296; Charles Gayarre, *Louisiana: Its History as a French Colony: Third Series of Lectures* (New York: John Wiley, 1852).

[43] "Address of the Jamestown Association," *Richmond Enquirer*, April 22, 1854; "Editor's Table," *SLM* 24 (March 1857), 236–7; "Memorials of the Past," *Richmond Enquirer*, September 6, 1857; "A Monument at Jamestown to Captain John Smith," *SLM* 27 (August 1858), 112–15; *Richmond Semi-Weekly South* May 15, 1857.

slaves into the colony, a dozen years after Smith first made landfall. The landing of "twenty negars" from a Dutch ship in 1619 had been part of the colonial story at least since Robert Beverley's 1705 Virginia history, though nineteenth-century historians like Robert Grahame, George Bancroft, and Richard Hildreth had since expanded upon this episode to note the ironic contrast between this "dark" landing and that of the Mayflower Pilgrims the following year. The contrast between the two ships, one bringing religious fugitives to freedom, and the other landing black captives for plantation labor, held an iconic potency in the struggle for the Pilgrim's moral pre-eminence. Whiggish New Englanders like Daniel Webster and Robert Winthrop proudly noted the juxtaposition, though the link with current sectionalism was only perfected when abolitionists adopted the Pilgrim past for their own uses in the 1850s.[44] In what was the first novel written by an African-American, William Wells Brown elaborated antislavery understanding of how sectional strife was a consequence of an original divergence.

Behold the Mayflower anchored at Plymouth Rock, the slave-ship in James River. Each a parent, one of the prosperous, labour-honoring, law-sustaining institutions of the North; the other the mother of slavery, idleness, lynch-law, ignorance, unpaid labour, poverty, and dueling, despotism, the ceaseless swing of the whip, and the peculiar institution of the South. These ships are representative of good and evil in the New World, even to our day. When shall one of those parallel lines come to an end? [45]

Whether or not they had ever heard of Brown's *Clotel*, culturally-attuned slaveholders responded to the intensifying rhetorical contrasts drawn between Jamestown and Plymouth. When, in 1860, the Virginia historian Charles Campbell revised his chronicle of the colonial period, he went out of his way to contextualize and excuse the 1619 landing of slaves. The former

---

[44] Robert Beverly, *The History of Virginia, in Four Parts* edited with an introduction by Charles Campbell (Richmond: J.W. Randolph, 1855), 37. While Winthrop's 1839 address was perhaps the strongest statement outside abolitionist tradition, it was Webster's 1843 contrast between Jamestown and Plymouth that raised southern ire. See Seelye, *Memory's Nation*, 278–81 and "Mr. Webster's Bunker Hill Oration" *SLM* 9 (December 1843), 749–55 and *SLM* 10 (January 1844), 25–31.

[45] William Wells Brown *Clotel; or The President's Daughter* Robert Levine ed., ([1853] Boston: Bedford St. Martins, 2000), 180. See also [Nathaniel Hawthorne], "Chiefly About War Matters," *Atlantic Monthly* 10 (July 1862), which claimed that the first African arrived on the Mayflower itself, a "historical circumstance, known to few" that "connects the children of the Puritans with these Africans of Virginia." Hawthorne's invention of this link, which had no basis in fact, led him to speculate about how the "monstrous birth" of slavery in America had given New Englanders "an instinctive sense of kindred" with slaves and stirred them to "an irresistible impulse to attempt their rescue, even at the cost of blood and ruin."

president John Tyler similarly reminded listeners on Jamestown's 250th
anniversary that the trade begun early in Virginia's history had mainly
enriched New Englanders. These strategies of justification and evasion
extended similar proslavery maneuvers undertaken by David Ramsay in
the histories of South Carolina that he wrote, and then revised, during
Jefferson's presidency. A few spokesmen went farther, and by redefining
a familiar contrast they provided a historical counterpart to the late antebellum sense of proslavery mission. James Barron Hope followed his sectional tribute to the Virginia Washington monument with a reflection in
1860 on Jamestown's part in launching the "beneficent institution" that
would eventually "open the fountains of a great human Nile," "fertilize
the vast Savannahs of the South," and "regulate the exchanges of two
hemispheres."[46]

Henry A. Washington, a professor at William and Mary and Beverly
Tucker's son-in-law, offered another means to overcome the damaging
rhetorical contrast between corrupt Jamestown masters and Pilgrim
worthies. His plea to historians was to go beyond the "romantic adventure,
bold achievement, and thrilling incident" that had dominated most accounts
of Virginia's mythic past and to approach those social developments of
bygone years in the way that Thomas Babington Macaulay had done for
England. "It is not in courts or camps, nor yet on battlefields that the life of a
people is spent, or their true history is discovered; but far away from scenes
like these, in the field, the workshop, and the factory." In these more ordinary surroundings, "causes which few eyes see and which are chronicled in
no records are silently, but steadily and irresistibly moulding the destinies of
the human race." Accordingly, Washington's major theme was not the
actions of government, but the formation of Virginia's peculiar society,
which had developed as "a sort of anomaly" paralleled only by "the other
slave-holding states of the union" and which had produced what he called a
"fragment of the feudal system floating about here on the bosom of the
nineteenth century."[47]

Washington pledged that every problem "connected with the past history
or present condition of the commonwealth" could be "found in the peculiar
elements which prevailed in her social organization during the colonial

---

[46] Compare Campbell's 1860 *A History of the Colony and Ancient Dominion of Virginia,*
144–5, with his *An Introduction to the History of the Colony and Ancient Dominion of
Virginia* (Richmond: B.B. Minor, 1847), 46–7; Tyler, "Celebration at Jamestown," *SLM*
24 (June 1857), 440; Arthur Shaffer, "Between Two Worlds: David Ramsay and the Politics
of Slavery," *JSH* 50 (1984), 175–96; Hope, *Social Development in Virginia,* 5–6.
[47] Henry A. Washington, "The Social System of Virginia," *SLM* 14 (February 1848), 65–81.

period," a perspective that helped him to move beyond icons and to instead address more gradual developments within early Virginia society. Though he suggested that more might be investigated in this regard, his own premature death prevented him from doing so. When Senator Robert Hunter ventured a similar theme in an address to the Virginia Historical Society, he thus had to rely on the familiar anecdote of Edmund Burke to explain how not only "the existence of African slavery contributed much to the settlement of this country" but had shaped the character of white Virginians over a long colonizing span.[48]

Some proslavery advocates longed for an even more affirmative view of colonial bondage, though they never produced a southern planter–historian on par with Edward Long and Bryan Edwards, two Caribbean authors who had woven proslavery arguments into what had become definitive histories of their respective colonies. In 1846, S. Henry Dickinson (himself a member of the Charleston New England Society) urged southerners to include the "inferior and subject race" in their histories "frankly ... fairly, and faithfully" and "without a blush." Though all history was "written in letters of blood," the South could pride itself on comparatively humane dealing with Indians and Africans, he argued. Others reminded Georgia historians to distrust the much-lauded philanthropy of their original colonial Trustees, noting that these men "allowed their eager benevolence to warp their judgment" in restricting slavery in the colony, which suffered "disastrous calamities" before African workers were introduced. William Henry Trescot argued that slavery's centrality in South Carolina history made that state, not Virginia, the "historical type of the great southern section of the United States."[49]

Calls for more stridently proslavery histories went largely unheeded, and most southern historians continued to approach the role of slavery as an

---

[48] Ibid.; Robert Hunter, *Observations on the History of Virginia: A Discourse Delivered Before the Virginia Historical Society, at their Eighth Annual Meeting* (Richmond, VA, 1854), 32; see also John L. Thompson's later echo of Henry Washington in "Colonial Life of Virginia," *SLM* 20 (June 1854), 330–42.

[49] S. Henry Dickinson, "An Essay on the Difficulties in the Work of the Historian," *SLM* 12 (February 1846), 110; H.W. Law, "Judge Law's Oration Before the Georgia Historical Society, Delivered on the Anniversary of Ogelthorpe's Landing" *Collections of the Georgia Historical Society* (Savannah, 1840); "Collections of the Georgia Historical Society," *SQR* 3 (January 1843), 40–93; William Henry Trescot, "Oration Delivered Before the South Carolina Historical Society"; J. Barrett Cohen, "Oration Delivered on the First Anniversary of the South Carolina Historical Society," *Collections of the South Carolina Historical Association, Volume 2* (Charleston, SC, 1856). The Maryland Historical Society sponsored a rare tribute to a free African-American, written by a prominent white supporter of African Colonization: John H. B. Latrobe, *Memoir of Benjamin Banneker* (Baltimore, MD, 1845).

original implantation whose main effect was to set the southern colonies on a distinctive path. There was a surprising reluctance to explore bondage within the larger currents of world history, or to acknowledge that its growth and development operated across four continents and over the course of centuries. Appreciating the nuance and the scope of this historical process would have required southern masters to look at the development of bondage in the same cosmopolitan terms they approached the more abstract fields of philosophy, religion, or ethnology. But with the exception of T. R. R. Cobb's 1858 history – a work that was not much noted or used – there was simply no southern equivalent to such synthetic overviews produced by the French writer Henri Wallon, or the Ohio free-soiler William O. Blake. George Frederick Holmes perceived danger in this oversight, predicting in 1855:

> Until we have canvassed and sifted the history as well as the philosophy of slavery, and discriminated the true lessons of the past from the mistaken or distorted inferences extracted from its archives, our cause is undefended, and we concede the vantage ground to our antagonists, and then affect to be surprised or indignant at the advantages they have gained from their position.[50]

Southern historians of the 1850s were less likely to delve into the particulars of colonial slavery than to explore, and to champion, the social heterogeneity of the Chesapeake, the Carolinas, and Georgia which they presented as these regions' most important feature. Developing this theme in the late antebellum period drew attention to New England's own insularity at a moment of supposedly "Puritanical" nativism and reclaimed the moral high ground that connected southern ancestors to present claims to lead an even more polyglot United States. George Frederick Holmes argued for the world-historical importance of the Jamestown settlement (and, by implication, the irrelevance of Plymouth) by insisting that this colony had initiated America's defining mission, which was to "attract, absorb, incorporate, and consubstantiate, as Rome did in antiquity, all the improvable races of mankind – all the tendencies of human progress – all the mature elements of modern civilization." A Louisiana historian was less philosophical in likening his state's white settlers to "the rich soil upon our great rivers" which was "composed of different colored strata, not yet perfectly amalgamated." South Carolinians tended to be most enthralled with their state's early ethnic variety, with Frederick Porcher marveling at "the various heterogeneous elements, which lay at the basis of our social polity." James

[50] George Frederick Holmes, "Ancient Slavery" *DBR* 19 (November 1855), 562.

L. Petigru likewise noted how "as every variety of living thing found refuge in Noah's ark, so in Carolina, there was a strange meeting of the human race." Both of these men claimed that social cohesion developed among white Carolinians during the colonial period, but insisted that it sprang from other forces than shared bloodlines.[51]

In heralding the varied nature of early southern society, many late antebellum historians effectively debunked the mythic predominance of Virginia "cavaliers." Hugh Blair Grigsby was especially pointed in discounting the influence of the small number of royalists who actually settled in Virginia. He blasted those who did come, insisting that "the cavalier was essentially a slave – a compound slave – a slave to the king and a slave to the church" and claimed that the heroes of the revolution did not descend from "butterflies of the British aristocracy" but were "the bone and sinew of that unconquerable people" who, in combining diverse strains from throughout northern Europe, "we call, for want of a better name, the Anglo-Saxons." James Barron Hope tried to cling to the mythic past, but even he admitted, with a nod to Grigsby, that other groups had a numerical predominance within the early history of his state. Hope argued that what set the royalists fugitives apart was the fact that they were natural masters, not the natural slaves that Grigsby had belittled.[52]

Attention to the Cavalier theme came fast and furious only during the presidential election year of 1860. This had far less to do with the work of southern historians than with the yearning for a deep-rooted explanation for the North's political consolidation within the Republican Party. Themes of

---

[51] George Frederick Holmes, *The Virginia Colony; or the Relation of the English Colonial Settlements in America to the General History of the Civilized World. An Address Delivered at the Annual Meeting of the Virginia Historical Society at Richmond, December 15, 1859* (Richmond, VA, 1860); Judge Henry Bullard, "Louisiana Historical Researches," *DBR* 3 (January 1847) 22–3; Porcher, "Address Pronounced at the Inauguration of the South Carolina Historical Society," 5; James L. Petigru, *Oration Delivered on the Third Anniversary of the South Carolina Historical Society, at Hibernian Hall* (Charleston, 1858), 10. For links between Puritan homogeneity and antebellum New England nativism see Jan Dawson, *The Unusable Past: America's Puritan Tradition, 1830–1930* (Chico, CA, 1984), 49–60.

[52] Hugh Blair Grigsby, *The Virginia Convention of 1776: A Discourse Delivered Before the Virginia Alpha of the Phi Beta Kappa Society, in the Chapel of William and Mary College* (Richmond, VA, 1855), 38–41; James Barron Hope, *Social Development in Virginia: An Oration Before the Society of the Hampton in Poem and Address Delivered on the First Annual Meeting of the Society of the "Old Boys of Hampton Academy" July 1860* (Richmond, VA, 1860), 5–6. William Henry Foote, *Sketches of Virginia* (New York, 1850); Samuel Kercheval, *A History of the Valley of Virginia* (Woodstock, VA: John Gatewood, 1850) took another tack by emphasizing the Scotch-Irish contributions to state history.

racial exclusivity and purity, of class and religious fervor, were swirled into
the mix during this period of transition. This odd enterprise drew equally
from the themes of fiction and from racial theory. Those who pushed the
argument to its logical conclusion postulated an ancestral blood feud that
conjured up memories of English strife at Marston Moor and Naseby 200
years earlier. Quickly enough, the echoes from the era of American colonization became far less important, however. As bloodshed mounted in the
early 1860s, white southerners realized that they had plenty of history and
heroes on fields of battle far closer to home.[53]

FUTURE MEMORIES OF THE HEROIC PRESENT

Americans' prevailing orientation toward the future made excessive attention to past achievements a source of anxiety no less than of pride. In 1858,
as historical echoes seemed to become louder and louder across the slave
states, the South Carolina poet Paul Hamilton Hayne registered skepticism
of what Ralph Waldo Emerson had called an age of "retrospection." In a
poem titled "National Decay," Hayne wrote that:

> A People whose true life is in the Past
> Whose fame is buried in ancestral tombs
> Cold as their ancient ash; no fresh blooms
> Of vigorous manhood have sprung up, and cast
> A Grateful shadow on the desert vast
> Of present degradation![54]

Hayne touched on a larger cultural problem, which involved the need to
imbue the present with historic associations while not obscuring or delaying
glories still to be won on behalf of later generations. Possessing a history was
an intrinsic need since, as Senator Robert Hunter put it "Without a history
of our own, we can expect neither unity nor consistency of national character, we may hope for no system of culture properly our own, we cannot
maintain even a just self-respect, nor have we a right to expect from our sons
a high ambition or noble aspirations." Contemporary understanding of

[53] Compare Robert E. Bonner, "Round-Headed Cavaliers? The Context and Limits of a
Confederate Racial Project," *CWH* 48 (March 2002), 34–59, with Ritchie Devon Watson
Jr., *Normans and Saxons: Southern Race Mythology and the Intellectual History of the
American Civil War* (Baton Rouge: Louisiana State University Press, 2008).

[54] Paul Hamilton Hayne, "National Decay," *Russell's Magazine* 2 (March 1858), 499. See
also Thomas M. Allen, *A Republic in Time: Temporality and Social Imagination in Nineteenth Century America* (Chapel Hill, 2008).

"historical peoples" even made a claim to past glories a sign of full human-ity. Conversely, the absence of historical achievements became a signal of collective shortcomings within the grand sweep of human existence. Lectur-ing before the New Orleans New England Society in 1845, S. S. Prentiss conveyed what was involved when he insisted that "he who lives only in the present is but a brute and has not attained the human dignity."[55]

Whatever the worth of possessing a history, the dead weight of the past seemed likely to induce paralysis if it were to become all-consuming. The editor James De Bow, who had been among those who founded the Loui-siana Historical Society in the 1840s, pointed out in 1858 that "people are easiest enslaved who, clinging to the traditions, the memories, and the fame of their country, are mindless, as to its present practical workings." One response to this, which furnished a distinct subtheme within proslavery historical writings, were histories of the future, a genre taken up and popu-larized by the same Virginians who had idolized Washington and who lent credence to the glory of colonial Cavaliers.[56] The cousins Beverley and George Tucker set the standard for future histories with *The Partisan Leader* and *A Century Hence*, two works that were written in the decade following the nullification crisis. Then on the eve of secession, John Beau-champ Jones composed *Wild Southern Scenes*, which offered an even racier bit of retrospective nostalgia. Jones' attempt to imagine a future Civil War immediately prompted the fire-eater Edmund Ruffin (who happened to be another Virginia cousin of the Tuckers) to write his own *Anticipations of the Future*, which appeared in 1860.[57]

These four efforts showed how the region's historical sensibility extended forward as well as backward, and was thus unlikely to dwindle into com-placency or mere romance. While none of these works represented particular literary merit, each involved an effort to put the institution of slavery, and those who bore the greatest responsibility for its continuance, within the larger flow of an ongoing heroic tradition. The politics of George Tucker's

[55] Hunter, *Observations on the History of Virginia*; Prentiss quoted in Seelye, *Memory's Nation*, 404.
[56] De Bow, "Disruption of the Federal Union" *DBR* 30 (April 1861), 429–35; this address was first delivered at the College of Charleston in 1858.
[57] George Tucker, *A Century Hence Or, A Romance of 1941* edited by Donald R. Noble. (Charlottesville, VA, 1977) [Nathaniel Beverly Tucker], *The Partisan Leader* (Washington, 1836); John B. Jones, *Wild Southern Scenes: A Tale of Disunion! And Border War!* (Philadelphia: TB Peterson and Brothers, 1859); Edmund Ruffin, *Anticipations of the Future to Serve as Lessons for the Present Time* (Richmond: J.W. Randolph, 1860). See also LCB, "The Country in 1950, or the Conservatism of Slavery," *SLM* 22 (June 1856), 426–39.

novel were the most oblique, though even he gave a nod toward slavery in showing how abolitionist "agitators" were still at work in the year 1941. The other three novels offered a far clearer preview of the impending catastrophe that would occur if decisive action were not immediately taken in defense of Southern Rights. Beverley Tucker and Edmund Ruffin both focused on the consequence of the presidency passing to a northern enemy (in the persons of Martin Van Buren and William Seward, respectively). In each case, the expected tyranny was met on the battlefield and from guerrilla hideouts by resolute southern fighters, supported by a loyal phalanx of slave retainers. Jones was a bit more fanciful, depicting an attempted northern secession, a coup in Washington, D.C., a gallows prepared beside the Washington National Monument for Jacobin-like executions, and the final restoration of southern control of the United States through armed force.[58]

This cluster of books featured actors whose pride in their own forebears made them willing to suffer and to create their own glorious history that subsequent generations might inherit. In showing how proslavery Southerners might realize their destiny within historical time, they thus reminded readers what future generations might think of the present. Such fantasies would gain new relevance as their scenarios seemed to transpire. Tucker's *The Partisan Leader* would be republished on the eve of secession, as would his 1850 call for disunion, foisting upon him the posthumous reputation as a secessionist prophet.

Slaveholders' broadening historical consciousness mattered most because of what it said about the present, which was implicitly set in conversation with both the past and the future. This tendency was evident in *De Bow's Review's* selection of articles during the last three months of 1860. Ruffin's *Anticipations of the Future* received a complimentary notice from the magazine, which promised to offer excerpts from it in future issues. George Fitzhugh contributed a plea for a proslavery version of George Bancroft's American colonial history while J. Quitman Moore emphasized William Gilmore Simms' accomplishments as a historical writer. Yet it was in a political essay written by the Mississippi planter J. B. Gladney that concerns about the past and the future were tied together. Situating American masters within the continuum of historical time, Gladney explained how "the brave men who hoisted the flag of independence in the face of Great Britain did not undertake that arduous struggle for their own rights and liberties alone" but

---

[58] Few of the texts have generated critical commentary; the exception is the discussion of *Partisan Leader* in John M. Grammer, *Pastoral and Politics in the Old South* (Baton Rouge: Louisiana State University Press, 1996).

also "looked to the welfare of their children." With a new crisis facing them, Gladney's slaveholding readers were likely to take their own descendents into consideration. Would the present-day heirs of the Revolution "do their duty in defending for themselves, and handing down to posterity, this great boon of rights?" Or would they instead be "like Samson ... enticed from their duty, bound while asleep, shorn of their locks of strength, and have their eyes put out?" A tradition of defiance, Gladney made it clear, mattered hardly at all if it did not evoke a struggle to transmit it forward in time.[59]

[59] "Editorial Notes" *DBR* 29 (October 1860), 543; Fitzhugh, "Mr. Bancroft's History and the 'Inner Light" *DBR* 29 (November 1860), 598–613; J. Quitman Moore, "William Gilmore Simms," *DBR* 29 (December 1860), 702–12; [J.B. Gladney], "The South's Power of Self-Protection, *DBR* 29 (November 1860), 551–2.

6

Yankee Apostates and Allies in the American 1850s

Late in 1856, Senator Robert Hunter of Virginia traveled to Poughkeepsie, New York, to rally free-state voters for the first time in his two decades as a politician. In venturing beyond his usual audience of Virginians and Washington Congressmen, Hunter became part of a wider trend. The previous winter, Georgians Robert Toombs and Howell Cobb had traveled north of the Potomac with hopes of quelling a free-soil insurgency and laying the groundwork for the upcoming presidential campaign. Following in their wake came William Barksdale of Mississippi, John Floyd of Virginia, John Slidell of Louisiana, and James Orr of South Carolina, each of whom argued that the Union was doomed if Americans did not elect the Pennsylvania Democrat James Buchanan to the presidency. Northern conservatives heard from slaveholding representatives of the nativist American Party during these same months, as Sam Houston completed a celebrated New England tour in 1855 and North Carolinian Kenneth Rayner stumped for the presidential candidate Millard Fillmore through November of 1856.[1]

Catering to free-state audiences was a natural response to the worst political crisis over slavery yet seen. As proslavery interests increased their lock on southern politics, southern allies in the North absorbed fiercer assaults than they had ever before experienced. Just four years after a wide-reaching compromise over the admission of a free-soil California,

---

[1] R.M.T. Hunter, *The Democratic Demonstration at Poughkeepsie* (n.p., 1856); Cobb, *Speech Delivered in Concord, N.H., at a Mass Meeting of the Democratic Party of Merrimac County* (n.p., 1856); Proceedings of the Merchant's Great Democratic Meeting at the New York Exchange ... Speech of Gov. Floyd (New York: John F. Trow, 1856); Gregg Cantrell, *Kenneth and John B. Rayner and the Limits of Southern Dissent* (Urbana: University of Illinois, 1993).

the Kansas-Nebraska Act overturned the 1820 restriction on slavery in the northern part of the Louisiana Purchase. With the Pierce administration and its northern allies crippled by charges of moral treason and political infidelity, a South Carolinian's caning of Massachusetts Senator Charles Sumner enflamed the North; the prospects of a Republican party based exclusively in the free states rose at an astounding pace. The looming menace of "geographical parties" lent new relevance to George Washington's warning in his famous Farewell Address of 1796. As the first president had predicted, sectional "jealousies and heart-burnings" seemed likely to "render alien to each other" those who had long been "bound together by fraternal affection."[2]

As northern audiences realized, appeals made by southern politicians in 1856 were even more attuned to the issue of slavery than usual. Nearly all of Hunter's address was focused either on the "disturbed question of African slavery upon this continent" or on the need for a basic change in northern attitudes toward this institution. Toombs addressed similar topics in Boston, where his mission would be hamstrung by rumors that he had boasted in Georgia of "calling the names of his slaves within earshot of Bunker Hill." Propagandizing on northern soil under such circumstances collapsed the distinction between political tours undertaken for partisan fortunes and the polemical exercises undertaken by provocateurs like George Fitzhugh, who debated the "failure of free society" before a New Haven audience in 1855. Sooner or later, all such missions presented white Northerners with a choice – either work to save the Union and slavery together, or realize that southern secession was imminent.[3]

If the 1850s witnessed fierce internal arguments among southern politicians about the allegiance of white immigrants and the wisdom of resuming the African slave trade, the key choice for southern voters concerned what sort of alliance with free-state voters might still be possible. Was there a critical mass of Yankees willing to allow the South to retain its political

---

[2] Washington, "Farewell Address" reprinted in Furman Sheppard, *The Constitutional Text-Book* (Philadelphia, PA: Sower, Barnes & Potts, 1855), 287. The politics of this period are developed in David Potter, *The Impending Crisis, 1848–1861* (New York: Harper and Row, 1976) and Roy F. Nichols, *The Disruption of American Democracy* (New York: Macmillan, 1948) while the cultural assertion of "Northern nationalism" can be traced in Susan-Mary Grant, *North Over South: Northern Nationalism and American Identity in the Antebellum Era* (Lawrence: University of Kansas, 2000) and Peter J. Parish, "Partisanship and the Construction of Nationalism," in Susan-Mary Grant and eds., *The North and the Nation in the Era of the Civil War* (New York: Fordham University Press, 2003), 113–28.

[3] Hunter, *Democratic Demonstration*; John Hope Franklin, *A Southern Odyssey: Travelers in the Ante-bellum North* (Baton Rouge: Louisiana State University Press, 1976), 218–43.

predominance, despite its lagging population rates? The answer to that question held enormous ramifications, since the free states had previously been unable to translate their majority status in terms of population into a corresponding dominance of political power. The Mobile editor John Forsyth Jr. crisply noted one likely result. "If we allow the North to master us, we cannot influence, guide or restrain the North for the common good," he argued. Once Republicans took control, the South would no longer be able to "teach our masters," and attempts to "council with and influence our equals" would thus be a thing of the past.[4]

PURITAN POLITICS AS YANKEE SUBVERSION

Robert Hunter's target audience in 1856 did not encompass the entire free-state populace. After singling out Democrats (especially those with an interest in the cotton trade), Hunter used his peroration to establish the geographical limits of the North that he hoped to rally. Just as Washington had during the darkest days of the Revolution made "the line of the Hudson" into the "greatest strategic line of the Union," so in 1856, it fell to "the democracy of the empire State" to "make good their possession" of this same "great point" and make it a boundary against enemy assault. With this concluding flourish, the Virginian suggested how easily defenses of the "real" America might dispense altogether with the Yankee heartland of New England.[5]

Hunter had earlier been more explicit about his animus toward New Englanders, denouncing their bid for political power as illegitimate and their sympathy for the battered Senator Charles Sumner as unbecoming. Such a tack had very deep roots in the politics of Virginia Democrats. Not long after George Washington's Farewell Address famously warned against all "geographical distinctions," Thomas Jefferson privately conveyed how a nationalist political partnership might make New England into a foil for more genuinely American values. Having witnessed what he took to be unmistakable reactionary tendencies in this seedbed of high "Federalism," Jefferson noted that Yankees were "marked, like the Jews, with such a perversity of character, as to constitute, from that circumstance, the natural division of our parties." Over the years that followed, southern Jeffersonians continued to make the five New England states into a sort of sectionalist scapegoat by drawing attention to the region's narrow distrust of the West, its unpatriotic

[4] John Forsyth, *The North and the South: A Lecture Before the Franklin Society of Mobile, May 23, 1854* (Mobile: Thompson and Harris, printers, 1854), 9.
[5] Hunter, *Democratic Demonstration*, 16.

opposition to nationalist military expansion, and its disturbing affinity with aristocratic British reformers. Proslavery secessionists could even cast aspersions on this deeply suspect region as a means of explaining their own disaffection from the Union. As an Alabama editor put it in 1850, "the spirit of American fraternity, so long the predominating and master-sentiment of the Southern bosom, would never have called up this image of separate nationality if the Pilgrim Race had been true to public faith and public honor."[6]

There was a dose of cultural insecurity that permeated these attacks on New England, whose dominance of historical memory had analogues in its unusually influential program of publishing and in its continuing leadership in educational endeavors. Sectional rivalries understandably emerged from such disparities, though these would have been managed far more easily had not New England antislavery become part of the equation. The physical proximity of radical abolitionists and a Whiggish political establishment led many proslavery spokesmen to conflate these two very different groups. Critics like the Georgia Methodist Augustus Baldwin Longstreet thus set the Massachusetts legislature's attempt to repeal the three-fifths clause of the U.S. Constitution beside the fiery denunciations of William Lloyd Garrison's Boston-based *Liberator*. He conveyed these as simply two different manifestations of "this Massachusettsia, this satanic Puritanism, this puritanical Satanism" that was "laying waste to all that is great, and glorious, and good, and beautiful and lovely, in our Heaven befriended land."[7]

As was the case with other critics of the New England, Longstreet's hostility to Yankee-inspired antislavery was borne of personal familiarity with the region. His Yale education and his legal training in Litchfield, Connecticut, did not hamper his alliance with Georgia's most radical state

---

[6] Hunter, "The Massachusetts Proposition for Abolishing the Slave Representation," *SLM* 11 (August, 1845); Jefferson to John Taylor, June 4, 1798 Paul Ford, *Works of Jefferson* (New York, 1904), 8: 432. *Dallas Gazette*, 1850 quoted in J. Mills Thornton, *Power and Politics in a Slave Society* (Baton Rouge: Louisiana State University Press, 1978), 228.

[7] [A.B. Longstreet], *A Voice from the South: Comprising Letters from Georgia to Massachusetts, and to the Southern States, with an Appendix* (Baltimore, MD, 1847), 26. For a sampling of relatively mild sectional animus that New England cultural pretensions bred, see [William Gilmore Simms], "A Passage with the 'Veteran Quarterly'" *The Southern and Western Magazine and Review* 1 (May 1845), 297–311; "The Edinburgh Review and the Southern States" *DBR* 10 (May 1851), 302; A Planter, "South Side View of the Union," *DBR* 23 (November 1857) and compare these to Kenneth S. Greenberg's discussion of the move from "Anglophobia to New Anglophobia" in *Masters and Statesmen: The Political Culture of American Slavery* (Baltimore: John Hopkins, 1985) and the more ambivalent portrait in Lewis P. Simpson, *Mind and the American Civil War: A Meditation on Lost Causes* (Baton Rouge: Louisiana State University Press, 1989).

rights forces during the 1830s. His turn to the Methodist ministry, a short time later, immersed him within new national networks that served to deepen his skepticism about antislavery attempts to politicize "prayers and hymns, and thanksgivings to God" intended to unite "the sons of the North and of the South." The bitter Methodist debate over slaveholding bishops pushed Longstreet to set aside his literary work as a Southwest humorist and perform a brief stint as a proslavery polemicist. A scriptural defense of slavery in 1844 anticipated his 1847 collection of letters to Massachusetts. These systematized anti-New England themes into an unusually coherent statement of a wider trend.[8]

Longstreet's 1847 letters to Massachusetts devoted most of their attention to those instances of "political witchcraft and diabolical incantations" that had erupted since the American Revolution. In ignoring the themes of the religious legacies from the colonial past, he thus tacitly agreed with the Rev. John Bocock (and a good many other proslavery evangelicals) who insisted that "never were two things of the same name much less identical in spirit and intrinsic character than the English puritanism of the seventeenth century, and the Yankee puritanism of the nineteenth." The story of declension could be as powerful as that of deeply rooted differences that purveyors of the Cavalier legend labored to establish. Even the secular-minded Henry Wise of Virginia could score points by contrasting the "vitality" and "spirituality" of colonial-era Puritanism – (which he noted had made "even the barren rock of Plymouth to fructify") with New England's latter-day fostering of "Unitarianism, Universalism, Fourierism, Millerism, Mormonism, – all the odds and ends of isms." Longstreet's assault on New England's "un-American" character thus did not move farther back than Yankee complicity in the eighteenth-century slave trade, after which he made his way through a familiar sequence of post-Revolutionary episodes. Anglophilic Federalists and treasonous Hartford Conventioneers dotted his narrative, as did greedy tariff exponents and jealous opponents of Southwestern expansion. Running through his account were a series of reflections on how a period of revolutionary-era unity (during which New England and the Deep South shared a commitment to ordered liberty) had given way to the provincial narrowness of apostate Yankees.[9]

[8] John Donald Wade, *Augustus Baldwin Longstreet: A Study in the Development of Culture in the South* (New York: Macmillan, 1924).
[9] *A Voice from the South*, 21; John H. Bocock, "The Martyrs of Scotland and Sir Walter Scott," *SPR* 10 (April 1857), 93; Wise quoted in James Pinckney Hambleton, *A History of the Political Campaign in Virginia in 1855* (Richmond: J.W. Randolph, 1856), 104.

Whether Massachusetts' un-American heresies were deep-rooted or of recent growth was incidental to Longstreet's main concern, which was the alarming upsurge of New England abolitionism during the mid-1840s. Initially, the Georgian saw little hope of reversing this tide, and he thus challenged Massachusetts to "cease your agitations, and calmly appeal to the States (not to Congress) to release you from the tie that binds you to them." Addressing the many benefits of a truncated Union, he declared: "Let us exhibit to the world two sublime political miracles, in less than that many years: the nuptials and the divorce of nations, by the omnipotent law of love on the one hand, and its kindred law of peace on the other." He counseled Southerners to "throw all our power ... about the Constitution that we may drive these malcontents to despair of a change or overthrow of Government." The most likely scenario for the exodus of New England would be for the Supreme Court to protect slavery in the territories, and act that would require Yankees to choose between compromising their honor or setting up on their own. By the election of 1848, he found another means of isolating New England, as he privately detailed how the elevation of Lewis Cass to the presidency might renew a South–West alliance that would "consign abolitionism to its merited contempt."[10]

In less than a decade, it would become increasingly difficult to associate antislavery and associated "isms" only with a New England core. As the Republican Party swept Cass's Michigan and a full ten additional free states in the 1856 presidential election, proslavery nationalists found themselves alternating between befuddlement, deep anxiety, and at times a grudging admiration of that "stern Puritanism" that typified the "universal Yankee nation." "Call them, if you will, meddlesome, inquisitive, underhanded, self-opinionated, parsimonious," a self-described "Planter" explained late in 1857. New Englanders clearly showed "a doggedness, a self-reliance, and hopefulness, and a resolution not to be beat" that had gained national influence through Yankee "preachers, lecturers, schoolmasters, pamphlets, reviews and newspapers." The spread of radical ideas through these media was, to be sure, partly offset by those "vast numbers" of the region's "most honest and earnest minds" who remained willing to stand with the South on the politics of slavery. But this writer wondered why masters should "love and cling to a Union our equality and rights in which hang by so precarious a thread?" "Had we not better part with our few sincere and honest friends?"

---

[10] *A Voice from the South*, 56–7; Longstreet to Calhoun, July 4, 1848, *PJCC* 25, 560–2; Cf. Caleb McDaniel, "Repealing Unions: American Abolitionists, Irish Repeal, and the Origins of Garrisonian Disunionism," *JER* 28 (2008), 243–69.

Any delay seemed likely to encourage New England allies "one by one" to
forsake their erstwhile southern partners, with some breaking ties "because
they could not serve us" and others doing so "because we could not serve
them."[11]

The stunning Republican ascendancy in the North invited new frameworks for understanding what lay behind these manifold Yankee "isms."
The most intriguing proslavery polemics of the late antebellum years took
up this challenge by shifting away from traditional themes of Puritanical
intolerance and neo-Federalist hostility to popular rule (two staples of the
Jeffersonian tradition) and focusing instead on the region's disruptive proclivity for social and religious radicalism. Recasting earlier proslavery
assaults upon the British, the essayist "Python" accused Yankees of pursuing
"property-robbery and political power" through the "cant of humanitarianism and the wild cries of a visionary religion." The language of republican
counter-subversion helped "Python" to minimize differences between insidious forces while maximizing the intricately intertwined threat. "Whether
the Protean shape assumed be that of the 'Roundhead' the 'Sans-Culotte,'
'Red-Republican,' or 'Black republican,' " the purpose of free-state agitators was simply "to make a law unto themselves, bend God to their purposes, and demand the world to worship at their altar."[12]

If "Python's" barbed assaults on the North generated considerable commentary, these would have made an even bigger impact had his true identity
been more widely known. The six fire-eating essays that appeared under
"Python's" name between 1857 and 1861 represented a new opportunity
for the third of President John Tyler's fifteen children to win distinction in
his own right. John Tyler Jr. wrote of the ways of Washington and of the
free states with some authority, having served as his father's secretary in the
White House before relocating northwards with his older brother, who was
a key leader of Philadelphia's Democratic machine beginning in the early
1850s. Tyler had launched his career as a proslavery polemicist in the aftermath of California's admission, though he pursued journalism with a true
sense of purpose only in 1857, just as his bid for a patronage job in the

[11] A. Planter, "South Side View of the Union," *DBR* 23 (November 1857), 465.
[12] "Python" [John Tyler, Jr.], "The Secession of the South and a New Confederation Necessary to the Preservation of Constitutional Liberty and Social Morality," *DBR* 28 (April
1860), 382. David Brion Davis, "Some Themes of Counter Subversion: An Analysis of Anti-
Masonic, Anti-Catholic, and Anti-Mormon Literature,'" in *From Homicide to Slavery:
Studies in American Culture* (New York: Oxford University Press, 1986), 137–54; and
idem, *The Slave Power Conspiracy and the Paranoid Style* (Baton Rouge: Louisiana State
University Press, 1969).

Buchanan administration faltered. His widely noted essays went well beyond Longstreet's letters in exploring the intrinsic antagonisms of the free North (whose "aggregational" tendencies and social corruption bred "agrarian" excess) and the "conservative" and "individualist" slave South. By drawing attention to differing modes of capital and labor, Tyler pursued a self-consciously voguish sociological analysis that rested on how a "dense, landless, day-laboring, no-property mass" had taken hold of northern politics, first in rallying the masses to the cause of nativism, and then in transforming them into the groundswell of free-soil Republicanism. The latest stage of this mania sought not only to push the southern states from slavery to a more exploitative system of free labor but also to forcibly establish "a general system of hybrid-peonage" by bringing Mexico, Central America, and the West Indies into a "Black Republican" American empire.[13]

Tyler supplemented his sociological and historical analysis with an especially striking discussion of those ethno-religious differences and affinities that drove the politics of party and section in the late 1850s. He recast the debate over New England religiosity by contrasting that region's "Calvinistic insubordinatism" (which he dubbed "iconoclastic" and hostile to all law) with the forms of "Episcopal subordinatism." The latter, in teaching "respect and reverence in all things," united the southern elite who still clung to Anglican traditions with northeastern Catholicism, which represented the last remaining bulwark of order left in free society. "Strike out episcopacy from the North," Tyler summed up in 1857, "and no conservatism would remain, no friendly aid to the South, no stay in support of the Constitution." This formula reflected his reliance, in writing from Philadelphia, on the Democratic Irish immigrants who formed his brother's political base. Far from being the font of propertyless discontent that nativists charged, the Philadelphia Irish were, in Tyler's mind, a profoundly stabilizing element. "The importance of naturalized citizens to the South" could not be overestimated, Tyler wrote in 1860, as he noted how these men's allegiance to the Democratic Party formed an "antagonistic political element to Abolitionism and Black-republican agrarianism." Even in the event of armed conflict, Catholic immigrants would likely "rush spontaneously by thousands and hundreds of thousands beneath the flag of the South" and

[13] "Python" [John Tyler Jr.], "The Relative Political Status of North and South," *DBR* 22 (February 1857), 113–32; idem., "The Issues of 1860, The Designs of Black Republicanism," *DBR* 28 (March 1860), Philip Gerald Auchampaugh, *Robert Tyler: Southern Rights Champion, 1847–1866: A Documentary Study Chiefly of Antebellum Politics* (Duluth: Himan Stein, 1934) provides many revealing details about John Tyler, Jr.

would then "hurl the tide of war back upon New-England and the Lakes."
Enlistment in a common cause would come "not only through a sense of
right and natural affiliation with the South, the section most committed to
religious liberty, but through the policy of preserving the integrity of Mexico
and Cuba from the Vandalism of Black-Republicanism."[14]

Such crosscutting tendencies and staunch free-state allies might have
bolstered Tyler's faith in the Union had it not been for what he considered
the corrosive moral example of northern society. Yet his greatest fears
were with a "social system of the North" that had sunk in a mere eighty
years to the same level that Rome had reached over six centuries of corruption. Degeneracy of northern households provided the best index to this
precipitous decline, which was evident in the warning of "parental obligation and filial affection" and in the "unceasing toil" and "unending
anxiety" inflicted on those white servants who were nominally free. By
far the most dangerous aspect of free-state individualism was the move
toward the "independency of women," who had gained access to property
rights and to "easy" divorce. As the example of female insubordination
spread beyond the free states, the Union threatened to "dethrone Southern
virtue" in destabilizing the respective roles of men and of women. The
conservative influence of slavery was not so much an end in itself as a
bulwark against the sort of gender confusion that had become a stock
image within anti-abolitionist assaults on New England (see Figure 6.1).[15]

Tyler was more advanced than most proslavery figures in resting hostility
to the Union on a diagnosis of northern society rather than on the political
threat posed by "black Republicanism." By 1860, a focus on northern devi-
ance had helped Tyler and like-minded extremists to blend Calhoun's critique of party with William Seward's notion of an "irrepressible conflict." In
this view, calls for partisan rather than sectional unity were little more than
"carefully prepared dust thrown into the eyes of the South, blinding the
people of the South to the real dangers around them, and entrapping them
to their ultimate destruction." Sensing an underlying antislavery radicalism
at work within both the northern Democracy and the Republican opposition, Tyler wondered "of what advantage is it to the South to be destroyed
by Mr. Douglas through territorial sovereignty to the exclusion of Southern

[14] "Python," "Relative Political Status," 127–8; "The Secession of the South," 378; "The
Issues of 1860, The Designs of Black Republicanism" *DBR* 28 (March 1860), 271. Not
surprisingly, a Virginia Presbyterian took exception to Tyler's High-church position in *DBR*
23 (October 1857), 446.
[15] "Python," "The Relative Moral and Social Status of the North and the South," *DBR* 22
(March, 1857), 225–48.

MEETING OF THE FRIENDS OF "THE HIGHER LAW."

FIGURE 6.1. Literary responses to *Uncle Tom's Cabin* routinely presented abolition-ism as an inappropriate forum for female assertiveness. This "Meeting of the Friends of the Higher Law" is taken *from "Vidi," Mr. Frank: The Underground Mail-Agent (Philadelphia, PA: Lippincott, 1853). Courtesy of Duke University: Rare Book, Manuscript, and Special Collections Library.*

institutions, rather than by Mr. Seward through Congressional sovereignty to the same end?" Whether slaveholders were "forcibly led to immolation by Seward, or accorded, in the alternative, the Roman privilege of selecting their own mode of death by Douglas," the end result was the same. Missing from this analysis was the fact that there were other partisan maneuvers then underway, which aimed to restore links with those northern conservatives who seemed the last best hope of a proslavery Union.[16]

---

[16] Python, "The Issues of 1860," 271.

SOUTHERN MATRONS AND THE PLANTATION SHRINE

John Tyler Jr.'s anxieties about women's rights were no doubt influenced by his father, who, in 1835, had warned that it was a misguided sex, not an aberrant section, that posed the greatest threat to American republicanism. In sketching the perils of popular antislavery petitioning, the elder Tyler explained how female sentimentalists might eventually become the "instrument of destroying our political paradise, this Union of States." Eighteen years later, with the sensational success of a female Yankee novelist, satanic abolitionists seemed more intent than ever on transforming "woman" into "the presiding genius over the councils of insurrection and discord" and making her "into a fiend, to rejoice over the conflagration of our dwellings and the murder of our people." In retirement, the former president remained alert to this danger, though he found a new reassurance in female mistresses who were then responding to Harriet Beecher Stowe. It was thus with his full blessing that his thirty-three year-old wife joined a cadre of southern women venturing for the first time their own powerfully nationalist vindication of American bondage.[17]

The immediate occasion for Julia Gardiner Tyler's public defense of slavery was neither *Uncle Tom's Cabin* nor any other American initiative. What inspired her public letter was a petition launched by a circle of well-placed British ladies inspired by "fictions" that passed for truth. Soon after the Duchess of Sutherland reached out to her "sisters in America" through a mass petition campaign, Tyler followed the example of James Henry Hammond, William Gilmore Simms, and other proslavery writers in depicting abolition as a foreign menace, borne of British jealousies and insidious attempts to embarrass the republican mission. By castigating Sutherland's aristocratic attempt to cripple a thriving transatlantic rival, Tyler thus spoke on behalf of "all the thinking women, not only of the South, but of the whole Union." With what had become a familiar stance of nationalist assertion, she urged British reformers to follow "the golden rule of life" that required "each to attend to his own business and let his neighbors alone!" Only through a sober reassessment could the "mother country" secure Americans' "peace, love and friendship" rather than their "hatred, ill will, and contention."[18]

---

[17] John Tyler Sr. quoted in Jean Fagan Yellin, *Women and Sisters: The Antislavery Feminists in American Culture* (New Haven, CT: Yale, 1989), 3; Julia Gardiner Tyler, "To the Duchess of Sutherland and Ladies of England," *SLM* 19 (February, 1853), 120–6; Robert Seager II, *And Tyler Too: A Biography of John and Julia Gardiner Tyler* (New York: McGraw-Hill, 1963).

[18] Tyler, "To the Duchess of Sutherland," 121, 126; Evelyn Pugh, "Women and Slavery: Julia Gardiner Tyler," *VMHB* 188 (1980), 186–202.

Julia Tyler's letter provided important clues why slaveholding women had delayed their entry into proslavery polemics up to that point. In her mind, American women who accepted the "sphere for which the God who created her seems to have designed her" had, by owning slaves, embraced a divinely ordained duty to "preside over the domestic economy of the estates and plantations of their husbands" and to "attend to the comfort of all the laborers upon such estates." Their complaint with Sutherland, and by extension, with Stowe, sprang less from a defense of the institution than from a sense that these women had belittled the dutiful paternalism practiced by females who would rather not speak out at all. Once drawn in by wanton assaults, southern women continued to present themselves in the guise of calming passions, leaving a vigorous defense of rights to slave-holding men. Their cue in this regard had come from the female antiabolitionism pioneered by none other than Catherine Beecher, who, in 1837, had instructed American women to "assume the office of a mediator and an advocate of peace." In her rejoinder to the outspoken abolitionism of the Grimké sisters of South Carolina, Beecher had explained how female influence should not be used "for the purpose of exciting or regulating public sentiment" but for "promoting a spirit of candour, forbearance, charity, and peace."[19]

Master-class women entered the fray only after Catherine Beecher's younger sister Harriet had managed, in the words of John R. Thompson, to "foment heartburnings and unappeasable hatred between the brethren of a common country" and thus "to sow, in this blooming garden of freedom, the seeds of strife and violence and all direful contentions." The most visible effort to blunt Stowe's work came in an outpouring of "Anti-Tom" fiction, a phenomenon that involved southern men and Northerners as well as slave-holding women. More intriguing was the rapid intrusion of female voices into previously all-male preserves. A month after Stowe's serialized novel appeared as a book, Louisa McCord transferred her energies from anonymous commentary on political economy and race (in essays she had signed only with her initials) to a self-consciously "womanly" rebuttal to Anglo-American feminism. In becoming the first female to write for *De Bow's*

---

[19] Tyler, "To the Duchess of Sutherland," 120–2; Beecher, *An Essay on Slavery and Abolitionism, With Reference to the Duty of American Females* (Philadelphia, PA: Henry Perkins, 1837), 128–9; Jean Fagin Yellin addresses both Beechers in "Doing It Herself: *Uncle Tom's Cabin* and Woman's Role in the Slavery Crisis," *New Essays on Uncle Tom' Cabin*, Eric Sundquist, ed., (New York: Cambridge, 1986); Elizabeth R. Varon, *We Mean to Be Counted: White Women and Politics in Antebellum Virginia* (Chapel Hill: University of North Carolina Press, 1998).

Review, McCord established herself as one of the liveliest proslavery polemicists. Like Julia Tyler, she directed her hottest fire toward British meddling rather than toward her wayward American sisters.[20] By issuing responses across the Atlantic rather than toward the free states, McCord and the others caught up in the moment launched what would be a peculiarly short-lived proslavery insurgency. When the furor over Kansas erupted in 1854, a more purely "political" issue returned slavery debate to the purview of southern men. The nationalist dynamic seen in female responses to Sutherland and Stowe was not easily transferred to disturbances over the territories, which were shaped almost entirely by domestic currents.[21]

Another opportunity for southern women's proslavery nationalism had already begun to emerge, however, in the patriotic campaign to preserve George Washington's homestead. The trajectory of the "Mount Vernon campaign" – which moved from sectional imperative to Unionist crusade – involved a wider swathe of southern masters than any other Washington-related project of the 1850s. Julia Tyler, Mary Jones, and dozens of other plantation women took the lead in spurring the action of some 75,000 Americans – most of whom had some tie to the slave South. These women's pioneer effort in historical preservation involved both a disproportionately southern constituency and a recognizably southern program of making an estate managed by black "servants" into

[20] Quotation from [J.R. Thompson], "Uncle Tom's Cabin," *SLM* 18 (October 1852), 630; Joy Jordan-Lake, *Whitewashing Uncle Tom's Cabin: Nineteenth-Century Women Novelists Respond to Stowe* (Nashville, TN: Vanderbilt University Press, 2005); Sarah Meer, *Uncle Tom Mania: Slavery, Minstrelsy, and Transatlantic Culture in the 1850s* (Athens, GA: University of Georgia Press, 2005); McCord "The Enfranchisement of Women" *SQR* 21 (April 1852), 322–41; idem, "Woman and her Needs" *DBR* 13 (September 1852), 267–91. These two pieces are reprinted in Richard S. Lounsbury, *Louisa S. McCord: Political and Social Essays* (Charlottesville: University Press of Virginia, 1995), as are her "Uncle Tom's Cabin," "British Philanthropy and American Slavery," "Charity Which Does Not Begin at Home"; and "Letter to the Duchess of Sutherland." The same transatlantic perspective prevails in "A Georgia Lady," "Southern Slavery and Its Assailants" *DBR* 16 (January 1854), 46–62; and Maria McIntosh, *Letter on the Address of the Women of England to their Sisters of America, in Relation to Slavery* (New York: T.J. Crowen, 1853).
[21] Baym, "The Myth of the Myth of Southern Womanhood" in *Hebrew University Studies in Literature and the Arts* 18 (1990), 27–47, provides a useful, if somewhat overstated, corrective to stubbornly persisting assumptions typified by Elizabeth Moss, *Domestic Novelists in the Old South; Defenders of Southern Culture* (Baton Rouge: Louisiana State University Press, 1992).

WESTERN FRONT OF MOUNT VERNON, AS IT APPEARED IN 1858.

FIGURE 6.2. Through their 1850s campaign to purchase Mount Vernon, slave-holding women established a working plantation as a site of nationalist nostalgia. *From Benson Lossing, Mount Vernon and its Associations (New York: W.A. Townsend and Co., 1859). Used with permission of Dartmouth College Library.*

a resonant national shrine.[22] As a major event in nineteenth-century cultural history, the Mount Vernon movement has attracted considerable attention, much of which has focused on the dogged organizing efforts

---

[22] Figures taken from *Mount Vernon Record, 1858–1860*. The most historically informed and scrupulously documented account of the movement comes in Patricia West, *Domesticating History: The Political Origins of America's House Museums* (Smithsonian Institution Press, 1999); the role of Virginia women is persuasively conveyed in Varon, *We Mean to Be Counted*.

of Ann Pamela Cunningham, the invalid daughter of a wealthy South
Carolina planter. What remains elusive, however, is how Southerners
from varied political perspectives jockeyed for control of the program,
how Cunningham's efforts revealed both the promise and the perils of a
bisectional conservative alliance, and how her navigation of sectionalism
and gender replicated, while it also reshaped, wider developments of
proslavery Americanism.[23]

Cunningham's shifting understanding of her constituency depended on
the basic mutability of Washington's legacy. Late in 1853, as the
controversies over Sutherland and Stowe were becoming old news,
Cunningham's "Southern Matron" appeal appeared in the fire-eating
Charleston Mercury. Using imagery laden with the vocabulary of the
Southern Rights' movement, she enlisted southern women's "warm, generous, enthusiastic hearts" to block Mount Vernon's "purchase by
Northern capital and its devotion to moneymaking purposes." Giving
new credence to a rumor that grasping Yankees would soon bid for the
estate, Cunningham put female patriots across the country on notice.
Soon enough, a group of "patriotic and generous ladies of Philadelphia"
offered to join forces, thus extending "the olive branch of sympathy and
kind feeling toward those who, all must admit, have had too much reason
to feel aggrieved by the acts and speeches of many of our Northern
representatives, and those of a large, reckless body of agitators who
are widely spread over our land." As the bitter struggles over Kansas
increased political tensions, Cunningham worked assiduously to retain
control of the effort, insisting that southerners would "move" the Vernon
cause while permitting "Sisters of the North" to only "offer aid."
The crosscurrents of Virginia politics were more important during this
early period than the infusion of sectionalism. The main objective of
Cunningham and her allies was to engineer the approval of the surprisingly prickly Washington family and to convince the Virginia state
legislature to grant two separate charters of incorporation. In 1858,
the movement had secured these necessary commitments, though it
still fell well short of its financial goals. Cunningham began in these
circumstances to write as the "American Matron," concluding that her

---

[23] David Moltke-Hansen, "Why History Mattered: The Background of Ann Pamela Cunningham's Interest in the Preservation of Mount Vernon," *Furman Studies* 26 (December 1980),
34–42.

stalled campaign proved that "Washington belonged not alone to the South!" nor to "one State alone!"[24]

The challenge of the Mount Vernon "Ladies" was to rally broad support from as many Union-minded conservatives as possible while avoiding political controversies that could derail the movement altogether. The question of who would lead and participate in the effort was fraught with tension, but so too were questions about who would ultimately manage the estate. In 1853, the antislavery representative Joshua Giddings of Ohio coyly implied that Congress might apply the Wilmot Proviso to Mount Vernon, a jab that caused Cunningham to sour on federal involvement and the prospect of turning Washington's gravesite into a "great yearly battle-ground of pro and anti-slavery antipathies." In the end, ownership passed not to any government entity but to the "Mount Vernon Ladies' Association of the Union" overseen by Cunningham and a small circle of "Vice-regents." These women used their authority to resolve even more basic representational disputes than those that had marked the Washington memorialization projects in Richmond (which resulted in Thomas Crawford's equestrian monument) and in the District of Columbia (which sought to erect a huge obelisk on the banks of the Potomac). What exactly would a "preserved" Mount Vernon become? The association ignored calls to make the grounds into a showplace for agricultural reform, a course that would almost certainly have focused attention on Washington as slaveholding wheat farmer. They showed no more interest in establishing a national cemetery there, a proposal that some hoped would result in an American version of Westminster Abbey. Washington's tomb remained a part of Mount Vernon's aura, having already become an iconic symbol of the revolutionary heritage. Yet through the work of the "Ladies," the public came to focus even more on "those green lawns and that 'modest mansion'" that had "gladdened the eye and cheered the heart of our great father" while he was still alive. Emphasizing the house (which the Association would take considerable pains to repair) and its gardens (which some suggested might be restored to their 1790s appearance) accentuated the domestic image of the first president. The movement thus offered an alternative to

---

[24] "To the Ladies of the South," *Charleston Mercury*, December 2, 1853; "To the Southern Matron," *Augusta Chronicle and Sentinel*, August 16, 1854; "To the Daughters of Washington," *SLM* 21 (May 1855), 320–1. Cunningham modified some of her 1853 letter's sharper inflections when she republished it, along with several other early documents in *An Appeal for the Future Preservation of the Home and Grave of Washington* (Philadelphia, PA: TK and PG Collins, 1855). Cunningham forthrightly detailed the tensions with the Pennsylvania women in *Proceedings of the Council of the Mount Vernon Ladies' Association Held in Washington Monday, November 19, 1866* (Baltimore, MD, 1866).

the Virginia-based militarism of the Richmond monument and to the awe-inspiring majesty of the Washington City obelisk project. A garden of tranquility and the refuge of a home worked in tandem with the Washington tomb to imbue this "American Mecca" with a distinctly sacred sense of nationalist repose and perspective.[25]

The Mount Vernon Association's search for suitable male allies threatened to disturb this image of calm and to open the project to ordinary politicking. Some of this was to be expected, since the so-called "knights" of the movement made little pretense of divorcing their patriotism from the partisan maneuvering that came with holding elected positions or planning to seek office in the future. No single party or perspective stood out among the movement's male patrons, however. In the Alabama Black Belt, Cunningham's cousin William Yancey gave the movement a distinctively fire-eating edge in his appeals to Washington as a "consecrated rebel." Though increasingly at odds with the organization's larger drift toward Unionism, Yancey worked to preserve the movement's defiantly proslavery associations. South Carolinian William D. Porter also pushed back against northern allies, rallying masters to take a special interest in "'the illustrious Southerner,' the man born on your soil and reared under the influences of the patriarchal civilization you cherish." In 1857, Porter helped elicit the largest Mount Vernon contribution to date by challenging his Charleston audience: "Be it yours to keep the whiteness of his fame!"[26]

Mount Vernon's most visible male support came not from southerners, however, but from that quintessential Massachusetts Yankee Edward Everett. After charming Cunningham personally, this former diplomat, Senator, and Harvard President ingratiated himself with the rest of the group by the simple achievement of shoring up their finances. Barely a year after he began to draw contributions through his Washington orations, Everett had convinced Susan Pellet of his unique power to "utter the 'open sesame' to the purses of the people." Pellet marveled at how

[25] Giddings speech of December 15, 1853, as reported in *CG* Thirty-third Congress, First Session, 53; "The Southern Matron's Letter to Virginia," *SLM* 21 (May 1855), 323; Cunningham, "To the Officers and Members of the Mount Vernon Ladies' Association," in *Mount Vernon Record* (November 1859). The notion of an agricultural use of the farm was discussed in *Richmond Enquirer* December 31, 1853, and January 5, 1854; among the several suggestions to emulate Westminster Abbey was Andrew H.H. Dawson, *Mt. Vernon a National Cemetery* (Savannah: EJ Purse, 1858).

[26] West, *Domesticating History,* Porter, *Semi-Centennial Address an Oration Delivered Before the Washington Light Infantry, in the South-Carolina Institute Hall, on Monday, February 23, 1857* (Charleston, VA: James and Williams, 1857), 27–8.

"his glowing words" could be "transmuted into golden tributes from North, South, East, and West, to be by patriotic pilgrims born and laid on that sacred shrine hallowed to every American heart." In the end, Everett's tours and his series in the popular *New York Ledger* accounted for more than one-third of the total purchase price of $200,000. Everett intended to accomplish "some good beyond the more immediate object" of preserving the estate, of course. In trying to rekindle the sort of nationalist conservative alliance associated with the late Daniel Webster, his Mount Vernon testimonials became a means of reassuring Southerners that at least some New Englanders were willing to seek common ground.[27]

Southern Rights' critics of the movement balked at Everett's ties to Mount Vernon, and their displeasure crested during his acrimonious reception at the Richmond Washington's Birthday celebration of 1858. Distrust of his motives persisted during his Deep South tour later that spring, forcing his Charleston host Richard Yeadon to sidestep the question of state, sectional, or national claims on Washington's legacy, and instead to plunge headlong into the politics of slavery. Yeadon used his position as editor of the *Charleston Courier* to chide "country editors" for taking swipes at Everett and urged them to recall how in 1826, the young Massachusetts Congressman had pledged to "buckle a knapsack to my back, and put a musket to my shoulder" rather than allow "any part of this fair America converted into a Continental Haiti." Reprinting the robust proslavery sentiments of this Congressional speech (which had already become a source of deep embarrassment to Everett across the North) cleared the way for Yeadon to note his soundness on other issues. Everett had taken reassuring action in support of the fugitive slave law, in his aloof response to the Kansas uproar, and in his earlier willingness to vindicate southern interests abroad.[28]

Everett's inclusion in the Vernon campaign cleared the way for further national cooperation that dominated efforts in 1858. The main challenge

[27] Susan Pellet, "Report of the Mount Vernon Association," *SLM* 25 (July, 1857), 70; Everett to Yancey, Everett Papers, MHS. For differing assessments of Everett, see George Forgie, *Patricide in the House Divided: A Psychological Interpretation of Lincoln and His Age* (New York: Oxford University Press, 1979); Paul Revere Frothingham, *Edward Everett Orator and Statesman* (Boston, MA, 1925); and Paul A. Varg, *Edward Everett: The Intellectual in the Turmoil of Politics* (Susquehanna University Press, 1992).

[28] *Charleston Courier*, April 12, 1857. Despite his public affirmations, Everett's "soundness" on slavery had been regularly questioned; see [Nathaniel Beverly Tucker], "Original Literary Notices," *SLM* 1 (February 1835), 307–12 and Abel Upshur to John C. Calhoun, November 8, 1843 in *PJCC* 17, 535.

that year lay in recruiting a core of northern women who might be as sound on the meaning of Mount Vernon as Everett had proved to be. As the Association expanded from its initial slaveholding enthusiasts into a total of twenty-nine state organizations, the issue of slavery simmered just below the surface. Cunningham tried systematically to identify in each northern state a vice-regent whose "social position would command the confidence of the State and enable her to enlist the aid of persons of the widest influence." Not surprisingly, she was loathe to include any women associated with antislavery politics, a criteria that spurred Everett to warn that "if it should get abroad, that you excluded Republicans, it would be all over with us in the nonslaveholding States." Anticipating his own stance as a vice-presidential candidate in 1860, Everett argued that "the only ground on which we can stand is that of rising above the party questions of the day." By invoking "sound Constitutional principles and interests," regardless of partisan affiliations, the group could "carry as large a portion of the population with us as possible in this great act of filial duty to the memory of the Father of his Country." Yet divisive issues could no more be excluded from this patriotic project that they could from politics. Cunningham learned this when a group of otherwise friendly supporters in New England lobbied for an exclusive use of free white labor at Mount Vernon once "national" possession of the shrine was complete.[29]

Such internal conflicts were largely confined to discussions within the organization, however. The Association's public image – which was burnished through a sophisticated publishing campaign and by successful marketing of every conceivable sort of Mount Vernon memento – positioned slaveholding women and their allies as patriots while marginalizing their detractors as bitter malcontents. Everett's stated goal was to "soften the asperity of sectional feeling, by holding up to the admiration of all parts of the country, that great exemplar which all alike respect and love." Proslavery partisans realized that doing so would force the North to acknowledge that their common country had been led to its independence by "an accursed slaveholder." The Rev. C.W. Howard of Georgia signaled the implications of Washington's status as master when he explained that Yankees could not "malign their brethren of the South, without in one in the same breath, parricides as they are, reviling the memory of the illustrious dead."

---

[29] The process of expanding to the free states is chronicled in the Mount Vernon *Record*. Cunningham to Horace Mann, September 3, 1858, and Everett to Cunningham, December 9, 1858, Everett Papers; letters from Mrs. C.A. Hopkinson and Mary Goodrich as quoted in West, *Domesticating History*, 29.

The Mount Vernon campaign's success in relocating the responsibility for sectionalism away from the South resonated with friendly foreign observers. By the fall of 1858, a Liverpool newspaper could hold up the relatively tepid free-state response to the Mount Vernon campaign as evidence of lagging Yankee patriotism. "Great as is the general reverence for Washington's memory" among Northerners, this paper reported that "the detestation of the south is still greater."[30]

Unlike even the most effective responses to Sutherland, the proslavery nationalism of the Mount Vernon enterprise based its appeal on the power of images and aura rather than words and arguments. It relied upon what the Rev. Howard termed "solemn eloquence, voiceless yet ceaseless as the flow of the Potomac" as the path toward sectional accord. The peace it sought to foster thus could be achieved by quieting "those insane men, who with worse than Ephesian fury, under cover of liberty, would fire the temple of liberty." Such an approach allowed slaveholding women to act within prevailing gender conventions, as they used their sense of matronly responsibility to quiet what Louisa McCord had termed the "noisy tongues" of "wordy boisterous debate" produced by *Uncle Tom's Cabin*. Charles Jones knew that it would diminish the moment to spell out exactly what was so special about the Mount Vernon chestnuts he melodramatically sent to his mother early in 1861. He showed what the native Georgia writer Maria McIntosh had predicted back in 1853, when she wrote how women might "close our ears to every voice which would introduced hatred and unholy rivalry in our hearts" and thus prepare the way for "the world's restoration to more than Eden's joys."[31]

Yet if the Mount Vernon women worked to quiet the conservation, they did not shield plantations from public view or remove slaves from the American imagination. On the contrary, the movement's primary effect lay in helping white Americans to visualize an archetypal southern household that was far more exalted than those so strikingly portrayed in antislavery fiction. As both proslavery friends and abolitionist enemies of the movement appreciated, attempts to ennoble the "domestic life of the Great

[30] Everett, *Orations and Speeches on Various Occasions* (Boston, MA: Little Brown, and Co., 1870), 3: 623; C. E. Howard, quoted in "Editor's Table," *SLM* 27 (September 1858), 231–2.; *Liverpool Post* quoted in *Charleston Courier*, October 15, 1858.
[31] Howard, in "Editor's Table," McCord, "Woman's Progress," *SLM* 19 (November 1853), 700; Maria McIntosh, *A Letter on the Address of the Women of England to their Sisters of America in Relation to Slavery* (n.p. 1853). The "silencing" both built upon gender conventions and rolled back the politicization of slavery's "aural landscapes" by the Grimke sisters, as explained in Mark Smith, *Listening to Nineteenth Century America* (Chapel Hill: University of North Carolina Press, 2001).

Chieftain" almost inevitably put bondage in a favorable context. Long before Cunningham's involvement, visitors to the estate had been welcomed by black slaves, who had, with little fanfare, ushered visitors around its sacred precincts. Though they had little choice in taking on this role of loyal retainers, Mount Vernon's multigenerational black community put actual black faces on the pretenses of proslavery paternalism and thus powerfully underlined southern claims that shared domestic settings allowed masters to glean "the nature of this negro people." Louisa McCord's 1853 response to the Duchess of Sutherland rested on this sense of personal experience. "With grey hairs beginning to cluster around my brow, I am still cheerfully served by many of the same faithful negroes who watched with hope my tottering baby steps; their children labor for me, and their grand children are cherished and reared by me." White Americans who claimed Washington as a national inheritance might feel something of the same in being greeted by African-Americans at a restored Mount Vernon.[32]

Presenting plantations in a more positive light was only part of the Mount Vernon movement's cultural legacy. At least as significant was its validation of female patriotic organizing, which proved that women could work as an independent force and offer a distinctive vision of national unity amidst a crisis. At its outset, a tone of apology prevailed among the movement's backers, who cautiously explained how "wherever there is a pure sentiment, there is woman's sphere." In 1854, an anonymous writer for the *Mobile Tribune* warned that any men who condemned female involvement in the patriotic crusade deserved "to die where there is no power of women to provide to men 'the gentle voice to soothe his passing moments.'" Five years later, in announcing the final payment to the Washington family, Cunningham showed a new spirit of confidence. "In the deep gloom now overspreading our political horizon, this noble sisterhood of the Mount Vernon Association stands as the chief 'beacon light' of the world," she cheered. Within a matter of months, lamentations returned, and conflicted women like Mary Jones found themselves turning instinctively to Mount Vernon paraphernalia as they said their goodbyes to the Union.[33]

---

[32] Quoted in West, *Domesticating History*; [McCord], "A Letter to the Duchess of Sutherland from a Lady of South Carolina," *Charleston Mercury*, August 10, 1853. The prevalence of African-Americans at Mount Vernon is established in Jean B. Lee, "Historical Memory, Sectional Strife and the American Mecca: Mount Vernon, 1783–1853," *VMHB* 109 (2000), 255–300; and is noted in Theresa Pulszky, *White, Red, Black: Sketches of American Society in the United States* (New York: Redfield, 1853), 132.

[33] *Mobile Tribune* March 8, 1854, quoted in *An Appeal for the Future Preservation*, 20–1; Cunningham, "To the officers and members," *Mount Vernon Record*, November, 1859.

The Vernon movement thus included both slavery and slaveholding women in a nationalist frame of harmony. Its effectiveness in doing so with the fewest words possible was lamented by northern critics, who bemoaned the conservative co-opting – and silencing – of Washington the man. A few months before being assaulted on the Senate floor, Charles Sumner insisted that any tribute to Washington must set the first president's Unionist professions aside his expressed aversion to slavery. To do otherwise would be as much of a "barren spectacle" as staging "the play of Othello without the part of Othello." In his 1860 tour of the east, Illinois Republican Abraham Lincoln made a similar point, though he used less provocative imagery to do so. Lincoln seemed to appreciate how beguiled many in his Cooper Institute audience had been by the "invocations to Washington" expressed in a powerfully patriotic register. But the Republican Party's rising star warned New Yorkers to be on alert for those who made political capital – and who compromised the nation's ideas – by "imploring men to unsay what Washington said, and undo what Washington did."[34]

PARTISAN NATIONALISMS AND THE PERIL OF NORTHERN UNITY

Three months after women from across the Union took control of Mount Vernon, a writer in *De Bow's* cast a critical eye on the worth of largely symbolic patriotic displays. The "mass meetings, patriotic resolutions, and conservative speeches" presented by men like Edward Everett were not objectionable in their own right. But they mattered little if such support could not "meet Black-republicanism at the polls and there manifest its actual strength." With a presidential election already underway, the times seemed ripe for an ultimatum. "If our Northern allies shall there prove their ability to rebuke and crush the lawless spirit of sectionalism, Southern men will be enabled to rest in quiet, confident that their rights will be preserved and protected." The triumph of "fanaticism" through the electoral process would convey a different lesson. Southerners would learn that "Northern friends, being unable to protect us, we must needs protect ourselves."[35]

---

[34] Sumner, "The Example of Washington Against Slavery Not to Be Forgotten Now: Letter to a Committee of the Boston Mercantile Library Association, February 19, 1856," in *Collected Works* (Boston: Lee and Shepard, 1875), 95–6; Lincoln, "Address at Cooper Institute," in *LSW*, 130.
[35] "The Conservative Men and the Union Meetings of the North," *DBR* 28 (May 1860), 514–23. See also [Randall Lee Gibson], "Our Federal Union," *DBR* 29 (July 1860), 38.

As this writer clarified, the ultimate test of free-state allies came not in shared nationalist endeavors but in the quest for working control of the federal government. Northern political muscle could bolster Southern Rights through a party system that had, despite the misgivings of Calhoun and others, successfully contained nearly every antislavery initiative that had arisen at the federal level. The rival partisan expressions of American nationhood that emerged in the 1850s would test this formula, suggesting both the possibilities and the limits of seeking to place slavery upon an unassailably national platform. While the majority of free-state voters joined a coalition based on containing the "slave power's" territorial expansion, Republicans would fall short of a national governing majority until late in 1860. Champions of slavery were ambivalent through these years, unsure whether they should relish the successes provided by northern alliances or prepare for what might happen if a starkly different future ever came to pass.[36]

Hovering over partisan maneuverings of the 1850s were disagreements about the implications of the Union-saving compromises that began that decade. Deep South voters reconciled themselves to California's admission as a free state only after extracting mutual commitments to slavery within the South. This Unionism was contingent upon prompt enforcement of a draconian Fugitive Slave Law and the cessation of free-soil efforts to impede slavery's further territorial expansion. Those who pledged their parties and their sections to the "finality" of the compromise helped to restore some semblance of order to the partisan system. By the presidential election cycle of 1852, the "Union" and "Southern Rights" parties that had made the Deep South elections a referendum on the compromise vanished, to be replaced by more familiar political alliances. Nationally-based Whigs and Democrats sought voters in every state of the Union during that year's election. To critics, such a reunion implied a deep partisan complicity in allowing masters to "nationalize" a system that had earlier been nothing more than a "local institution, existing only in a portion of the States."[37]

Beneath the surface, the rival presidential tickets of Winfield Scott and Franklin Pierce showed signs that slavery's purported "nationalization"

---

[36] Calhoun's warnings about parties during the 1830s continued to resonate in "Publicola," "The Present Aspect of Abolition," *SLM* 13 (July 1847), 429–36; Sydenham Moore, "The Irrepressible Conflict and the Impending Crisis," *DBR* 28 (May 1860), 531–51. Proslavery domination of the party system can be followed in Leonard Richards, *The Slave Power: The Free North and Southern Domination, 1780–1860* (Baton Rouge, 2000).

[37] Potter, *The Impending Crisis*, 121–41; Giddings, *Baltimore Platforms: Slavery Question* (Washington: 1852), 6.

might yet produce fissures, however. After the southern Whigs failed to secure Winfield Scott's explicit endorsement of the Fugitive Slave Law, many withheld their support and began to plan for a restoration of Millard Fillmore to the White House in 1856. Northern Democrats proved to be stronger allies, generally supporting a Fugitive Slave law that could be understood, in its restoration of blacks to their southern masters, as a reaffirmation of the white supremacist strain of Jacksonian racialism. Factionalism within the Democratic Party resulted less from slavery politics than from the decision of President-elect Pierce to dole out high-level appointments to party members with fundamental differences about the future of slavery and the legitimacy of secession. Critics such as Sam Houston of Texas were quick to note how a party filled with secessionists, free soilers, and conservatives alike had thus acquired "more wings than the beast of Revelations."[38]

A toxic mix of northern Democratic factionalism and southern Whig defensiveness about their proslavery "soundness" each contributed to the political catastrophe of the 1854 Kansas–Nebraska Act. This measure, which voided the 1820 restriction of slavery from most of the Louisiana Purchase, rescrambled northern politics even more decisively than Winfield Scott's wavering over the Fugitive Slave Law had spurred a southern realignment of the Whig Party. Proponents of "popular sovereignty" argued that they simply applied a new formula tacitly established by the 1850 Compromise (and which logically flowed from free-soil refusal to run the "1820 line" through the Mexican Cession all the way to the Pacific). In standing for reelection, northern supporters of Kansas popular sovereignty learned how controversial their departure from earlier compromises could be. Hardest hit was the free-state delegation of House Democrats, which dwindled from a contingent of ninety three in 1854 to only twenty two in the succeeding Congress.[39]

The damage inflicted on the Democratic Party's free-state wing might have inspired a resurgence of Whiggery had not the makings of a new conservative alliance already begun in the guise of "Know-Nothingism." This manifestation of political nativism had swept across American cities in 1853 and 1854, propelled by an influx of Catholic immigrants from Ireland

[38] Houston, "Speech at Austin Mass Meeting, 1855," 227; Michael Holt, *The Rise and Fall of the American Whig Party: Jacksonian Politics and the Onset of the Civil War* (New York: Oxford University Press, 1999), 726–37; John Ashworth, *Slavery, Capitalism, and Politics in the Antebellum Republic Volume 2: The Coming of the Civil War* (New York: Cambridge University Press, 2008), 339–470.

[39] Richards, *The Slave Power*, 190–7.

and Germany. Duff Green, whose proslavery Anglophobia had informed the antiabolitionism of the 1830s and the Texas annexation crisis of 1844, publicly speculated how this new organization might be perfectly situated to "allay sectional feeling" in even more dangerous circumstances. Green's idea was to build up a new patriotic party devoted to counteracting "British intrigue" which he considered "the most potent and active element of the abolition movement." At the core of his message was the conviction that "the best way to put down one excitement is to get up a stronger," a perspective shared by others who hoped to overcome anti-Kansas furor by stoking fears of immigrant newcomers or of British outsiders. Concluding that it was foolish to "surrender that organization with the power and influence which 'philosophy,' 'true religion,' and 'patriotism' must give, into the hands of northern fanaticism," Green insisted that "instead of wasting our energies in a fruitless war upon the American party, it is much better to unite in the movement, and give it a right direction."[40]

Green's injection of British abolitionism into the nativist repertoire hit an odd note, especially in neglecting to appreciate how Irish-American had already mixed stalwart partisan loyalties and deep-rooted hostility to Anglo-American reform within the Democratic Party. Green was more sensible in reporting how "those who trade in politics hate a minority as nature hates a vacuum." As he realized, white rural Southerners might become part of a new nativist majority even if they did not regularly encounter Catholic immigrants. The effectiveness of conjuring up distant enemies had a precedent in the success of those northern racists who had fixated on the menace of faraway African-Americans. Nativist concerns about Catholic influence had an indigenous base of support among prominent proslavery evangelicals, who had long fretted about "papist" inroads. One route for a conservative party in the South to revive itself would be to combine Protestant pride with the visceral xenophobia of this period of American expansiveness and then link both of these tendencies to escalating qualms about majoritarian excess. The Alabama lawyer Samuel Rice showed how antiabolitionism could be turned toward a new indictment of immigrants, whom he warned would soon "increase the social evil, and tend to establish the ascendancy of the lawless and fanatical" across the country. Allowing the

---

[40] Duff Green to Robert Hunter, *American Organ*, February 28, 1855; William Darrell Overdyke, *The Know-Nothing Party in the South* (Baton Rouge: Louisiana State University Press, 1950) has been supplemented by John David Bladek, "America for Americans: The Southern Know Nothing Party and the Politics of Nativism, 1854–1856" (PhD dissertation, University of Washington, 1998).

flow of impoverished Europeans to continue would "bring no good to any portion of the people of the Union," Rice pointed out, "except to those who are willing to participate in the scheme of the Abolition party and acquire rewards or greatness by the ruin of the country."[41]

Beginning in the late fall of 1854, Southern-leaning operatives in the American Party worked to transform what had begun as a grassroots upsurge in the nation's commercial cities into an organization capable of contesting the presidency. Several strategists aimed to move "Americanism" beyond its urban base by reassembling the coalition of Middle States conservatives and southern slaveholders that in 1851 had rallied to Millard Fillmore's vindication of the Compromise measures. This "law and order" strategy sought to maximize its chances of success by scoring a victory in the decisive Virginia campaign of 1855. Even without a large urban population, the state seemed well positioned for such a realignment. Late in 1854, a prominent Richmond lawyer hailed Know-Nothingism as "one of the most important political and social movements of the day," as he informed readers of the *Southern Literary Messenger* how "viewless as the wind," the secret party had "swept before it every obstacle that grappled with its strength, and has lain prostrate in its path alike the oldest and best established political organizations and mushrooms of the hour."[42]

Though voter turnout soared to historic levels in Virginia in the spring of 1855, the firebrand campaign of Democrat Henry Wise narrowly beat back an unexpectedly lackluster American Party ticket. This setback was the worst part of a bad year for those who had hoped to establish the new American Party's soundness on slavery. The New York party's willingness to endorse William Seward's reelection in February of that year to the Senate weighed down Know-Nothingism at least as much as Winfield Scott's nomination had damaged the Whigs in 1852. The Virginia editor William Burwell responded by pledging the party to an unequivocally proslavery position, a strategy that failed to overcome widespread Deep South skepticism about the Party's northern flank. The worst blow of all came when free-soiler Nathaniel Banks of Massachusetts was elected Speaker of the House early in 1856, in large part

---

[41] James Henley Thornwell, *The Arguments of Romanism From the Infallibility of the Church* (New York: Leavitt, Trow, 1845); Robert Breckenridge, *Papism in the United States in the Nineteenth Century* (Baltimore: D. Owen, 1841); William G. Brownlow, *Americanism Contrasted With Foreignism, Romanism and Bogus Democracy, in the Light of Reason* (Nashville, TN, 1856). Samuel F. Rice, *Americanism and Southern Rights: An Address* (Montgomery: Barrett and Wimbish, 1855), 4–6.

[42] Alexander Hamilton Sands, "A Calm Discussion of the Know Nothing Question," *SLM* 20 (September 1854), 540–3.

because of the unwillingness of southern Americans to support any representative of the Democratic Party. Albert Pike, the most prominent Arkansas nativist, mourned how such developments proved that "no such thing as a national party can any longer exist." "If one is formed, or seems to continue, the league between its members will be a mere hollow truce," he complained, adding that the "slavery question shatters all parties in turn; and each, as it dissolves, swells the ranks of the Republican party with new recruits; while its leaders daily increase in boldness, and more industriously throw up their earthworks, and plant their batteries against the ramparts of the Union."[43]

Among the unintended consequences of the American Party's brief ascendancy was a proliferation of nationalist rhetoric among proslavery Democrats. Henry Wise's barnstorming campaign set the tone by affirming Jeffersonian liberalism as an alternative to the secretive exclusivity of the nativists. Fire-eaters like William L. Yancey joined regular Democrats in attacking the Know-Nothings, observing that "nothing can be more anti-American, more European, more in accordance with kingcraft and despotism, more analogous to the secret and fearful tribunals of the Inquisition" than the religious test established by the new party. Such a message would become the party doctrine during the 1856 quest for the presidency and in the run-up to the next election season. In 1857, Gideon Pillow of Tennessee proudly explained how "the Democrat party stands now, where it has always stood, upon the Constitution, as embodying the rights of all classes of citizens." The future Confederate general concluded that latter-day Jacksonians formed "the only true American party – while the party assuming that name, occupies anti-American ground."[44]

Once Democrat James Buchanan assumed the presidency and backed the Supreme Court's Dred Scott decision, gauzy Union-saving appeals gave way to new northern concerns about slavery's imminent "nationalization." In denying Congressional power to legislate slavery in the territories, the Supreme Court elevated the absolutist position of John C. Calhoun to the status of constitutional law. Such a stunning coup prompted as much southern gloating as Republican Party outrage. Henry W. Hilliard, a "Clay Whig" of Alabama who had aligned himself with the Democrats, noted that "the position of the South in the Confederacy is

---

[43] Bladek, "America for Americans"; [Albert Pike], *Letters to the People of the Northern States* (n.p. 1856), 4–6.

[44] Wise letter to *Richmond Enquirer*, February 2, 1854; John Witherspoon DuBose, *The Life and Times of William Lowndes Yancey* (Birmingham: Roberts and Son, 1892), 296; *Letter from Gen. Gideon J. Pillow on the Politics of the Day: Addressed to a Committee of Democrats or Lawrence County* (Nashville,TN: G.C. Torbett, 1857), 3–7.

better than it has been for thirty years." Thomas Clingman, another recent convert to conservative "Buchananism," likewise informed slaveholding constituents that "for the first time since 1820, you and your institutions have, in all respects, the same recognition and the same rights under the Federal Government as those of any section of the Union." Congressional muscle lent substance to these boasts, as Democrats in 1857 replaced Banks of Massachusetts with a new House speaker from South Carolina.[45]

A Buchanan administration identified with slavery's constitutional triumph held enormous appeal for many former southern Whigs. Among the most prominent in a wave of party-switchers were Robert Toombs and Alexander Stephens of Georgia and Judah Benjamin of Louisiana. South Carolinian Benjamin Perry greeted such recruits as the consummation of John C. Calhoun's "great wish" to "see the South united and at the head of the Government, with enough of the Northern states to give her the power to carry on its operations." Early in 1857, Perry saw how the strategy of southern unity had been "realized to the fullest extent" by a Democratic Party that had won an extraordinary 56 percent of the slave-state vote in the presidential election. With such strength, victory could be assured by even the thinnest of majorities in Pennsylvania, New Jersey, Indiana, and Illinois. In speculating how such a pattern might continue indefinitely, Perry charged that "if the past unrivalled growth, prosperity, power, wealth, and grandeur of the American republic is not enough to satisfy us as to the future, nothing can."[46]

The presidential election of 1860 would feature growing Republican Party strength in the free states, however, just as it placed even more choices than usual before alarmed southern voters. Of the three candidates running against the Republican nominee that year, none would break 45 percent of the slave-state vote. In a more successful replay of their 1855 proslavery feint, former Deep South Whigs stayed competitive by bolstering their proslavery credentials. Their insistence that the Dred Scott decision required a territorial slave code provided a proslavery subtext to the "Constitution, the Union and the Laws" campaign of Tennessee planter John Bell and Edward Everett of Mount Vernon fame. On election day, this ticket ran nearly as strongly in the wealthy plantation districts of

[45] William W. Freehling, *The Road to Disunion* 2: 109–22; Hilliard, *Letter on the Political Issues of the Day* (Montgomery: Confederation Book and Job Office, 1858), 7; Clingman, *Valedictory Address to the Freemen of the Eighth Congressional District* (n.p., 1858).
[46] Lillian Adele Kibler, *Benjamin F. Perry: South Carolina Unionist* (Durham, NC: Duke University Press, 1947), 287.

the Cotton Kingdom as it did in those upper south states of Kentucky, Tennessee, and Virginia, the three states that the Constitutional Unionists carried outright.[47]

Meanwhile, proslavery dissatisfaction with Stephen A. Douglas put two rival Democratic tickets before southern voters. Douglas had begun 1858 by railing against what he saw as a proslavery version of "higher law" at work in Kansas. In a sharp break with Buchanan and his proslavery allies, Douglas championed local jurisdiction as an alternative to the insidious attempt of the Lecompton Constitution to "nationalize" bondage. Cool to the implications of the Supreme Court decision in Dred Scott, Douglass blasted southern demands that slavery be treated as a "national and not local" institution that would go "everywhere under the Constitution of the United States and yet is higher than the Constitution." His position preserved his standing in the North while it pushed proslavery critics of "squatter sovereignty" to work on behalf of Buchanan Vice President John C. Breckinridge, who would run as a "Southern Rights Democrat" against Douglas' "national Democrat" candidacy.[48]

The three candidates who sought southern votes sketched quite similar paths to victory. If Bell gestured toward New England in his choice of Everett, his private strategizing calculated that a win depended on his sweep of all the slave states and the addition of at least a few protariff states such as Pennsylvania. John C. Breckinridge put his hopes on uniting the slave states behind his more forthright candidacy while using the Buchanan machine to rally cotton-friendly conservatives of New York. Douglas worked on a similar version of this map, though in reverse. He would make sure to hold the slim northwestern component of the Buchanan coalition while swinging the South as a unit back to the wisdom of his "nonintervention" program. His supporters made much of the notion that the Northwestern states offered "the only alliance between the South and any part of the North which is likely to be permanent, apart from mere government connections."[49]

[47] *Senator Benjamin H. Hill of Georgia: His Life, Speeches and Writings* (Atlanta, GA: H.C. Hudgins, 1891), 229–37; John V. Mering, "The Slave-State Constitutional Unionists and the Politics of Consensus," *JSH* 43 (August 1977), 395–410.

[48] *Speech of Senator Douglas of Illinois against the Admission of Kansas under the Lecompton Constitution: Delivered in the Senate of the United States, March 22, 1858* (Washington, D.C., 1858), 6, 25–6.

[49] Bell to Boteler, in Boteler Papers, Duke University; Charles W. Russell to R.M.T. Hunter, May 13, 1860, in C.H. Ambler, "Correspondence of R.M.T. Hunter, 1826–1876," *Report of American Historical Association* (Washington, D.C., 1918), 324.

In the end, there was little that slave-state politicos could do about the constrained electoral geography of the 1860 campaign. The changing map of American politics resulted less from those candidates friendly to slavery than from powerful forces at work within the North, which were especially evident in the upper tier of New England states and across the Great Lakes region. Jefferson Davis might make a rousing appeal to the Democratic voters of Maine, as he did during the summer of 1858. Stephen Douglas might make a plea to Minnesotans to follow his lead in assuring the continued strength of a Jacksonian alliance. And Edward Everett might convey, by his very presence, the sense that proper Boston was still committed to the property rights of southern slaveholders. But a different story was evident when one shifted from the top echelon of leaders to more popular demonstrations across a North intent on asserting its own vision of the future. The enthusiastic response given by New England towns to John Brown's raid spoke volumes, as did the hostility of Chicagoans to "slave catchers" and Wisconsin's challenge to the Fugitive Slave Law's constitutionality in the case of *Ableman v. Booth*. Each testified to Republican success in consolidating the political program of the North.[50]

Even the most politically cautious slaveholders appreciated the danger that such trends would bring. Most realized that current circumstances could not be blamed on scheming abolitionists or meddlesome foreigners. Their future within a Union that had increasingly catered to their interests was imperiled by what one proslavery observer called "a dominant and most formidable sectional party combination, formed and organized for the sole purpose of waging a ferocious, savage, and relentless war against the South and the Constitution." The Republican pledge merely to break the South's lock on power seemed to betray a deeper design which in the end would "subvert her institutions – dissolve her society – deprive her of her property, and all her constitutional rights." In Republican victory would come not simply a shift in national power, but a destruction of proslavery political capital that had been decades in the making.[51]

---

[50] *Speeches of the Hon. Jefferson Davis of Mississippi Delivered During the Summer of 1858* (Baltimore, MD, 1859). Potter, *Impending Cirisis*, 294–5, 378–80.
[51] "American Slavery in 1857," *SLM* 25 (August 1857), 94.

PART THREE

CONFEDERATE NATIONHOOD AND
THE REVOLUTIONS OF WAR

W ar has converted all of the citizens of each of the Confederacies into
aliens and enemies. It has disrupted all church connections and all
charitable associations, not previously broken up. It puts an end to inter-
marriages and traveling into the separate nations. It breaks up all private
correspondence and friendship. It creates separate systems of municipal laws
and all the usages, legal, political, and pecuniary, become distinct and divergent. It individualizes the blood and race of each branch. It sifts the people of
the two nations, and has driven or will drive Northern men, with Southern
ideas and Southern proclivities to the South, where they properly belong.
It has driven or will drive all men in the South, having Northern ideas
and proclivities to the North, where they properly belong. The war is thus
making the whole people in the South homogeneous and the people in the
North homogenous.

"The Northern and Southern Confederacies"
Nashville Union and American, July 11, 1861

You are not merely Southern heroes, but American heroes; and as in the
olden time, the Ark was removed from the Tabernacle into the temples,
so, by your agency, if faithfully executed, the true ark of American freedom
will pass from the temporary tabernacle which it occupied, and find a
permanent resting place in that temple of which you are called to be the
architects.

"Cincinnatus", *Address of the Atlanta Register to the People of the Confederate
States*, 1864

At certain periods ... [God] causes the whole nation to pass into the furnace, melts it down, and pours it into new moulds of thought and character. Do we not behold something of that sort now among ourselves?

Rev. Richard Hooker Wilmer, *Future Good: The Explanation of Present Reverses*, 1864.

7

The Anatomy of Confederate Nationhood

In a single day of balloting late in 1860, proslavery separatism ceased to be a marginal idea and became a mainstream solution to the greatest crisis in the history of the American South. More than any other event since the American Revolution, the election of Abraham Lincoln changed all earlier calculations and recast all imagined futures. Most importantly, this shift in power effectively ended the prospects for achieving proslavery Americanism within the federal Union. As masters stood on the brink of a new world, even advocates of compromise admitted that the slaveholding South would soon be "not only without power, but without influence in the government."[1]

The most committed radicals appreciated that aftershocks of this electoral earthquake could sway many slaveholders who had earlier opposed severing ties with the Union. Through six months of uncertainty, the efforts of such fire-eating activists assured that eleven slave states would withdraw from the United States and join together in creating a new slaveholding Confederacy, which would start to equip itself for war. Masters who had long reconciled bondage with republicanism clung to the mantel of Americanism across this divide. War injected new energy in their condemnation of Yankee betrayal and their claims that they alone could maintain previously shared ideas and commitments.

Each step in the formation of Confederate nationhood was taken deliberately, albeit with little coordination. Those who lived through the dizzying half year that followed Lincoln's election often noted the sense of being overtaken by mysterious forces that remolded destinies and redrew boundaries. Shortly before South Carolina declared its independence, the

---

[1] Archibald Roane, "A Plan of Present Pacification, or, a Basis for the Reconstruction of the Union, If It Be Dissolved," *DBR* 30 (January 1861), 105.

Rev. William Prentiss noted with awe how Charlestonians stood "between the hearse and the cradle, touching as we do the shroud and the swaddling bands of national death and national infancy." A few months later, Gertrude Clanton Thomas recorded the bracing sensation of being "in the midst of what all of us have read of – thought of – and dreamed of before, but never realized." An anonymous writer in the *Southern Literary Messenger* marveled about the sacred process through which nations were "not made, but born." This writer concluded that "treaties, leagues, constitutions" mattered little in shaping new national governments, which were best understood as creatures "of nature and of God."[2]

Participants found comfort in the notion that the new Confederate nation was a gift from on high or the result of a mystical awakening. Such rhetoric obscured how the most calculating nationalists guided events through the secession crisis and then across the four difficult years of war that followed. A fairly compact group of proslavery nationalists maneuvered amidst the whirl of change and acted in concert with an upsurge of popular patriotic verse, ritual, and worship. An interplay of bold political initiatives and emotionally powerful cultural expressions helped to structure the new republic's arrangement of powers, to launch a debate over the country's territorial limits, and, most importantly, to establish the religious framework in which supporters understood the Confederacy's struggle for existence. Ever-mounting battlefield casualties injected a sacred dimension into a bid for nationhood that would mark the last American defense of bondage.[3]

Those who formed the proslavery republic of 1861 shared many concerns with the Federal Union's founders who had gathered in Philadelphia three-quarters of a century earlier. Slaveholders' quest for security within a hostile world had been made all the more urgent by a successive wave of New World emancipations. The growing expanse of "free soil" in the Americas isolated southern whites from potential allies at the same time that successive emancipations showed how easily antagonistic authorities could undermine slaveholding regimes. As the Mississippi lawyer

---

[2] Rev. William O. Prentiss, *A Sermon Preached at St. Peter's Church, Charleston and Repeated on Sunday, and at Meeting of Legislature* (Charleston, SC: Evans and Cogswell, 1860), 3; Virginia I. Burr, ed., *The Secret Eye: The Journal of Ella Gertrude Clanton Thomas, 1848–1889* (Chapel Hill: University of North Carolina Press, 1990), 185; "Disfederation of the States," *SLM* 32 (February 1861), 119.

[3] Drew Gilpin Faust, *The Creation of Confederate Nationalism: Ideology and Identity in the Civil War South* (Baton Rouge: Louisiana State University Press, 1988); Gary Gallagher, *The Confederate War* (Cambridge, MA: Harvard University Press, 1997) offer two particularly influential introductions to this process.

Thomas J. Wharton put it, recent history proved that "slavery, of all property in the world, most needs the protection of a friendly government." His audience of Tennessee delegates need only to have imagined the fate of Saint Domingue or of Jamaica to grasp his warning: "as well commit the lamb to the protection of the wolf, as slavery to the protection of a Government hostile to it."[4]

The dire prospects faced by slaveholders in a Republican-governed nation convinced many Deep South Unionists to back a separatist program they had long opposed. The Rev. James Henley Thornwell led the way, presenting Republican victory as "nothing more nor less than a proposition to the South to consent to a Government, fundamentally different on the question of slavery, from that which our fathers established." Thornwell urged southern Christians to understand "that the Constitution, in its relations to slavery, has been virtually repealed" and he predicted that within a matter of months the federal government would assume "a new and dangerous attitude upon this subject" as it formulated "new terms of union submitted to our acceptance or rejection." With an election guaranteed to instigate radical change, the time had come to preempt disaster with a counterrevolutionary strike for separation.[5]

The change in heart of Deep South Unionists allowed fire-eaters to intensify the crisis and to translate an intricate reordering of loyalties into new political realities. To accelerate the tempo, radical spokespersons demanded that individual states take action before Lincoln assumed office. On Christmas day, a Georgia newspaper proclaimed how membership in the Union should be relinquished "before a fanatic has been placed in command of the army and navy of the United States." While the Lower South heeded this call, uncertainty still prevailed in Virginia, the largest of all the slave states. On the first day of Lincoln's presidency, the *Richmond Examiner* noted how "we stand today between two worlds. Here a past ends, here a future begins." The paper realized that its own vision of separate southern nationhood was being stymied by Unionists who were as committed to slavery as radicals were. Virginia clergymen like Robert L. Dabney clung to the Union long after their Deep South counterparts had given up hope.

---

[4] Wharton address to the Tennessee legislature in *Journal of the House of Representatives of the State of Mississippi* (Jackson: E. Barksdale, 1861), 55.

[5] Rev. James Henley Thornwell, *The State of the Country: An Article Republished from the Southern Presbyterian Review* (Columbia, GA: Southern Guardian Steam Press, 1860), 26. James M. McPherson has influentially developed the notion of the Confederacy's "preemptive counterrevolution" in *Battle Cry of Freedom: The Civil War Era* (New York: Oxford University Press, 1989), 245.

In their view, bondage might still be safeguarded with another round of compromises within the framework of a continental United States.[6]

The process of federal dissolution that began with Lincoln's election culminated with his first major decision as commander-in-chief. In mid-April, in the wake of the Confederates' prolonged assault on Fort Sumter, Lincoln called upon state governors to provide him with 75,000 troops. This turn toward war sparked a second wave of state secession, which would more than double the white population of the new Confederate republic. As the prospect of invasion grew imminent, most border-state clergy closed ranks with proslavery evangelicals in the cotton South. Military leaders from the border states (and especially from Virginia) also rallied to the cause of what was popularly understood as a defensive struggle. Mexican War veterans like Robert E. Lee and Thomas J. Jackson came late to the cause, but these men would be enormously important to the articulation of Confederate purpose, especially once the capital of the new republic was relocated from Montgomery to Richmond, thus assuring that Virginia would be a major theater of military operations.

This rapid course of events gave die-hard secessionists grounds for satisfaction. As they appreciated, Lincoln had done more to unite the South over the course of several months than they had managed through far more considerable efforts over a span of decades. Yet there was a more ominous fact about this new Republican presidency that few Confederates bothered to note. From the federal city established in 1800, Lincoln would perfect what he took to be the principles of Thomas Jefferson and would do so under the auspices of a state vastly more powerful than foreseen by Alexander Hamilton. Augmenting the already considerable resources of the federal government would depend on shaping the energies of those same white northern citizens who had shown themselves willing to tolerate slavery within the South throughout the 1850s. At the same time that wartime developments injected new intensity into masters' proslavery imagination, the force of American nationalism took a different tack, setting the basis for the destruction of all that slaveholders had managed to achieve in their long dominance of the federal Union.

AN ASSEMBLAGE OF SOUTHERN REPUBLICS

As 1861 opened, Americans' saw their transcontinental republic dissolving into an ever-growing number of smaller constituent parts. Those who

---

[6] Athens *Watchman*, December 25, 1860; *Richmond Enquirer*, March 4, 1861; Bertram Wyatt-Brown, "Church, Honor, and Secession" in Harry Stout, et al. eds., *Religion and the American Civil War* (New York: Oxford University Press, 1998), 89–109.

pushed such disintegration forward were well aware of the novelty of the moment. By the year's second week, for instance, a Tallahassee convention dominated by cotton planters introduced the world to their own "sovereign and independent nation," which they imagined might vindicate the claims of roughly 80,000 white citizens to the rest of the world. After delegates tallied a lop-sided vote for disunion with a formal ordinance of secession, they presented the parchment to Thomas Jefferson's twenty-seven-year-old great-granddaughter, who agreed to "embellish" this homegrown Declaration of Independence with a blue ribbon of her own design. Such symbolism captured the outsized aspirations of a body that moved Florida past its history as a mere colony, then a territory, then a coequal federal state. Florida poets took up their pens, seamstresses stitched new Florida flags, and clergy led their congregations to pray for this newest member of the community of nations. Those in charge worried over the future of federal ports and installations while they speculated how they might mobilize a separate Florida army and a naval force capable of guarding the Peninsula's extensive coastline. There were plenty of skeptics who lampooned what they took to be self-important posturing. One critic even poked fun at how ambassadors might soon institute a Floridian foreign policy, which would outlandishly seek an audience before what would surely be the dismissive court of Emperor Louis Napoleon.[7]

Each of the seven Deep South states that left the Union before Lincoln's installation similarly dramatized the fundamental shift in proslavery geopolitics. For Texans, a tinge of nostalgia accompanied calls to raise the Lone Star flag and to "enter once again upon a national career." The other seceding slave states lacked any real experience with plenary sovereignty, and thus considered alternatives to the Union by looking to the future rather than the past. Sectional and state-rights fervor of the late antebellum period had never encouraged South Carolinians to claim the right to "levy war and make alliances," as their convention did in late December of 1860. Nor had Alabamians granted passports, Louisianans established separate Custom Houses, or Mississippians run a state-based postal system. Exponents of Southern Rights had tended to exceed their state-rights predecessors in calculating the gains to be accomplished through a powerful central government. With secession, new doubts arose about what had been

---

[7] *Journal of the Proceedings of the Convention of the People of Florida* (Tallahassee, 1861), 1130; *Oration Delivered by Thomas J. Boyton, at Key Point, July 4th, 1861* (Key West, 1861), 14.

an emerging proslavery consensus that a vigorous executive administration was a crucial means of securing masters' property.[8]

The bewildering range of alternatives during the secession winter resulted from the intricate divisions of responsibilities that had prevailed within the Madisonian republic. While largely agreeing that a state had the right to secede, proslavery constitutionalists found little common ground about what new arrangements should follow the Union's dismemberment. That North America would become a continent filled with the same "petty republics" that dotted Europe seemed possible, especially for those who shared William J. Grayson's opinion that federal alliances by their very nature had a tendency to "fly, one or another, from their appropriate places." It even seemed possible that in the upheaval counties and even cities such as Manhattan might set up on their own. The cohesive tendencies associated with imperial and sectional programs offset the centrifugal forces at work. Jefferson Davis and others imagined a new Union continuing upon a course of Caribbean expansion. An even greater number imagined a republic made up only of those slaveholding states of the old Union. More novel proposals also emerged, such as the flurry of attention given by some Georgians to a scheme to seize their own state's imperial future by absorbing weaker neighbors like Florida.[9]

The pace of rapid change in these months generated an air of expectancy and uncertainty. Week after week, actions undertaken by representatives in an array of political settings altered expectations, pushed events past one threshold after another, and redrew the map of American nationhood. A lame-duck Congress and James Buchanan's presidential administration proved no more successful at guiding events than the so-called "Peace Congress" that assembled in Washington D.C. to venture a comprehensive compromise regarding slavery's future. Far better suited to decisive action were sovereign state conventions assembling across most of the South. These had, at least since the days of Calhoun, been associated with sovereign authority to act on behalf of those they represented.[10]

[8] Sam Houston to J.M. Calhoun, January 7, 1861 in OR Series 4, Vol. 1: 72; Judge O.M. Roberts, *Speech at the Capitol Upon the Impending Crisis* (Austin, 1860), 5.

[9] William Grayson, *Reply to Professor Hodge, on the "State of the Country"* (Charleston, SC: Evans and Cogswell, 1861), 32; "The Republic of Georgia," Augusta *Chronicle and Sentinel*, January 20, 1861; "The Southern Congress," Augusta *Chronicle and Sentinel*, January 26, 1861; Davis to Anna Ella Carroll, March 1, 1861 in *PJD* 7: 64–5.

[10] D. W. Meinig lays out the variety of geopolitical alternatives in *The Shaping of America: A Geographical Perspective on 500 Years of History* Vol. 2 (New Haven, CT: Yale University Press, 1993), 489–501. For the state conventions see Don E. Fehrenbacher, *Constitutions and Constitutionalism in the Slaveholding South* (Athens: University of Georgia Press, 1989) and Mark E. Brandon, *Free in the World: American Slavery and Constitutional Failure* (Princeton: Princeton University Press, 1998).

What such conventions might do after untethering themselves from allied states remained an open question. Even as a majority of delegates to the Virginia convention clung to the Union, secessionists found themselves split between those who counseled cooperation with the Montgomery Convention and those who were open to the idea of a border-state league or an Ohio Valley Confederacy. The former governor Henry Wise led those interested in a still more radical project, which involved the renewal of his scheme (first ventured in 1856) for an armed *coup d'etat* that would forcibly prevent Republicans from assuming those federal offices that Wise believed should remain in the hands of southern whites.[11]

This range of options unnerved even those who had set the crisis in motion. In late December, the *Watchman* of Athens, Georgia, followed a string of arguments on behalf of secession by warning readers about the "stupendous folly of splitting into petty, contemptible little republics, from whose internecine strifes, in the not far distant future, a despotism would be preferable." William Henry Trescot of South Carolina expressed similar anxieties about what he termed the "condition of weakness and confusion which will result from four or five states floating about." In a private letter to Senator Robert Toombs of Georgia, Trescot stressed the need to "meet Lincoln with a president of our own" and urged state delegates at Montgomery to "weld them together while they are hot." His hope was to translate the passions for secession into the basis of a new nationality. To undertake such work would be the business of the interstate commissioners sent by South Carolina, Mississippi, Alabama, and Georgia across the entire slave South in the weeks that followed. The ability of a sovereign power to treat with other sovereigns thus ceased to be a theoretical claim, and became the basis for a loosely coordinated process of reconfederation.[12]

---

[11] Compare the public debates included *in Proceedings of the Virginia State Convention of 1861* (Richmond, VA: Historical Publications Division, 1965) with Daniel W. Crofts, *Reluctant Confederates: Upper South Unionists in the Secession Crisis* (Chapel Hill: University of North Carolina Press, 1989).

[12] Athens *Watchman*, December 25, 1860; Trescot to Toombs, January 14, 1861, in *TSC Corr.*, 529; Charles Dew *Apostles of Disunion: Southern Secession Commissioners and the Causes of the Civil War* (Charlottesville: University Press of Virginia, 2001) lays out the importance of the commissioner's mission, which can be followed in OR Series 4, Vol. 1; William R. Smith, *The History and Debates of the Convention of the People of Alabama* (Montgomery, 1861); *Journal of the State Convention, with an Appendix* (Jackson, MS 1861); *Journal of the People of the Convention of the People of South Carolina* (Columbia, SC, 1862) and Allen D. Candler (comp.), *The Confederate Records of the State of Georgia* (Atlanta, GA, 1909), Vol. 1.

Such interstate diplomacy achieved its primary objective by laying the
basis for the Montgomery convention that commenced in early February
1861. Delegates from six cotton-growing states immediately went to work
there to "bind together the broken fragments of a separated, but homogenous people," as a participant from Mobile later put it. These Confederate
founders managed their most notable achievement in selecting Senator
Jefferson Davis of Mississippi as the president of a new southern republic,
which Texas joined in early March. Over the course of several weeks,
delegates committed much of each day to the business of the provisional
government, while a select committee spent a series of evening sessions
establishing a permanent constitutional framework. Some proslavery radicals hoped that secret sessions might permit a set of fundamental revisions to
the Federal Constitution, which they hoped might lift the ban on the African
slave trade, replace the three-fifths clause with full slave representation, and
require that all Confederate states commit themselves to the absolute rights
of masters to hold slaves. These most sweeping attempts to "nationalize"
slavery in a constitutional sense failed, despite the fact that there was a
backing away from "state rights" in other areas, such as the more uniform
provisions on naturalization, territorial policy, and taxation that were
implemented.[13]

Advocates of an overtly proslavery Constitution found grounds for hope
in the "safety valve" of a modified amending process, which many believed
would allow for a pristine slave republic to be implemented in the future.
The same Montgomery delegates who gestured toward the inheritance of
1787 lay the basis for continuing speculation about constitutional innovation simply by lowering the threshold needed to call a new constitutional
convention and decreasing the number of states needed to ratify amendments.[14] While this new calculus did not in the end produce any wholesale

---

[13] Robert H. Smith, *Address to the People of Alabama, on the Constitution and the Laws of
the Confederate States of America* (Mobile: Daily Register Press, 1861) 4; William C.
Davis, *A Government of Our Own: The Making of the Confederacy* (New York: Free
Press, 1994); David P. Currie, "Though the Looking Glass: The Confederate Constitution
in Congress, 1861–1865," *Virginia Law Review* 90 (September 2004), 1257–399.

[14] *Charleston Mercury*, March 15, 1861; the Montgomery delegates agreed that three states
could initiate change (rather than the two-thirds of the U.S. model) and they required only
two-thirds (rather than three-fourths) to ratify any such changes. For Union's more hesitant
wartime move toward constitutional amending, see Michael Vorenberg, *Final Freedom:
The Civil War, the Abolition of Freedom, and the Thirteenth Amendment* (Cambridge:
Cambridge University Press, 2001). For an early frank discussion of the need for broad
constitutional reform, see E. Delony, "What of the Confederacy? The Present and the
Future," *DBR* 31 (December 1861), 517–20.

changes, it injected a note of uncertainty into the discussion of constitutional structures for the rest of the war. Early in 1862, Thomas Bocock of Virginia used his opening speech before the first Confederate House of Representatives to consider whether the new country's constitution could "without injury to its own integrity, supply the machinery and afford the means requisite to conduct this war to that successful conclusion which the people in their hearts have resolved on." Having just been unanimously chosen as House Speaker, Bocock insisted that if the current constitutional order proved incapable of winning the war, then "it must perish," presumably according to the amending process established the previous year. He expected Confederate congressmen to be both "custodians of the nation's life" and "the guardians of the Constitution's integrity," though his remarks indicated that he was more intent on the former duty than the latter. Supporters of the Davis administration continued to sound similar themes, following William Barksdale in vowing to "throw aside the Constitution rather than that the South should be subdued and brought under the dominion of the North."[15]

There was even more openness to basic constitutional change beyond the confines of Congress. At the same time that Bocock spoke to the Confederate Congress, the editor George Bagby reflected in the *Southern Literary Messenger* how "the blood of the slain has moistened and the fire of battle has warmed the germ" of a more distinctive governmental form. "The investing substance of the old system is felt to be all too narrow and cumbersome," he explained, concluding that "our difficulties are but the symptoms that attend the absorption and transformation of the decayed Yankee polity that clogs us." A writer for the *Southern Field and Fireside* revisited the issue of constitutional modification two years later, as he lamented an inbred conservatism that was responsible for "repressing" the people's "aggressive energy" and "binding them down to hereditary ideas and usages." The lingering aversion to basic change worked great mischief, this writer concluded, because it "deadens their aspirations" and prevented Confederates from achieving their destiny within a suitably distinctive polity.[16]

Military necessity would become the most important theme among those who advocated a radical break from inherited constitutional forms. Their pleas for centralization and an enhanced executive authority typically

---

[15] Bocock in *SHSP* 44 (June 1923), 12–13; Barksdale quoted by "Hermes" [George Bagby], *Charleston Mercury*, September 16, 1862.
[16] Bagby, "Editor's Table," *SLM* 34 (February–March 1862), 192; "Southern Conservatism" *Southern Field and Fireside*, January 23, 1864.

emphasized raising troops, expending money, and directing complicated military campaigns more effectively. A few of the most outspoken centralizers supported nationalization as the best basis for slavery's long-term safety as well and expected such trends to continue even after Confederates had won the peace. There were precedents to such forecasts in stray antebellum comments about a "consolidated" slave republic that would "put slavery under the control of those most interested in it" and in the "sociology" of Henry Hughes, who advocated a stark form of proslavery authoritarianism during the 1850s. John Eakin, the reactionary editor of the Washington Arkansas *Telegraph*, applied similar perspectives to the Confederate war, as he explained how "states rights" had concluded its sole mission by securing slavery from the "numerical majority of that set of fanatics" who sought free soil ascendancy within the United States. In directing their own republic, proslavery leaders might do well to consolidate central power over the entire domain. "Who knows but that in the new order of things which is to be inaugurated after the declaration of peace (which will assuredly come) we may find it to our advantage to lay this venerable doctrine [of state rights] on the shelf," Eakin wrote. An independent slaveocracy could then "adopt a stable and centralized system; adjusted to preserve the personal respect of every citizen, and free from the fluctuations of popular caprice."[17]

Pleas for proslavery centralization drew sharp retorts from a far larger group of Confederates who insisted that inherited principles of state sovereignty had been perfected through the process of state secession and reconfederation. Even amidst the whirl of war, most proslavery southerners retained a residual distrust of nationalization as framed in constitutional terms. Terminology mattered as a check on ambitious governance from the center, just as it had in the days of Spencer Roane and John Taylor. Those who drafted the Confederate Constitution followed the Philadelphia framers in avoiding the word "nation" and even qualified their preamble's opening words "We the people of Confederate States" with a stipulation that they were speaking for "each state acting in its sovereign and independent character." Self-appointed censors remained on guard against what William Yancey termed "the introduction into our political vocabulary of such a phrase as 'the National Life'." Even the newspaper writers of the Richmond press, whose journalists played a pivotal role in inculcating Confederates

[17] Henry L. Benning to Howell Cobb, July 1, 1849 in *TSC Corr.*, 171; Douglas Ambrose, *Henry Hughes and Proslavery Thought in the Old South* (Baton Rouge, LA: Louisiana State University Press, 1996); *Washington Telegraph*, quoted in Arkansas *State Gazette*, June 28, 1862.

with a set of nationalist loyalties, warned that "nation" was a "mischievous word" that had "led the North into its present wicked attempt" to quash Confederate separatism. In 1864, a flurry of suggestions to bestow a more inspiring title on the Confederate republic than "Dixie" caused the *Richmond Examiner* to lash out at the same "old freemasonry of 'nationalism'" it had similarly scorned when patriots proposed national names during secession winter. While it might be the policy of the Yankees "to keep alive that feeling" of ultimate patriotic unity, Confederates were bound "to suspect, to discredit to destroy" a similar encroachment of nationalist heresies within the borders of their avowedly confederal Union.[18]

Newspaper controversies over Confederate names hinted at a broader phenomenon of popular culture shaping wartime debates over federal and national allegiances. Jefferson Davis may have been as nuanced as Madison or Calhoun when he purposefully vindicated Confederate conscription in a series of public letters to the Georgia Governor Joseph Brown. He likely appreciated how founding a Confederate Supreme Court might vindicate wartime centralism upon the same principles that John Marshall introduced in the arena of economic nationalism. But such efforts were ultimately less important to Confederates' sense of themselves and their common undertaking than the President's poetic flourishes, which he offhandedly issued every time he noted national or state symbols, or paid homage to heroes who brought glory to both the state and nation. Especially evocative was Davis' early 1861 image of a new alliance that would make the slaveholding republics "as distinct as the billows though as one as the sea." This catch phrase – which Davis casually lifted from antislavery poet Thomas Campbell – became the most widely circulated image of unity and diversity within the Confederate compound republic. This conceit, which showed a deep underlying unity among Confederate states, updated and made more dynamic federal imagery that had pictured the Union as a heavenly constellation of individual stars.[19]

---

[18] *Speeches of William. L. Yancey, Esq., Senator from the State of Alabama* (Montgomery: Montgomery Advertiser, 1862), 23; "Too Much Nationality," *Southern Monthly* (October 1861), 86–8; *Richmond Examiner*, April 13, 1864. The wisdom of adopting a more "national" name for the Confederacy sparked wide discussion, as could be seen in *Montgomery Weekly Mail*, December 6, 1860; *Memphis Avalanche*, February 22, 1861; *Richmond Enquirer*, August 9, August 15, and October 27, 1862; "Editor's Table," *SLM* 37 (February 1863), 124; *Richmond Sentinel*, October 21, 1864.

[19] Davis Address in Richmond, June 1, 1861 in *PJD*, 7: 184. Davis' lengthy interchange with Governor Brown was among the most thorough Confederate forays into constitutional argument; the letters appear throughout *OR* Series 4 while larger context is provided in Paul Escott, *After Secession: Jefferson Davis and the Failure of Confederate Nationalism* (Baton Rouge: Louisiana State University Press, 1978).

Ordinary Confederate followed Davis' lead in simultaneously stoking nationalist passions and attending to state-level patriotic themes. Harry Macarthy's "Bonnie Blue Flag" told the story of a "band of brothers" by explaining how the Southern Confederacy grew a state at a time, until it reached its full strength. The federalist inclinations of this popular anthem were echoed by James Randall's "Maryland, My Maryland," James Phelan's "Men of Alabama," and countless other songs and poems that celebrated individual states. The key site for blending state and national glory was the Confederacy's massive army, of course, which would be compromised of state regiments, organized by state officials, and motivated alternately by a hatred of Yankees and competition with Confederate units from rival slave states. When Governor Thomas H. Watts noted in 1863 that the "name Alabamian has become immortal to history," he was conjuring up martial associations rather than any memories of the political self-determination undertaken in 1861. A wartime federalism that established the constitutional relationships between component parts thus functioned as a crucible of broader political identities. There was as much harmony as discord in the simultaneous intensification of white civic pride at the state and at the Confederate level. In the vortex of war, a state's reputation depended less on its historical legacies, or even on present events transpiring within its boundaries. A Florida patriot could best contribute to state pride by dying in Tennessee, just as a Texan could add to his state's honor by taking the fight to a faraway front in Virginia.[20]

THE BOUNDARIES OF A SLAVEHOLDERS' NATION

Disputes over the Confederacy's territorial extent generated nearly as much controversy as matters of state sovereignty and of wartime centralization. Such a concern for marking frontiers was to be expected, given earlier proslavery interest in buffer zones and in warnings that "southern institutions" had either to expand or face extermination. Secession fundamentally reconfigured Confederates' outlook, by encouraging most commentators to set aside warnings about Republicans' free-soil policies and to dampen speculation about the Caribbean, Mexico, and the far west, lest such

---

[20] Watts quoted in *Montgomery Advertiser*, December 9, 1863. Among those works that set state and Confederate loyalties into a basic tension, thus looking past opportunities for harmony, are Frank L. Owsley, *State Rights in the Confederacy* (Chicago: University of Chicago Press, 1925); Curtis Arthur Amlund, *Federalism in the Southern Confederacy* (Washington, D.C.: Public Affairs Press, 1966); and Richard Beringer, et al. *Why the South Lost the Civil War* (Athens: University of Georgia Press, 1986).

expansionism arouse international hostility. Over the course of the war's first two years, proslavery radicals focused attention on another issue – whether former free state allies might someday be incorporated into the Confederate republic. Slavery's most zealous defenders were on guard against the sort of "reverse reconstruction" that they feared would undermine bondage and set the stage for future conflict. Those committed to achieving a "pure" slave republic would try to convince fellow Confederates that growth no longer heralded the future, as it had when the United States embraced its imperial destiny. Once the separatist path was chosen, expansion took on new connotations, and could easily appear to be an ignoble retreat to a degrading past.

The long debate over the Confederacy's possible northward expansion began at the Montgomery convention, when radicals unsuccessfully tried to limit membership in the new federation to slave states. After Alexander Stephens took a leading role in defeating this proposal, he publicly celebrated how "our growth, by accessions from other States" would depend solely on "whether we present to the world, as I trust we shall, a better government than that to which neighboring States belong." To Stephens, this new "Southern" Confederacy might become "the controlling power on this continent" by welcoming into its fold the "great States of the North West." "Our doors are wide enough" to admit all the states along the Mississippi River, this former supporter of Stephen Douglas added, before he quickly made the proslavery concession that such an alliance was only possible after these states were "ready to assimilate with us in principle." Jefferson Davis staked out a far more cautious approach, writing that "to increase the power, develop the resources, and promote the happiness of the Confederacy" required "so much of homogeneity that the welfare of the portion shall be the aim of the whole." Using purposefully vague language, Davis sanctioned confederating with all states that made slavery part of the social order, while suggesting that overture toward even the most antiabolitionist free states was unwise.[21]

By the late spring of 1861, the Confederate debate over admission of free states escalated, and several newspapers predicted that this issue would furnish the basis of the new country's party divisions and ultimately determine who would succeed Davis as president in 1868 (See Figure 7.1). The Mobile politician Robert Handy Smith spoke for one side of an increasingly

---

[21] Alexander Stephens, "Cornerstone Speech," in Jon Wakelyn, *Southern Pamphlets on Secession, November 1860–April 1861* (Chapel Hill: University of North Carolina Press, 1996); Jefferson Davis, "Inaugural Address," CMPC 1, 35.

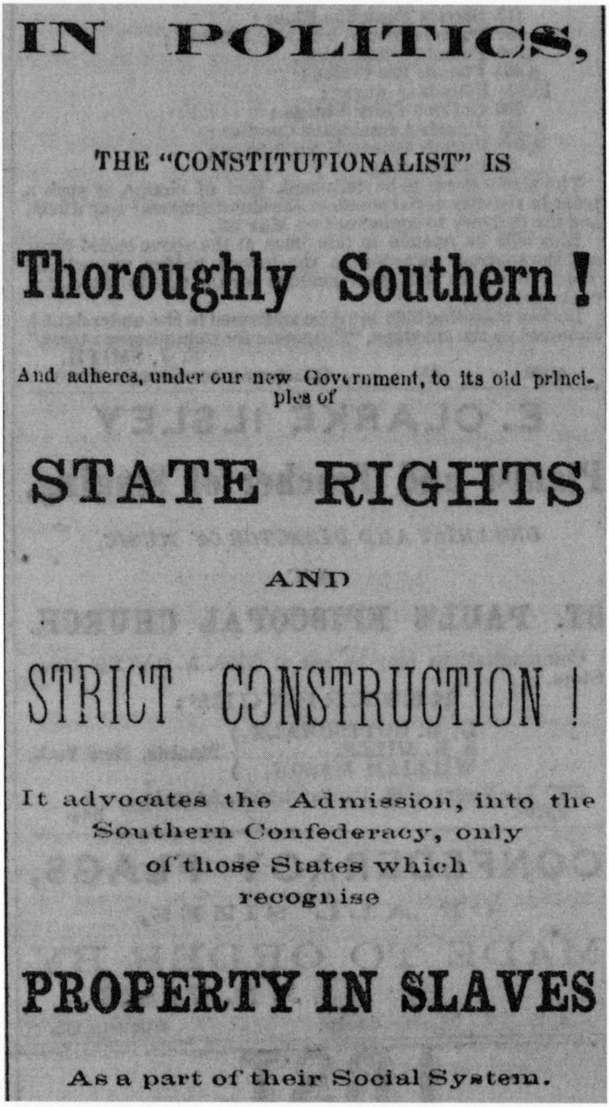

IN POLITICS,

THE "CONSTITUTIONALIST" IS

Thoroughly Southern!

And adheres, under our new Government, to its old principles of

STATE RIGHTS

AND

STRICT CONSTRUCTION!

It advocates the Admission, into the Southern Confederacy, only of those States which recognise

PROPERTY IN SLAVES

As a part of their Social System.

FIGURE 7.1. As this prospectus from a Georgia paper indicated, the future admission of free states formed an early dividing line in Confederate politics. *Augusta Daily Constitutionalist, April 21, 1861. Courtesy American Antiquarian Society.*

heated controversy when he speculated how the "great Northwestern States, watered by the Mississippi" might be "drawn by the strong current of that mighty river" into the new Confederate republic. Such a development, Smith predicted, would allow slaveholders to "grasp the power of empire on this continent and announce to the startled North that it has reached its western limit, and must spread, if spread it can, towards the frozen sea." Opponents of what Thomas Cobb of Georgia termed this "specious guise of reorganization and assimilation" compared this "suicidal policy" to the Israelite longing for "the flesh pots of Egypt." He concluded: "For forty years more, God may lead us through a wilderness of cares and troubles, if at their end, our children may be brought under some chosen Joshua into the promised land of a purely slaveholding Confederacy."[22]

Like much else during this initial stage of Confederate nationhood, the prospect of war informed considerations of the optimal size of the new proslavery republic. The threat of Union armies caused many of the most committed Deep South radicals to rethink earlier misgivings about the border slave states. Francis Pickens was typical in concluding that union among the entire "slave holding race" was necessary to "secure the protection and development of our civilization in any emergency that may arise." While Pickens insisted that the new government reach out even toward those wavering masters in Maryland and Delaware, Governor Henry Rector of Arkansas cast his eyes upon the Indian Territory, where he identified our "red neighbors to the West" as an underappreciated part of a geographically-dispersed slaveholding class. Securing the "sympathy and cooperation" of these "valuable allies" would be made easier by the fact that the Indian masters held some 10,000 black slaves. Soon enough, the Confederate loyalties of leading Cherokee factions validated Rector's prediction that these tribes would seek "protection against the abolitionist crusade that is held in store for them by the northern government."[23]

The outbreak of war only partially satisfied Confederate ambitions to extend its jurisdiction over the entire slave South. Among the four states to accede to the Confederacy after the bombardment of Fort Sumter, Virginia was easily the most important, since it offered its sizeable population, the site of a new national capital, and, perhaps most importantly, what Alexander Stephens termed "the very prestige of the name of the old Commonwealth." For Confederates to assert control of the southern banks of the Potomac bolstered the perception that they would become what Governor

---

[22] *Augusta Chronicle and Sentinel*, March 28, April 16, 1861; Smith, *Address to the People of Alabama*; T.R.R. Cobb, *Substance of an Address of . . . to his Constituents of Clark County*, April 6, 1861 (n.p., 1861), 2.

[23] Pickens to Jefferson Davis, January 23, 1861, in *PJD* 7, 25; *Message of Henry M. Rector, Governor of Arkansas, to the State Convention* (Little Rock: Johnson and Yerkes, 1861), 6; see also *The Arkansian*, January 13, 1860 and, for continuing resistance to the border South, the [Columbus, Georgia] *Cornerstone* April 2, 1861.

R. W. Johnson of Arkansas called "the real United States." As Johnson put
it, Lincoln's "rump" Union seemed as likely as not to become "a narrow slip
of country as straggling as that of Prussia, and are soon to fall to pieces."
Holding the Potomac might even clear the way for Pennsylvania to gravitate
toward the new Confederate alliance.[24]

The main hindrance to such growth came, of course, in the post-Sumter
wavering of four border slave states, whose Unionism would frustrate those
Confederates who were intent to govern all territory south of the Mason-
Dixon Line and the Ohio River. The commitment to bondage shown in these
border zones seemed less important than their considerable white population,
which was nearly equal to that of the states making up the "original" Confederacy, and only a bit smaller than that of the states who joined the cause
after Lincoln's call for troops (See Table 7.1). A combination of shrewd Union
policy and Confederate blundering allowed federal commanders to stage the
initial military invasions of the rebellious states from "slave soil." When
secessionists in Kentucky and Missouri used extralegal conventions in 1862
to ally their states to the Confederacy, most of this "Southern" territory was
already under firm Union control. Delegates from these two states would be
sent to Richmond, sustaining a fascination in Confederate popular culture for
the irredentist "liberation" of these areas from Union occupation.[25]

Maryland became the most important focus of the Confederacy's irredentist imagination. This state's allure was enhanced rather than diminished by
the fact that proslavery elements there never managed to push through even a
spurious secession from the Union. The attack of a Baltimore mob upon
Massachusetts troops in April 1861 changed the image of the slave South's
second largest city from a nest of free soil radicalism into a Confederate *cause
célèbre*. Thereafter, the image of "Maryland in Chains" became an endur-
ingly popular topic for Confederate patriotic poetry, music, and theater.
Before the end of 1861, the Provisional Congress had formally registered
its sympathy for the "outrages" of the "foreign despotism" that ruled the
state with an iron grip, while the same body asserted how the state was tied to

[24] Alexander Stephens, "Speech Before the Virginia Secession Convention," in Henry Cleveland, ed., *Alexander Stephens in Public and Private* (Philadelphia, PA: National Publishing
Company, 1866), 735; *Captain Maury's Letter on American Affairs: A Letter Addressed
to Rear-Admiral Fitz Roy, of England* (Baltimore, MD, n.p., 1862), 10; [George
McHenry], *Why Pennsylvania Should Become One of the Confederate States of America*
(London: J. Wilson, 1862).
[25] Contrast Bettie Lane Clark, "Appeal to Kentucky," in *Jackson Mississippian*, August 14,
1861 with J.R. Barrick, "Kentucky, She Is Sold" in William Gilmore Simms, *War Poetry of
the South* (New York: Richardson and Co., 1867), 98–9.

TABLE 7.1. 1860 *Population and Territorial Extent of Slave States, Categorized by Secession-era Stance*

	7 States Represented at Montgomery (February 1861)	4 States Joining CSA at Richmond (May–July 1861)	4 Slave States Remaining in Union as of July 1861
Total population	4,968,277	4,143,813	3,136,908
White population	2,619,114	2,828,106	2,589,480
* Slaveholders	181,521	134,111	77,335
* Slaveholding households	36.7%	25.2%	15.6%
Enslaved population	2,312,352	1,208,758	429,401
Free black population	36,811	95,949	118,027
Territory (sq.miles)	578,507	216,149	125,016

Source: U.S. Census, Eighth Census, Population, Agriculture Summaries.

their own new nation "by geographical situation, by mutual interests, by similarity of institutions, and by enduring sentiments of reciprocal amity and esteem." As Congress insisted that any peace negotiations include a method for Maryland to choose its own destiny free of outside compulsion, Jefferson Davis paid his own tribute to a people who were "already united to us by hallowed memories and material interests." Faith in this state's considerable body of Confederate sympathizers led to the exemption of all Marylanders from the "Alien Enemies" act and later led to a fierce debate whether conscription would extend to those exiles within Confederate lines.[26]

Geopolitical contests elsewhere turned less on legislative pronouncements, flights of rhetoric, or even policy-making than on the march of armies. As federal invasions brought sizeable chunks of Tennessee, Arkansas, and Louisiana under Union control, leaders in Richmond supported General Henry Hopkins Silbey's campaign into New Mexico, imagining that it might secure the newly created Confederate territory of Arizona. This

---

[26] "Appeal to Maryland, by a Dying Solider at Manassas," *SLM* 33 (October 1861), 314; Robert E. Holtz, "We'll Be Free in Maryland," in Frank Moore, ed., *Rebel Rhymes* (New York, 1864), J.D. M'Cabe Jr., "The Maryland Line" in Simms, *War Poetry of the South*, 395–6; Randall "There's Life in the Old Land Yet," *New Orleans Delta*, September 1, 1861; "Resolutions Relating to Maryland," in *JCC* 1: 589; Davis "Inaugural Address, *JDC* 5: 200.

adventure caused the *Houston Telegraph* to mix enthusiasm for how a western "cordon of free states" might allow slavery's indefinite safety with speculation how the Pacific coast as a whole might ultimately fall into Confederate hands. Administration officials were less eager, however, and they expended little interest in this far frontier between late March of 1862 (when Confederate troops were turned back at the Battle of Glorietta Pass) and the creation of a semiautonomous Trans-Mississippi Department a year and a half later. Of far greater consequence to the government were efforts taken during the summer of 1862 to repel the Union army from the outskirts of Richmond and then to send Robert E. Lee's army across the Potomac in September.[27] Acting upon a presidential directive, Lee announced to Maryland locals during the early stage of that campaign that "our army has come among you, and is prepared to assist you with the power of its arms in regaining the rights to which you have been despoiled." With a tone of reassurance, Lee added that "while the Southern people will rejoice to welcome you to your natural position among them; they will only welcome you when you come of your own free will." Such an appeal roused scant support in the western, largely nonslaveholding part of the state, making the Antietam campaign a clear political failure, even if its military significance was decidedly more mixed.[28]

The lengthier Confederate thrust into Kentucky the same month had greater geopolitical consequences. The state capital at Frankfurt was a primary destination for General Braxton Bragg, whose Confederate troops oversaw the installation of pro-Confederate Richard Hawes as Kentucky's "legitimate" governor. While residents of the slaveholding Bluegrass region around Lexington proved to be far more receptive than western Marylanders, Bragg's recruiting goals still fell far short of his expectations. He admitted shortly before his retreat that "enthusiasm runs high but exhausts itself in words." Edmund Kirby Smith was blunter in explaining that Kentuckians were "slow and backward in rallying to our standard" because "their hearts are evidently with us, but their blue-grass, and fat cattle are against us." Without greater popular support, Bragg's retreat was

---

[27] *Houston Telegraph,* quoted in *Richmond Daily Dispatch,* April 20, 1862. See also *Richmond Daily Dispatch,* June 17, 1862.

[28] Lee proclamation quoted in *Richmond Enquirer,* September 18, 1862; Davis to Lee, Bragg, and Smith [c. September 7, 1862] in *JDC* 7: 338–9. For a lucid discussion of how these invasions fit into larger strategic thinking see Herman Hattaway and Archer Jones, *How the North Won: A Military History of the Civil War* (Urbana: University of Illinois Press, 1983), 2025–269. Also of note is Richard R. Duncan, "Marylanders and the Invasion of 1862," *CWH* 11 (December 1965), 370–83.

only a matter of time. Yet, he did linger long enough in Kentucky to issue a late-September address "To the People of the Northwest" that would emphasize how the Confederacy and the Upper Midwest were bound by the Mississippi River, which he termed a "grand artery of their mutual national lives which men cannot sever." Bragg combined an anti-New England animus that had long informed Democratic Party politics with a more timely observation of how the Northwest was "being used" by meddling Easterners "to fight the battle of emancipation, a battle which, if successful, destroys our prosperity, and with it your best markets to buy and sell."[29]

Bragg's appeal to western antiabolitionism anticipated the Confederacy's renewed interest in pushing its advantage in the Mississippi and Ohio River valleys. The Congressional renegade Henry S. Foote had already begun to court peace elements in Illinois, Indiana, Ohio, and Iowa with his vow to restore peaceful commerce on the "inland sea" that marked these states' borders. Political developments in the fall of 1862 encouraged General P.G.T. Beauregard to hint how a Memphis conference of Confederate and northwestern governors might lead to a peace treaty. Beauregard's plan, while it gained little traction, signaled a broader Confederate fascination with the resurgence of the Democratic Copperheads, whose rising fortunes resulted from Lincoln's stalled military efforts (made all the worse by the December debacle at Fredericksburg), from a broad discontent about Republican policies of martial law and conscription, and, most pertinent to Confederate observers, from the racist backlash sparked by the president's preliminary Emancipation Proclamation in September. Tying all these programs together was the prospect that Copperheads and Confederates might work together to contain the excesses of New England-inspired fanaticism.[30]

The Rev. Joseph W. Tucker, a South Carolina-born St. Louis editor and ordained Methodist minister, became the key figure in this campaign to convert the northern divisions into an expanded Confederacy. Early in 1863, Tucker established the *Southern Crisis,* in Jackson, Mississippi, in order to recast the Confederacy's lingering "question of boundary" in light

---

[29] Bragg to Jefferson Davis, October 2, 1862 *PJD* 8: 417; Kirby Smith quoted in Grady McWhiney, *Braxton Bragg and Confederate Defeat* (New York: Columbia University Press, 1969), 295; Bragg, "To the People of the Northwest," *OR* Series 1, Vol. 52 (Part 2): 363–5. Most historians credit John Forsyth Jr. (former Stephen Douglass backer, Alabama editor, and Bragg confidante) with the authorship of this public letter.

[30] *JCC* 5: 314–15, 334–5, 405–7 and 6: 79–81 (for debate on Foote's proposals); H.S. Foote, "The Great Northwest" in Jackson *Daily Southern Crisis,* March 3, 1863; Beauregard to William Porcher Miles, October 21, 1862 in *OR* Series 4, Vol. 2: 137–8.

of new political opportunities. Nearly every issue of his newspaper addressed the Confederacy's geographical borders which, as he explained, had not yet been "determined by any organic act of the government." Combining fire-eating politics with a commitment to imperial dominion, Tucker considered the "liberation" of Kentucky, Missouri, and Maryland as but the first step toward a Confederacy presiding over all American territory "south of the lakes." "We want the balance of power on this continent. We want to have done with the capture and theft of our negroes. We want rest and peace," Tucker wrote. Those newspapers that heeded his call reminded their readers of the primary issues of the 1850s. The editor of the Columbus *Mississippi Republican* once more rallied around "our rights in the territories" and dismissed as mere foolishness the Confederacy's apparent willingness to "sacrifice hundreds of thousands of lives" merely to enjoy "the privilege of keeping our own property where it is."[31]

Pleas for cooperation with the free states and for additional growth drew sharp replies both in letters to Tucker's *Southern Crisis* and from such proslavery stalwarts as the *Charleston Mercury*, the *Augusta Constitutionalist*, and the *Jackson Mississippian*, where distrust of a "greater Confederacy" was just as vigorous as it had been in 1861. A combination of war weariness and hopes for an impending northern schism changed the terms of debate and indicated a popular willingness to rethink the matter, however. The Mississippi poet Margarita Conedo balanced proslavery disavowal of hasty reconstruction with the provocative question:

> South and West are truly brothers, children of a common mother
> Why then slaughter one another, at a stranger's dark behest?[32]

---

[31] [Tucker], "The Cloud in the Northwest," Jackson *Daily Southern Crisis*, January 20, 1863; Tucker, *The Importance of the Upper Mississippi Valley to the Peace and Prosperity of the Confederate States. What Is the Truth of the Case?* (Jackson: Southwestern Confederate Printing House, 1863); Columbus *Mississippi Republican* in Jackson *Daily Southern Crisis* March 9, 1863. For a commentary on the breadth of discussion of the Northwest issue, see *SIN*, March 12, 1863. This Tucker should not be confused with Joel W. Tucker, another Methodist who delivered an important sermon on providence in Fayetteville, North Carolina, in 1862.

[32] "War or Peace" in *Charleston Mercury*, February 24, 28, 1863; "The Northwest," and "The Way to Perpetuate Slavery," in Augusta *Daily Constitutionalist* January 27 and March 12, 1863; *Jackson Mississippian*. At the end of Canedo's "Appeal to the States of the Northwest" (first published in the February 9, 1863 issues of the *Daily Southern Crisis*) came the note "The writer of these lines would not be understood to advocate any reconstruction of the old Union. A thousand times No! that such a result follow our glorious Revolution. Nor even that we should accept the Western States as our natural allies, unless with our Government they accept our Institutions."

The *Selma Reporter* noted how the Northwest could provide a "break-water" for abolitionist attacks and even come to "the practical accept-ance of slavery as a matter of convenience as well as of right" once they entered into formal alliance with the Confederate states. E. W. Cushing's *Houston Telegraph* wavered in its response to the issue while admitting that it would "rather have Illinois with a proslavery con-stitution than Delaware, North Maryland and North-west Virginia with their proclivities." John Tyler Jr. framed the ultimate issue of how reun-ion with the Midwest could only be accomplished on Confederate terms, which would reverse the ban on slave property established by the 1787 Northwest Ordinance. "The South cannot be carried to them," Tyler wrote of the Ohio Valley States. "But they can be brought to the South."[33]

Confederates' early 1863 debate over the Northwest was built upon shaky assumptions about Copperhead secessionism, which Tucker and others vastly exaggerated. It revealed far less about the nature of northern opposition to Lincoln than about the continuing fascination of proslavery Confederates about the consequences of Republican emancipation.[34] George Bagby was skeptical about states that would be "nominally slave" while having "the worst elements of Yankeeism in immense excess in them." He concluded that these would be "but so many Pandora's boxes" if brought into the Confederacy. The *Atlanta Intelligencer* agreed, finding the prospect of formerly free states joining the Confederacy "repugnant" and an affront to the fact that "we are fighting this war for southern independence and for a government of Southern States, recognizing African Slavery as an institution ordained of God, beneficial to mankind, a neces-sity to our social and political relations as states, and in our intercourse with all other nations and states." Tucker met such objections by offering a sweeping view of how a northwestern "revolution" would begin with toleration of slavery, move to a formal incorporation of that institution across the northwest, and then move toward a still broader advocacy.

---

[33] Selma *Daily Reporter*, March 12 1863; [Cushing], "Worth a Thought," Houston *Tri-Weekly Telegraph*, February 23, 1863; John Tyler Jr., "Peace between the Sections or War to the World," January 27, 1863 in Jackson *Daily Southern Crisis*; later excerpted as "Python," "Our Present Confederate Status: Foreign and Domestic," *DBR* 34 (August 1864), 1–33.

[34] For an especially overstated account of Copperhead separatism see "Programme in the Northwest," *Daily Southern Crisis*, February 10, 1863, which also appeared in Richmond *Daily Dispatch*, February 16, 1863. Compare with Jennifer L. Weber's now-authoritative *Copperheads: The Rise and Fall of Lincoln's Opponents in the North* (New York: Oxford, 2006).

Not content with replacing Republicans with friendlier Democrats or with Northwestern states detaching themselves from the East, Tucker predicted that the Northwest was on the cusp of a "purification of their society by a baptism of blood" which would be effected by "the expulsion from these commonwealths of that element which, to some extent, has infested Virginia, Kentucky, Tennessee, Missouri, Arkansas, Texas, the city of New Orleans, and, indeed, every state of the Confederacy." Another writer agreed that the northwestern alliance would increase the long-term prospects for slavery. If the institution "survives the shock of this war, all the Puritanic fanaticism of Christendom will not be able to shake it again," while "the Northwest, even if so inclined, will have too much sad experience to reopen a dangerous wound."[35]

Such visions of a how a "purified" Northwest might join the proslavery republic echoed a debate underway at the very same time about the Confederate basis of citizenship. The *Charleston Mercury* identified a common danger between the public's apparent openness to territorial expansion and what it considered to be overly permissive naturalization laws inherited from the United States. Lax citizenship requirements threatened to be "nothing but a form of reconstruction of our Union" the paper wrote, since "after the war is over, ten Yankees will enter the Confederated States for one European." In the flurry of 1861, similar warnings had come from proslavery doctrinaires like George Fitzhugh and from former nativist supporters of the American Party such as William Bilbo of Tennessee.[36] But in 1863, as Confederates began to contemplate future relations with the North, there seemed to be new urgency in considering how victory might be a prelude to an influx of troublesome Yankees. William Schley of Augusta recommended that political rights after the war be extended only to those born within the slave states. Outsiders were "not only opposed to the institution of slavery, but are strangers to those

[35] "Hermes" in *Charleston Mercury*, September 23, 1862; *Atlanta Intelligencer*, January 20, 1863; Tucker, *The Importance of the Upper Mississippi Valley*; "Confederate," *Annexation of the Northwest* (Savannah, 1863). Governor John Milton sent this last broadside to Jefferson Davis with comments included in OR Series 4, Vol. 2: 493.

[36] *Charleston Mercury*, May 7, 1863; George Fitzhugh, "The Perils of Peace" *DBR* 31 (October–November, 1861); *Montgomery Mail*, January 13, 1861; William M. Bilbo, *The Past, Present and Future of the Southern Confederacy: An Oration Delivered in the City of Nashville* (Nashville, 1861); J. Nathan Ellis, "Our Country," in *Southern Field and Fireside* August 30, 1861. Notably, the *Mercury's* argument on this issue pushed it to employ the sort of nationalist rhetoric it usually held at arms length. "This Confederacy will never be recognized as an independent nation – never – until we first have the spirit to recognize ourselves," it wrote, insisting that a bill before Congress "affirms the right of this nation – if it is a nation – to define as other nations do, the terms of its own citizenship."

sentiments of personal honor, integrity and high-toned and chivalric feelings and views which characterize the people as a class in these Southern States." Frank Alfriend, who would soon be named the editor of the *Southern Literary Messenger*, also hoped to "strengthen slavery by every possible appliance" by limiting political power to those who were "born in the South" and who were "engaged to appreciate the character and understand the operation of our system."[37]

Responding to popular pressure, Congress debated a modified citizenship law in the spring of 1863, a year after it had repealed all U.S. legislation on the subject. The earlier step had championed the principle of state sovereignty, but it also contradicted the Confederate Constitution, which had centralized Congressional power over this issue by changing the old stipulation that it had the sole power to enact "rules" for naturalization to the more significant power to enact "laws" on the subject. Jefferson Davis, whose 1845 maiden speech in the U.S. Congress had blasted northern nativism for its "sordid character and arrogant assumption," promptly vetoed the 1862 act, wondering aloud "whether legislation intended to effect the entire exclusion from citizenship of all who are not born on the soil will be deemed in accordance with the civilization of the age." Hoping to avoid a similar veto in 1863, the president encouraged the bill's opponents to frame their criticism as a possible diplomatic blunder rather than a violation of liberal principles, an approach that assured the measure's defeat.[38]

Before the spring of 1863 drew to a close, Confederate debates over the Northwest and over stricter naturalization had subsided and public attention quickly shifted from northern politics to battlefield campaigns. J.W. Tucker bitterly blamed the sneering tone of the Richmond press for undermining Confederate aspirations north of the Ohio River. Such a dismissive attitude, he complained, revealed how far such voices were "removed from the heart of the country." *The Southern Illustrated News* instead blamed Tucker and others for subjecting to public discussion those matters whose

[37] William Schley, *Our Position and True Policy* (Augusta, 1863), 9–10; Frank Alfriend, "A Southern Republic and a Northern Democracy," *SLM* 37 (May 1863). An intriguing working-class intervention into this nativist discussion could be seen in B.W. Rumney, *Address to the Laboring Men of Georgia* (n.p.).

[38] For Davis' 1845 speech, see William C. Davis, *Jefferson Davis: The Man and His Hour: A Biography* (New York, 1991) 120–1 and for his veto, exercised on February 4, 1863, see *JCC* 1: 758–9. Maneuvering over the 1863 bill can be reconstructed through the private correspondence reprinted in Ruth K. Nuermberger, *The Clays of Alabama, A Planter-Lawyer-Politician Family* (Lexington: University of Kentucky Press, 1958).

delicacy required careful diplomacy.³⁹ It hardly mattered who was to blame
for the passing of Confederate interest in the Northwest, however. The
Union capture of Vicksburg in early July gave the federal government the
upper hand in the quest to reunite the Mississippi River Valley. Thereafter,
Confederates would be less involved in expansion – even into the border
states – than in reconnecting with a Trans-Mississippi region severed
from Richmond for the war's final two years. Tucker would again
take an interest in northern political divisions during the 1864
presidential election, but he pursued plans in private letters to leading
officials rather than in the pages of the daily press. The few who continued
to imagine a reunion of slave and free states along the Mississippi took
pains to emphasize how this Union could only be accomplished "in the
course of years," after "mutual interests shall have healed animosities."⁴⁰

As the cumulative effects of war inscribed indelible limits to Confederate growth, the geographical "South" assumed greater conceptual fixity
that was at odds with the Confederacy's waning hold on its territory.
Military events played a key role in this process, both in determining
effective military control over contested areas and in undermining Confederate interest in accepting reunion on any other basis than military
subjugation. In the midst of debate over the Northwest, the *Jackson
Mississippian* had argued that: "If free-soil states are to be admitted into
this Confederacy, our revolution, the sea of blood and treasures, the
horrors, sacrifices, and deprivations which our people have suffered to
accomplish the severance of the slave States from those of free soil States
is worth nothing." Such reasoning only gained strength as Confederates
absorbed the dramatic bloodletting at Gettysburg and the still more costly
campaigns of 1864.⁴¹

By the fall of 1863, the *Charleston Mercury* was thus able to celebrate
how bitterness engendered by war had rescued the proslavery republic
from the degradation of free-state contagion. "If, after the publication of
the Confederate Constitution, the northern states had offered us their

³⁹ "The Northwest – Once More," *Daily Southern Crisis*, March 28, 1863; *SIN*, March 14,
   1863; For a sampling of Richmond opposition to the Northwestern alliance, see *Enquirer*
   and *Whig* coverage throughout the spring of 1863.
⁴⁰ Tucker to Jefferson Davis March 14, 1864 in *JDC* 6, 204; "A Gentleman of Mississippi,
   [Alexander H. Handy], *Parallel Between the Great Revolution of England in 1688 and
   the American Revolution of 1860–61* (Meridian: Daily Clarion, 1864), 39. Among the
   exceptions to the pattern of disinterest in the border states were the operations of John
   Morgan's cavalry, who crossed the Ohio in 1863, and General Sterling Price's 1864 raid
   into central Missouri.
⁴¹ *Jackson Mississippian*, March 6, 1863.

union on its terms, we have not a doubt that a majority of the public men of the South, especially those familiarized with Washington would have readily accepted it" the paper reflected. "But the war has settled the hankering after a reconstruction of the old Union on any terms" and nearly all Confederates had thus come to see that "we must be entirely independent of them or perish as a people." William Henry Trescot expressed no less ambivalence about ultimate consequences, but he employed more memorable language. "If an earthquake had cleft this continent in twain, we could not be further separated than we are," he noted in a letter enthusiastically published in the *Mercury*. As Trescot sensed, the division of former allies had ceased to be merely a matter of waterways, political boundaries, or even the divisions between slave and free territory. To die-hard Confederates, the most important fact was that "great, red river of kindred blood, which swollen by dismal streams from Manassas and Murfreesboro, Antietam and Fredericksburg, now rolls its fearful border between hostile nations."[42]

PROVIDENTIAL GORE

To many patriots, Trescot's "great red river" of sacrifice not only divided the Confederates from eternal enemies but also consecrated the slave South with the blood of the heroic fallen. "The martyred dead have taken possession of this Southern soil for the Southern people," the Rev. Joseph Atkinson explained in 1862, before he predicted that "this land will be endeared to us and to our posterity" by becoming "the earthly resting-place of our immortal dead." Confederates were borrowing from larger perspectives when they pondered a divine order that linked their nation's destiny, its newly sanctified territory, and the willing deaths of countless soldiers. Supporters of the new Richmond government offered many of the same themes of nationalist suffering and holy redemption that Julia Ward Howe and Abraham Lincoln rendered in classic form. The Confederate version of "providential gore" played a distinctive role in the anatomy of proslavery nationalism, however, since it animated a newly fashioned body politic by operating simultaneously as the country's motive power and its collective soul. The powerful wartime associations between death and collective purpose would outlive the Confederate state and provide the groundwork for the "Lost Cause." The mass carnage allowed whites to

---

[42] *Charleston Mercury*, September 9, 1863; William H. Trescot, "Letter to Hon. J.R. Ingersoll," printed in *Charleston Mercury*, October 16, 1863.

replace the earlier peacetime emphasis on mastery with a new fixation on suffering, defeat, and communal chastisement.[43]

It would take time for wartime sacrifices to reorient the proslavery imagination and to establish a Confederate vocabulary of holy martyrdom. During the secession crisis, concern for violence came mostly from Unionists like the Alabama delegate Jeremiah Clemens, who warned that "no liquid but blood has ever filled the baptismal fount of nations." In tacitly responding to the fire-eating pledges to drink all the blood spilled in the cause of Southern independence, Clemens insisted: "he has read the book of human nature to little purpose if he expects to see a nation born except in convulsions, or christened at any altar but that of the God of battles." The Virginia radical George Bagby was among the relatively few secessionists willing to display a similar frankness about the human cost of decisive action. Even before the assault on Fort Sumter, Bagby admitted that a "number of good, hard-fought battles" might be a necessary to "get rid of the black, bad blood in the veins of both sections."[44]

As imagined deaths gave way to actual ones, nationalists shifted ground, sanctifying bloodshed and endowing mounting losses with a mystical significance. Confederate commentators paid as much attention to ordinary martyrs for independence as they did to political leaders and to victorious generals of the first successful battles. Newspaper verse celebrated the June 1861 death of James Jackson, whose defense of the Confederacy's "Stars and Bars" flag atop his hotel had resulted in his death. A similar outpouring of poetry lamented fallen battlefield heroes like Francis Bartow and Bernard Bee (the two most prominent casualties of Manassas), the Tennessean Felix Zollicoffer (who was shot by his own men at Cumberland Gap), and Albert Sidney Johnston (who bled to death while commanding the western army at Shiloh in the spring of 1862). The Mobile editor H.L. Flash provided a particularly resonant understanding of these losses, noting in an ode to Zollicoffer how:

---

[43] Joseph M. Atkinson, *God, The Giver of Victory and Peace: A Thanksgiving Sermon Delivered in the Presbyterian Church, September 18, 1862* (Raleigh, 1862), 15. For more on the themes of bloodshed, see Robert E. Bonner, *Colors and Blood: Flag Passions of the Confederate South* (Princeton: Princeton University Press, 2002); Franny Nudelman, *John Brown's Body: Slavery, Violence and the Culture of War* (Chapel Hill: University of North Carolina Press, 2004); Drew Gilpin Faust, *This Republic of Suffering: Death and the American Civil War* (New York: Knopf, 2008); the postbellum persistence of Confederate loyalties (expressed as a politicized form of nostalgia rather than as a platform for separatism) is a main theme of Anne Sarah Rubin, *A Shattered Nation: The Rise and Fall of the Confederacy, 1861–1868* (Chapel Hill: University of North Carolina Press, 2005).

[44] Clemens quoted in William R. Smith, *The History and Debates of the Convention of the People of Alabama, Begun and Held in the City of Montgomery, on the Seventh Day of January, 1861* (Montgomery: White, Pfister and Co., 1861), 29; George Bagby, "Editor's Table," *SLM* 32 (January 1861), 74–5.

the blood that flowed from his hero heart,
On the spot where he nobly perished,
Was drunk by the earth as a sacrament
In the holy cause he cherished.[45]

Placing battlefield casualties within a sacred framework extended political leaders' earlier efforts to build national unity on the basis of Protestant religiosity. A sizeable contingent of proslavery evangelicals at the Montgomery Convention successfully included a "faith clause" in the preamble of the country's new Constitution, thus showing how their new republic had literally "begun in prayer." Executive proclamations immediately followed at both the national and the state levels and these proclamations initiated what would be an ongoing series of widely noted days of prayer, fasting, and thanksgiving. While the Confederate clergy already had experience in leading congregations in collective public worship, political independence suggested how Bible-based Christianity might become the lynchpin of a new nationalist culture. Fast-day and Thanksgiving sermons that were published and circulated helped to inject considerable self-consciousness into these potent new traditions. One clergyman greeted the first fast day as an "inspiring sentence which opens the book of our national history," while another thanked "the master builders of our national edifice" for "laying its foundation in humility and contrition, and cementing its stones with faith and prayer." Once established, the nationalist appeals to the Almighty helped to sustain an ongoing dialogue about the country's fidelity to God. With each national day of worship (there would be a total of nine before the war's end), clergy measured wartime developments since the last such occasion, thus encouraging citizens to understand the Confederate war as the unfolding of a sacred history.[46]

---

[45] "Memoria in Aeternia," *Southern Field and Fireside*, August 30, 1862; "H.C.B" "Gen. Albert Sydney Johnston," *Southern Field and Fireside* April 26, 1862. Quotation from Flash, "Zollifcoffer" in "Bohemian" [William G. Shepperson], *War Songs of the South* (Richmond: West & Johnston, 1862), 197. The following May, Flash sealed his reputation as the poet laureate of dead Generals by comparing the death of Stonewall Jackson – that hero of all martyred Confederate heroes – to that of the Hebrew leader Moses.

[46] Charles Jones, Jr. quoted in Robert Manson Myers, ed., *The Children of Pride: A True Story of Georgia and the Civil War* (New Haven, CT: Yale University Press, 1972), 101; Rev. Alfred Magill Randolph, *Address on the Day of Fasting and Prayer Appointed by the President of the Confederate States, June 13, 1861 Delivered in St. George's Church, Fredericksburg, VA;* (Fredericksburg, 1861), 2; Rev. Henry Niles Pierce, *Sermons Preached in St. John's Church, Mobile, on the 13th of June, 1861...* (Mobile, 1861), 3. Incisive recent discussions of these fast days include Faust, *Creation of Confederate Nationalism*; Mitchell Snay, *Gospel of Disunion: Religion and Separatism in the Antebellum South* (New York: Cambridge University Press, 1993) and Harry S. Stout, *On the Altar of the Nation: A Moral History of the Civil War* (New York: Viking, 2006).

Citizens responded enthusiastically to the new pattern of public devotion, recognizing how a collective "prayer of faith" would "ascend as from one heart and one voice, although ten thousand knees have bowed in humble supplication." These spectacles, by dramatizing a national collectivity, were among the surest signs that Confederates represented what Benjamin Morgan Palmer called "an incorporated society" which "possesses a unity of life resembling the individuality of a single being." Religious rituals were better suited than political rallies or troop mobilizations to the participation of both masters and slaves, a fact that prompted the *Charleston Mercury* to observe "how much more vividly would the patriarchal feature of the institution be therefore realized" if only African-Americans joined white Confederates in attending to government-sponsored worship. Widely publicized religious holidays linked civilians with those in the army, generating what one clergyman called "a deep undercurrent, a warm gulf stream of piety" that would roll "from the social circle, from the family altars, from the place of secret devotion, from thousands of sympathizing hearts" and, in the end, would fortify the country's "gallant armies." Poets took up the theme of national prayer by setting images of lone (typically female) individuals aside reminders that corporate worship extended across divisions of bondage and military service. For women barred from all-male armies, prayer became a way to mobilize energies and publicly enact their patriotic devotion (see Figure 7.2).[47]

Confederates who observed these days of prayer initially marveled about the power and self-determination these occasions implied. Some clergy encouraged listeners to think mostly of the utility of public devotion, explaining how "prayer touches the nerve of Omnipotence" and "moves the hand that moves the world." Invocations to the Divine could provide pious Confederates with "the rod in the hand of faith, that extracts the fiery curse from the burning bosom of the dark storm-cloud, and turns from our country and our homes the thunder-bolts of divine wrath." Such appeals were less persuasive when the Confederacy's fortunes dimmed and the new nation appeared to be more the object of Divine chastisement than protection. By 1863, fast days observances tended to concentrate on how citizens should supplicate themselves, regardless of what benefit might come in

---

[47] *The Children of Pride*, 992, 1054; *Charleston Mercury*, quoted in Savannah *Morning News*, June 11, 1861; Rev. Mr. M'Clure, "War and Victory: A Sermon at Grace Church, August 11th 1861" in *Memphis Avalanche*, August 17, 1861; Annie Chambers Ketchum "Nec Temere, Nec Timide" in Simms, *War Poetry of the South*; "The Great Fast Days in the South. June 13," *SLM* 33 (August 1861), 151–2; "Fast and Pray," in [Shepperson], *War Songs of the South*, 148–9.

FIGURE 7.2. This sheet music, published in 1864, asked "Maidens" who had already regularly observed days of fasting to pray even more, so that Providence might bless the Confederacy's "starry cross." *Courtesy of Duke University Special Collections.*

return. Such advice bred what one army chaplain called "an almost universal feeling of dependence upon the Heavenly Providence and a common reference of our cause to the control of the Infinite Mind and the support of the Almighty Arm."[48]

Confederates thus came to appreciate how even the hardest tribulations of war might be part of a Divine plan. The clergy's providential perspective was well suited to explain suffering as a path toward a greater good. As the South

---

[48] Rev. John T. Wightman, *The Glory of God the Defense of the South. A Discourse Delivered in the Methodist Episcopal Church, South, Yorkville, SC July 28th, 1861 the Day of National Thanksgiving for the Victory at Manassas* (Charleston, SC, 1861), 20; Rev. Jos. Cross, "Confederate Fast," in *Camp and Field: Papers from the Portfolio of an Army Chaplain Book Second* (Macon, GA: Burke, Boykin, and Company, 1864), 27–8.

Carolina Methodist John Wightman reminded listeners, "no work of God, no reformation can be accomplished without resistance, revolution and blood." After invoking the example of Moses, Luther, and Washington, he sealed his case by recalling how "even he who won our liberty on the cross died in the achievement." After the Battle of Manassas, the Richmond Presbyterian Rev. T.V. Moore was more specific, conveying how God had intended to put Confederates "into the furnace of war, that they might be welded into one great, united, and loving people, fused together by common weakness, common suffering, and common triumphs, having a common heritage of grief, and a common heritage of glory." This congealing process was a means of overcoming what Moore saw as potentially fatal "diversities that existed between border, and cotton, and gulf, and western States," which would otherwise have driven white southerners apart, despite their shared commitment to slavery. George Fitzhugh assured readers of the benefits of struggle using a slightly different perspective. Looking to the armies as a crucible of national sentiment, he explained how their common afflictions would not only "knit society more closely together for the present, but it will cement it in bonds of friendship and affection for half a century to come."[49]

The drama of war engrossed Confederates and inspired them to ponder the connections between providential will and the contingencies of battle. "The war which we are fighting for our liberties and independence," Governor Zebulon Vance pointed out in his 1862 inaugural address, "is indeed the sea which will receive our every stream of thought." By following the intricate details of distant battles, Confederates found themselves convinced that "the destinies of nations" really did "hang on the most minute and apparently casual incidents," as a South Carolina minister had insisted during the secession crisis. The momentous consequences of seemingly minor events fostered a widely shared belief that God alone had the power to guide the course of history. "Millions of souls should wrestle this night in prayer to the Great Disposer of events, for with Him is the issue," George Bagby wrote during the Union's 1862 advance on Richmond. "The courage of our soldiers, so often tried, so often proved, and the skill of our Generals, what are they against the thousand mischances of battle?" Battlefield particulars seemed to be too important to be driven by capricious fortune. These were an invitation for Confederates to "search the history of present events for the place and mission of the South" and to appreciate how "in searching for the traces of the finger of God, the student will often

---

[49] Wightman, *The Glory of God the Defense of the South*, 9; T.V. Moore, *God Our Refuge and Our Strength*; [Fitzhugh], "The Times and the War," *DBR* 31 (July 1861), 8.

discover in a single event the germ of a nation's history and a hint of the eternal mind."[50]

In attempting to discern and explain providential design, the Confederate clergy differed among themselves whether humans could comprehend an inscrutable and all-powerful God. Some offered elaborate readings of Biblical prophecy, hoping to discern how the fate of the new country had been foretold in dense scriptural allegories.[51] Most orthodox clergy conveyed greater humility, however, agreeing with James Henley Thornwell that it would be "presumptuous for any one, independently of a special revelation, to venture to decipher" what he termed "the whole end of Providence." Thornwell still expected the faithful to attend to those "tendencies which lie on the surface," and argued that these seemed to have been "designed for our guidance and instruction." He agreed with Benjamin Palmer, who, in 1864, explained that "providence is always hard to be interpreted, when we are in the very current of events, drifting and whirling us along too rapidly for the comparison and thought which are necessary to scan the mysterious cypher in which God writes his will upon the page of human history." To grapple with destiny required calm meditation, openness to God's suggestions, and a willingness to reflect on the course set by a higher power. Such perspective could be achieved only by suppressing those wartime passions that many clergy believed had "imparted too much of a morbid feature to the national character in the present struggle."[52]

---

[50] Vance quoted in Joe A. Mobley, *"War Governor of the South": North Carolina's Zeb Vance in the Confederacy* (Tallahassee: University of Florida Press, 2005), 33; Rev. W.C. Dana, *A Sermon Delivered in the Central Presbyterian Church, Charleston, SC ...* (Charleston, 1860), 11; "Hermes" [Bagby] in *Charleston Mercury*, June 2, 1862; Wightman, *The Glory of God the Defense of the South*.

[51] Rev. V. C. Spencer, *A Sermon. God in the Land of Magog, against Israel; or Southern Confederacy Triumphant* (Waco, TX, 1861); W.H. Seat, *The Confederate States of America in Prophesy by Rev. Seat, of the Texas Conference* (Nashville, TN, 1861); J.P. Philpott, *The Kingdom of Israel: From its Inception under Joshua, its First President, in the year of the World 2353, to the Second Advent of Christ* (Fairfield, TX, 1864). All three of these works acknowledge the influence of the Southern Methodist Rev. Samuel Davies Baldwin's well-known explications of prophesy of the antebellum period: *Armageddon; or The United States in Prophecy* (Nashville, TN, 1845) and *Dominion; Or, the Unity and Trinity of the Human Race ...* (Nashville, TN, 1858); the correspondent Samuel Chester Reid set forth similar themes under the pen name "Ora"; see his series of letters in the *Montgomery Advertiser*, June, 1864.

[52] Thornwell, "Our Danger and Our Duty," *DBR* 33 (May–August 1862), 50–1; Palmer, "Letter to Congregation, May 20, 1864" in Thomas Cary Johnson, *The Life and Letters of Benjamin Morgan Palmer* (Richmond, VA: Presbyterian Committee of Publication, 1906), 280; Rev. D.S. Doggett, *The War and Its Close: A Discourse Delivered in Centenary Church, Richmond, Va. Friday April 8th, 1864 on the Occasion of the National Fast* (Richmond, VA: Macfarlane and Ferguson, 1864), 7.

   While the clergy warned against drawing hasty or self-serving conclusions
about God's will, they generally agreed with Congressman Samuel Ford
(himself a Baptist minister) that during war, "God's voice speaks in thrilling
eloquence" that demanded believers open themselves to His will. Most
practicing Christian thus agreed that a Divine plan existed, even as they
differed as to human reckoning with all its complexities and essential mys-
teries. Pulpit pronouncements typically came with a strong disclaimer about
the level of certainty even a man of God could attain. But underlying this
was a basic agreement that history was "no mass of arbitrary, disorganized
events," to use the words of the Rev. James Warley Miles. Indeed, Miles
argued that it was "amid the most stormy convulsions and the fiercest
ebullitions of human passion" that the faithful might best step back and
appreciate "a Divine Providence directing with steady and intelligent hand
the development of its plan, and making that plan subservient to the cause of
humanity." Privately, Miles admitted by late 1864 that he found "no really
profane history, for it is all a manifestation of Providence."[53]
   Efforts to reckon with Almighty purposes paid particular attention to the
outcome of ever more spectacular battles. In this way, proslavery ideologues
recast their understanding of how they and the institution of slavery developed in harmony with a larger plan. Earlier invocations of Providence had
typically addressed the gradual processes of slavery's expansion toward the
tropics and the long-term Christianization of "Heathen" Africa. War made
the Divine presence far more immediate – and also more unpredictable. As
news registered the repulse of armies, the capture of cities, the destruction of
plantations, and the deaths of thousands of fighters, Confederates could
reflect upon how "transition periods are always convulsive," as an Atlanta
editor put it late in 1863. His call to arms offered up the elaborate promise
that "a splendid future is ours if we will be co-workers with Providence."
Readers who had just suffered a series of grave setbacks could take solace in
the promise that "our political creed is written for us by the hand of heaven,
and our part is to accept its principles as final." In one of the war's most

[53] Rev. Samuel Ford, *Address to the Confederate Soldiers of the Southwest* (Grenada,
   Mississippi, 1862); Rev. W. Knox, "Trust in God: A Sermon the Occasion of the Fast
   Appointed by the Governor of Georgia Delivered in Trinity Church, Savannah" in *Sav-
   annah Morning News* March 15, 1862; James Warley Miles, *God in History: A Dis-
   course Delivered Before the Graduating Class of the College of Charleston on Sunday
   Evening, March 29, 1863* (Charleston, 1863), 30; Miles to Mrs. Thomas John Young,
   August 21, 1864, quoted in Ralph E. Luker, "God, Man, and the World of James Warley
   Miles: Charleston's Transcendentalist," *Historical Magazine of the Protestant Episcopal Church* 39 (June 1970), 101–6.

chilling images, the pamphlet dramatized how national destiny and corpo-
real suffering were intertwined. "If like Niagara, this stream of blood pours
over its precipice, like Niagara, its white cloud of incense rises towards the
heavens of God," to be "wreathed with the rainbows that prophesy the
advent of a most blessed peace."[54]

The association of wartime sacrifice with "disciplinary providences"
grew more intense as the war's human toll mounted. By late in 1862,
Alexander Stephens was already marveling that Americans' participation
in the gargantuan clashes at Shiloh, during the Seven Days' Battles at Virginia, and at Antietam were introducing them to war "on the greatest scale
of any since the birth of Christ, the history of the world – not excepting the
crusades – furnishing no parallel to it in the present era." After two more
years of even more deadly clashes, the former U.S. War Secretary Charles M.
Conrad asked his colleagues in the Confederate Congress to contemplate
Americans' bloodbath and to consider "what are the pigmy wars of Europe
in comparison with our mighty struggle shaking the whole continent from
its breadth to its circumference involving the rights and property of every
man, woman, and child?" The tens of thousands killed in the weeks immediately following Conrad's query caused Henry Timrod to speculate that
"perhaps almost as many sleep beneath the sod as are now marching above
to defend it." This calculation was not far off the mark, for at the time that
Timrod wrote, fewer than 200,000 Confederates soldiers were present for
duty – a number that fell well short of the total losses that rebel armies
would suffer by the conclusion of hostilities just a year later.[55]

As might be expected, Timrod wrenched a positive message from this
grim comparison of the Confederate dead with those still in the ranks. In
discussing how the South had "laid a whole army in the earth," he relied on
a new nationalist mysticism rather than on the Christian doctrine of Providence. This was a means of assuring all readers that patriots might "still
count [this dead army], not without reason, as a component part of our
existing force." As he explained:

... of the myriads of graves, [this army's] blood cries unto God and the nations on
our behalf; the plants which wrap their roots around the bones of its heroes whisper,
with all their leaves, lessons of solemn self-sacrifice, and make the air heavy as with

---

[54] Wightman, *The Glory of God the Defense of the South*, 20; *Address of the Atlanta Register*.
[55] Alexander Stephens, "Address at Crawfordville, November 1, 1862," in Cleveland, ed., *Letters and Speeches*, 762; Conrad speech of May 21, 1864 in *SHSP* 51 (1958), 124; [Henry Timrod], "The Patriotic Dead," *South Carolinian*, July 15, 1864.

the fragrance of noble deeds; and in the hour of battle, when to the stirred soul and excited fancy metaphors becomes fact, and the cherished memories of the heart are ready to take bodily shape, the ghosts of the shadowy columns seem to float above our standards, and fight once more upon our sides.

"If there be any truth in moral and spiritual influences," Timrod concluded, "the might of that dead army remains with us yet. Their deeds and their fate transmuted into history and poetry" could hardly help but provide "an entire national education in themselves."[56]

Timrod's wartime musings signaled how central loss had become to the Confederate imagination, a development that would furnish mourners of the "Lost Cause" a readymade set of associations. Timrod himself resisted the temptation to consider what conclusive military defeat might mean for the Confederate cult of martyrdom. Others were ready, however, to acknowledge how the logic of providential design – and the larger framework of unwavering Divine Will – meant that even God's chosen people might find themselves accepting the triumph of their most bitter and undeserving enemies. In one of the most sweeping proslavery pleas of the secession crisis, William Henry Holcombe conceded "if it be possible, in the mysterious providence of God, that we should fail and perish in our sublime attempt [to leave the Union], let it come! Our souls may rebel against the inscrutable decree of such a destiny, but we will not swerve a line from the luminous path of duty." In a more popular vein, the poet Margaret Junkin Preston prepared the way for her postwar "Acceptance," by sounding themes during the second half of the war about supplicating oneself and the aspirations of one's nation to the will of a higher power.[57]

This sensibility that divine judgments might run counter to collective desires was new to many proslavery nationalists, who had for two generations been touchy about ceding control of their "sacred" institutions to outside forces. This is not to say that providential perspectives bred defeatism, or even fatalism. But the tendency to see cosmic forces at work restructured slaveholders' sense of their own power in important ways. In one of the last Confederate sermons to be published, the Rev. Charles Minnegerode of Richmond warned that "in the heat of action, under the fire of ambition, a world of courtiers or of slaves bowing before them: men may forget that they are but instruments in God's hand." A war of humiliating invasion and the

---

[56] [Timrod], "The Patriotic Dead."

[57] Holcombe, "The Alternative: A Separate Nationality or the Africanization of the South," *SLM* 32 (February 1861), 88; Margaret Junkin Preston, "Hymn to the National Flag" in *Richmond Sentinel*, January 17, 1865; idem, *Beechenbrook* (Richmond, VA, 1865).

increasing loss of mastery at home dissolved many of those pretensions to invulnerability that white Southerners had instinctively expressed prior to 1861. As slaveholders puzzled over what it meant to be tools of a higher power, they realized how a war largely of their own making had brought about their utter destruction. They would be taught by military defeat what the proslavery clergy had long preached – that they too had a master in heaven.[58]

[58] Rev. Charles Minnegerode *Power, A Sermon Preached at St. Paul's, Richmond, on the 13th November, 1864* (Richmond, VA: W.H. Clemmitt, 1864), 9.

8

Reckoning with Confederate Purpose

A few weeks before the Civil War's first major battle, William Falconer of Alabama urged Confederates to devote as much energy to divining their national mission as they had expended in forming a government, mobilizing their armies, and invoking the favor of the Divine. "The South finds itself engaged upon a course of civil war and revolution without a properly defined idea of any particular purpose to be advanced, and apparently without any just conception of the great social and philosophic truths that lie concealed beneath." By "permitting the present great move in society to assume the appearance and actual form of an ordinary civil war," partisans of the new republic fatefully ignored how "the present occasion is by no means a purely military one" and was at most "but a mixed one, in which the intellectual, by far, predominates over the physical." Falconer thus called out for what he termed the "Southern mind" to "direct its attention to a full and clear discovery of the great social, political, and philosophical principles involved, and set them forth quickly and prominently, so that the people shall feel, as with one thrill, the objects to be advanced – and move with one motive."[1]

Three years earlier, Falconer's appeal had been set forth in pithier form by his political nemesis, the fire-eater William L. Yancey, who explained how an effective proslavery revolution required not simply "firing the southern heart" but "instructing the southern mind" about its destiny apart from the Union. Establishing a clear, detached perspective was a challenge during the secession crisis, when passion rather than reason was the order of the day. Emotional energies were further stoked by the outbreak of war. The

---

[1] [Falconer], "The True Question: A Contest for the Supremacy of Race, as Between the Saxon Puritan of the North, and the Norman of the South," *SLM* 33 (July 1861), 21.

neglect of deeper issues confounded the Rev. Benjamin Morgan Palmer, who built upon his sensational Thanksgiving Day address of 1860 by lecturing slaveholders about "the duty of this new-born nation to consider the part assigned it in the great drama of History." Palmer's theological training equipped him to offer a particularly sophisticated understanding of how a national mind might turn the ligaments and blood of nationhood to higher purposes. On the occasion of the Confederacy's first national fast, Palmer explained how each truly historic nation "has its own precisely defined character, fulfills its appointed mission, is developed through a providential training, and is held to a strict providential reckoning." Before long, some in the daily press joined the clergy to venture a similarly rarified understanding of how nations embodied world-historical ideas that transcended any narrow defense of shared interests. A contributor to the *Richmond Sentinel* offered late in 1864 what had become a truism, noting that "nationality is the necessary protector of a distinctive idea" and that every "germ of social development, or of civilization (to use a better term) requires for itself a distinctive nationality."[2]

As the war dragged on, Confederates continued to gravitate toward explanations that were simple enough to be widely understood and inspiring enough to span human history and reverberate across the globe. Mounting casualties injected considerable urgency in reckoning with national purpose. By 1864, the Richmond journalist Edward Pollard implored that "we have not poured out our tears – we have not made a monument of broken hearts – we have not kneaded the ground with human flesh, merely for the poor negative of a peace, with naught higher or better things of the past." Despite his concerns about the Davis administration's "ruin and confusion," Pollard held fast to the conviction that "from the scattered elements will arise a new spirit of beauty and order." A similar mixture of assurance and hope came from an anonymous writer in the *Atlanta Register*. An editorial of New Year's Day 1864 urged Confederates: "you cannot fight this battle for yourself alone" but must cast their gaze "into something grander than a sectional triumph." Within a few months, the Rev. William A. Hall undertook a series of public lectures that he hoped would convince his fellow Confederates to "survey this great movement, not as politicians merely, not

---

[2] Yancey to James Slaughter quoted in *National Intelligencer*, July 20, 1858; Palmer, *National Responsibility Before God: A Discourse on the Day of Fasting, Humiliation and Prayer* (New Orleans: Price Current Book Shop, 1861); "Bland," "The Great Issue," in *Richmond Sentinel*, December 2, 1864 and reprinted in *Memphis Daily Appeal*, December 17, 1864.

as religionists, not even as *Southrons*, but as thinkers, controlled by the noble spirits of the philosophy of history." He urged his audience to appreciate how they were "leading a great battle for the sum of modern history" and to realize that "eighteen Christian centuries" were "looking down" upon their efforts. Such attempts to fix a cosmic perspective pleased those in the press who hoped that Confederate fortunes depended on replacing the "twaddle of petty politicians" with "the higher range of thought and survey, and disquisition."[3]

Explorations of Confederate purpose were hardly confined to learned pamphleteers or metaphysically-inclined theologians. In exploring and probing how this new political creation was a missionary redeemer no less than a sovereign polity, antebellum variants of proslavery Americanism converged and overlapped as never before. The overheated atmosphere of a nationalist war caused Presidential proclamations to inspire popular poetry and commercial reviews to reprint clerical reflection. Political columns that first appeared in literary magazines would become the topic of soldiers' campfire discussions. The future of republicanism and slavery inspired searching reflections upon the will of God; these same topics would become the occasion for frivolous song and festive display. Out of such intense cultural activity, three narratives of purpose arose, and each of these situated the 1860s within the larger sweep of history. The most prevalent and persistent strain identified southern rebels as the true inheritors of the American Revolution. Alternatives to this account appeared in two paired understandings of the Confederacy's status as the world's first proudly and self-consciously slaveholding republic. Some who focused on bondage associated the proslavery departure with a new dawn of reaction while others saw national independence as a precursor to the perfection of republican paternalism. Reckoning with collective purpose helped to shape the way slaveholders understood their loss of mastery, even if slaves' own understanding of American nationhood worked to usher in a world wholly beyond Confederate imaginings.[4]

---

[3] E. A. Pollard, *The Two Nations; A Key to the History of the American War* (Richmond, GA: Ayres and Wade, 1864), 22; "Cincinnatus," *Address of the Atlanta Register to the People of the Confederate States* (Atlanta, GA: 1864), 13; Rev. William A. Hall, *The Historic Significance of the Southern Revolution A Lecture Delivered by Invitation* (Petersburg: A.F. Cruchfield, 1864), 4; *Charleston Courier,* quoted in *Richmond Daily Dispatch,* May 11, 1864.

[4] Approaching Confederate nationalism as a matter of process and narrative rather than as attribute or measurable quality is detailed by Drew Gilpin Faust, *The Creation of Confederate Nationalism* (Baton Rouge 1990); idem, "Altars of Sacrifice: Confederate Women and the Narratives of War," *JAH* 76 (March 1990), 1200–28; and Reid Mitchell, "Nationalism" in *The Encyclopedia of the Confederacy* (New York, 1993) 3: 1111–16.

REVOLUTIONARY ECHOES DURING THE SECOND AMERICAN FOUNDING

Confederates wasted little time in making the "first" American Revolution the most important touchstone of their own campaign for national independence. Pairing 1861 with 1776 came naturally to those who had for decades circulated proslavery tributes to the American founding. Themes first popularized by South Carolina nullifiers and Unionists in the early 1830s thus reemerged as fire-eaters and compromisers of 1860 debated the relative worth of an abstract or embodied revolutionary heritage. Once Confederates formed a government and returned to a familiar constitutional order, nullifiers' defiant radicalism seemed more likely to hinder than to foster nationalist development and lost some of its allure as a result. The demands of modern war and the exigencies of government centralization recast broader understandings of the connection between the present and the formative Revolutionary period of American history. If bloodshed for the cause of Confederate independence continued to recall a tradition of political rights, it became increasingly tied to the devastation inflicted upon earlier white Southerners by King George III of England.[5]

Confederates were notably theatrical in drawing out the Revolutionary parallels between their ancestors' war of defense and that which they waged against the Yankee invaders. Shortly after the bombardment of Fort Sumter, James De Bow alerted his readers that they were "acting upon the stage the same great drama which was acted by our fathers in 1776–83." Lest anyone mistake his meaning, De Bow elaborated how "conscious of our right, we have accepted the arbitrament of the sword, and before it is sheathed a perfidious enemy will find that the spirit of a glorious ancestry survives, and that Washington and Lee, Randolph and Jefferson, Marion, Moultrie, Sumter, and Jackson still live." As events unfolded, the spirit of the founders seemed to revive in their actual progeny, many of whom held positions at the highest echelons of Confederate leadership. Among the sons of Revolutionary veterans were President Jefferson Davis (whose father had served in the patriot ranks during the 1780s), and the Virginia Generals Robert E. Lee

---

[5] George Rable, *The Confederate Republic: A Revolution against Politics* (Chapel Hill, NC: University of North Carolina Press, 1994) and Anne Sarah Rubin, *A Shattered Nation: The Rise and Fall of the Confederacy, 1861–1868* (Chapel Hill, NC: University of North Carolina Press, 2005) each emphasize Confederates' fixation on their Revolutionary legacy; the salience of military violence in such recollections is considered in Charles Royster, *The Destructive War: William Tecumseh Sherman, Stonewall Jackson, and the Americans* (New York: Vintage Books, 1991).

and Joseph Johnston (whose fathers had each achieved considerable fame under the command of George Washington). A still larger group of Revolutionary grandchildren included George W. Randolph (the Confederacy's third Secretary of War and grandson of Thomas Jefferson) and James Murray Mason (the chief Confederate diplomat and grandson of the author of the Virginia Bill of Rights). If Gulf State Confederates fell short of Virginians in the caliber of iconic forbears, Octavia Le Vert and Maria McIntosh each claimed direct descent from signers of the Declaration of Independence. Wade Hampton and Francis Pickens extended family traditions that began when their grandfathers gained military fame during the first American fight for republican independence.[6]

It was not simply the personnel but the stage that instilled a sense of history repeating itself. Shortly after De Bow grandly declared that "every field within our limits will prove a Yorktown – every fortification a Moultrie!" some of the same troops that initiated hostilities in Charleston Harbor quickly relocated to the lower James Peninsula, and established fortifications where Cornwallis had surrendered to the Continental Army eighty years earlier. As Confederates defended this history-laden territory, they did so with an expanded awareness of historical parallels and a sense that new locales were being added to a distinctly southern geography of patriotism. Late in 1861, one North Carolina Confederate vowed that the previously obscure Manassas Plains was "destined, in all times to come, to be as famous in history as Bunker's Hill, Yorktown, or New Orleans." Appreciating how Confederates contributed to broader American traditions, this writer noted how "some of the heroic patriots, who fought so bravely at those battles, had sons and grandsons at Manassas on the 21st of July, 1861." Conjuring up a distant future, he predicted that "the whole particulars of this battle will form a large book of history, when all shall have been known."[7]

Despite these distinguished bloodlines and familiar locales, enemies continued to attack Confederates' declension from founding virtues. As slaveholders themselves realized, claiming the Revolutionary mantle would mean little if echoes were not accompanied by efforts to perpetuate those commitments, principles, and endeavors first formulated in 1776. This initiative was complicated by earlier proslavery attempts to qualify the Declaration of Independence's affirmation of human equality. Even as Jefferson Davis and others focused attention on the "American idea" of toppling

---

[6] "Editorial," *DBR* 31 (May, June 1861), 68.
[7] T.N. Ramsey, *Sketches of the American Revolution of 1861* (Salisbury, NC: J.J. Bruner, 1861), 14.

governments that violated rights, a certain dissonance remained. The tensions were especially pronounced during the Fourth of July holiday, when newspaper columnists, diarists, and a handful of orators glossed over the particulars of the Declaration while lambasting the hypocrisy of those who would deny this latest episode in the self-determination of peoples. An Independence Day editorial in the *Charleston Courier* maintained: "we challenge the world to approve the Declaration of Independence and to show wherein the secession of the South fails in finding fuller and larger justification." There were, to be sure, a few skeptics who questioned continued observance of this "Yankee" holiday at all. In the wake of those July 1863 military disasters at Gettysburg and Vicksburg, the editor James Addison Turner of Georgia called for the "abolition" of this festive "bond" with the North, insisting that "the day that witnessed our deliverance from Yankee bondage is the time for our national holiday." Turner's suggestion drew little response, primarily because the process of separate state secessions meant that there was no one single birth date of "Southern" independence. Henry Timrod offered a sounder strategy in 1864, when he urged Confederates to continue to honor the Fourth of July and the principles of self-government established on that date, but to do so with more sober celebrations that would give the occasion a suitably distinctive character. By dispensing with the oratory that had been a staple of antebellum observances (and which still seemed to characterize Union celebrations), Confederates might alter their inheritance, establish a more serious attempt to match principles and actions, and put to shame the comparatively shallow Yankees.[8]

The experience of war was a key factor in altering Confederates attitude toward both the rituals and the substance of American patriotism. Once the Confederacy was established, the legitimizing principles of self-government seemed far less important than the self-sacrifice of Revolutionary heroism. Late in 1862, editor John Daniel did not even mention the Declaration of Independence when he reflected on "the historical idea of revolution," which he linked not to principles but to what he called the "mental excitement with which it was inaugurated; the upheaving of the masses; the close

[8] Davis, "Inaugural Address" *PJD* 7, 46–7; A. W. Terrell, *Oration Delivered on the Fourth Day of July, 1861, at the Capitol, Austin, Texas* (Austin, TX: John Marshall, 1861); Turner, *Countryman*, July 14, 1863; Timrod, *Daily South Carolinian*, July 8, 1864. Confederates joined other "new states" in elevating the Declaration's principles of self-determination over its embrace of human equality, a point established in David Armitage, *The Declaration of Independence: A Global History* (Cambridge, MA: Harvard University Press, 2006).

sympathy between the army and the people; and the desperate spirit" that was then everywhere on display. Deeds that had inspired civic devotion in peacetime took on new significance in the frenzied context of Union invasion and occupation. Confederates who were asked to subordinate their own individual fortunes to the cause of national independence took inspiration less from what the Continental Congress had done in its defiance of Parliament than what citizens had endured during the early 1780s, a period that had long been remembered as the hardest times of the Revolution. In 1862, the *Charleston Mercury* referred to this period as the "textbook of patriotism for all coming ages" and insisted that "its lessons can never be too often studied – nor its precepts too often inculcated – nor its principles too often held up for the example and admiration of mankind."[9]

Nationalists who sustained Revolutionary comparisons urged ordinary citizens to internalize the shared hardships of the founding period, to emulate the constancy displayed by earlier wartime patriots, and to achieve fame through their own death-defying risks. Soldiers marching from their camps were reminded less of the leadership of George Washington or the idealism of Thomas Jefferson than of the daring of Sergeant William Jasper, whose heroic reputation had been sealed in 1776 when he had bravely hoisted the Crescent Flag in Charleston Harbor. Southern women likewise heeded the example of the adventurous matrons who had shown their resolution and grit during the American struggle against England. Augusta Jane Evans used her best-selling novel *Macaria* to juxtapose the tale of Emily Geiger, a hero of the Low Country resistance in 1781, with a young female Confederate who had secretly carried a letter to the commanders at Manassas before that major battle of 1861. After explaining how this still anonymous heroine had assured Confederate victory that day, Evans speculated how posterity would eventually remember her. "When our national jewels are set up," her name would be set "between those of Beauregard and Johnston in the revolutionary diadem" and the three of them would together "blaze through coming ages, baffling the mists of time."[10]

As Evans' novel suggested, Revolutionary recollections held special meaning for Confederate women, whose desire for public acclaim accompanied their

---

[9] *Richmond Examiner*, November 25, 1862; "Original Journals of the Siege of Charleston," in *Charleston Mercury*, June 5, 1862.

[10] Robert E. Bonner, *Colors and Blood: Flag Passions of the Confederate South* (Princeton: Princeton University Press, 2002), 90–1; "The Daughters of Our War of Independence," *New Orleans Delta*, March 24, 1861; Augusta J. Evans, *Macaria, or, Altars of Sacrifice* (Richmond, VA: West & Johnston 1864), 146–7.

perception that posterity would lavish most of its attention on the men who joined and fought in the armies. The 1850s campaign of slaveholding women on behalf of Mount Vernon provided little guidance under these new circumstances. As the Union dissolved, so too did the credibility of that patriotic cause and of the personnel who had led the most visible campaign of female nationalists prior to 1860. A generational passing from Unionist mothers to Confederate daughters seemed underway as Ann Pamela Cunningham and her closest allies warned both southern and northern troops not to sully Washington's Virginia estate with their presence. Subsequently, these women implied that the sacred historical site be jointly owned by the Confederacy and the Union after the slave-South's independence, a notion that raised doubts about the ultimate allegiances of those who had worked so hard to calm sectional discord.[11]

Into the void left by the waning Mount Vernon campaign, a younger group of Confederate writers like Evans introduced a sharply different version of patriotism, which they based on a combination of literary output and widely-reported heroic exploits. A fairly sizeable group of female writers blended patriotic exhortation with an inspiring model of defiance. In the case of Evans, her dangerous trip to the front and subsequent interactions with generals and statesmen bolstered what was already a considerable reputation as a literary stylist. Other Confederate writers emerged from obscurity as they inspired their fellow countrywomen to emulate the "first revolution," to perfect proslavery domesticity, and to commiserate about the suffering despicable Yankees inflicted. Constance Cary translated her refugee status (which had followed her expulsion from Maryland) into prominence within Richmond society. After Cary began to write as "Refugitta" for the literary press, she assumed a presence across Confederate culture more generally. Exile and dispossession similarly established the celebrity of Confederate poets Mary Jane Cross (who was driven out of Louisville along with her husband, a Methodist minister), Susan Archer Talley (a deaf Virginia poet who had been imprisoned at Fort McHenry for her pro-Confederate loyalties), and

---

[11] C. Vann Woodward, ed., *Mary Chesnut's Civil War* (New Haven, CT: Yale University Press, 1981), 71; Gerald W. Johnson, *Mount Vernon: The Story of a Shrine* (New York: Random House, 1953), 24–33. Ambivalence was not universal among the Mount Vernon leadership, as was clear in the staunch support for secession given by Georgia Vice-Regent Philoclea Edgeworth Eve, as reported in Augusta *Daily Constitutionalist*, January 22, 1861.

Susan Blanchard Elder (who fled her native New Orleans to become a refugee in Selma, Alabama).[12]

Linking examples from the past with the heroic suffering of the present allowed Confederates to evaluate their own fortitude. In 1861, the Texas politician A. W. Terrell explained the importance of establishing "whether we have drifted away from the faith bequeathed to us by the apostles of '76." Some politicians used comparisons between the "First" and "Second" Revolution to rally enthusiasm, following Senator William Yancey's boast late in 1862 that "we present to the world a greater unity in numbers, in confidence in each other, and in adherence to our cause, than our forefathers presented in the revolution." Jefferson Davis used a similar means of motivating the crowds two years later, when, in surveying the actions of both male and female Confederates, he concluded that "our people are even better than were our honored ancestors," since "they have fought more and bloodier battles, and there are fewer who are lukewarm now, than existed in the days of the Revolution." Such positive evaluations were not universal. The acerbic *Charleston Mercury* noted in 1863 that "We are by no means such martyrs to Liberty's cause as the first American Revolution produced, and we fear, many of us, will never become such unselfish patriots." A similarly gloomy assessment came from the *Richmond Whig* late in 1864, when it insisted that Confederates could either match the fortitude of their ancestors or witness a defeat that would "unmask us to the world as a people of charlatans, and exhibit our attempted revolution as a sorry imitation of those nobler episodes which have adorned the history of the human race."[13]

[12] Mary Tardy, *Living Female Writers* (Philadelphia, PA: Lippincott, 1867); Rebecca Grant Sexton, *A Southern Woman of Letters: The Correspondence of Augusta Jane Evans Wilson* (Columbia: University of South Carolina Press, 2002); "Refugitta" [Constance Cary], "A Blockade Correspondence," *SIN*, August 8 through November 14, 1863; Cross story conveyed in "Chapter of Unparalleled Atrocity," Atlanta *Southern Confederacy*, August 31, 1862; Talley information from *Nashville Dispatch*, July 6, 1862; Elder quoted in Selma *Morning Reporter*, June 12, 1864. Margaret Junkin Preston, another emerging Confederate poet, publicly experienced exile in reverse, after her celebrated Unionist father was forced to relocate to the North. For an incisive view of the larger vibrant literary scene that helped these poets to craft new personas, see Alice Fahs, *The Imagined Civil War: Popular Literature of the North & South, 1861–1865* (Chapel Hill: University of North Carolina Press, 2001).

[13] A. W. Terrell, *Oration*, 3; *Speeches of William L. Yancey, Senator from the State of Alabama* (Montgomery: Montgomery Advertiser, 1862), 12–13; Jefferson Davis, "General Orders No. 19," February 10, 1864 in *CMPC* 1, 414; *Charleston Mercury*, March 4, 1862; *Charleston Mercury*, October 7, 1864; *Richmond Whig*, "The Price of Independence" December 24, 1864; see also *Richmond Whig* "The Attitude of the South," December 28, 1864.

Confederates realized that in terms of military scale and scope, their own struggle clearly did surpass that of their Revolutionary forebears. James McCabe referred to this basic fact when in 1862 he referred to the patriots of 1776 as having fought through "that other and lesser revolution." Arresting war commentary provided by the popular *Southern Illustrated News* tallied the comparatively minor casualties of the Revolutionary years and set these figures aside the gore of the early 1860s. When viewed in this context, it seemed that the most apt comparison of Lee's campaigns was not to Valley Forge or Yorktown but to the continental exploits of Napoleon and Wellington. A few commentators ventured as far back as the ancient battles fought at Pharsalia and at Platea to find examples that had the same world-historical significance as Confederate victories did.[14]

As Confederates wove themes from the Revolution throughout their political, military, and diplomatic commentary, episodes from America's heroic period emerged as a critical ingredient of their wartime vocabulary. Yet while historical echoes saturated public dialogue, most Confederates did not push themselves beyond stock phrases, sound bites, and patriotic boilerplate to grapple with how a Revolutionary inheritance complicated Confederates' desire to formulate their own distinctive mission. In the early summer of 1861, the Rev. Benjamin Morgan Palmer drew attention to the relative superficiality of southern tributes to the American Revolution. "The parallel which has been drawn" had "not been seen in its full significance by many even of those who have suggested it," he observed, before providing his own convoluted explanation that showed how cumbersome this task could be. "The principles involved in this conflict are broader and deeper than those which underlay that of the Revolution, rendering it of far greater significance to us and to our posterity and to mankind at large." Palmer backed up his claim by explaining how the colonists had taken up arms for political independence in defense of chartered English rights; Confederates, by contrast, fought for the far more exalted principles of self-government.[15]

The notion that Confederates pursued more glorious ends than their forefathers tempted Palmer to extend the notion that the current generation

[14] William Gordon McCabe, "Political Corruption" *SLM* 34 (February–March 1862), 89; "Battles of the Revolution," and "Parallel Between Lee's Campaigns in Maryland, and Wellington's Campaign of 1809, in Spain," both in *SIN* September 13, 1862; "Austerlitz and Manassas," *SIN* November 22, 1862; "The Illustrious Dead," *SIN*, May 16, 1863; Fitzhugh, "The Great Day of Manassas" *DBR* 32 (September 1861), 282; [J. Michard], "Pharsalia – Manassas." *SLM* 33 (October 1861), 296–303.

[15] Palmer, *National Responsibility Before God: A Discourse on the Day of Fasting, Humiliation and Prayer* (New Orleans: Price Current Steam Book, 1861).

would surpass the achievements of their forbears. But as most of his readers
would have recognized, he grounded his evaluation not on any set of
uniquely Confederate convictions but on his new country's fidelity to the
doctrines set forth in Jefferson's Declaration of Independence. In this sense,
sweeping rhetoric masked what was at heart a quintessentially conservative
preference for preservation over innovation. Most Confederate ministers
who addressed the legacy of the American Revolution reached similar conclusions. James Henley Thornwell exemplified the clergy's intricate pattern
of avowals and denials when he explained how efforts to "perpetuate and
diffuse the very liberty for which Washington bled, and which the heroes of
the Revolution achieved" demonstrated how Confederates were "not revo-
lutionists" but were "resisting revolution." Stephen Elliott and Thomas
Smyth alternated between praising the American Revolution (which both
contrasted to the excesses of French innovation) and expressing deeply-felt
qualms about the rights-based Jeffersonian philosophy that elevated human
desires over divine commands. The Rev. Thomas E. Peck set his understanding of the Confederate mission to "maintain" and to "restore" in
conversation with a similar set of goals proposed by leaders of the Protestant
Reformation and of the Glorious Revolution of 1688. In establishing a
tradition of renewal, he concluded that "we need no new principles; but
we do need to review and to remember the old, to refresh ourselves and
renew our youth at the fountain of truth."[16]

The pairing of Confederate rebellion with a traditional defense of rights
figured in secular commentary upon the Revolutionary legacy as well.
Edmund Walthall of Alabama denied that Confederates pursued "a mere
vulgar 'revolution' in the sense in which that term has been degraded by
Jacobinical, red-republican usage." A fight undertaken "on behalf of all that
is sacred and divinely sanctioned in human government" assured that Confederates had the "rare privilege" of being "called to defend their firesides
from tyranny, invasion, desecration" while simultaneously "being summoned to the maintenance of government authority, and order, against
insurrection, anarchy, or lawless violence." The Confederate Congress similarly blurred the line between "legitimate" revolt and order in the most
widely publicized of its several joint addresses, which appeared early in
1864. "As in the English Revolution of 1688, and ours of 1776," state
secession sparked by Lincoln's election had involved "no material alteration
in the laws beyond what was necessary to redress the abuses that provoked

---

[16] Rev. James Henley Thornwell, "Our Danger and Our Duty," *DBR* 33 (May–August,
1862), 44; Rev. Thomas E. Peck, "Church and State," *SPR* 16 (October, 1863), 129.

the struggle." From these orderly beginnings, Confederates had proven themselves consistent conservatives, the address continued.

No attempt was made to build on speculative principles. The effort was confined within the narrowest limits of historical and constitutional right. The controversy turned on the records and monuments of the past. We merely resisted innovation and tyranny, and contended for our birth-rights, and the covenanted principles of our race ... When the sovereign States met in council, they, in truth and substance, and in a constitutional light, did not make, but prevented a revolution.[17]

By the time the Congress articulated this nuanced stance, George Fitzhugh had already punctured the logic of a conservative revolution by altogether disassociating the Confederacy from its American predecessors. In what would become his signature wartime essay, the Virginia polemicist traced the disruptions of 1688 and then of 1776 through the revolutionary turmoil of late-eighteenth-century Europe, and finally to the ascendancy of Abraham Lincoln's Republican Party. In this genealogy, responsibility for current troubles ultimately lay with the natural rights theorist John Locke, whose doctrines of equality and consent consisted of a "tissue of the grossest and most palpable absurdities and puerilities" that Fitzhugh could imagine. The Revolutionary founders were complicit in having incorporated "false and unnecessary theories" into the American constitutional order and had thus "most officiously and unwisely" erected their "splendid political edifice" upon "powder-cask abstractions." With Lincoln's inauguration came "the grandest explosion the world ever witnessed" which the "reactionary and conservative" South was uniquely situated to resist. The formation of a new Confederate republic would "roll back the Reformation in its political phases" and thus overcome that "universal spirit of destructiveness" that had undertaken "a profane attempts to pull down what God and nature had built up."[18]

At first glance, much of Fitzhugh's assault on America's revolutionary doctrines was familiar. His outrageous polemics against individualism and equal political rights during the 1850s had featured essentially the same formulations. Yet unlike his antebellum writing, Fitzhugh's efforts to frame issues in the broadest possible terms and to situate the Confederacy as the pivot between a distant past and a future global destiny, were far less

---

[17] W. T. Walthall, "Letters to an Englishman," *SLM* 34 (January 1862), 8; [J.L.M. Curry], "Address of the Confederate Congress to the People of the Confederate States," Adopted January 22, 1864, in *OR* Series 4, Vol. 3: 128.

[18] Fitzhugh, "The Revolutions of 1776 and 1861 Contrasted," *SLM* 37 (November–December 1863), 718–26.

idiosyncratic in 1861 than they once had been. His incisive rhetoric and embrace of polarizing alternatives had a vigor notably lacking within the qualified and cautionary asides expressed by those who ambivalently clung to a Revolutionary inheritance. For first time, then, this provocateur represented not a marginal form of reaction but a mainstream variant of proslavery writing. Fitzhugh had thus improbably placed himself at the forefront of a second major attempt to discern Confederates' collective national purpose.

"SLAVERY, SUBORDINATION, AND GOVERNMENT"

The sharp rightward shift of the early 1860s was particularly evident in those journals that had nurtured George Fitzhugh's antebellum extremism. In the June of 1860, the young Mississippi lawyer John Quitman Moore began a series of articles for *De Bow's Review* that would surpass any other body of nineteenth-century American writing in their thirst for counterrevolutionary absolutism. In addition to situating Confederates in a long tradition of feudalists, royalists, and conquering Normans, Moore found time to propose how a hereditary senate, a permanent executive, and a standing army might assure the triumph of southern "institutionalism" over the ills of modern society. From Alabama, William Falconer sounded similarly reactionary themes in a series of contributions to *Southern Literary Messenger* that began the same month as Moore's debut. Though Falconer initially condemned secession as illegitimate, he soon championed a "patrician republic" that might replace the "quadrennial revolution" of presidential elections with a "strong government" capable of implementing the will of those southern whites bred to rule free of most restraint. Among his most consequential efforts was his claim that the slave South has been peopled from colonial days by an autocratic "Norman" race whose destiny called them to rule white-skinned "Saxon" inferiors no less surely than they governed black-skinned slaves.[19]

In the Confederate pulpits, an only slightly more temperate strain of reaction strove for a sanction higher than history, race, or nature could provide. A clergy dominated by former Unionists explained the catastrophe

---

[19] Moore, "The Past and the Present," *DBR* 29 (February 1861), 187–98; [Falconer], "The Difference of Race Between the Northern and Southern People," *SLM* 30 (June 1860) 401–9; "An Alabamian," "The One Great Cause of the Failure of the Federal Government," *SLM* 32 (May 1861), 329–34. For more on Falconer see Robert E. Bonner, "Roundheaded Cavaliers? The Context and Limits of a Confederate Racial Project," *CWH* 48 (March 2002), 34–59.

of secession as a consequence of democratic excess no less than of encroaching abolition. New School Presbyterian Charles Henry Read of Richmond numbered Americans' excessive pride in popular government as one of their gravest sins, thus leveling a critique as applicable to southern voters and politicians as to free-soil Republicans. In prescribing a more authoritarian variant of politics, Read observed that "men who make and unmake Presidents, Senators and Judges,– by so simple a process as putting a little billet of paper into a plain wooden box" were "in danger of losing sight of the true idea and ends of government, and of being puffed up with a sense of self-sufficiency." President William A. Smith of Randolph Macon College, a leading Southern Methodist, agreed that "wrong ideas on the subject of human liberty" and a foolish commitment to the "widest and wildest political liberty" were ultimately to blame for America's current troubles.[20]

It remained for the Old School Presbyterians to bundle anxieties about what the Rev. James Henley Thornwell termed "democratic absolutism" into a proposal for constitutional reform. Late in 1861, as the Presbyterian Church in the Confederate States of America was established in Augusta, Thornwell crafted a petition to the Richmond Congress that condemned "the fatal delusion that our government is a mere expression of human will" and insisted instead that the new republic, like all previous governments, was by its very nature "the creature and institute of God." As the leading voice of South Carolina Protestantism, Thornwell urged leaders to incorporate the Christian scriptures as the basis of the State's "organic life" and thus place the public actions of its leaders "under the authority of Jesus Christ and the restraints of His holy Word." Perhaps sensing how his suggestion encroached on a still cherished Jeffersonian heritage, Thornwell devoted much of his appeal to anticipating possible objections. He denied that Presbyterians had any intention of establishing a state Church or of regulating the private belief of citizens; he even insisted that one need not be a Christian to be an effective president of the new country. Such reassurances did little to mask the theocratic impulse within Thornwell's doctrine that "the Will of God, as revealed in the Scriptures ... conditions and restrains the discretion of rulers within the bounds of the Divine law." Turning to fear as perhaps a more effective prod than theological subtlety, Thornwell took pains to remind Congressmen that "God is the ruler of nations; and the people

[20] Rev. Charles Henry Read, *National Fast a Discourse Delivered on the Day of Fasting, Humiliation, and Prayer, Appointed by the President of the United States*, January 4, 1861 (Richmond, VA: West and Johnson, 1861), 15; "Address of President Smith, Delivered Before the Students of Randolph-Macon," *Richmond Enquirer*, August 4, 1861.

who refuse Him their allegiance shall be broken with a rod of iron, and dashed into pieces like a potter's vessel."[21]

In the secular press, counterrevolutionaries set aside religious injunctions and proposed instead to invest earthly rulers with greater powers. In the wake of an anonymous Georgian's call for constitutional monarchy, the Augusta editor William S. Jones joined "some of the best and wisest citizens" in pondering the advantages of a hereditary sovereign. Over a period of several weeks, his paper listed the pros and cons of what most would have considered to be the ultimate repudiation of American republicanism. Trying to navigate through the emotional issues involved, Jones calmly drew examples from Italy and from Brazil (in the latter instance, openly placing the needs of slavery above the desires of the southern white citizenry). Given the upheavals produced by the recent presidential election, at least some local planters were open to profound political changes in the interest of social stability. Crypto-royalists typically relegated their thoughts to private correspondence, where they muttered about the tendency of republics to "go down into democracy" even as monarchical empires proved their ability to "last a thousand years and more."[22]

The fate of republicanism continued to generate controversy after Confederates adopted a frame of popular government modeled on that of the United States. Enemies who sought to contest the Confederacy's claims of "Americanness" drew attention to sporadic pleas for monarchy and did their best to amplify these. But enough white Southerners joined in this haphazard public debate to suggest that there was an actual basis for worrying about masters' long-term commitment to republicanism. Early in 1862,

---

[21] "Relation of the State to Christ," (1861) in *The Collected Writings of James Henley Thornwell*, ed., John B. Adger and John L. Giradeau (1871–73) Vol. 4, 549–66. The immediate context in the convention can be followed in *Presbyterian Historical Almanac and Annual Remembrancer* (Philadelphia, PA: Joseph Wilson, 1863); while two broader perspectives on "Thornwellian" theocratic centralization are provided by Jack Maddex, "Presbyterians in the South, Centralization, and the Book of Church Order, 1861–1879" *American Presbyterians* 68 (Spring 1990), 24–45 and Douglas Ambrose, "Statism in the Old South: A Reconsideration" in Robert Louis Paquette and Louis A. Ferleger, eds. *Slavery, Secession, and Southern History* (Charlottesville: University Press of Virginia, 2000), 101–25.

[22] Augusta *Chronicle and Sentinel* December 8, 1860, January 20, January 26, January 31, 1861; William McKinley to David C. Barrow, March 29, 1861, quoted in J. William Harris, *Plain Folk and Gentry in a Slave Society: White Liberty and Black Slavery in Augusta's Hinterlands* (Hanover, NH, 1985), 139. See also *Richmond Daily Dispatch*, December 10, 1860, January 17, 1861 and coverage of William Russell's reports of South Carolina monarchism, as discussed in *Augusta Chronicle*, June 28, 1861, and *Richmond Dispatch*, June 28 and October 8, 1861.

Professor George E. Dabney of Virginia admitted to fellow Confederates that it had become a "fashion" to "deride republics, and especially confederacies, as wanting in dignity, concentrated vigor and permanence." A year later, Judge A.W. Dillard of Alabama insisted that it was "an indisputable fact" that many white Southerners "really desire to see a monarchical government founded." Prior to the war, Dillard continued, "the least intimation of a preference for monarchy, would have ensured the political ostracism of the most popular person, and have aroused the indignation of the entire press of the country." Such republican wavering saddened Augusta Jane Evans, who, early in 1864, found herself worrying about those who had lost "their former firm faith in democratic republicanism." Though war had taught her that "Universal Suffrage is an effete theory of Utopian origin," she was still "pained and astonished" to consider "how many are now willing to glide unhesitatingly into a dictatorship, a military despotism" or "even into a state of colonial dependence" to some distant European ruler.[23]

Richmond journalists linked the new suspicious about democracy and individual freedom more to local circumstances than to the allure of European courts. Early in 1862, the widely circulated *Dispatch* contrasted Richmond's earlier placidity (which had been disturbed only by the occasional "arrest of some predatory African") with an influx of population that had brought "ruffianism, drunkenness, and bloodshed" to city streets. "We scarcely meet a familiar face in the streets, or in any of the public places of amusement and resort," the paper noted, in celebrating how "the civil law, with its gracious courtesy" had been "unceremoniously kicked from the pavement" and replaced by martial rule that the *Dispatch* speculated might remain the norm even after peace was won. Editors like John M. Daniel pushed Confederate mobilization with the kind of brio that few Deep South fire-eaters could muster. Daniels' appointment during the 1850s as a European ambassador opened him to "Continental" affinities for standing armies, energetic executives, and invasive police forces. A similar worldliness marked the contributions of such outspoken Richmond authoritarians as Edward Pollard, Basil Gildersleeve, John Mitchel, and Littleton

---

[23] George Dabney, "Confederated Republicanism or Monarchy," *DBR* 32 (January–February 1862) 113–9; A. W. Dillard "Monarchical Leanings," in *Southern Field and Fireside*, January 3, 1863; Evans to J.L.M. Curry, October 16, 1863 and January 27, 1864 in Sexton, *A Southern Woman of Letters*, 77, 92. Among the few historical studies to note this trend is Elizabeth Fox-Genovese and Eugene Genovese, *The Mind of the Master Class: History and Faith in the Southern Slaveholders' Worldview* (New York: Cambridge University Press, 2005), 700–6.

Washington. While these men overtly argued the benefits of dictatorial power early in the war, their deeply personal aversion to Jefferson Davis after 1862 caused them to balance a plea for a "strong government" against a concern that Davis was wielding power too capriciously to render his office effective.[24]

George Fitzhugh took satisfaction in this new thirst for authority, which seemed to dovetail with the sort of proslavery principles he had endorsed over the preceding decade. Late in the summer of 1861, he urged the Confederacy to "at once take the lead, in thought, of all the nations of the earth" in creating "a new civilization" in which "negro slavery" would become a "great controlling and distinctive element." With victory at Manassas, Fitzhugh cast his gaze more widely, praising the Confederacy as "the bright exemplar and model government of the world" whose "institutions will be imitated" both in a greater appreciation for bound labor and by a return of all governments to their "natural historical and biblical form, never again to be disturbed by rash experiment." By 1863, Fitzhugh did his best to minimize differences between conservatives across the globe. The forces of reaction in North America, he argued, were at one philosophically with Tory Party principles, as had been expressed in the antireformist broadsides of the *London Quarterly Review*.[25]

Homegrown Confederate authoritarianism was tarnished in the eyes of foreign observers by its inextricable proslavery associations. To stake out a principled opposition in the face of such global hostility was precisely the point for the Rev. Calvin Wiley of North Carolina, who reasoned how "the just defence of our society implies a condemnation of that of many other nations." Though Wiley had stayed aloof from extremist politics prior to secession, he appreciated the power of nationalist self-assertion in his call for masters "to cease to occupy the attitude of criminals arraigned before the bar of civilization, and assume our true position of teachers of the unalterable truths of Revelation." George Bagby's decidedly more radical politics made him relish any opportunity to provoke outside critics. Early in 1861, the influential editor of the *Southern Literary Messenger* whimsically upped the ante (and knowingly invited outrage) when he questioned the loyalty of any Confederate who was unwilling to "love slavery for its own sake, as a

---

[24] *Richmond Dispatch*, March 12, 1862. Harry Stout and Christopher Grasso, "Civil War, Religion, and Communications: The Case of Richmond," in Harry Stout, et al. eds., *Religion and the American Civil War* (New York: Oxford University Press, 1998), 313–59.

[25] [Fitzhugh], "The Future of the Confederacy" *DBR* 31 (July 1861), 41; *idem*, "The Great Day at Manassas" *DBR* 31 (September 1861), 286; *idem*, "The Revolutions of 1776 and 1861."

divine institution" to "worship it as the corner stone of civil liberty," to "adore it as the only possible social condition on which a permanent Republican government can be erected." The true apostle of slavery should desire "in his inmost soul" to see bondage "extended and perpetuated over the whole earth, as a means of human reformation second in dignity, importance, and sacredness, alone to the Christian religion."[26]

Confederates' bold sense of mission encouraged speculation that their republic might inspire other nations to emulate similarly reactionary principles. Rather than emphasize the harmonizing effect that slavery had on the relationships of capital and labor, many Confederates broadcast how their country's stark embrace of racialism might be exported across the globe. Affirming white dominance thus became the main theme of Alexander Stephens' sweeping vision of Confederate mission expressed in his oft-quoted "Cornerstone Address" delivered at Savannah in the spring of 1861. Realizing the certainty of having "arrayed against us the civilized world," Stephens rallied nationalist sentiment by declaring that "I care not who or how many they may be against us, when we stand upon the eternal principles of truth, *if we are true to ourselves and the principles for which we contend,* we are obliged to, and must triumph." The predictable foreign outcry at such defiance did not discourage the Rev. James Warley Miles of Charleston from echoing Stephens' point two years later. Confederates had "a great lesson to teach the world with respect to the relation of races," Miles insisted, as he placed this mission as a crucial part of how "the history of our Confederacy will be another great chapter in the theodicy of nations, justifying the ways of Providence to man."[27]

The most thorough-going Confederate reactionaries moved beyond race and slavery to present themselves as bulwarks against a democratic age run to excess. George Bagby captured this tendency in asking "where is the thinking man who now believes that universal suffrage is not subversive of all free institutions?" Bagby distanced himself from the most extreme formulations percolating within Confederate culture, and even ridiculed the stray "crack-brain, who cries out for an Emperor" as "mere gibberish and book-worm nonsense, uttered in profound ignorance of things as they

---

[26] C.H. Wiley, *Address to the People of North Carolina* (n.p); Bagby, "Editor's Table," *SLM* 32 (March 1861), 344.

[27] A.H. Stephens, "Speech Delivered on the 21st March, 1861," in Henry Cleveland, ed., *Alexander Stephens in Public and Private* (Philadelphia: National Publishing Company, 1866), 721–3; James Warley Miles, *God in History: A Discourse Delivered Before the Graduating Class of the College of Charleston on Sunday Evening, March 29, 1863* (Charleston, SC: James S. Burgess, 1863), 26.

are and of the genius of the people." Yet both his editorials and his letters to newspapers across the Confederacy continued to express disdain for excessively popular governance. He opened a magazine that had long been a voice of moderation to counterrevolutionary voices such as that of Fitzhugh, who became a *Messenger* contributor after *De Bow's Review*, his usual outlet, suspended publication in 1862. The editorship of the young Frank Alfriend, who replaced Bagby in 1864, perpetuated the counterrevolutionary streak of this venerable southern magazine. Having already contrasted the "Southern Republic" with a "Northern Democracy," Alfriend used his editorship to identify the war as a "struggle between Infidelity, Intolerance, and Anarchy on the one hand, and Heaven's established ordinances of Order, Obedience, and dutiful Allegiance on the other."[28]

Among the most sensational efforts to laud Confederate reaction came from an anonymous Richmond journalist who celebrated the upturn of military fortunes early in 1863. This oracle built upon earlier proslavery assaults upon the French Revolution, as he grandly announced that not only was the founding of Confederacy "a distinct reaction against the whole course of the mistaken civilization of the age" but one that hoped to replace the triad of "Liberty, Equality and Fraternity" with a commitment to "Slavery, Subordination and Government." Confederates who wanted to avoid those "social and political problems which rack and torture modern society" should hold fast to the ancient dicta that "among those who are naturally unequal, equality is chaos" while they affirmed the more recent notion that there were "slave races, born to serve; master races, born to govern." In a flourish that most hostile commentators condemned as sacrilegious, this same writer then insisted that "reverently we feel that our Confederacy is a God-sent missionary to the nations with great truths to preach." The country had a duty to "speak them boldly" so that "who hath ears to hear" might be instructed.[29]

This Richmond writer echoed Fitzhugh and Bagby both in his embrace of authority and in his reflection upon that "baptism of sacrificial blood"

---

[28] [Bagby], "The Union: Its Benefits and Dangers," *SLM* 32 (January 1861), 1–4; Alfriend, "The Great Danger of the Confederacy," *SLM* 37 (January 1863) 39–43; *idem*, "A Southern Republic and a Northern Democracy," *SLM* 37 (May 1863) 283–90; *idem*, "Editor's Table" *SLM* 39 (February 1864), 124.

[29] In republishing this piece in full on June 2, 1863, the *New York Times* reported its initial appearance in the May 28 edition of the *Richmond Examiner*. As it circulated, some dated it to May 30 and others attributed it to the *Richmond Enquirer*. In surveying several extant runs of both these papers (which exist only in scattered holdings), I have yet to locate the original.

without which "our position at this day" would not have been "so high and clear." For Confederates to have achieved political independence without a struggle would have assured that they would "never have lifted our thoughts up to the height of our great argument, and our national life would have been but a half life, an abortionate compromise." In the face of such spectacular sacrifice, some leaders stubbornly continued to misunderstand and underappreciate "the true nature of that career and that destiny, and the responsibility it imposes." A prosperous Confederate future would rely on victory being extended upon by those "who have long deeply felt and earnestly striven to express, though timidly and speculatively, on what foundations of fact, with what cornerstones of principles, our social situation was one day to be build up fair and bright."[30]

Such counterrevolutionary advocacy of greater government authority welcomed military mobilization as both a means of repelling invasion and as a route to a more stable regime during peacetime. Quitman Moore predicted during the summer of 1861 that "the sword will share the supremacy of the spade, the rudder and the distaff" within the slave South, as Confederate armies came to "contribute no less to the national glory than the forum and the Senate." Early in 1864, the constitutional theorist John Scott supplemented his Southern Rights program of the late 1850s with a consideration of how Confederates might modify their government once military victory over the Union was complete. As a proud leader of a partisan cavalry unit, Scott looked to the "inquisitive and able minds of the army" to take the lead, reasoning that their "valor and heroic constancy" in combat would help them to fulfill the "high moral duty" of providing their country with "a free, stable government" thereafter. Trusting that the army could check any "domestic tyrant" that might arise in the future, Scott disavowed those anti-republican schemes of dictatorship or monarchy that he reported as being rife among the army brass. He instead made the case for a parliamentary form of government based closely on that of the United Kingdom. A distinguishing feature of his plan was the establishment of a stable group of Senators whose term of office would be made to approach "the ordinary term of human life."[31]

The clergy articulated their penchant for proslavery order within the framework of militarization as well. The Rev. William A. Hall was serving

---

[30] As quoted in *New York Times*, June 2, 1863.
[31] Moore, "The Belligerants," 72; Scott, *Letters to an Officer in the Army; Proposing Constitutional Reform in the Confederate Government after the Close of the Present War* (Richmond, VA: A. Morris, 1864), 7, 53.

as a chaplain of the illustrious Washington Artillery of New Orleans when he crafted a uniquely detailed explication of the Confederacy's "remarkable historic protest against philosophic infidelity and disorganizing wrong." Though he believed that "the doctrine of domestic slavery and the system of labor which time has built upon it are in a true sense divine," Hall had begun to sense by the spring of 1864 that war "may be intended to produce in us a willingness to part with the institution when God's time shall have come." The Confederate mission might lie less in perpetuating human slavery than in marking a pivotal stage in global history. Hall sketched the progression of human society from ancient times through the period of Reformation before he discerned how the Confederacy was leading in "one form or other against the extremes of individual authority." With "an intensity and rapidity which mark no previous era," Hall grandly announced that a "new era of Conservatism" was at hand.[32]

Hall's musings on the Virginia front were echoed a few months later by Bishop Richard Hooker Wilmer of Alabama. In preparing his civilian listeners for the onset of the third year of combat, Wilmer explained what enlisted men instinctually appreciated – that war was "a time when heroism is cultivated and when great ideas connected with human progress are generated and set free." Wilmer drew attention to social order in lecturing how "the leading ideas connected with the progress of the human race have been cradled in the storms of revolutions." Yet, rather than follow those of his Episcopal brethren in addressing the master–slave relationship, Wilmer anticipated the sociologist Max Weber in drawing attention to that "stern discipline of war" that had proven a remedy to the earlier lack of "good domestic training" among Southern-born whites. "A war of such dimensions" had been required "to include all our young men in the ranks in order to discipline the present generation of young Americans." Army life and the imperatives of command under fire had imbued Confederates with skepticism about democracy deeper than what had been taught by nature or even by divine Revelation. "The few must rule – the many do the work, but the few must guide their hands," Wilmer proclaimed, adding that "war teaches men this truth, if it accomplishes nothing more." Though he did not underline the point, his audiences no doubt appreciated how whites were undergoing a set of disciplinary

---

[32] Hall, *The Historic Significance*, 12, 41; Hall was shortly thereafter captured and then escaped, thus showing how the chaplaincy corps were themselves exposed to war's dangers; see *Richmond Dispatch*, June 13, 1864.

processes during war that had earlier been reserved for enslaved southern blacks.[33]

How much of this newspaper speculation and pulpit oratory filtered down to the Confederate white populace at large is difficult to gauge. An extraordinary letter written by a young Tennessee soldier in 1863 suggests that the rarified political discussion reached the ranks sooner than one might assume. "I notice a disposition on the part of some of our leading politicians and some of the newspapers to spring a new revolution before this one is closed," noted James Hamner to his mother before he quoted an extensive passage that Frank Alfriend had just published in the *Southern Literary Messenger*. Though Hamner found the case that Alfriend had laid out to have some merit, he believed that "such articles as this should be kept from the eyes of the troops, at any rate until the war is over." In this, he was thinking as much about practicality as ideology. Proposals to narrow the suffrage for white men then needed in the ranks accomplished "no good," he declared. Private Hamer then glumly reported that "I know of one man who deserted, on the belief that such would be our policy hereafter."[34]

MARTIAL PATERNALISM AND CONFEDERATE DESTINY

The Louisiana physician, poet, and religious mystic William H. Holcombe had little patience with reactionary attempts to link black slavery with the reawakening of neofeudal autocracy. In one of the most widely circulated pamphlets of the secession crisis, Holcombe drew a sharp distinction between the "wise and just subordination of an inferior to a superior race" and those "old systems of oppression and tyranny, which stain the pages of history and have excited the righteous indignation of the world." As a harbinger of the future, slavery was to Holcombe "an integral link in the grand progressive evolution of human society as an indissoluble whole."

[33] Rev. Richard H. Wilmer, *Future Good – The Explanation of Present Reverses, A Sermon Preached at Mobile and Sundry other Points in the State of Alabama, During the Spring of 1864* (Charlotte, NC: Protestant Episcopal Church Publishing Association, 1864); Walter Claiborne Whitaker, *Richard Hooker Wilmer, Second Bishop of Alabama* (Philadelphia, PA: George W. Jacobs, 1907). Weber's exploration of how "military discipline gives birth to all discipline" can be found in *Economy and Society: An Outline of Interpretive Sociology* trans. Guenther Roth and Claus Wittich (Berkeley, CA: University of California Press, 1978) 1: 1155.

[34] James Hamner to his mother, April 11, 1863, in Annette Tapert, *The Brothers' War: Civil War Letters to Their Loved Ones from the Blue and Gray* (New York: Vintage Books, 1988), 135–7.

Confederate independence, far from providing the occasion to "roll back" modern history, instead invited masters the opportunity to elevate those familiar proslavery principles of domestic reciprocity, harmony, and good feeling between white and black and to fashion these into a nationalist ideal. The vision of a paternalist slave republic embraced by Holcombe and others partook in the same utopian elements as the radically reactionary programs conjured up by Fitzhugh, Falconer, and Quitman Moore. In furnishing the theme of clerical addresses, newspaper commentary, and poetic, anecdotal, and visual celebrations, the attention to the Confederacy's "faithful slaves" became at once more enticing and even more divorced from reality than other elements of collective mission. Masters who cast themselves in the role of heroic paternalists at war, and who entrusted the Confederacy with the very survival of the "black race," articulated a third aspect of national purpose that achieved wider resonance, and displayed greater permanence, than even Confederate reckoning with their Revolutionary inheritance from 1776.[35]

Holcombe's own experience demonstrated both Confederates' fascination with black loyalty early in the war and the ultimately self-deceiving nature of these evaluations. Just before authoring his secessionist appeal, Holcombe had argued in his distinctively Swedenborgian "Spiritual Philosophy of African Slavery" how black slave's "peculiar and remarkable genius" was best achieved within the "well-regulated, cultivated Christian family" governed by a paternalist master. He closed 1861 by revisiting the scientific basis of African-American docility in "The Character and Capacity of the Negro Race." In addition to these pieces – which displayed a willingness to blend religion and scientific racialism – Holcombe offered two dramatizations intended for wider audiences. The first, offered to readers of the New York *Knickerbocker* in the summer of 1861, drew sketches of "plantation life" from a diary Holcombe had kept while practicing medicine in Tensas, Louisiana, during the mid-1850s. His widely circulated poetic tribute to "Uncle Jerry" (which he clearly wrote for fellow Confederates) featured the voice of a white master who refused to sell a slave who had, from childhood, become particularly dear. We do not know whether Holcombe's three slaves conveyed their own attitudes about such presumed emotional bonds within southern households. By 1865, Holcombe had been stripped of all legal claims to their loyalty, however, as his patriarchal world was dashed by armies that had forced him to

---

[35] Holcombe, "The Alternative: A Separate Nationality or the Africanization of the South," *SLM* 32 (February 1861), 82; this article would later appear as a pamphlet.

relocate twice, first to Natchez and then to the federally occupied city of New Orleans.[36]

At the same time that Holcombe and thousands of other masters witnessed slaves making history on their own terms, Confederates paradoxically adapted proslavery domesticity as the defining feature of their embattled republic. At the center of their imaginative vision was a conviction that the interrelations of black slaves and their white superiors might be capable of furnishing the basis of a national ideal. In the wake of Lincoln's election, the Rev. A.H. Boyd recast well-worn proslavery themes (which extended back to proslavery retorts to Jeffersonian "boisterous passions") and applied them to new circumstances. After boasting that there was "perhaps no country where the family relationship is more valued than in these States," Boyd imagined how the "mighty power" of household stability might soon work "to bind us together in indissoluble bonds" and "make us feel that, having common interests, we should live for each other's good, for our mutual elevation, and to disseminate throughout the world the principles bequeathed to us by our fathers!" Boyd's call to achieve a familial nationalism within the Union gave way after war began to even grander visions from those who trumpeted the racial solidarity of southern plantation life. "If we become two separate nations," an anonymous essayist in the *Southern Literary Messenger* proposed, "that noble and sacred gift of the Creator, the family, complete and pure would be preserved to us." A future in which the South achieved separation and peace from Yankee enemies would be one in which "our servants would be truly domestics, not hireling enemies; our roofs would be the shelter of our households, of innocence and peace and every virtue, and not theaters of every disorder and magazine of rapine."[37]

Paternalists established their own missionary zeal by insisting that Confederate nationhood would best shield family "servants" from the fate of extinction suffered by Indians, Caribbean freedmen, and the other "dark races" that had withered in open and unequal competition with more powerful whites. A few Deep South masters acknowledged that black

---

[36] Holcombe, *The Spiritual Philosophy of African Slavery* (New York, 1860), 22; idem, "The Characteristics and Capabilities of the Negro Race," *SLM* 33 (November–December 1861) 401–10; idem, "Sketches of Plantation Life," *The Knickerbocker, on New York Monthly Magazine* 57 (June 1861), 619–34; idem, "Uncle Jerry," in William G. Shepperson, *War Songs of the South* (Richmond, VA: West & Johnston, 1862), 183.

[37] Rev. Andrew H.H. Boyd, *Thanksgiving Sermon, Delivered in Winchester, Va., On Thursday, 29th November, 1860* (Winchester: Office of the Winchester Republican, 1861), 8; "The New Republic" *SLM* 32 (May 1861), 397.

liberation might cause Confederate masters themselves to "become the executioners of our own slaves," as the Mobile radical Edmund Dargan explained during the Alabama secession convention. The wealthy Mississippian Charles Dahlgren speculated how a society mobilizing for war might meet slave insurrection with lethal force, as he coolly calculated how "any ten thousand of our men would be more than sufficient to exterminate the negro race." Such veiled threats were far less common, however, than accounts of how impersonal forces of providence and the intrinsic helplessness of a servile race would assure black destruction if slavery ever were to end. Benjamin Morgan Palmer's Thanksgiving Day sermon of 1860 captured the humanitarian gist of this argument in warning how black freedom "in the presence of the vigorous Saxon race, would be but the signal for their rapid extermination before they had time to waste away through listlessness, filth, and vice." Removing southern slaves to Africa through a program of colonization provided no better solution, Palmer argued, since in suffering through that "most refined cruelty," black Southerners "must perish with starvation before they could have time to relapse into their primitive barbarism."[38]

Paternalist appeals to save African-Americans from destruction coexisted uneasily with the specter of black violence that secessionists had stoked. As war drew slaveholding men away from their plantation homes in the spring of 1861, the anxieties of white southern women stirred particular concern, since wavering within households seemed likely to dampen army enlistment and thus reveal a wider crisis of planter confidence. One female writer in Louisiana warned that the "vague rumors of insurrection" that circulated through patriotic sewing circles might doom Confederate independence even before local armies left for distant battlefields. "The utterances of idle tongues, like a faint thrill of wind of the coming storm, forces a vacuum in the still atmosphere of confident security which pervades Southern society," this correspondent noted. She then urged her countrywomen to "join with the men in frowning down with the very essence of contempt those weak-minded men who are inventing constantly these startling rumors."[39]

---

[38] Dargan quoted in William R. Smith, *The History and Debates of the Convention of the People of Alabama* (Montgomery: White, Pfister, and Co., 1861), 94; *Letter to His Excellency Gov. Harris, of Tennessee, on State Rights and Secession from C.G. Dahlgren* (Natchez, MS, 1861); Rev. B.M. Palmer, *Slavery a Divine Trust: The Duty of the South to Preserve and Perpetuate the Institution as it Now Exists* (New York, 1861). Similar rhetoric among Europeans in this period is the theme of Patrick Bratlinger, *Dark Vanishings: Discourse on the Extinction of Primitive Races, 1800–1930* (Ithaca, NY: Cornell University Press, 2003).

[39] "Grace Hopper," Baton Rouge *Daily Advocate*, May 9, 1861.

The nationalist image of Confederate womanhood developed in light of these and other chidings that slaveholding mistresses be brave even when abandoned by white guardians. Most patriotic appeals sanctioned female vulnerability to distant armies while at the same time minimizing concerns about potential threats lurking from the "domestic enemy" within plantation households. It thus became a mark of female patriotism to avoid public discussion of slave insurrection and to relegate anxieties to the privacy of a diary, if expressed at all. Many of the poets who gave voice to the defiant femininity of this "Second American Revolution" bolstered their celebrity status by dramatizing in verse the staunch loyalties of slaves to their masters. Lutha Fontelle recalled the "first" Revolution at the same time that she featured a "faithful, white-heared servant" sobbing at Yankee destruction and calling out "'Dis nigger can't endure dis orful sight!/ O lubly mansion, lost in flamin strife,/ Where us been libbin all our glorus life!" The poetic efforts made by Fontelle and other female writers sparked endless imitations, and thus attained even greater cultural currency than female-written proslavery fiction had done in their scattered responses to Stowe's *Uncle Tom's Cabin.*[40]

Poetic tributes to faithful servants built on the proslavery fiction of the 1850s in many respects, not least in alternating between humor and sentimentality in their depiction of black characters. In the widely circulated "A Scene from Southern Life" that first appeared in 1861, an anonymous female poet employed "negro dialect" to show how a female "mammy" might respond to Lincoln's supposed inclination for black freedom. This figure met a young charge's questions about her opinion of emancipation by asserting the religious grounds of her enslavement and by belittling the Union president:

> De good God says it mus' be so,
> An' honey, I, for one,
> Wid tankful heart will always say
> His holy will be done!
> I tanks Mass' LINKIN all de same,
> But when I wants for free,
> I'll ask de Lord for Glory,
> Not poor buckera like he.

Such poetry drew on more prevalent themes to reassure whites about the docility of slaves indoctrinated by religion. As a writer for the *Richmond*

[40] Lutha Fontelle, "Liberty or Death," *SLM* 34 (June 1862), 381–4.

Examiner put it in 1863, "The South can never be a St. Domingo, in spite of all that the ingenuity of Yankee hate can do; for our negroes are better Christians and truer gentleman than their would-be liberators."[41]

As military conflict escalated and the strains of war increased, Confederate anecdotes of trusted servants on besieged plantations increased, as did dramatic episodes of black heroism performed by slaves who served their masters in the army. Images of slaves facing enemy fire alongside their owners had already appeared in the proslavery novels of Beverley Tucker and Mary Davis, both of whose works were reissued by Confederate publishers two decades after their original appearance.[42] The homegrown examples were initially bolstered by broader perspectives on slave docility. The Latinist John L. Reynolds combined extensive examples from the classical texts of Homer, Virgil, and the Greek and Roman dramatists with similar evidence from the history of colonial South Carolina. These allowed him to conclude that "we may confidently anticipate the undisturbed continuance of a relation, which, however beneficial to the master, confers its chief blessings upon the slave." The racial theorist Samuel Cartwright invoked the still more obscure authority of the French historian Pierre Charlevoix in privately assuring Jefferson Davis that the Federal troops were no more likely to spark slave insurrection than the Spanish fighters had when they launched a war of invasion in the eighteenth-century Caribbean.[43]

As time passed, the regular accounts of black loyalty that appeared in the daily news would be gathered in compilations that served as repositories of Confederate nationalist lore.[44] These anthologies, and the poetry that they inspired, connected the image of loyal slaves to the military saga that would captivate not only the white South but also the many international observers

---

[41] "Southern Scene" first appeared in *Jackson Mississippian*, but was later reprinted in [Shepperson], *War Songs of the South*, 180–3; [Basil Gildersleeve], "The Tontine," *Richmond Examiner*, November 4, 1863.

[42] [Beverley Tucker], *The Partisan Leader: A Novel and an Apocalypse of the Origin and Struggles of the Southern Confederacy* (Richmond, VA: West & Johnson, 1862); Mary Elizabeth Moragne Davis, *The British Partizan: A Tale of the Olden Time* (Macon, GA: Burke, Boykin, and Co., 1864). These were first published in 1836 and 1841, respectively.

[43] J.L. Reynolds, "The Fidelity of Slaves," *DBR* 29 (November 1860), 569–83; Cartwright to Jefferson Davis, April 17, 1862 in *PJD* 8, 143–4.

[44] Published compilations such as Henry W.R. Jackson, *The Southern Women of the Second American Revolution, Their Trials, etc.* (Atlanta, GA: Intelligencer Steam Power Press, 1863); and Personne [Felix G. De Fontaine] *Marginalia; or, Gleanings from an Army Note-Book* (Columbia, SC: F.G. Fontaine & Co 1864) were supplemented by individual efforts to assemble newspaper clippings about faithful slaves. George Bagby collection of what he termed "loyal darky" stories remain among his papers at the Virginia Historical Society.

who looked on the South from afar (see Figure 8.1). Several of these vignettes featured the devoted black followers of exemplary martial heroes such as Robert E. Lee, J.E.B. Stuart, and Stonewall Jackson. The poet Catherine Warfield adapted what she termed a "well-authenticated incident" to depict "Stonewall's Sable Seers," one of whom explained "whenever de masta's wakeful, / And whenever he prays and groans, / Why dem dat lies by his camp fire / Feel battle in dere bones!" Dramatizing the adulation of black subordinates bolstered the image of Confederate martial heroes while bearing out the assertion, made by a Richmond essayist in 1861, that slaves sought masters who could "satisfy the sentiment of worship or the ideal of grandeur, by the manifestation of a splendour transcending any vows which the negro has ever made, or is capable of making in the future."[45]

Confederates broadcast their own wartime paternalism so as to alter foreign opinions of southern masters. In the wake of Abraham Lincoln's Emancipation Proclamation, the Rev. Stephen Elliott argued that Confederate claims to respectability rested on the docility of their slaves. "Let their quiet subordination thro' all this fierce conflict speak trumpet tongued to the world of their treatment," he urged, visiting a theme that would prominently appear in each of his subsequent fast-day sermons. Edward Pollard boasted how the "quietude" of the black population was working to remove the "cloud of prejudice, defamation, falsehood, romance, and perverse sentimentalism through which our peculiar institution had been formerly known to Europe." The absence of a Haitian-style revolt, Pollard insisted, had become "a better vindication of our system of slavery than all the books that could be written in a generation," since such apparent harmony showed how "the institution of slavery had withstood the shocks of war" and revealed how slaves had "been a faithful ally of our arms, although instigated to revolution by every art of the enemy, and prompted to the work of assassination and pillage by the most brutal examples of the Yankee soldiery."[46]

---

[45] Catherine Anne Warfield, "Stonewall's Sable Seers," in Emily V. Mason, ed., *The Southern Poems of the War* (Baltimore, MD: John Murphy, 1867), 291; [Lazarus Marx], "Boston Notions'– A Letter and a Reply," *SLM* 33 (October 1861), 289. Other notices of famous generals depending upon slaves while in the army include Lawley's note about J.E.B. Stuart in *London Times*, January 1, 1863; and John Brown Gordon's recollection of Robert E. Lee in *Reminiscences of the Civil War* (New York: Charles Scribners', 1904), 383–4.

[46] Elliott, *Ezra's Dilemma: A Sermon Preached in Christ Church, Savannah, on Friday, August 21st, 1863* (Savannah: George N. Nichols, 1863), 12; Pollard, *The Second Year of the War* (Richmond, VA: West and Johnson, 1863), 187–8.

FIGURE 8.1. Late in the war, the popular *Southern Illustrated News* used its masthead to convey the domestic ties that war had brought to both black and white families. The clustering of soldier and sweetheart on the right suggests the wartime context of paternalist themes; that of the slave couple beside it echoed calls to "reform" slavery by protecting the marriages of loyal black Confederates. *By permission of the Houghton Library, Harvard University, Call Number TR 1165.*

Avowals of black loyalty failed to resonate abroad as loudly as many Confederates hoped, however. Henry Timrod exaggerated only slightly when he admitted in the fall of 1864 that "three years of fearless fighting and noble self-sacrifice, and whole volumes of discussion, have hardly yet sufficed to convince the world that we are not a nation of negro-drivers, wading fiercely to the knees in blood only to maintain the privilege of flogging, flaying, and fettering human creatures like ourselves." Proslavery paternalism of the early 1860s mostly worked to discredit the Union abroad by introducing themes that found favor among foreign audiences ambivalent about the Confederacy. Late in 1863, Napoleon III's most important pamphleteer maintained that it had become "thoroughly understood in Europe" that the "northern idea of the abolition of slavery" involved either "making the negro food for powder" or "exiling him from his home to die of hunger." Such an assessment followed the war's most dramatic development – the flood of black refugees toward Union lines and the massive enlistment of African-American men in the U.S. Colored Troops in 1863 and 1864.[47]

The rallying of southern African-Americans to the Union cause seemed to be such a direct contradiction of paternalist claims that one might expect it to have undermined earlier professions. But Confederates responded to this development by emphasizing the mistreatment that black Southerners received at the hands of their new Federal "masters." In 1863, the Rev. Alexander Gregg explained how black and white Southerners alike should celebrate the repulse of Union armies, since these Confederate victories had saved untold numbers of blacks from "certain wretchedness and poverty... homeless wandering... unheard appeals" and a "subjection to those who had never learned to love or appreciate them." Jefferson Davis more concisely lamented Union efforts to "pervert menservants and maidservants into accomplices in their wicked designs." Not long after Federal troops occupied his own Mississippi River plantation, Davis reported to Congress (and thus to a far wider public audience) how "unrelenting warfare" had "been waged by these pretended friends of human rights and liberties against the unfortunate negroes." The president cannily drew from northern antislavery complaints about the wretchedness of contraband camps to predict that fewer than half of the freedmen would survive the war. This was the same figure that would be echoed by several leading Confederates over the next two years. Governor Henry Watkins Allen lashed out early in 1865 at the "false, pretended friends who have taken [the slave] away from a kind master and comfortable home," and who "now treat him with criminal neglect, and permit him to die without pity." Governor Allen even began to document his claims by assembling

---

[47] Timrod, *South Carolinian* September 27, 1864; [Michel Chevalier], *France, Mexico, and the Confederate States* (New York: E.B. Richardson, 1863), 7, 12.

sworn testimony about Federal conduct toward freedmen in western Louisiana.[48]

The wartime image of the contented slave and the contrasting image of the suffering freedmen extended beyond Confederate public relations. Just as the antebellum myth of the plantation had cheered northern audiences by offering an alternative to wrenching economic changes, so the image of tranquil plantations provided Confederates with an appealing alternate reality, located, at least in imaginative terms, far from the chaos of war. Confederates beset by conflict were likely to welcome efforts like "A Sketch of Plantation Life in Louisiana" which appeared in the *Southern Literary Messenger* in 1863 as a sort of wish fulfillment. As the following passage suggests, this poem moved away from antebellum efforts to contrast the slave system with the class struggle of free labor societies and instead presented plantations as a refuge from a martial world where the brute force of armies governed all relationships.

> Peace breathes all around!
> Sweet peace pervading all
> Calm nature's scenes – the cottage, and the hall!
> Faith, mutual service, and good will unite
> The white race and the black; Not tyrant might
> On one side – on the other, abject fears.
> Such a tale is false. Society appears
> Like one vast family. No anxious cares
> Gnawing his soul, the thoughtless negro bears,
> But, like a trusting child, his wants he leaves
> To one who ne'er his simple trust deceives.[49]

This harmonious depiction of the Confederate plantation anticipated themes of the postwar "Lost Cause," in which black folk stood with their racial betters to fend off the Yankee onslaught. Such narratives would attribute deep racial enmity to the expansion of black civil rights during

---

[48] Rev. Alexander Gregg, *A Sermon Preached in St. David's Church, Austin, on Sunday, March 15th, 1863* (Austin, TX: Texas Almanac Office, 1863), 10–1; Davis "Proclamation, February 27, 1863," and "Message to Congress, December 7, 1863," in CMPC 1: 325, 380; *Annual Message of Governor Henry Watkins Allen, to the Legislature of the State of Louisiana January, 1865* (Shreveport: Caddo Gazette, 1864); idem, *Official Report Relative to the Conduct of Federal Troops in Western Louisiana, During the Invasions of 1863 and 1864* (Shreveport, 1865). See also Elliott, *"Vain Is the Help of Man" a Sermon Preached in Christ Church, Savannah, on Thursday, September 15, Georgia* (Macon, GA: Burke, Boykin, and Co., 1864) and Pollard, *The Rival Administrations: Richmond and Washington, in December, 1863* (Richmond, n.p.), 20–1.

[49] C.L. "A Sketch of Plantation Life in Louisiana," SLM 37 (September 1863), 532–3.

radical Reconstruction rather than to the upheavals of wartime emancipation. Yet during the war itself, the image of the loyal slave played a different sort of role in Confederate self-understanding, as was evident in a series of remarkable attempts to incorporate the mutuality of masters and slaves into a providential framework of national mission. As several historians have shown, the crisis of plantation authority encouraged southern evangelicals to amplify their calls to "reform" slavery by sanctifying slave marriages and decriminalizing slave literacy. This movement cleared the way for some of the most prominent proslavery clergy to speculate that the Confederacy's providential mission might have less to do with the liberation of white masters from Yankee dominion than with the role that whites might play as the divinely chosen custodian of black destiny.[50]

Over the last half of the war, the Rev. Benjamin Morgan Palmer balanced his continuing vindication of Confederate republicanism with an even more heartfelt consideration of how "the presence of the helpless African" might be "a sign of the Divine protection and blessing." Late in 1863, he worked through this issue with great care, applying themes from his Thanksgiving Day sermon of three years earlier to the subsequent history of the war. "With [the slave's] fate bound up so entirely with our own, I believe that for his sake at least we shall be preserved" he declared, before he continued:

I cannot doubt that one of the compensations of this bitter conflict will be to sanctify, and to endear, the tie by which these two races are linked together. The timid amongst ourselves will be reassured, when they discover this relation, regarded by many so unstable, unshaken by the rockings of this terrific tempest: and in the sweeping away of these groundless fears, the way will be prepared for the more faithful discharge of all the duties which slavery involves. Relieved of those embarrassments which a hypocritical fanaticism has interposed, we shall be able, with greater freedom, to give them God's blessed word, to protect their persons against the abuses of capricious power, and to throw the shield of a stronger guardianship around their domestic relations.

Then, in reaching for the ultimate explanation of why war had come, Palmer concluded that "it may be for this that our people are now passing under the severe discipline of this protracted war – on the one hand to

---

[50] Faust, *The Creation of Confederate Nationalism*; Clarence Mohr, *On the Threshold of Freedom: Masters and Slaves in Civil War Georgia* (Athens, GA: University of Georgia Press, 1986), 235–71; Eugene Genovese, *A Consuming Fire: The Fall of the Confederacy in the Mind of the White Christian South* (Macon, GA: Mercer University Press, 1998).

chasten us for past shortcomings, and on the other to enlarge our power to protect and bless the race committed to our trust."[51]

The Rev. Stephen Elliott crafted an even more effective link between Confederate mission and the fate of black slaves, by drawing upon perspectives he had developed as an antebellum advocate of African colonization. As early as 1862, Elliott, then the Episcopal Bishop of Georgia, marveled that "as Egypt was the land of refuge and the school of nurture for the race of Israel, so were these Southern States first the home and then the nursing mother of those who were to go forth and regenerate the dark recesses of a benighted Continent." Two years later, Elliott's understanding of black Southerners' salvation had transformed, and African-American destinies in distant Liberia were eclipsed by the matter of the Confederacy's collective mission. "The only purpose which makes a struggle for independence worth the cost of blood and feeling which it always demands is that it should bring out of its fermenting and convulsed elements an earnest people," Elliott explained. In searching for a defining collective responsibility that might rise to the appropriate level of seriousness, Elliott, like Palmer, set aside the question of republicanism, and concluded that "We have been entrusted with the moral and religious education of an inferior race, made more sacred to us by the events of this war, because we have been made to see what will be their miserable fate should they pass out of our nurturing hands."[52]

As Elliott sought to discern the particulars of this providential scheme of black salvation, emancipation was developing an irreversible momentum as the most profound social revolution in American history. There was thus a sense of stubbornness to Elliott's insistence in 1864 that God was using war to show abolitionists "how little the slaves care for such freedom as [Yankees] can offer." Setting aside the mounting evidence of slave flight from Confederate plantations toward the Union lines, Elliot praised African-Americans for having "never gone to our enemies in any numbers" and even noted how "their quiet has been wonderful even to ourselves, and has caused the world not only to wonder, but to reverse its settled judgment about their treatment and condition." A global audience, he continued "even now sees

[51] Palmer, *A Discourse Before the General Assembly of South Carolina, on December 10, 1863, Appointed by the Legislature as a Day of Fasting, Humiliation, and Prayer* (Charles P. Pelham, State Printer, 1864), 16–19.
[52] Elliott, *Our Cause in Harmony with the Purposes of God in Christ Jesus: A Sermon preached in Christ Church, Savannah, on Thursday, September 18th, 1862* (Savannah: John M. Cooper, 1862), 11–12; idem, *Gideon's Water-lappers: A Sermon Preached in Christ Church, Savannah, on Friday, the 8th day of April, 1864* (Macon, GA: Burke, Boykin, and Co., 1864), 20.

and acknowledges that the slaves have gained nothing by their emancipation, and are beginning to be satisfied that it has made a grievous mistake in attempting to remove these people from their normal condition of servitude." Placed within the long history of proslavery defenses, Elliott's was perhaps more thoroughly divorced from objective reality than anything that had come before.[53]

In seeking to discover the providential meaning of wartime suffering, paternalists offered an understanding of Confederate nationhood focused as much on the fortunes of black slaves as on the independence of white masters. In 1863, a writer for the *Southern Presbyterian Review* summed up a broader tendency by remarking that "African civilization in America, to the thoughtful student of events, must appear the transcendent fact connected with our continent since the discovery of the new world." Within this broad perspective, the travails of a deeply rooted past seemed mysteriously to be transforming into a divinely ordained future. Black salvation would in fact be the most dramatic result of this bloody war over American nationhood, just as paternalists foretold. Where these partisans went astray was in their failure to realize that it would be Union victory that would bring about this result. Confederate defeat thus allowed for consequences unimaginable in the event of Confederate victory, as former slaves took part as never before in the quest to redefine the deepest assumptions of American nationhood.[54]

---

[53] Elliott, *"Vain is the Help of Man,"* 11.
[54] "A Slave Marriage Law," *SPR* 16 (October 1863), 160.

9

Liberty, Slavery, and the Burdens of Confederate Nationhood

If order was the leading principle within the proslavery intelligentsia, liberty retained its hold, even during war, as the chief idiom of Confederate popular politics. During the spring of 1864, John P. Murray boiled the matter down to its basics. "The strength of the Confederate Government," he told his fellow Congressmen, "exists in the idea that we are fighting for freedom." Speaking as a slaveholding Democrat, a former Tennessee judge, and a Colonel wounded at Shiloh, Murray maintained that since "the battalions of the enemy are heavier than ours," the country's only hope lay "in the fact that 'Ideas fight more terrible battles than men.'" What animated the Confederate enterprise was not its providential calling, its defiance of outsiders, or even the attainment of separate nationhood, Murray argued, but its undying commitment to the rights of all white citizens. President Jefferson Davis's plan to extend his suspension of habeas corpus endangered such liberties and risked support for the cause. Those who were already unnerved by Confederate centralism and a seeming drift toward martial law thus rallied with Murray against their own government for betraying its central idea. In doing so, they hoped to check the Davis administration's march past those constitutional boundaries that had formed the core of proslavery politics.[1]

As the Confederacy's bid for nationhood demanded more and more from its white supporters, the intricate proslavery reckoning with freedom and bondage took on new layers of meaning. Early in 1863, the *Richmond Enquirer* explained to its readers how a war for independence from the

---

[1] *Speech of Hon. John P. Murray, of Tennessee, in Favor of Repealing the Act Suspending the Privilege of the Writ of Habeas Corpus* ([Richmond, 1864]), 4.

North had reshaped the very "meaning of the term Liberty" by giving rise to two competing – and perhaps incompatible – standards by which "a nation may be called a Free Nation." During peace, southern whites had often boasted of how their slaveholding society best secured the blessings of limited government and what the *Enquirer* approvingly termed the "equality of all citizens before the law." Amidst war, the paper's editors concluded that such rights – the same that dominated Representative Murray's understanding of liberty – had become "not so essential to national well-being as the first kind of liberty; namely, national independence." The struggle to throw off all "foreign domination" required an unwavering focus on "possessing and exercising autonomy" in the collective sense of that term. Preserving individuals' freedom from government interference would be irrelevant if the Confederacy lost its standing among the countries "whose laws are made at home; whose citizens have a national type of character and thought; who form and develop their institutions for themselves, and, who protected by national arms, and under the shadow of a national flag, dare to call their souls their own."[2]

The notion that national freedom trumped long-held commitments to individual rights became an increasingly contentious issue over the four-year campaign for Confederate nationhood. Two years before Representative Murray stood before Congress, Vice President Alexander Stephens had railed against the idea of "getting independence first and looking after liberty afterward." As he ominously warned, "Our liberties, once lost, may be lost forever." Stephens and other critics of Confederate policy were motivated both by distrust of the Davis administration and by deeper misgivings about the consequences of military mobilization. The *Charleston Mercury* summed up a widespread complaint in the spring of 1863 when it wrote that "all wars are adverse to liberty" and that "even wars to establish or vindicate it are dangerous to its continuance." A year and a half later, Congressman W. W. Boyce of South Carolina explained how military authority had shown itself to be incompatible with the rights of masters. As Boyce privately worried how the continuation of war would destroy "both slavery and freedom," he concluded that "another campaign" would cause "the social system of the South" to be "broken up, and despair will settle in every heart."[3]

[2] *Richmond Enquirer*, March 20, 1863.

[3] Stephens, "Address at Crawfordville, November 1, 1862," in Henry Cleveland, ed., *Alexander H. Stephens in Public and Private* (Philadelphia, 1866), 760; *Charleston Mercury*, May 25, 1863; Boyce to Davis, in *Charleston Courier*, October 13, 1864; Boyce to James Henry Hammond, October 5, 1864, quoted in Rosser H. Taylor, "Boyce–Hammond Correspondence," *JSH* 3 (August 1937), 354.

Scholars have marshaled conflicting evidence about whether intrusive government and accompanying political discord hastened Confederate defeat by simultaneously sapping white freedom and compromising masters' interests.[4] However one frames the ultimate issue, it seems clear enough that war and the dissolution of plantation discipline gave new urgency to the Confederate dialogue about liberty and slavery. Southern Rights enthusiasts like Albert Pike had early in 1861 found it easy enough to argue that Lincoln's election presented a choice between being "state or province, bond or free." A year and a half of wartime experiences taught Pike that freedom might face perils from an independent South no less than from a Yankee-dominated Union. Pinched by the arbitrary power of renegade Confederate generals, the eccentric Arkansan condemned the tyranny of the Richmond administration and warned Jefferson Davis that "bye and bye the people will regain their reason" and come alive "to the great truth, which now seems almost obsolete, that the way to Liberty does not run by the road to Slavery." For the final two years of the war, Pike found refuge in the Arkansas mountains, thus removing himself both from the clash of rival armies and from the no less dramatic overthrow of chattel bondage.[5]

Confederate critics like Pike questioned whether a national venture sanctified by wartime sacrifice and providential mission was a good in and of itself. Many of slavery's most stalwart defenders insisted that political independence be judged by the benefits it delivered, and they implied that their support for the cause was contingent on its upholding of earlier landmarks. Their utilitarian approach to national sovereignty assumed new significance late in 1864, when Confederates faced the climactic moment of proslavery nationalism. Near the end of his government's costly separatist venture, Confederate president Jefferson Davis concluded that military and diplomatic pressures required the enlistment of slaves in the army and perhaps even a tentative program of emancipation. If slavery's fiercest defenders had reached little consensus about the erosion of other personal rights, they closed ranks to face this dramatic challenge to their claims on human property. Those who

---

[4] For differing opinions on whether "internal" disaffection had a greater impact on Confederate fortunes than "external" Union force, see Paul Escott, *After Secession: Jefferson Davis and the Failure of Confederate Nationalism* (Baton Rouge: Louisiana State University Press, 1978) and Gary Gallagher, *The Confederate War* (Cambridge: Harvard University Press, 1997).

[5] [Albert Pike], *State or Province? Bond or Free?* (Little Rock, 1861); Pike, *Letter to the Chief Magistracy of the Confederacy, Calling His Attention to the Enclosed Orders of Major General Hindman, Commanding the Trans-Mississippi District* ([Fort McCulloch], 1862), 4; Mark E. Neely, Jr. *Southern Rights: Political Prisoners and the Myth of Confederate Constitutionalism* (Charlottesville: University Press of Virginia, 1999).

remained true believers in bondage rallied for one last time, agreeing with the *Charleston Mercury* that a final crisis removed earlier ambiguity. "Slavery and independence must stand together, or they must fall together." And fall was exactly what bondage and nationhood together did.[6]

WARTIME GOVERNANCE AND THE EROSION OF WHITE FREEDOM

Alexander Stephens' skepticism of Confederate governance developed from his idealized understanding of earlier American norms. Stephens had gloried during the secession crisis how "the influence of the Government on us is like that of the atmosphere around us" in that "its benefits are so silent and unseen that they are seldom thought of or appreciated." The wartime transformation of his Middle Georgia community showed how quickly circumstances might change. While Stephens suffered the political slings and arrows of office-holding, his real despair came as master of "Liberty Hall," as he had rechristened his Crawfordville homestead in 1860. War's burdens impinged on daily life well before William T. Sherman's 62,000 troops penetrated the Deep South in the late autumn of 1864. The Confederacy's own armed guards monitored nearby railroad stops, where they prodded suspicious characters and prevented recently drafted men from deserting from the army. Mounting taxes and goods impressed for army use flowed toward Milledgeville and Richmond along these same roads. In return came dictates about how much cotton could be planted and how high prices for basic foodstuffs would be allowed to rise.[7]

It is important to exercise care in assessing planters' aversion to state and central governments, since these had long worked to secure their mastery of slaves and facilitate planters' easy interaction with world markets. Slaveholders were unlikely to be libertarians in any meaningful sense, any more than plantation homes like "Liberty Hall" were the citadels of freedom they proclaimed themselves to be. Even so, peacetime routines and republican

---

[6] *Charleston Mercury*, February 1, 1865.

[7] "Alexander Stephens' Unionist Speech, Wednesday Evening, November 14," in William Freehling, *Secession Debated: Georgia's Showdown in 1860* (New York: Oxford University Press, 1992) 64; J. William Harris, *Plain Folk and Gentry in a Slave Society* (Middletown, CT: Wesleyan University Press, 1985). For a broader view, see Richard F. Bensel, "Southern Leviathan: The Development of Central State Authority in the Confederate States of America," Karen Orren and Stephen Skowronek, eds., *Studies in American Political Development* (New Haven, CT: Yale University Press, 1987), 2: 68–136; and *Yankee Leviathan: The Origins of Central State Authority in America, 1859–1877* (1990).

idioms had nurtured an ingrained touchiness about official dictation from distant authorities, and this sensibility had flourished in those formal defenses of slavery that identified bondage as the primary basis of liberty. Proslavery republicanism bred not only a penchant to be "let alone" but a pervasive "longing for order" that would, as the historian Mark Neely has argued, become more important during war than ever before. Both critics and defenders of the Confederacy's intrusion into daily life confronted the contradictions between popular distrust of interference and popular demands for internal security.[8]

In some areas, the Confederate government simply extended local routines of mobilizing coercive power and expelling potentially subversive persons. The informal policing of whites who seemed insufficiently enthusiastic about slavery had grown more intense over the antebellum years, as Southern Rights partisans expanded practices that had, during the 1820s, focused attention on the passage of free persons of color through seaports and other points of contact with the wider world. During the chaotic secession period, ad hoc "committees of safety" gave newfound attention to "enemies within" as they rooted out white dissenters through mass ceremonies of oath-taking to the new Confederacy. By the fall of 1861, the Confederate government committed its administrative energies to identifying those "Alien enemies" who, if male, aged 14 years or older, and unwilling to pledge loyalty to the new regime, were given forty days to leave Confederate territory before they faced prosecution on charges of spying. Such draconian measures lacked effective mechanisms of enforcement, and the main penalty that Confederates inflicted on southern supporters of U.S. authority was a sequestration system that was riddled with inefficiencies.[9]

---

[8] Compare the discussion of "libertarianism" in George Rable, *The Confederate Republic: A Revolution against Politics* (Chapel Hill: University of North Carolina Press, 1994), 174–94 with *Southern Rights* and *idem, Confederate Bastille: Jefferson Davis and Civil Liberties* (Milwaukee, WI, 1993).

[9] Atlanta *Southern Confederacy*, August 17–18, 1861; Memphis *Avalanche*, September 6, 1861; New Orleans *Crescent*, December 16, 1861; Jefferson Davis, "Proclamation of August 14, 1861," *CMPC* 1: 131–2. Neely's work has inspired new attention to Confederate exclusionist policies, though most of these skirt the dynamic tension between the proslavery basis of Confederate order and political hostility to government intrusion. See Brian R. Dirck, "Posterity's Blush: Civil Liberties, Property Rights, and Property Confiscation in the Confederacy," *CWH* 48 (September 2002), 237–56; Mark A. Weitz, *The Confederacy on Trial: The Piracy and Sequestration Cases of 1861* (Lawrence: University of Kansas Press, 2005); and Daniel W. Hamilton, "The Confederate Sequestration Act," *CWH* 52 (December 2006), 373–408. A less vibrant discussion of whether free blacks should also be expelled from the Confederacy was raised by Americus Featherman, "Our Position and That of Our Enemies," *DBR* 31 (July 1861), 32.

Confederate officials continued to monitor the region's inhabitants long after the 1861 flurry of coerced oaths and forced banishments. Nationalized armies provided Confederate policy-makers a set of readymade tools to supersede local efforts. The military authority of provost marshals, especially those who governed urban areas, both secured the pledge of enlisted men and extended control over whites who would have earlier been deemed "safe" by neighbors who knew them best. There were calls to extend state and federal loyalty oaths from soldiers to the entire white population, though such measures were never implemented, even on the restricted basis attempted during the South Carolina nullification crisis. Confederate officialdom probably lacked the requisite administrative capacity to initiate an intrusive national system of civilian oath-taking. Even if there had been the will to attempt such a program, a bitter political fight would surely have ensued. A fiery dissent by North Carolinian William Graham made clear that such oaths betrayed both inherited Anglo-American liberties and, perhaps more important, the Protestant freedom of conscience. By seeking to "control by force that conscience, which the God who gave it designed to be free, and avows its purpose to drive men to perjury or self-accusation," governments that relied on these techniques crossed a line. Graham was not alone in denouncing as impious those efforts to coerce an individual's political volition. Late in the war, prominent Confederate clergy would make the same point about the limits of government intrusion, as they warned Confederate loyalists in occupied districts against swearing false oaths of allegiance to federal authority.[10]

The Confederate press by and large acquiesced to new modes of military power and gave their enthusiastic backing to novel measures, such as the ban on alcohol imposed by military authorities in many southern cities. An increasingly ambitious system of internal passports furnishes one of the most instructive examples of shifting attitudes. Prior to 1861, white men and women associated demands to carry a pass with despotic Old World regimes or, more likely still, with the degrading requirement that both free

[10] The oath of allegiance required for Confederate soldiers appears in OR Series 4, Vol.1: 164; *Richmond Enquirer*, September 24, 1861; William A. Graham, *Speech in the Convention of North Carolina, on the Ordinance Concerning Test Oaths and Seditions* (Raleigh: W.W. Holden, 1862), 8; B.M. Palmer, *The Oath of Allegiance to the United States, Discussed in Its Moral and Political Bearings* (Richmond: Macfarlane and Fergusson, 1863); Rev. W.H. Ruffner, *The Oath: A Sermon on the Nature and Obligation of the Oath with Special Reference to the Oath of Allegiance Delivered in the Presbyterian Church, Lexington, VA* (Lexington, VA; The Gazette Office, 1864); William A. Smith quoted in Charlotte *Western Democrat*, February 14, 1865.

and enslaved blacks carry at all times proof of their identity. The *Charleston Mercury* continued to offer this critique early in the war, insisting that the passport system established by Lincoln's Secretary of State evoked "the most obnoxious of all 'European tyrannies.'" Yet while such parallels continued to flare up after the Confederacy began to institute its own set of internal controls, these fostered less outrage than might have been expected. The *Richmond Examiner* typically observed that "it used to be that negroes only were required to carry 'their papers' but now their masters are bothered with them as well." As one of the most fervent supporters of "strenuous" government, the *Examiner* was fatalistic on the topic, offering little more than a reflection of "what a tyrant war is" and "how much should we appreciate peace!" Though there were sporadic appeals to Congress to amend the system, both the passport regulations and the organization of provost marshals were left largely untouched by civilian authority.[11]

Congressional sanction of martial law generated far more political discord, launching successive legislative debates and providing the target for several state governments to issue official protests. Each time the suspension of habeas corpus came up for debate, pleas grew louder that the military effort against the Union required the sacrifice of rights at home. As a consistent supporter of this suspension, the *Richmond Daily Dispatch* implored: "If we are to have a despot, had he not better be one of our own people than a Yankee?" Opponents chafed at such logic, preferring the stance taken by the *Charleston Mercury*, which lectured readers that "those are fit to be slaves who voluntarily seek a master." In hoping to protect traditional legal rights from the pleas of military necessity, the paper boldly concluded that "if we are to have a Despotism, let it be the result of force." At stake for such critics was both Davis' inability to monitor generals who implemented martial law and a desire to hold the Richmond government to the same standard established by Confederate attacks on Lincoln's violation of civil liberties in 1861. On a still deeper level was the disturbing sense, as Sam Houston wrote in his last public letter, that "Acquiescence to usurpation is – SLAVERY!" and that "necessity

---

[11] "Our Foreign Policy," *Charleston Mercury*, October 29, 1861; "The Passport Office," *Richmond Examiner*, July 16, 1863; "Hermes" [George Bagby], "Letter from Richmond," *Charleston Mercury*, October 14, 1862. For an antebellum travelers complaint about European passports, see Michael O'Brien, *Conjectures of Order: Intellectual Life in the American South, 1810–1860* (Chapel Hill: University of North Carolina Press, 2004), 146 and, for more information about Confederacy passes, Neely, *Southern Rights*, 2–8; Paul Escott, *Military Necessity: Civil–Military Relations in the Confederacy* (Westport, CT: Praeger Security International, 2006), and Kenneth Radley, *Rebel Watchdog: the Confederate States Army Provost Guard* (Baton Rouge: Louisiana State University Press, 1989).

is the plea of tyrants, and the exercise of unrestrained will is the throne of Despotism!" To Robert Toombs, any "compromise with slavery under the delusive hope of aiding liberty" was bound to fail. "We had as well attempt to reach Heaven through a compact with the Devil."[12]

Hyperbolic complaints of government "enslavement" sparked a backlash, however, in the full-throated vindications of martial law that followed. Proponents of military rule often drew upon the same autocratic principles set forth by those Confederate reactionaries who perceived war as an opportunity for a counterrevolutionary curtailment of democracy and disorder. When Congress first suspended habeas corpus during the spring of 1862, John M. Daniel of the *Richmond Examiner* affirmed that "the Government, into whose hands the people, when in their right minds, have intrusted all their power, should use it like a bar of iron." He urged the administration to proceed "by military order, and without consulting any-body" and concluded: "To dogs with Constitutional questions and moder-ation!" A year and a half later, the editor Henry St. Paul of Mobile called the newly elected Second Confederate Congress to "initiate vigorous measures, nay, arbitrary ones, if needed, to bring out the whole power of the nation." "Let those playthings of peacetime, Constitutions, Habeas Corpus, be for-gotten for the stern realities of public safety and national independence," St. Paul argued. "Let our Congress rule and govern as any absolute Monarch would rule and govern, responsible only to God for the abuse or misuse of their power."[13]

Antebellum assumptions about white freedom in a slaveholding republic were undermined both by the critics' denunciations of Confederate tyranny and by the sweeping endorsements of unfettered central power by reaction-ary editors. Compounding the Confederate challenge in reconciling liberty and government was the increasingly uncertain status of chattel slavery, which was subjected to the enormous pressure of those Union military forces that moved deeper into southern territory. In 1863, William Cabell Rives maintained that suspending habeas corpus would not hinder Confederates from pursuing the same goals of "national independence and political rights" that had been established by the American founders eighty years

---

[12] *Richmond Daily Dispatch*, April 1, 1862; *Charleston Mercury*, April 7, 1863; Houston to Gov. Lubbock in Houston *Telegraph*, March 9, 1863; Toombs quoted in Augusta *Daily Constitutionalist*, June 8, 1864. A thorough account of this issue can be found in John B. Robbins, "The Confederacy and the Writ of Habeas Corpus," *Georgia Historical Quarterly* 55 (Summer 1971), 83–101.

[13] *Richmond Examiner*, February 26, 1862; Henry St. Paul, *Our Home and Foreign Policy, by Henry St. Paul, November, 1863* (Mobile, 1863) 12, 19–21.

earlier. But he quickly noted how neither nationhood nor liberties were as important as the all important need to secure "everything precious to the human affections" that were threatened by "the vindictive and brutal passions of an uncivilized race" then being unleashed "in this unholy crusade against us." Rives was not alone in justifying military power as the only alternative to race war. Testifying to the persistence of secession-era paranoia, Rives was treading familiar ground when he argued that it was "impossible for the imagination to picture a fate more horrible than ours would be, if we were once subjugated."[14]

Peacetime liberties were in shortest supply among the hundreds of thousands of men who joined the Confederate armies. Those who enlisted justified the deprivations of army life in terms of securing more important freedoms in the future. Their private testimony demonstrates a mixture of commitments to Confederate national independence, to the rights of white men in general, and to masters' particular interest in maintaining control of human property. But at the same time that Confederate military service summoned up powerful strains of liberty, it also provided the most appropriate site to consider how war curtailed the freedoms of those who were not used to such subordination. Edward Ward of Memphis was so perturbed by soldier life that he wrote his sister "I often wish I was a negro with a good master." What he described as his own blackening face and "crisped and wirey" hair testified to his new status, no less than the expectation that he perform those demeaning military chores like washing and cooking, which were usually reserved for African-Americans.[15]

While white soldiers privately complained about the "slavishness" of enlisted life, Confederate newspapers cast light on the issue by tracking white deserters in advertisements earlier used to identify fugitive slaves. (see Figure 9.1). The Confederacy's turn to conscription in the spring of 1862 increased the basis for comparisons between white soldering and the most degrading forms of unfreedom. A few months before this measure became law, the *Richmond Enquirer* had explained that "volunteering is emphatically an Americanism, and grows out of the fact that ours is a

---

[14] Rives, "Letter to Francis Deane" in Milledgeville *Confederate Union*, July 15, 1863.

[15] Ward's 1862 letters are reproduced in Robert E. Bonner, *The Soldier's Pen: Firsthand Impressions of the Civil War* (New York: Hill and Wang, 2006), 59–60. James McPherson, *For Cause and Comrade: Why Men Fought in the Civil War* (New York: Oxford University Press, 1997) emphasizes Confederate soldiers' commitment to republican freedom while their commitment to racial subordination is taken up convincingly in Chandra Manning, *What this Cruel War Was Over: Soldiers, Slavery, and the Civil War* (New York: Knopf, 2007).

FOR DESERTERS !!

THIRTY DOLLARS will be paid for the apprehension and delivery, at the Augusta Arsenal, of the following deserters :

WILLIAM WHITTEN enlisted at Macon, on the 11th of April, 1861 : height 5 feet 8 inches, complexion fair, hair light, eyes blue, 30 years of age.

THOS. C. McDANIEL enlisted at Macon, on the 11th of April, 1861 : height 5 feet 10 inches, complexion dark, hair black, eyes brown, 30 years of age.   By order.

Col. E. W. CHASTAIN,
Com'g 2d Reg't., G. A.
G. B. LAMAR, Adj't.

☞ Macon Telegraph copy 1 month.   d1m   ap19

LOST,

A GOLD PEN, with Ebony Holder. The finder will be rewarded by leaving it at this office.   1   ap17

$25 Reward !

DISAPPEARED, on the night of the 1st of September, my Negro Woman ABBEY. Supposed to be decoyed off. Said woman is about 35 years old ; of copper color. Has lost all of her front upper teeth ; speaks like a low country Negro; and has some deficiency in her walk. The above reward will be paid for her apprehension and delivery, or lodgment in any jail where I can get her.   WM. MILLER.
sep5   dtf

FIGURE 9.1. Within a week of the bombardment of Fort Sumter, rewards for Confederate deserters were being offered with the same sort of advertisements previously associated with runaway slaves. *Augusta Daily Constitutionalist, April 25, 1861. Courtesy of the American Antiquarian Society.*

citizens' Government." The paper went on to conclude that "our system of Government will have failed" if the army depended on any measure other than appeals to patriotic sentiment. In Congress the next fall, Williamson Oldham accused draft supporters of embracing a system foreign to the spirit of American republicanism and charged that it was a crucial mistake to assume that "soldiers should be mere machines, not citizens." The Texas Senator saw danger in having an army that was "a vast mass of iron unthinking *vis inertiae*, to be hurled at the will of the commander with irresistible force against the columns of the enemy." He even echoed earlier proslavery critiques of free society in conjuring up a "vast military establishment of pyramidal form and proportions" that promised to make "the common soldiers, composed of the free citizens of the States" nothing more than "the mud sills, the substratum, the foundation" of the Confederate war effort.[16]

Proslavery polemicists similarly reflected on the parallels between soldiering and servitude, though for quite different purposes than Oldham had. A year before the Confederacy instituted a draft, the Louisiana botanist Americus Featherman reasoned how "the common soldier, either from inclination or necessity, barters away this inalienable birthright of liberty for a mess of pottage, and suffers himself to be used as an automatic machine of an exacting despotic power, effectively exercised by means of rigid disciplinary regulations." Featherman's point was not to question the worth of soldiering but to justify what he understood as slavery's more "natural" form of subordination according to innate racial characteristics. This line of argument had precedent in the efforts of planter-politicians in the first U.S. Congress to vindicate their region's military strength. In the midst of the 1790 fight over antislavery petitions, William Smith of South Carolina had argued that "discipline may make a black soldier as good as a white" given that "the soldier was a mere machine." His question of whether "a black machine was not as good as a white one" would be revisited, in strikingly similar fashion, during the final months of the Confederate war.[17]

Those who commanded Confederate soldiers had grounds to worry whether such proslavery flourishes (and the authoritarian inclinations from which they drew) would cast a pall over white military subordination within a racist slaveholding regime. Many army officers developed strategies to prevent wartime political opposition from moving beyond sporadic grumblings about a "rich man's war" becoming a "poor man's fight" so as to become the basis of a broader critique that equated enlisted life with a form of white servitude. As Peter Carmichael has recently shown, second tier

---

[16] "New Laws for Volunteers," *Richmond Enquirer*, December 14, 1861; *Speech of Williamson Oldham Upon the Bill to Amend the Conscript Law, Made in the Senate, September 4, 1862* (Richmond, 1862), 7–9.

[17] Americus Featherman, "Our Position and That of Our Enemies," *DBR* 31 (July 1861), 24; William L. Smith in *DHFFC* 10: 753. Cf. Joseph Addison Turner's insistence that "soldiers are nothing but machines, put up for the purpose of shooting and being shot at," in Jackson (Mississippi) *Daily Clarion*, January 28, 1865.

officers in Virginia's "last generation" established a basis of martial paternalism between white leaders and subordinates in the Army of Northern
Virginia, in large part by appealing to a common Christian ethos of hierarchical authority. Such bonds of solidarity across the ranks helped to assure that
Lee's "gallant army" would not become the "Botany Bay for ruffians or
cowards" that some Richmond officials feared when they authorized an infusion of conscripts into the ranks mid-way through the war. Whether or not
similar patterns prevailed outside the Army of Northern Virginia remains an
open question. West of the Appalachian mountains, Confederate policy was
complicated by the bitter conflict among John Preston, Gideon Pillow, and
Braxton Bragg over the best means to fill their armies through forcible conscription. Each of these men had a slightly different understanding of what
forms of compulsion would most effectively replenish the army with effective
fighters. All three generals had earlier managed their own large plantations,
and their experiences as masters seemed to have played at least some role in
how they understood effective discipline and how the coercive techniques of a
slave society might be adapted to the mobilization of a free white citizenry.[18]

As armies became an increasingly key element of Confederate self-
understanding, it became ever more important for leaders to reassure the
country's fighting men that they were "not hired mercenaries, or the floating
scum of a half-barbarous mongrelism" but "a citizens' soldiery" whose
service simultaneously accomplished their country's freedom and their
own glory as patriotic citizens. When Joseph Echols offered this tribute to
the troops in 1865, a roiling controversy had already developed that would
test his assertion that Confederate fighters "know no master and are not
ready to purchase independence by making slaves of freemen." Military men
had already begun to contemplate a national army in which freeborn whites
would fight alongside black plantation slaves. Understanding how leaders of
the slaveholding republic were driven to consider such a plan requires venturing beyond military necessities and the tenets of proslavery polemics. The
final crisis of the slaveholders' rebellion resulted from a confluence of two
factors – the steadily increasing disparity between Union and Confederate

---

[18] Peter Carmichael, *The Last Generation: Young Virginians in Peace, War, and Reunion*
(Chapel Hill: University of North Carolina Press, 2005). James A. Seddon to G.J. Pillow,
October 12, 1863 in *OR* Series 4, Vol. 2: 489. Albert Burton Moore, *Conscription and
Conflict in the Confederacy* (New York: Macmillan, 1924) and Armstead L. Robinson,
*Bitter Fruits of Bondage: The Demise of Slavery and the Collapse of the Confederacy,
1861–1865* (Charlottesville: University Press of Virginia, 2005) both discuss conflicts over
the draft, though I base my own understanding on the dozens of relevant documents contained in *OR* Series 4, Vols. 2–3.

enrollments and a set of diplomatic difficulties that suggested Confederate
nationhood might only be achieved by taking dramatic action to mitigate the
slave South's global isolation.[19]

ENTANGLING ALLIANCES AND DIPLOMATIC INTRIGUE

At the same time that white southerners experienced the pinch of wartime
government at home, the Confederacy's foreign representatives overseas lost
most of the advantages that U.S. diplomats had long taken for granted.
Among the signal failures of the Confederacy as a nationalist project was
its government's inability to secure foreign recognition and thus to operate
as a sovereign state in the international community. The Confederacy's
global isolation proved to be one of the greatest disappointments of the
war, even if it never burdened ordinary white citizens as directly as did
loyalty oaths, soaring taxation, martial law, or conscription. Uncertain
standing as a mere "belligerent" nurtured disillusionment and revealed
how a government that regularly intruded into daily life might be hollow
at its core. Aggravating this blow to self-confidence was a widely shared
perception that slavery represented the most important barrier to international support and acceptance.[20]

As many historians have recognized, Confederate foreign policy was
hampered from the outset by misplaced confidence in the global clout of
slave-grown produce. There was a near infatuation with "that little attenu-
ated cotton thread, which a child can break, but which, nevertheless can
hang the world," as Senator Benjamin Hill of Georgia put it in 1861. James
Henry Hammond had popularized the diplomatic potential of "King
Cotton" in 1858, when he had boasted that the South's leverage in global
markets furnished better protection from foreign pressures than did a viable
and expansive federal Union. Like other elements of proslavery polemics,
the perception of commercial omnipotence soon hardened into orthodoxy.
In 1861, John Quitman Moore ventured a commonplace when he marveled
how "one single plant" had "revolutionized the diplomacy of the world and
now dictates the policy of cabinets." The intoxicating sense of power
dimmed judgment over the crucial early period of hostilities. In retrospect,

[19] *Speech of Hon Joseph H. Echols* (Richmond, 1865), 2–3.
[20] Frank Lawrence Owsley, *King Cotton Diplomacy: Foreign Relations of the Confederate
States of America* (Chicago: University of Chicago Press, 1931), 550–2, Charles
M. Hubbard, *The Burden of Confederate Diplomacy* (Knoxville: University of Tennessee
Press, 1998); Gregory Louis Mattson, "Pariah Diplomacy: The Slavery Issue in Confederate
Foreign Relations" (PhD dissertation, University of Southern Mississippi, 1999).

Confederates like James De Bow would appreciate the foolishness of assuming that "any clever gentlemen" sent abroad would be able to secure European recognition simply by displaying a willingness to "affix their names" to treaties presumably "ready prepared and awaiting their signatures."[21]

If Jefferson Davis shared these misguided assumptions about cotton diplomacy, he was more clear-sighted in appreciating international discomfort with Confederate bondage. Though he did not completely shy away from references to slavery, these were regularly couched with a disarming insistence that "all we ask is to be let alone." This cautious stance, which worked in tandem with attempts to draw foreign attention to other elements of Confederate purpose, pleased the planter-polemicist William Falconer, who believed that "to come before the world right in the beginning of our national career, as the piddling defenders and advocates of a slave republic, would denude the subject of all dignity and importance, besides putting ourselves in a wrong position – a position that would at once array against us all the ill-founded prejudices of the age." Falconer realized that not all shared his own proslavery convictions and that Europeans, in particular, had "no sympathy with African slavery – for the simple reason that they do not understand it, have never been associated with it, do not feel the force of its domestic ties, nor appreciate its appropriate, singular and tremendous physical power and climatic endurance." Avoiding controversy seemed increasingly politic as time passed. In 1861, the *Charleston Mercury* reasoned that proslavery diplomats, in establishing "the true characteristics of the people of the Confederate States," should embrace their callings as "quasi-missionaries of truth." Yet two and a half years later, these same editors were convinced that "the less said about slavery the better." Confederates should postpone any efforts to "champion the beauties of our domestic institutions" until "our cause of independence is established and we have nothing better to do."[22]

[21] Hill in *Atlanta Southern Confederacy*, July 18, 1861; Hammond, "Speech Before the U.S. Senate, March 4, 1858," in *CG* 35th Congress, 1st Session, Appendix, 68–71; Moore, "The Belligerents," *DBR* 31 (July 1861), 75; Moore "Our Domestic and Foreign Relations," *DBR* 31 (September 1861), 293. See also Jay Sexton, *Debtor Diplomacy: Finance and American Foreign Relations in the Civil War Era, 1837–1873* (Oxford: Clarendon Press, 2005), 134–57; Gordon H. Warren, "The King Cotton Theory," in Alexander DeConde, ed., *Encyclopedia of American Foreign Policy: Studies of the Principal Movements and Ideas* (New York: Scribner's, 1978), 2: 515–20.
[22] Davis, "Message to Congress, April 19, 1861," in *CMPC*: 1, 82; Falconer, "The Slave Trade," *SLM* 33 (August 1861), 112; "The Diplomatic Policy of the South," "Reply to the Address of the Confederate Clergy," both in *Charleston Mercury*, June 3, 1861; January 27, 1864.

To many Confederate nationalists, suppressing proslavery propagandism was a demeaning compromise of true conviction, at odds with the defiant stance of the 1850s. William Gilmore Simms castigated attempts to distance the new republic from black bondage as cowardly "subterfuge" and termed official silence as "not only wrong, but, politically, an error." He believed that "either we are capable of independence, or we are not" and argued that "to endeavor to purchase its recognition by a sacrifice of right or principle" was "a great blunder which will, no doubt, exact its penalties in the end." The New Orleans native Eugene Musson made a similar point in a public letter he sent to Louis Napoleon of France a short time later. Hearkening back to John C. Calhoun's bold opposition to abolition petitioning, this self-identified "Creole" reasoned that "having right on our side, it is our duty not to draw back an inch, but to hold on to the end without fear and without reproach; to do nothing, to say nothing which could pass for the slightest concession to public opinion." For Confederates to relinquish their defense of a discredited institution "might perhaps be diplomacy," Musson conceded, but it "would certainly be bad diplomacy."[23]

As cotton failed to work its magic and as international debates over slavery's future continued, Confederates increasingly realized that they would be the servants rather than the masters of New World geopolitics. Early in 1862, George Bagby expressed a growing consensus that while "we look to cotton and to the immediate present," foreign leaders "look to vast movements on the continental chessboard and to important changes in the map of Europe." Confederates thus had little choice but to accept the fact that "the relations of the great civilized powers in Europe and America will be intimate and complicated" for the foreseeable future. Drawing attention to a new world of international relations, Bagby believed that "the Monroe doctrine is very dead for all time to come" and that slaveholders' fortunes would be aided by embracing a hemispheric balance of power that a powerful Union had henceforth sought to diminish. A dispute over Spanish San Domingo early in 1861 had already directed Confederate attention to the potentially vital role of developments to their south. George Fitzhugh pointed to the impending shift in Caribbean geopolitics as evidence of how "we of the South strengthen ourselves by multiplying rival nations, and thus preventing the undue preponderance of any one of them." He conceded that it might be less important to lead an international tide of

---

[23] Simms, "Our Commissioners to Europe: What Are the Facts?" *DBR* 31 (October–November 1861), 413–14; Musson, *Letter to Napoleon III on Slavery in the Southern States, by a Creole of Louisiana* (London: W.S. Kirkland, 1862), 100.

reaction (which had been his goal in the 1850s) than to be adept at capitalizing on favorable circumstances as they developed.[24]

Confederacy policy-makers devoted a disproportionate amount of attention to lobbying Great Britain. England's self-image as the patron of international antislavery was complicated by the heavy dependence of its textile industry on southern cotton, a factor that gave Confederates an opening, if not the lock that some had expected. An inexplicably poor choice of initial personnel squandered the expected diplomatic benefits of the Montgomery Convention's constitutional ban of the foreign slave trade, which was framed as a concession to British no less than to border-state sensibilities. Robert Toombs, the first Confederate Secretary of State, compromised this gesture by identifying the 1842 Webster-Ashburton agreement, which would have required the Confederacy to patrol the coast of Africa, as the only U.S. agreement the new government would explicitly renounce. William Yancey, the leading figure of the 1861 foreign delegation, then petulantly refused to discuss "the question of the morality of slavery" with any foreign power. After concluding that British abolitionism would foreclose any aid, Yancey returned to America to be replaced by James Mason, whose service as chief diplomat was hampered by his authorship of the 1850 Fugitive Slave Law.[25]

Some Confederates abroad openly ventured plans to reshape international attitudes toward slavery and racial subordination. Late in 1861, Ambrose Dudley Mann of Virginia reported that "the Britishry are not yet prepared to give their sanction to such an advocacy, warmly as their feelings are enlisted in behalf of the Confederate States." Nonetheless, he believed that "the time is not distant, in my opinion, when they will cease to rail at our cherished institution." After Mann relocated to Belgium, he sporadically called for the government to issue an "executive manifesto"

---

[24] "Hermes" [Bagby], "Letter from Richmond," in *Charleston Mercury*, February 3, 1862; Fitzhugh, "Hayti and the Monroe Doctrine" *DBR* 31 (August 1861), 131–6. Fitzhugh had given qualified support to Monroe Doctrine in "Acquisition of Mexico – Filibustering," *DBR* 25 (December 1858), 614. For the Caribbean, see "Napoleon is Coming! Maximilian is Coming!: The International History of the Civil War in the Caribbean Basin," in Robert E. May, ed., *The Union, the Confederacy, and the Atlantic Rim* (W. Lafayette: Purdue University Press, 1995): 101–30. Secession's impact on geopolitics on both sides of the Atlantic is the theme of [Robert Ridgeway], "The Foreign Aspect of Our Difficulties," *Richmond Whig*, April 3, 1861.

[25] Toombs directive, March 16, 1861, OR-N, Series 2, 3: 195; Yancey et al. to Earl Russell, August 14, 1861, OR-N Series 2, Vol. 3: 244; London *Times*, October 7, 1861; Eric H. Walther, *William Lowndes Yancey: The Coming of the Civil War* (Chapel Hill: University of North Carolina Press, 2006). Mason's reputation might have been worse had he not been primarily associated with his detention aboard the *Trent*.

that would announce "our inflexible purpose to remain forever free of the North and to preserve inviolate and cherished and, as I more religiously believe than ever benign institutions." He was particularly insistent that only an explicit embrace of slavery by Confederate officialdom would prevent Europeans from using intervention in American affairs as a pretext for emancipation. Most Confederate propagandists opted for a more nuanced approach, following the lead of the Alabamian Henry Hotze, who in editing the *Index* of London directed attention away from bondage to the shared Anglo-American commitment to white supremacy.[26]

The prospects of British aid caused Anglophilia to spring up in unexpected places. During the fall of 1861, editor George Bagby seemed resigned to the slaveholding South's position as a global *"bête noir"* and to Confederates' status as the "Ishmaelites of the whole earth." Just a few months later, however, he optimistically predicted a "fast alliance" with those Britons he dubbed "the foremost people of all the world." Though English "faults" were "many, great and glaring," these seemed minor in comparative terms. "We want to see the people of the South – debauched hitherto by Yankee association – take pattern after the English in their houses, their homes, their solid comforts, their honest wordmanship, their manly sports. We wish especially to see some features of the British constitution grafted on our own," Bagby wrote.[27] Accompanying such flattery came attempts to introduce themes of Confederate martial paternalism into international circulation. British opinion-makers regularly expressed admiration of Confederates generals and martyrs, a trend that the *Index* sought to exploit on behalf of slavery's dim international reputation. "We need hardly say that the corps of Stonewall Jackson was not composed of men who were accustomed to force their female servants, by the terror of the lash, to become mothers of mulattoes, to be sold hereafter for their father's profit or worked to death on his plantations," Henry Hotze wrote shortly after Britons had begun a campaign to establish

[26] Mann to Davis, November 4, 1861, *PJD* 7: 395–6; Mann to J.P. Benjamin, June 13, 1862, September 1, 1862, and June 5, 1863 all in "Records of the Confederate States of America, 1859–1872" (also known as "Pickett Papers,"), Library of Congress Manuscript Division. Robert E. Bonner, "Slavery, Confederate Diplomacy and the Racialist Mission of Henry Hotze," *CWH* 51 (September 2005), 288–316.

[27] [Bagby], "Editor's Table," *SLM* 31 (September 1861), 238; "Editor's Table," *SLM* 32 (February–March, 1862), 195. A broader view emerges from the various essays contained in Joseph P. Ward, ed., *Britain and the American South: From Colonialism to Rock and Roll* (Jackson: University of Mississippi, 2003). For similarly complicated Anglo-American dynamics at work among New England men of letters, see Leslie Butler, *Critical Americans: Victorian Intellectuals and Transatlantic Liberal Reform* (Chapel Hill: University of North Carolina Press, 2007).

a memorial to Stonewall Jackson. As editor of the *Index*, Hotze learned that the image of slaveocratic treason might be neutralized by emphasizing the martial heroism of the Confederacy's white warrior class.[28]

Despite the international vogue enjoyed by "warriors in gray," the Confederacy's identification with proslavery propagandism continued to breed foreign skepticism. The continuing reluctance of the Palmerston government to grant recognition caused several well-placed southern sympathizers in England to lobby for greater Confederate flexibility regarding slavery's future. Secretary of State Judah Benjamin summarily rejected all suggestions that his government give ground and even resolved to make the transatlantic slave trade a "forbidden topic" in future diplomatic negotiations. He instructed ministers that any discussion of this sensitive matter was the exclusive prerogative of officials in Richmond. Benjamin's prickliness toward those who provided unsolicited antislavery advice was not uniform, however. He was notably reluctant to reign in the "unduly conspicuous" case for Confederate emancipation made by the Liverpool merchant James Spence, a major figure in Confederate finance who mixed outspoken sympathies for the South with the concession that the "age has gone past for the sale of men as cattle." Lincoln's Emancipation Proclamation spurred him to predict that disunion would begin a new period in American history, in which slavery would "soon be altered into serfdom, and freedom eventually follow" regardless of Confederate desires. Benjamin waited more than a year to renounce such apostasy, finally aligning himself Henry Hotze, who chided Spence in noting how "no cause has every prospered which its supporters did not fully espouse."[29]

By late 1863, Confederate frustration with the British government mounted, as Palmerston's aloofness generated the same sort of Anglophobic conspiracy theories that John C. Calhoun and Duff Green had proffered two decades earlier. Into the void came renewed interest in other European powers, who seemed, as the editor Henry Timrod put it, to be "actuated neither by colonial selfishness, the imperial pride, or the political hatred of

[28] Mann to Benjamin, April 10, 1863, Pickett Papers; [Hotze], "Colonel Lamar at Chertsey" *Index*, October 22, 1863; Hugh Dubrulle, " 'We Are Threatened with . . . Anarchy and Ruin': Fear of Americanization and the Emergence of an Anglo-Saxon Confederacy in England during the American Civil War," *Albion* 33 (Winter 2002), 583–613.

[29] OR-N, Series 2, Vol. 3:567, 597, 648; Spence, *The Recognition of the Southern Confederacy* (London: Richard Bentley, 1862), 22; [Hotze], "The Foul Blot," *Index* February 18, 1864. Despite several factual errors, the most succinct treatment of Benjamin's handling of slavery remains John Bigelow, "The Confederate Diplomatists and Their Shirt of Nessus: A Chapter of Secret History," *Century Magazine* 42 (May 1891), 113–27. For Spence's importance as an organizer of Confederate finances, see Sexton, *Debtor Diplomacy*, 161–2.

our institutions, which animate England and direct English policy." Early in
the war, Confederates had sporadically considered making a common proslavery front with Spain or with Brazil. During the final two years of combat,
such plans drew little attention, however, in part because Confederates
realized the folly of subjecting their proslavery inclinations to international
scrutiny. Public attention instead turned to the possibilities of a Franco-
Confederate alliance, which had been given new life with Napoleon III's
successful occupation of Mexico City the week before Confederate defeat at
Gettysburg. Though the French emperor repeatedly insisted that he would
only act in concert with Great Britain, many Confederates expected him to
play the decisive role in ratifying international acceptance of their
independent nationhood.[30]

There was a sentimental aspect to Confederate yearnings for what
Jefferson Davis termed the "ally of days of old." The financial, moral,
and naval resources of the Second French Empire seemed capable of rekin-
dling the same victorious partnership that had linked the "first" American
Revolutionaries with Louis XVI's Bourbon monarchy. French support in
1859 for Piedmont's independence from Austria suggested that Napoleon
III might be less interested in replaying the American founding than in
extending his antirepublicanism variant of a nationalist "self-determination
of peoples." Napoleon's widely publicized support for New World "Latins"
(a phrase that would lead over the course of the early 1860s to the notion of
"Latin America") increased his reputation as a nationalist liberator, while at
the same time it inspired a flurry of quasiracialist distinctions of Anglo-
Saxonized Yankees from "Panlatinist" Confederates. The Louisiana editor
Henry St. Paul boiled down such racialist mysticism to its geopolitical
essence, explaining how in "cementing together all the Republics and States
of South America, as he has cemented together the fragments of a
United Italy," Louis Napoleon would establish "a power fully equal in
magnitude to that of the United States." In urging Confederates to court
European powers, St. Paul noted that "our territory is too vast, our

---

[30] "The Reasons Why We Have Not Been Acknowledged by Great Britain," *SIN* October 4,
1863; *Montgomery Advertiser*, January 13, 1864; [Timrod], "To See Is Nothing; to
Foresee Is Statesmanship," *South Carolinian*, February 2, 1864. For considerations of an
explicitly proslavery alliance with Spain and Brazil, see Fitzhugh, "Cuba: The March of
Empire and the Course of Trade," *DBR* 30 (January 1861), 30–42; R.M.T. Hunter "Cir-
cular," August 24, 1861 in *OR-N* Series 2, Vol. 3: 250–1; "The Balance of Power,"
Richmond Daily Dispatch, October 21, 1861; 783; P.G.T. Beauregard to C.J. Villere,
February 9, 1863 *OR* Series 4, Vol. 2: 291; Henry Hotze to J.P. Benjamin, June 6,
1863, *OR-N* Series 2, Vol. 3: 786; Augusta *Daily Constitutionalist*, August 9, 1863.

population yet too sparse, and our domestic institutions too precarious to allow us to stand alone before the world."[31]

St. Paul joined a host of other proslavery commentators who had already established Louis Napoleon's "safety" on the central issue of bondage. The *Charleston Mercury* led the way in noting how the emperor was "no fanatic" and had rarely "talked nonsense about negroes." His authoritarian regime drew even more admiring commentary from reactionaries such as J. Quitman Moore (who had embraced his coup during the 1850s) and George Fitzhugh (whose Tory inclinations did not keep him from praising Napoleon as a "wise, amiable, prudent, far-seeing man"). The only slightly less extremist Richmond press had also burnished the Emperor's image, with John Daniel's *Examiner* hailing him as "the only ruler in Europe who has the intellect to comprehend the occasion or the nerve to play a grand coup."[32]

Napoleon's perceived disdain for abolitionism convinced the proslavery pamphleteer John Tyler, Jr. to link France's Mexican adventure not only to Confederate independence but to the continued southwestern drift of American slavery. Comparisons between Confederate slavery and Mexican peonage dated at least from 1861, when Secretary of State Robert Toombs had noted that "a similarity in their systems of labor" would prevent Mexicans and Confederates alike from disregarding the "feelings and interests of the other." Two and a half years later, Tyler used his position as a Confederate major to encourage Texas authorities to welcome a French military incursion. An effort to stabilize Mexico might also protect bondage in Texas, he argued, suggesting that in the early 1860s, no less than in the mid-1840s, slavery's

---

[31] Davis address in Mississippi, December 26, 1862 *JDP* 8: 576; "The War of Independence: Watchman What of the Night?" *DBR* (February 1864), 55–6; Henry S. Foote, House Speech of January 16, 1863, in *SHSP* 47 (1930), 918; "How to Close the War," *Savannah Republican*, August 14, 1863; Henry St. Paul, *Our Home and Foreign Policy* (Mobile: Daily Register and Advertiser, 1863). Louis Napoleon broadcast his support for New World "Latins" his letter to General Forey (as quoted in *Richmond Daily Dispatch*, February 6, 1863) and in [Michael Chevalier], *La France, le Mexique at les Etats-Confederers* (Paris, 1862); notable Confederate responses include Edwin De Leon, *Verite sur des Etats Confederes* (Paris: E. Dentu, 1862); Alfred Mercier, *Du Palatinisme* (Paris: Librarie Centrale, 1863); and "Panlatinism," *The Age* (February, 1864). For broader views, see Hanna, *Napoleon III and Mexico: American Triumph over Monarchy* (Chapel Hill: University of North Carolina Press, 1972).

[32] "Our Commissioners to Europe," Charleston *Mercury*, June 29, 1861; Fitzhugh, "Reminiscences of Zouave Life," *DBR* 30 (June 1861) 660–1; *Richmond Examiner*, August 3, 1863. Ambrose Mann's dispatches from Belgium (contained in the "Pickett Papers" cited above) displayed a persistent distrust of Louis Napoleon, who he termed in a September 15, 1863, letter "as rabid an abolitionist as there is in Europe."

providential destiny would be determined by who controlled the "Lone Star" republic. This plea gained little favor among those Confederate officials who feared how French annexation of the entire Trans-Mississippi would undermine their government's own national project. Yet Tyler continued to see more promise than peril in Napoleon's desire to "re-establish the empire of his illustrious uncle." In a widely noted 1864 article for *De Bow's Review*, Tyler predicted that Mexican peonage might be transformed into chattel slavery outright, especially if bound labor were replenished by a renewed African slave trade. Converging labor systems might thus encourage Napoleon to frame a "secret alliance with the South, relying upon the South, as a slaveholding community, to support his policy in the direction of slavery, and in negation of the Monroe doctrine." While self-consciously replaying the attempts of his own father (the former U.S. President) to secure slavery's southwestern flank, Tyler found himself also considering how Louis Napoleon might repeat the actions of his uncle, the first French Emperor, who re-enslaved the freedmen of Guadeloupe and Martinique, even as he had lost Haiti and Louisiana with the 1803 destruction of his army in St. Domingue.[33]

Confederate interest in murky Mexican developments peaked during the winter of 1863–4, when a rupture with England and a downturn in military fortunes suggested that battlefield efforts alone could not secure national independence. Judah Benjamin was well aware that Napoleon's role in the establishment of a Mexican empire under Maximilian I would have a "deep and permanent influence over affairs on this continent" and thus seemed willing to bide his time to see what might transpire. James De Bow was more active in publicly noting that Napoleon's "movement upon Mexico is but that of a dotard and a fool, if it does not involve recognition and intervention" on behalf of the Richmond government. "The hour is not yet, but approaches. The historical moment will not be allowed to pass," De Bow wrote, repeating a growing sense that the destinies of a New World monarchy and of a separatist Southern Confederacy had become effectively intertwined. De Bow clung to the idea of Louis Napoleon's pro-Confederate leanings longer than most. As late as February 1865, he speculated that

---

[33] Toombs to John T. Pickett, May 17, 1861 in *OR-N* Series 2, Vol. 3: 203; Tyler memo of October 27, 1863, in Charles W. Ramsdell, ed., "The Last Hope of the Confederacy – John Tyler to the Governor and Authorities of Texas," *Texas Historical Association Quarterly* (1911) 129–45; "Python" [John Tyler, Jr.], "Our Present Confederate Status: Foreign and Domestic," *DBR* 34 (July 1864), 10–11. For the background of these maneuverings, see Kathryn Abbey Hanna, "The Roles of the South in the French Intervention in Mexico," *JSH* 20 (February 1954), 3–21.

informal negotiations conducted by Lincoln and Confederate representatives at Hampton Roads, Virginia, would bring "French politicians to the
point of action" and force them to take action before Americans united in a
coordinated vindication of the Monroe Doctrine. In his mind, the same
fortuitous alignment of international politics were at work that had assured
the U.S. acquisition of Louisiana in 1803 and the final push in 1845 for
Texas annexation to the Union.[34]

By the summer of 1864, Napoleon and Maximilian had resolved that
their own shaky imperial projects would be better served by avoiding
conflict with the United States than by offering quixotic aid to an imperiled
Confederacy. In pursuing friendly relationships with the Lincoln
administration, the upstart Mexican empire and its French sponsor sparked
enormous anger among Confederates. Secretary of State Judah Benjamin
captured the mood in railing against the "bad faith and deception in the
course pursued by the Emperor, who has not hesitated to break his promises
to us in order to escape the consequences resulting from his unpopular
Mexican policy." Benjamin pledged that henceforth Confederates would
not "allow ourselves to be made use of in this matter as a convenient
instrument for the accomplishment of the designs of others."[35]

Manipulations and double-crossing seemed to generate even more anger
toward Napoleon than toward Palmerston in England, but hard feelings did
not keep Confederates from completely disregarding "the designs of
others." Benjamin's angry vow notwithstanding, Confederates remained
alive to the prospect of European aid through the closing months of war,
and some even began to argue that white Southerners would fare better
under a "foreign protectorate" than as a defeated section within the Union.
The logic of this "die-hard" position persisted in post-Confederate
campaigns by masters to relocate to Maximilian's Mexico or to Dom
Pedro's Brazil. Amidst this feverish speculation, the possibilities of two more
distinctively republican alliances arose as alternatives to foreign help. The
first of these options sought to reach an understanding with friendly allies in
the free states of the Union and to use their cooperation to halt the revolutionary transformation from slavery to freedom. A second choice inverted
these priorities, looking to a military mobilization of southern blacks (and a

---

[34] Benjamin to Slidell, August 4, 1863, *OR-N*, Series 2, Vol. 3: 854–5; [De Bow], "The War of
Independence;" De Bow quoted in Henry Blumenthal, "Confederate Diplomacy: Popular
Notions and International Realities," *JSH* 32 (May 1966), 165. In this same letter, De Bow
hailed the Hampton Roads meeting as "the first diplomacy exhibited by our country."

[35] Benjamin to John Slidell, June 23, 1864, *OR-N*, Series 2, Vol. 3: 1057.

corresponding modification of Confederate bondage) as a last remaining route to national independence.[36]

A far-flung cast of characters had reached across the North–South divide throughout the war and such informal contacts, as we have seen, even stirred speculation early in 1863 that the northwestern states might be brought into the slaveholding Confederacy. In 1864, a new round of contacts, schemes, and proposals emerged during a presidential electioneering process that many expected to re-kindle the same sort of cross-sectional ties that had shaped late antebellum politics. Defeating Lincoln at the polls might overthrow what Senator Benjamin Hill of Georgia termed "the idea, the power, and the hopes of abolitionism and the spirit of Puritanic intermeddling." In a private letter to Confederate Vice President Alexander Stephens, Hill insisted that "any thing [sic] attained with abolitionism crushed is better than any thing [sic] possible with abolitionism not crushed." It remained to be seen how Lincoln's loss of the presidency would affect either the conduct of the war or the geopolitical future of North America. Confederate independence was only one scenario imagined by white southern leaders who cheered northern Democrats' electoral prospects. Perhaps more realistic was the notion (that echoed similar proposals put forth during the secession crisis of 1860–1) that a convention of all the states might establish "state sovereignty" as the fundamental principle of a restored American constitutional order. This formula appealed equally to northern Democrats (who saw it as a means of establishing "The Union as it was and the Constitution as it is") and to leading anti-Davis Confederate figures, especially those clustered in areas of Georgia where slavery remained largely intact. Early in 1864, the Confederate Congress seemed to provide an opening for this controversial "convention movement" by publicly expressing its readiness to consider any terms that were "consistent with the honor and dignity and independence of the States, and compatible with the safety of our domestic institutions."[37]

The domestic diplomacy that emerged among white Americans took on heightened importance as the Union's military advances stalled during the

---

[36] I borrow here terminology from Jason Phillips, *Die-Hard Rebels: The Confederate Culture of Invincibility* (Athens: University of Georgia Press, 2007).

[37] Hill to Stephens, March 14, 1864, in *TSC Corr.*, 635; "Address of Congress to People of the Confederate States," and "Manifesto of the Congress of the Confederate States," both in *OR* Series 4, Vol. 3: 131, 486–88; Larry E. Nelson, *Bullets, Ballots, and Rhetoric: Confederate Policy for the United States Presidential Contest of 1864* (University: University of Alabama Press, 1980); Edward Chase Kirkland, *The Peacemakers of 1864* (New York: Macmillan, 1927), and George Rable, *The Confederate Republic: A Revolution against Politics* (Chapel Hill: University of North Carolina Press, 1994).

late spring of 1864. In responding to this apparent stalemate, Confederate peace advocates argued that a regulated assembly of autonomous states might reestablish social order by modifying the nature of a reconstituted federal Union. Both Jefferson Davis and Abraham Lincoln rejected such proposals out of hand, considering them to be a repudiation of the nationalizing projects they each oversaw. But despite the attempt of these two executives to belittle the convention movement as naive, there was nothing inherently far-fetched in the notion that a war of centralization might foster a reaction that would result in a Union loosened rather than consolidated by war. Confederates like George Fitzhugh and William M. Burwell thus touched upon an important point in proposing how "nationalizing" both free and slave states could function as a war-ending panacea. Their vision of a reformulated community of powerfully autonomous states drew sustenance from inherited state sovereignty constitutionalism and from a sense that wartime politics had already produced alternatives to centralism. A sign of persistent federalism in the slave South was evident in a set of regular meetings held late in the war among the Trans-Mississippi governors at Marshall, Texas, and in the agreement among eastern governors to counsel with one another in the fall of 1864. A similar tendency toward the autonomy of normally localized polities seemed to be at work in northern Mexico, where governor Santiago Vidaurri established a base of power largely independent from those who warred for control of the central government in Mexico City. Such trends made it more understandable for convention advocates to see 1864 as a crucial moment not only for slavery and freedom, but for federal alternatives to nationalist consolidation.[38]

In fashioning rejoinders to this escalating peace sentiment, Lincoln and Davis clarified their respective policies toward slavery no less than toward their nationalist commitments. Even as military setbacks eroded Lincoln's political standing, he placed a comprehensive program of emancipation among his nonnegotiable demands, a stance that hostile peace advocates condemned for sacrificing national concord to "fanatical" principles. Once Federal military victory in Atlanta guaranteed Lincoln's reelection in November, the president's course was set. As Republicans prepared for a second executive term (based on a far more durable popular mandate than their first victory), continued talk of reconstituting the Union as a customs league or a mutual defense pact took on an air of unreality. Lincoln insisted upon a free-labor, continental, national

---

[38] Fitzhugh "State Rights Among the Yankees," *DBR* (July 1864); Fitzhugh in Richmond *Enquirer*, September 28, 1864; William M. Burwell, in Richmond *Sentinel*, November 22, 1864; Ronnie C. Tyler, *Santiago Vidaurri and the Southern Confederacy* (Austin: Texas State Historical Assoc., 1973).

Union when he traveled secretly to the Hampton Roads conference early in 1865. There, he showed little willingness to compromise what had become core principles.[39]

For his part, Confederate President Jefferson Davis passed up the chance to sow northern internal discord and to pursue the possibility of a negotiated peace. He did so by denouncing speculation that slavery might be saved through an alliance with northern conservatives. During a Richmond interview with Union soldiers James Jaquess and James Gilmore in the summer of 1864, Davis declared that "we are not fighting for slavery, we are fighting for independence." Confederate commentators instantly recognized how this eminently quotable position modified Davis's earlier tendency to downplay but not deny slavery's importance. His colloquy with Jaquess and Gilmore in July, by contrast, subordinated bondage to the pursuit of national independence in unqualified terms. The *Richmond Examiner* agreed with the president on the main point but wondered why he had not developed this crucial distinction "in some message, or some other State paper, which would have carried it round the world, and repeated it in all languages of civilized nations, instead of leaving it to be promulgated through the doubtful report of an impudent blockade-runner." Several Deep South newspapers, by contrast, attacked Davis' concession and urged Confederate slaveholders to cling to their prerogatives to the bitter end. Even before the Davis-Jaquess interview became widely known, the *Augusta Constitutionalist* had argued that "slavery in the South should be nationalized" so as to "stand as a part of the bill of rights, on the same footing as the right of trial by jury." The institution was not simply the concern of masters but was "an inheritance to the people, whether owned by all or not – a something not to be tampered with by meddling politicians, or be made a subject of debate or argument in our Legislative bodies." Shortly after Davis elevated Confederate nationhood above the cause of bondage, the paper dug in further. "To the large body of soldiers fighting this battle for liberty and State Rights, independence gained without our system of slavery, is to them no independence at all – and the quarrel is not worth the blood."[40]

---

[39] James M. McPherson, "No Peace without Victory, 1861–1865," *AHR* 109 (February 2004), 1–18; Michael Vorenberg, " 'The Deformed Child': Slavery and the Election of 1864," *CWH* 47 (September 2001), 240–57.

[40] Summary of the July 17, 1864, meeting of Davis appears in *PJD* 10: 533–4; quotes from *Richmond Examiner*, August 2, 1864; Augusta *Constitutionalist*, July 29 and August 7, 1864. Davis' comments appeared in the Northern press as early as the July 22 issue of the *Boston Evening Transcript*, but would not be featured in Confederate papers for another ten days, and were still being reported as "news" as late as the August 29, 1864, issue of the *Charleston Mercury*.

Davis's insistence that Confederate independence was of greater value than even slavery followed a familiar pattern of "founding fathers" like George Washington and Simon Bolivar, both of whom came to appreciate the inverse relationship between national prestige and a new country's discrediting association with bondage. Yet Davis made clear in his conversation with Jaquess and Gilmore that a set of more personal factors was also involved. The Confederate President appreciated how the Union army had "already emancipated nearly two millions of our slaves" and that it was inclined to use the same force to "emancipate the rest." His own loss of a valuable Mississippi River plantation workforce had been part of this process. "I had a few [slaves] when the war began," Davis noted, bitterly adding "I was of some use to them; they never were of any to me." This sense of disaffection from his slaves was complicated by a nod towards paternalism, which Davis conveyed when he insisted that "against their will you 'emancipated' them; and you may 'emancipate' every negro in the Confederacy, but we will be free!" With this sweeping challenge, the president hinted that he had already begun to consider how he might rally support for the most dramatic proposal of his administration. This plan, made public just a few weeks later, would propose black enlistments as the key to achieving two key nationalist imperatives – securing international approval while sustaining the military viability of Confederate armies. Davis's proposals would test his political skills, requiring him to convince a populace already alarmed by his disregard for white liberties to alter their assumptions about black bondage. Skeptical Confederate audiences might agree in principle that "We will govern ourselves!" as Davis put it to Jaquess and Gilmore during their interview. It remained to be seen whether they would truly agree with his pledge that "We will do it, if we have to see every Southern plantation sacked, and every Southern city in flames!"

"DIED OF A THEORY?"

A week after Abraham Lincoln won a second term as U.S. president, the newspaper correspondent "Larkin" reported from Richmond that "the question of extending the conscription act to the negro population of the Confederacy" was "being extensively canvassed in private circles." Jefferson Davis's proposal to add 40,000 black laborers to the Confederate military quickly found "many supporters among the prominent men." Much had changed in the ten months since a more expansive program of black enlistment had been urged by high-ranking members of the Army of Tennessee. In that stretch of time, the Union's manpower advantages over the

Confederacy had expanded, while its occupation of the railroad center of Atlanta opened the way for still more recruiting from southern plantations. The dwindling possibilities of foreign alliances and the declining fortunes of potential friends within the United States lay the basis for a final turn inward. As the program of white conscription failed to add meaningful numbers to the armies, the cause of Confederate independence seemed to depend on a newly invigorated partnership of masters and slaves.[41]

Supporters of a biracial military effort hoped to build upon the previous incorporation of southern African-Americans into the Confederate military machine. Impressing slaves for the most onerous army tasks had already bolstered southern confidence in their society's stability and had spurred some Confederates to identify the "preservation of the black race" as the new nation's providential mission. Davis's late 1864 suggestion staked out new ground, however, which even avowedly patriotic masters found hard to swallow. As "Larkin" informed his readers, "the rock upon which the friends of the measure split" was "the bond of freedom for honorable discharge of their duties." Davis had advised that black Confederates with guns should march into battle on behalf of their own emancipation. In hinting how such a step might even lead to a still broader program of black freedom, the Confederate president pushed proslavery nationalists to reckon with exactly how much they had lost in dissolving the bonds of Union.[42]

To term the response to Davis's proposal a "debate" implies more deliberation than actually occurred. The winter of 1864–5 witnessed a noisy, overheated upheaval of possibilities that marked what editors of the *Southern Christian Advocate* aptly recognized as the Confederacy's "crisis of thought, of sagacity, of sacrifice." The fevered unpredictability of this final episode involved the same dizzying range of options that had confronted masters during the secession crisis four years earlier. The loudest voices overcame initial concerns that discussion itself might foster more assertiveness from the slave quarters. Rumors escalated about developments both at home and abroad, especially as a faltering telegraph service produced a vacuum of reliable news. Hyperbole and sharply posed alternatives between

---

[41] "Larkin," "Letter from Richmond," in *Augusta Daily Constitutionalist*, November 18, 1864. Bruce Levine, *Confederate Emancipation: Southern Plans to Free and Arm the Slaves During the Civil War* (New York: Oxford University Press, 2006) provides a superb recent account of this controversy, though useful first-hand perspectives are threaded through Philip Dillard, "Independence or Slavery?: The Confederate Debate over Arming the Slaves," (PhD Dissertation, Rice University, 1999) and Robert F. Durden, *The Gray and the Black: The Confederate Debate On Emancipation* (Baton Rouge: Louisiana State University Press, 1972).

[42] "Larkin" "Letter from Richmond."

liberty and slavery reached higher levels of intensity than they had in the rancorous fight over suspension of habeas corpus. Howell Cobb summed up the stakes by memorably insisting that "the day you make soldiers of [slaves] is the beginning of the end of the revolution." Sensing a threat to fundamental convictions, Cobb warned that "if slaves will make good soldiers, our whole theory of slavery is wrong."[43]

Cobb's evocative turn of phrase about "our whole theory of slavery" looked past the actual content of proslavery polemics of the preceding eighty years. Had Cobb recurred to debates in the first federal Congress, or to the canonical writings of William Harper, James Henry Hammond, William Gilmore Simms, Beverley Tucker, of even those of his own brother (who was the South's foremost legal scholar of slavery), he would have found ample testimony about slaves' potential as "good soldiers," fully able to protect their masters in a war launched by hostile invaders. Loyal members of the planter class had staked out this position from the earliest days of the Confederate war and had drawn the theoretical agreement (if not official approval) from Richmond bureaucrats like Albert Taylor Bledsoe, who recalled the willingness of Revolutionary leaders such as George Washington to sanction the use of black troops in America's struggle for independence. The apparent willingness of some planters to lead their slaves into battle had become a theme of private correspondence between Samuel Cartwright and Jefferson Davis and was validated in print by the likes of George Fitzhugh, who in 1861 had bragged that Confederate blacks would, if given the opportunity, "fight side by side with us to expel the filthy foreigners and roughish Yankees who come avowedly to steal our lands and to drive both master and slave from the fair fields of the South."[44]

The proslavery justification of black military service rested on owners' insistence that they might use their slaves however they pleased. As the Louisiana governor and sugar planter Henry Watkins Allen put it late in 1864, "if a master may, with the help of his faithful slaves, drive thieves from his corn-crib, incendiaries from his cotton-gin, and marauders from his house, why may not many masters, helped by their many slaves, act in concert to drive away armies of thieves, incendiaries, and assassins?"

---

[43] *Southern Christian Advocate*, February 2, 1865; Howell Cobb to James A. Seddon, January 8, 1865, OR Series 4, Vol. 3: 1009–10.

[44] Bledsoe to W.S. Turner, August 2, 1861 in OR Series 4, Vol. 1: 529; George Fitzhugh, "The Times and the War," *DBR* 31 (July 1861), 11; Levine, *Confederate Emancipation*, 60–2. Washington's sanction for slave troops would later be taken up by Davis supporters such as William Barksdale, whose lengthy comments on the Revolutionary debate are featured in Durden, *The Gray and the Black*, 244–9.

A cartoonist for the *Southern Illustrated News* had already demonstrated this point the previous winter. His crude fantasy had broadcast to tens of thousands of readers how the command of whites over blacks might be made into a Yankee "nightmare." Such imagery furnished striking evidence that a "harder" view of racial domination persisted alongside those paternal arguments popularized by the clergy and patriotic poets (see Figure 9.2).[45]

The crisis faced by Confederates late in 1864 altered the meaning of proposed black enrollments and moved considerations well past the proslavery orthodoxies of the past. As the editor H.L. Flash put it, the sweep of the Davis proposal was "emphatically an indication of the future – pointing to a change in the organic structure of society, and giving a new phase to the current of our civilization." Confederate leaders who coupled black enlistments with emancipation were "evincing a desire for a readjustment of our social system which, in its operation, would convert the whole structure into a fabric widely different from what it now is." Even a slight modification of the all-white fighting force signaled a broader transformation, he warned, foreseeing how "the old land-marks determining the relation between master and slave" would be "effectually swept away forever." In helping the South Carolina legislature submit a formal objection to Davis's suggestion, Congressman William Porcher Miles agreed, explaining how even a modest reliance on slaves in the army would be nothing less than a "fatal stab" that would "overturn the whole social fabrick [*sic*] of our country."[46]

Critics of the Davis plan worked hard to disassociate a program of black conscription (which many prominent masters would come to support) from a wider program of black freedom. Turning to ancient and modern history allowed them to consider how proslavery Confederates might emulate those Hebrew patriarchs, Roman generals, and West Indian planters who had used enslaved fighters to secure their mastery and to perpetuate chattel bondage.[47] Flash considered how the same might be done for the Confederacy, albeit with at least some important modifications. Themes of paternalism seemed to

---

[45] *Annual Message of Governor Henry Watkins Allen, to the Legislature of the State of Louisiana* (Shreveport, 1865), 17; "The Yankee's Worst Nightmare," *SIN*, February 20, 1864.

[46] [H.L Flash], "Negro Soldiers," *Macon Daily Telegraph and Confederate*, October 18, 1864. Flash's opinion, which preceded the Davis message, was sparked by a widely noted article in the *Richmond Enquirer* from October 6, 1864.

[47] "Ozina," in Milledgeville *Confederate Union*, January 17, 1865; Rev. Charles Minnigerode, *He that Believeth Shall Not Make Haste: a Sermon Preached on the First of January, 1865, in St. Paul's Church, Richmond* (Richmond, 1865), 10; *Inaugural Address of Governor Henry Watkins Allen, to the Legislature of the State of Louisiana* ([Shreveport, 1864]), 7. Brown and Philip Morgan, eds. *Arming Slaves: From Classical Times to the Modern Age* (New Haven: Yale University Press, 2006).

THE YANKEE SOLDIERS' NIGHTMARE.

A VISION OF THE BLACK–HORSE CAVALRY!!!

FIGURE 9.2. This sharply satirical image came closer to the spirit of abolitionist ridicule than to the paternalism that marked most contributions to the *Southern Illustrated News*. The underlying message of the image – that masters might be able to make slaves a military advantage while keeping them firmly under their control – became a central part of the Confederate's nationalist imaginings during the final months of Civil War. *From Southern Illustrated News, February 20, 1864, The Gilder–Lehrman Collection, on Deposit at the New York Historical Society, New York, GLC 5959.76.*

inform his assumption that slave veterans would forego personal freedom as long as they were granted the right to choose their master and their state of residence upon their release from the army. Henry Timrod considered another means of illustrating the "tremendous vigor and elasticity" of Confederate slave society. Along with the *Richmond Whig* and the *Columbia Times*, the South Carolina editor found a glimmer of hope in the suggestion that Congress "buy and present to each soldier in the field a young and able-bodied negro man, armed and equipped – to be instructed by his new master in the art of handling his weapon, and to be carried into battle by his side." After other papers weighed in, Tennessee Representative John Atkins placed the measure before Congress, though that body gave even less consideration to using slaves as bounties than Revolutionary Virginians had in considering a similar measure back in 1781.[48]

Redistributing slaves to army privates, and thus increasing the number of Confederate masters, was presented as a way to swell the ranks with blacks without undermining the allegiance of unpropertied white soldiers. This issue of nonslaveholder discontent emerged as a major theme of the entire episode. Robert Toombs privately spelled out how the most objectionable feature of Davis's program of black enlistment was its degradation of white troops. "If you put our negroes and white men into the army together, you must and will put them on an equality," and this would assure that both races would "be under the same code, the same pay; allowances and clothing" while also being eligible for the same "promotions for valor." Masters may have been willing to subject their slaves to the "protective custody" of the Confederate army, which might have become a sort of "overseer of last resort." Yet as Toombs appreciated, even measures that secured white control of African-Americans were likely to fan the smoldering resentments within the nonslaveholding rank and file. Earlier discussions of the degradations of military service took on new relevance as newspapers suggested how "in drilling negroes" officers might finally learn "how to discipline the whites" as well. A West-Point-educated Brigadier General pushed this theme further, basing his endorsement of black troops on his conviction that "real soldiers come to have no will of their own" and that such men obeyed commands less out of duty or patriotism but "simply because they are ordered by proper authority." The sense of powerlessness among white troops was exacerbated when officers who had long commanded them to fight orchestrated unit-by-unit endorsements of the Davis plan. Evidence suggests that the widely noted expressions of regimental votes in favor of black enlistments relied more on coercion from above than on a groundswell of support from ordinary infantrymen.[49]

---

[48] [Flash], "Negro Soldiers;" Timrod in *Daily South Carolinian*, January 17, February 3, 1865. *Richmond Whig* January 30, 1865; "A Bonded Man" in Columbus (GA) *Times*, January 10, 1865; Atkins proposal in *SHSP* 52 (July 1952), 294; L. Scott Philyaw, "A Slave for Every Soldier: The Strange History of Virginia's Forgotten Recruitment Act of 1 January 1781," *VMHB* 109 (2001), 367–85.

[49] Toombs to Mann, printed in *Liberator*, June 9, 1865; Ira Berlin, et al., eds., "The Confederacy," *Freedom: A Documentary History of Emancipation* (Cambridge University Press, 1985) Series 1, 1:681; Richmond *Enquirer*, February 18, 1865; Francis A. Shoup, *Policy of Employing Negro Troops* ([n.p.]). For commanders' role in shaping regimental resolutions, see Levine, *Confederate Emancipation*, 113–17; related evidence of the tepid response of the rank and file is convincingly assembled in Chandra Manning, *What this Cruel War was Over*.

Most proslavery writers focused less on dampening class conflict among whites, however, than on reconciling black enlistment with the preservation of slavery. The Confederate chaplain Robert F. Bunting turned to well-worn themes of the evangelical clergy in a letter published in Texas' most widely circulated newspaper. This Princeton-trained Presbyterian was serving with Terry's Rangers in the Army of Tennessee when he systematically addressed how Confederates "must employ slavery if we expect to perpetuate slavery." Failure to increase the size of the army, he reasoned, would hasten Federal victory and result in the imposition of a program of emancipation that defied his sense of possibility. "Whatever may be the future fortunes of slavery, it is very clear that it should survive the war," Bunting wrote, noting how "Humanity, Philanthropy, Christianity all indicate this as essential to the well-being of all parties." The challenge lay in working to "manfully discharge all our pre-possessions, our hereditary modes of logic, and examine the light which the Providence of the Present not the Providence of the past, shed upon it." To reframe accepted understandings would allow Confederates to conclude that "duty to ourselves, to the negro, to the civilization of the continent demands of us the immediate arming of our slaves." Bunting believed that a mixture of personal sacrifice from owners and commitment of all Confederates to Scripture would assure that the institution of bondage would "emerge from this Revolution with yet higher and holier claims upon our Christian care and sympathy."[50]

Other proslavery advocates of black troops addressed the resilience of bondage through the lens of demography rather than of providential design. In February 1865, the stalwart proslavery journalist Edmund Ruffin lamented that the voluminous "talking & publishing" about black troops was "as likely to impair the strength of the institution, & to induce discontent and disobedience among the slaves, as the enlisting of 200,000 with the promise of their prospective emancipation." Faced with the prospect of "subjugation" and attuned to the disruptions that this frothy dispute had already produced, Ruffin was ready "not only to enlist negro soldiers, but to give up the institution of slavery itself (which I would still deem one of the greatest evils)." Working his way into the details allowed him to venture a slightly different alternative, however, as he calculated how forty years in the future, all black Confederate veterans would be dead, while the remaining slave population would, through the process of natural growth, be "but few less if the 200,000 emancipations had not been made." While Ruffin's forecast merely projected current rates of

---

[50] "RFB," "Letter of Feb. 17, 1865," *Houston Tri-Weekly Telegraph*, April 7, 1865; Thomas W. Cutrer, ed., *Our Trust Is in the God of Battles: The Civil War Letters of Robert Franklin Bunting* (Knoxville: University of Tennessee Press, 2006), 309–11.

population growth, that made by the Georgia editor Joseph Addison Turner factored in prospective patterns of postwar migration. In Turner's scenario, Confederates would capitalize on their victory by replacing those slave soldiers who had helped achieve nationhood with new recruits from "the slave coast of Guinea." Black veterans themselves would likely be kept under arms, and turned either toward the Confederate conquest of Mexico and Central America or encouraged to plunder the "fat store houses of northern villages and cities." The main concern, in Turner's mind, was that these black troops not become a disruptive presence by returning to the plantation states.[51]

Expectations that black enlistments would bolster slavery's long-term prospects were not confined to such written speculations. At least a few slaveholders devoted themselves during the spring of 1865 to putting the master–slave relationship on a military footing through direct action. Prior to the Davis proposal, Confederates who had offered up their plantation work force had usually stipulated that either they or their white sons would exercise actual command. Sporadic newspaper commentary echoed this point in affirming how "masters and overseers" would be able to "marshal them for battle by the same authority and habit of obedience with which they are marshaled to labor." By early in 1865, the Texas master William Sledge applied this principle more generally, publicly calling for the "slave owners of the South to raise an invading force of one hundred thousand blacks to be officered by their owners." More specific plans were soon undertaken by several prominent planter families. Even Howell Cobb overcame his earlier objection to black troops as he authorized some of his family's slaves to be readied for combat under the supervision of their overseer. How much discussion of the postwar future passed between master and slave is impossible to determine. But such isolated instances gave at least some credence to James De Bow's postbellum recollection that Confederates had at war's end begun to "receive [the negro] into the ranks of the army, without dissolving the bond of slavery."[52]

[51] Ruffin entry of February 13, 1865, in William Kaufmann Scarborough, ed., *The Diary of Edmund Ruffin* (Baton Rouge: Louisiana State University Press, 1989), 3: 748–50. Turner, "Negro Soldiers" quoted in Jackson *Daily Clarion*, January 28, 1865. Similar demographic calculations, along with a proposal to deport the "enfranchised" black veterans to either Mexico or Central America, appeared in "Native Georgian" to James Seddon, September 29, 1864, OR Series 4, Vol. 3: 693.
[52] W.S. Turner to L.P. Walker, July 17, 1861 in OR Series 4, Vol. 1: 482; Houston *Tri-Weekly Telegraph*, September 21, 1863; *Mobile Register*, November 29, 1863; Houston *Tri-Weekly Telegraph*, January 20, 1865. The Cobb episode is discussed in Clarence Mohr, *On the Threshold of Freedom: Masters and Slaves in Civil War Georgia* (Athens: University of Georgia Press, 1986), 285; De Bow, "Memories of the War: Negro Slavery – Emancipation – Conduct of the Negroes" *DBR* n.s. 3 (March 1867), 226.

Despite the objections and counterproposals that proliferated over the closing months of the war, Davis and his Secretary of State Judah Benjamin were resolute that black enrollments would only be effective if accompanied by a gradual loosening of slavery's bonds. The most prominent military authorities agreed. Like Davis, Robert E. Lee argued that southern blacks would desert to the enemy if not motivated by a promise of ultimate freedom. Lee's public support of the Davis plan provided a nudge to the Confederate Congress, which authorized legislation in March. In defiance of civilian and military leaders, Congressmen (many of whom were among the country's leading slaveholders) included a proviso that "nothing in this act shall be construed to authorize a change in the relation which the said slaves bear toward their owners, except by the consent of their owners and of the States in which they may reside, and in pursuance of the laws thereof." In implementing the law, the War Department established a policy closer to what Davis and Lee desired, requiring masters who volunteered a slave to issue a "written instrument" that would confer upon him the "rights of a freedman."[53]

The Davis administration's inflexibility about the status of black recruits stemmed in part from a desire to coordinate the public campaign for black soldiers with a secret, and even more daring, diplomatic program. Benjamin forthrightly explained to correspondents how even a gradual move away from slavery would "be of more value to us abroad than any diplomacy or treaty making." If Confederates were able to retain their hold on the machinery of government by winning the war, they might institute an "intermediate stage of serfage or peonage" to be followed by a program of "ultimate emancipation." By "vindicating our faith in the doctrine that the negro is an inferior race and unfitted for social or political equality with the white man," this scenario would provide a stark alternative to a Union-sponsored freedom that had already begun to address the extension of civil and even of political rights for former slaves. By contrast, Confederates were likely to do little more than "modify and ameliorate the existing condition of that inferior race" by providing black Southerners with "certain rights of property, a certain degree of personal liberty, and legal protection for the marital and parental relations." The key point was that relinquishing slavery on Confederate terms would "relieve our institutions from much that is not only unjust and impolitic in itself" but from pressures that were "calculated to draw down on us the odium and reprobation of civilized man." The spectacle of transforming slaves into soldiers might shift international opinion, Benjamin reasoned. Once foreign hostility was neutralized, Confederates

[53] Levine, *Confederate Emancipation*, 118–20; Durden, *The Gray and the Black*, 268–70.

could facilitate the inevitable transition from the chaotic overthrow of bondage to a sharply qualified variant of black freedom.[54]

Davis and Benjamin kept quiet about how they were working to link their
plan to replenish the armies with a final bid for foreign recognition. Yet at
the same time that they rallied Congressional support for placing black
Confederates in the ranks, they recruited Louisiana sugar planter Duncan
Kenner for a covert mission to Europe. Like Davis, Kenner had already seen
most of his own considerable investment in human property liquidated by
Federal invasion of the Mississippi Valley. This experience might have
encouraged him to communicate to foreign audiences what Davis had told
Jaquess a few months earlier – that Confederate slavery had already suffered
grievous blows and had thus become far less valuable than the attainment of
a separate nationality would be. This stance, which betrayed as much des-
peration as any real change in heart, alienated chief Confederate diplomats
like James Mason and John Slidell and fell flat before its intended audience
of European policy-makers. The Kenner mission's primary significance lay
in the rumors that it set off in the Richmond press beginning late in 1864. As
speculation about how emancipation might serve to placate foreign governments, the perception hardened that slavery was no more likely to survive
Confederate victory than it would survive Confederate defeat.[55]

Confederates devoted the final months of their war, then, to an extended
consideration of the relative merits of national independence and chattel
slavery. Late in 1863, a few newspaper commentators had begun to
formulate the basic issue by insisting: "Let it never be said that to preserve
slavery we were willing to wear the chains of bondage ourselves." The
following summer, Davis's interview with Colonel Jaquess extended
an equation that would by 1865 become routine. As the Union military
pushed into the plantation districts of the Deep South, some Confederates
adopted a new standard for patriotic sacrifice, rallying to calls that it would
be "better to throw over part of the cargo than to lose the ship and cargo
together." J.H. Stringfellow was ready to dispense altogether with what he
still considered the most beneficial relationship that capital and labor could
assume toward one another. Yet he confided to Davis that "the teachings of
Providence as exhibited in this war dictate conclusively and imperatively

---

[54] Benjamin to Fred. A. Porcher, December 21, 1864 in OR Series 4, Vol. 3: 959–60.
[55] *Richmond Enquirer* linked manpower needs and slavery's international isolation as early as
November 11, 1864, and continued to reflect on the diplomatic potential of emancipation in
early January. For a sampling see Bagby's letters to the *Charleston Mercury* printed on
January 4, 5, 10, 1865, and Craig A. Bauer, "The Last Effort: The Secret Mission of the
Confederate Diplomat, Duncan F. Kenner," *Louisiana History* 22 (1981), 67–95.

that to secure and perpetuate our independence we must emancipate the negro." The only remaining choice was "between emancipation for our independence or subjugation and emancipation, coupled with negro equality or superiority, as our enemies may elect."[56]

Those who resisted such revolutionary changes conveyed no less conviction. The *Charleston Mercury* termed the Davis proposal simple "lunacy." It warned: "Falter and hack at the root of the Confederacy – our institutions – our civilization – and you kill the cause as dead as a boiled crab." A letter to a Georgia paper condemned emancipation as "tantamount to defeat" adding that "every life that has been lost in this struggle was an offering upon the altar of African Slavery." For Confederates even to venture emancipation demonstrated how dramatically "revolutions hurry men away from the landmarks of their political faith." In denouncing news that foreign negotiations might offer a Confederate-led program of emancipation, George Bagby insisted that "a surrender of slavery is a surrender of everything. It is subjugation by the Yankee idea." National independence achieved on such terms would quickly collapse upon itself. "Subjugated by the Yankee idea, we become Yankees. If we are Yankees, why not be in the Union with the rest of the Yankees? Indeed how will it be possible to keep out of that Union?" Bagby wondered.[57]

A decade and a half later, Jefferson Davis recounted his own version of this dramatic finale. He remembered his impatience with Congressmen who did not respond quickly enough to his plan for arming the slaves and even recalled lecturing a Senator that "if the Confederacy falls, there should be written on its tombstone, 'DIED OF A THEORY.'" He seemed to stand by this evaluation through the postwar period, though he surely realized that there were many other factors that contributed to his government's collapse. In any event, Davis expected more from his slaveholding constituency than he had reason to. The "theories" henceforth expressed about slavery's virtues, and about its adaptability, were far older, and would prove to be far more durable, than any commitment to separate nationhood. The racist underpinnings of the proslavery argument would survive the war and become newly relevant to the challenges of the postemancipation order. Given this pattern, a North Carolina Congressman sounded a closer version of the truth when he insisted late in 1864 that "when the president arms the

---

[56] Jackson *Mississippian*, 1863, as quoted in Durden, *The Gray and the Black*, 31; J.H. Stringfellow to Jefferson Davis, OR Series 4, Vol. 3: 1067–70.
[57] *Charleston Mercury*, January 13, 1865; "Q," in *Macon Telegraph*, January 6, 1865; Bagby, "Richmond Gossip," in *Augusta Chronicle and Sentinel*, January 8, 1865.

slaves he seals the doom of the Confederacy." Such a national leader might thereafter "speak to the undertaker, and write its epitaph."[58]

What stands out about this final episode was not the adaptability of some masters like Davis or the recalcitrance of others. The remarkable aspect was the pace at which considerations of slavery changed once proslavery nationalists transferred their allegiances from the Union to the Confederacy. "Such an idea as abolishing slavery by the General Government advocated five years ago, would have made people stare," noted Governor Zebulon Vance of North Carolina when he responded to the Davis proposal. To meet an emergency by pursuing a new plan of freedom was, in Vance's view, "to surrender the entire question which has ever separated the North from the South." Another young Carolinian agreed, complaining privately how "the opinions of a lifetime must now vanish in a day." Far from gaining favor, Confederate action against slavery seemed to threaten a loss of credibility with slaveholding citizens and with outside observers. The world had over time come to expect at least consistency from the enthusiastically American champions of bondage. In this respect, Vance argued that Confederate emancipation promised the same thing as defeat, as it worked merely to "stultify ourselves in the eyes of the world, and render our whole revolution nugatory – a mere objectless waste of human life."[59]

---

[58] Davis, *The Rise and Fall of the Confederate Government* (New York, 1881), Vol. 1, 518; Josiah Turner, quoted in Richard E. Beringer, et al., *Why the South Lost the Civil War* (Athens: University of Georgia Press, 1986), 384.

[59] Zebulon Vance, "Message to the Legislature" in *Charlotte Western Democrat*, November 24, 1864; Walter Clark to mother, April 10, 1865, in Aubrey lee Brooks, ed., *The Papers of Walter Clark* (Chapel Hill: University of North Carolina Press, 1950), 1: 140.

Epilogue: "A People Brought to the End of a Given Cycle"

In 1864, having endured two years of "weary exile" from his adopted home of New Orleans, the Rev. Benjamin Palmer resumed ties with his Lafayette Square congregation. He did so by writing a lengthy pastoral letter that attracted none of the attention stirred by his 1860 Thanksgiving sermon. Yet despite clear differences in the substance and timing, there was an underlying unity to these two efforts, both in the providential framework that each employed and in the nationalist ends each sought to advance. At this point in the conflict, Palmer's Confederate patriotism was no more shaken than was his conviction that there was "undoubtedly a meaning of the most solemn significance in all this, which we must strive to understand." Indeed, the upheavals that had brought destruction to southern battlefields and to slave plantations suggested that Confederates were living through one of God's "special epochs," those periods of transition that every century or so allowed the Almighty to disclose his "terrible majesty." With the chaos of the war, invasion, and emancipation challenging human comprehension, Palmer counseled patience for those who longed for a transcendent perspective. "By and by" Confederates would gain peace and security and would only then be able to "look leisurely back upon these tangled and perplexed scenes" and understand how the war for national independence "has been throughout a discipline of love and not of wrath."[1]

---

[1] Palmer, "Letter to Congregation, May 20, 1864," in Thomas Cary Johnson, *The Life and Letters of Benjamin Morgan Palmer* (Richmond: Presbyterian Committee of Publication, 1906), 280. See Guyatt, *Providence and the Invention of the United States, 1607–1876* (Cambridge University Press, 2007).

Palmer's letter accurately predicted that "the closing act" of war was "not far off which shall give the moral to the whole." What he did not foresee (or at least what he did not publicly venture) was that within little more than a year the curtain would fall not only on the war but also on the Confederate republic and on the system of slavery it had been framed to protect. This tripartite finale was a heavy burden for the white South's most celebrated preacher, who returned to New Orleans with the remnants of a family chastened by defeat and loss. Palmer postponed any assessment of cosmic designs in favor of more pressing challenges. He devoted his energies to his pastoral ministry (at least as it involved the white members of his Church) and commenced ecclesiastical jousting with erstwhile northern allies that would establish him over the next three decades as the most recalcitrant exponent of Southern Presbyterianism.[2]

By the early 1870s, Palmer's proclivity for reflection had returned, first in a crowd-pleasing tribute to the vanquished Confederacy and then with a lengthier reconsideration of the course of events that he shared with a Virginia audience. "The State still rocks beneath the ground-swell" of the late war's "fearful agitation," Palmer commiserated in 1872, as he explored how Americans remained "within the jaws of an amazing crisis." His journey from the violence of New Orleans to the calm of Washington and Lee University was noteworthy in several respects. A school that had served as a breeding ground of proslavery nationalism from the 1790s through George Junkin's leadership of the 1850s was emerging, in the wake of the late Robert E. Lee's celebrated postbellum presidency, as a key node in a developing network of the "Lost Cause." To ascend to such a stage inspired Palmer to rise above issues associated with the upcoming presidential election and to take up more knotty issues. Unlike 1860, when a looming shift in executive power had required a preemptive counterrevolution, new circumstances called for a more cautious policy of guiding a transitional period toward its most suitable conclusion. The immediate problem hinged on the comparatively simple matter of "how a people brought to the end of a given cycle, may safely tide over the bar, and find the deeper sea-room lying beyond."[3]

---

[2] Johnson, *Life and Letters,* for a suggestion that Palmer may have begun to despair of slavery late in 1864, see Woodward, ed., *Mary Chesnut's Civil War* (Yale University Press, 1981), 644.

[3] Palmer, *The Tribunal of History: A Lecture Delivered Before the Historical Society of New Orleans, February 16, 1872* (Columbia: Presbyterian Publishing House, 1872); Palmer, *The Present Crisis and Its Issues: An Address by Rev. B.M. Palmer D.D. at Washington and Lee University* (1872). James K. Hogue, *Uncivil War: Five New Orleans Street Battles and the Rise and Fall of Radical Reconstruction* (Baton Rouge: Louisiana State University Press, 2006).

Just as the drama of Palmer's 1860 sermon was enhanced by its New Orleans locale, so his 1872 Virginia oration was geared to the particularities of its setting. Instead of gazing across the continent and toward the future (as he had in his Lafayette Square performance), this occasion found Palmer retrospectively summoning the "immortal shades" of Revolutionary and Confederate heroes and asking them to gather on newly sacred ground. Before an audience lately accustomed to linking the example of Virginia demigods Washington, Jefferson, and Madison with the more recently martyred Lee and Jackson, Palmer gestured toward continuity. The "principles of our Fathers are our principles to-day; and the stones upon which the temple of liberty was first built" were "the only stones upon which it shall ever be able to stand." The white Confederacy's quarter of a million dead haunted the scene no less than the South's statesmen and generals did. It was, after all, their blood that had sanctified Virginia soil. "This land of ours, furrowed by so many graves and overshadowed with such solemn memories" was a cause for inspiration as well as sorrow. Such mass sacrifice seemed capable of nurturing a far more powerful set of regional devotions than had been available in 1860. A landscape defined by death could nudge the white South to make a "consecration of the heart" that would be "equal to its grief." As befitted a providential mystery, the very losses suffered by Confederates during war had thus produced a crucial gain. A war whose main results included forcible re-Union and the destruction of slavery would also, as the historian David Potter would later sum up, do "far more to produce a southern nationalism which flourished in the cult of the Lost Cause than southern nationalism did to produce the war."[4]

The post-Confederate "Lost Cause" as elaborated by men like Palmer at places like Washington and Lee represented one strand in a larger complex of white regional solidarity. The men and women who spearheaded this commemorative tradition fashioned coherence from a messy set of wartime experiences and in doing so launched an even wider array of magazines, organizations, and observances than proslavery nationalists had managed to do at the height of their influence in the 1850s and 1860s. Yet when placed beside that earlier program, which had united a recognizable set of geopolitical initiatives with a broad series of cultural endeavors, the Lost Cause

---

[4] Palmer, *The Present Crisis*; David Potter, *The Impending Crisis: 1848–1861* (New York: Harper and Row, 1976), 469. Palmer's invocation of Confederate dead was part of a larger process, explored by Bill Blair, *Cities of the Dead: Contesting the Memory of the Civil War in the South, 1865–1914* (Chapel Hill: University of North Carolina Press, 2004) and Susan-Mary Grant, "Raising the Dead: War, Memory and American National Identity," *Nations and Nationalism* 11 (October 2005), 509–29.

was far more disparate, disjointed, and modest in its aims. Its proponents regularly faced competition from other manifestations of what might be termed "Southern Americanisms." These alternate visions would play themselves out in the burgeoning social, political, cultural, and religious realms of the late nineteenth century American republic.[5]

Without the overriding issue of slavery – and without the outside emancipationist pressures on the slave South's "peculiar" vindications of bondage – the postures assumed by former masters in defeat tended toward fragmentation rather than toward unification. The so-called "solid" politics of the New South were thus more apparent than real. If region had become a more palpable entity as a result of secession and war, the circuits of political maneuvering and of cultural production increased in their complexity. Understandings of what made former Confederates both "Southern" and "American" were broad enough to encompass a stunning array of darkly racist fears and escapist fantasies. Reflections on regional and national destinies sparked a conversation between expressions of hope about a fresh start and a yearning to transmit important elements of the past to future generations. Shifting political alliances and emerging patterns of economic development at home intersected with the willingness of the international community to take a new look at white southern character. The outside world listened attentively as even proslavery stalwarts like Palmer came to associate wartime emancipation with the "the heroic boldness of American legislation."[6]

Even in its most defiant forms, the Lost Cause version of "Southern Americanism" would be especially constrained when evaluated a form of

---

[5] While varieties of New South "Americanisms" have attracted little scholarly attention, suggestive guides to the content and broader context of this phenomenon can be found in Steven Hahn, "Class and State in Postemancipation Societies: Southern Planters in Comparative Perspective," *AHR* 95 (February 1990), 75–98; Anne Sarah Rubin, *A Shattered Nation: The Rise and Fall of the Confederacy, 1861–1868* (Chapel Hill: University of North Carolina Press, 2005); Jane Turner Censer, *The Reconstruction of White Southern Womanhood* (University of North Carolina Press, 2005); Edward Blum, *Reforging the White Republic: Race, Religion, and American Nationalism, 1865–1898* (Baton Rouge: Louisiana State University Press, 2005); David Blight, *Race and Reunion: The Civil War and American Memory* (Cambridge: Harvard University Press, 2001); Charles W. Calhoun, *Conceiving a New Republic: The Republican Party and the Southern Question, 1869–1900* (Lawrence: University Press of Kansas, 2006) and Desmond King and Stephen Tuck, "De-Centring the South: America's Nationwide White Supremacist Order After Reconstruction," *Past and Present* 194 (February 2007), 213–53.

[6] Palmer, *The Present Crisis*, 25. Edward L. Ayers made variety even among whites a central theme of *The Promise of the New South: Life after Reconstruction* (New York: Oxford University Press, 1993); his emphasis has been confirmed by an outpouring of studies in the fifteen years since his book appeared.

nationalist assertion. The men and women who had sought to "nationalize" slavery in the Union and who afterward became staunch Confederates devoted their energies over the last third of the nineteenth century to fostering a sense of group identity and establishing a common sense of purpose. Even those who harbored great bitterness toward former Yankee enemies were reluctant, especially after Reconstruction had run its course, to engage in any sustained discussions of a geopolitical destiny apart from the Union. They appreciated that if the federal government had proved capable of maintaining its integrity against armed insurgency in the early 1860s, its growth over each succeeding decade forestalled visions of a renewed southern "rising." The most recalcitrant former rebels thus pursued their prerogatives largely as a matter of regional autonomy within the confines of an increasingly nationalized United States.

In 1872, Palmer was more skeptical than many were about the durability of the "American empire," but he was fully within the emerging consensus when he addressed that "problem of race" that marked the most perilous of all postbellum transitions. The work of "adjusting the relations between two distinct peoples that must occupy the same soil" was not an issue that could be skirted, Palmer insisted, as he noted how this challenge "stares us in the face whenever we turn." Earlier visions of redistributing the black population across space (whether in the guise of African colonization or of westward expansion) seemed irrelevant to current circumstances. Such a "solution" had no more chance of success than the failed Confederate program of perfecting a "paternalist" form of bondage. Clinging to the idea that Americans might find glory in accomplishing God's larger purposes, Palmer went to the Bible to see how new forms of "racial adjustment" might, with an appropriate providential twist, prove to be "the most conspicuous proof of the vigor of national life." Rather than search out scriptural descriptions of bondage or of liberation, Palmer asked former Confederates to turn to the stories of Noah and Nimrod, and to stitch these together to understand a supposed Divine imperative to "break the human family into sections." Melding scriptural injunction with warnings of how a "mongrelized" American Union might sink to the level of South American republics, Palmer insisted that whites and blacks should thereafter "stand apart in their own social grade."[7]

Palmer engaged in a rhetorical trick in distancing himself, and his God, from white dominance of the "black race" and instead elevating a "social division" that would carve out spaces for former masters and the New

---

[7] Ibid, Stephen R. Haynes, *Noah's Curse: The Biblical Justification of American Slavery* (New York: Oxford University Press, 2002); Blum, *Reforging the White Republic*, 160–5.

South's freed people to operate independently from one another. Framing issues as a matter of benign "separation" masked the continuing relationships of power that would structure everyday experience in the postemancipation South. Palmer's language was no less powerful for its duplicity, however. The understanding he helped to popularize disguised the ferocity with which white Southerners regained control of their region's political and economic destiny. At century's end, this same formula would make the federal government, through the auspices of the Supreme Court, as complicit in a Jim Crow system of "separate but equal" as it had been fifty years earlier in a powerful slave system that was never merely "Southern" in its character and its underpinnings.

Yet beneath the apparent continuity in nationally sanctioned structures of "white supremacy," there was a sharp break in the transformation of a fight for "home rule" toward an overriding concern with "who shall rule at home." The re-organization of power that this shift entailed revealed something important about the diminished ambitions of former slaveholders on whose behalf Palmer spoke. In having sought to master not only their plantations but the American nation as a whole, these men and women had set in motion a process that would lead toward a new world. For the next hundred years, they and their progeny would claim the prerogatives available to junior partners of more powerful northern allies. With the cycle of proslavery nationalism having run its final course, former Confederates would have little choice but to relinquish their earlier ambitions and to allow new forces and new figures to shape the next stage of America nationhood.

Acknowledgments

The project began during my graduate school training, when I was taught to approach the past with a healthy spirit of skepticism and a suspicion of easy answers. Research seminars directed by David Montgomery, Nancy Cott, the late John Blassingame, Jon Butler, and John Demos gave me the first opportunities to raise questions about "Southern nationalism" as an interpretive approach to the mid-nineteenth-century crisis of Union. Collaboration with a superb cohort of historians-in-training helped me to consider how a dissertation might be launched to reconsider the context, pace, and trajectory of slaveholders' path to independent nationhood. When David Brion Davis agreed to serve as the director of the dissertation, he began what he has remained – this project's most important guide. Jon Butler and Harry Stout completed an exemplary dissertation committee and have served, along with David Davis, as true friends and constant supporters of my work and career. A better group of mentors is hard to imagine.

In addition to my fellow graduate students and teachers at Yale, the project has benefited from continued input from faculty colleagues, co-panelists at conferences, and from audiences at public presentations who have helped me, in ways both large and small, to refine the research of the dissertation, to hone my analysis, and to sustain my energies during further research and revision. Standing out among a very large group are David Bailey, Peter Beattie, Tom Brown, Eileen Cheng, Laurent Dubois, Drew Faust, George Forgie, Gaines Foster, Bill Harris, Gary Johnson, Wim Klooster, Peter Knupfer, Jack Maddex, Jr., Reid Mitchell, Laurence T. Moore, Susan O'Donovan, Michael Parrish, Lewis Perry, Paul Quigley (who was among the last to read the entire manuscript), Patrick Rael, Anne Rubin,

Marni Sandweiss, Harlow Sheidley, Manisha Sinha, Mitchell Snay, Tom Summerhill, David Waldstreicher, and Charles Reagan Wilson.

Three additional opportunities deserve special mention. The hospitality shown to me by the Civil War Center at Penn State in 2001 was remarkable, as was the seriousness with which Bill Blair, Mark Neely, and a group of their graduate students provided commentary. That same year, Frank Smith and two anonymous readers for Cambridge University Press helped me to undertake revisions for what would become a much better book. Then in 2005, Chris Wohlforth generously arranged a review of a revised manuscript at the John Sloan Dickey Center of Dartmouth College. That group (which notably included John A. Hall, James Roark, Mike Vorenberg, Judi Byfield, and Roberta Stewart) collectively helped me to adopt a new title and clarify the stance I would take during an important final round of revisions.

Along the way, this project has received generous financial assistance from Yale University (in the form of a John T. Roberts fellowship, a Mellon and an Enders travel grant, and a Robert Leylan fellowship) and from the Yale history department (which provided travel stipends to conferences and financed an invaluable six-week trip to southern archives). The Beinecke Library and the Pew Foundation for the Study of American Religion provided two successive summers of uninterrupted research while a James C. Caillouette Research Fellowship at the Huntington Library in San Marino, California, and a Mellon Fellowship at the Virginia Historical Society in Richmond helped me to complete the dissertation. More recently, a lengthy period in residence at the American Antiquarian Society (made possible by funding for a separate project, supported by the NEH) helped me to secure several illustrations. The University of Southern Maine, Michigan State University, Amherst College, and Dartmouth College have each provided much appreciated (and not easily catalogued) institutional support in the years since I left graduate school.

In addition to thanking the staffs at the Beinecke, Huntington, Virginia Historical Society, and American Antiquarian Society, I wish to acknowledge the helpfulness of those at the Seeley G. Mudd, Law School, and Divinity School Libraries at Yale and the guidance of the expert staff at Yale's Sterling Library. I have depended on the aid of librarians and archivists at the Alabama Department of Archives and History; the Hoole Special Collections at the University of Alabama; the Robert Woodruff Library of Emory University; the Special Collections of the University of Georgia; the South Caroliniana Library at the University of South Carolina; the Virginia State Library; the Alderman Library of the

University of Virginia; the Presbyterian Historical Society repositories at Montreat, North Carolina, and Philadelphia, Pennsylvania; the Perkins Library at Duke University; the Wilson Library at the University of North Carolina; the Tennessee State Archives; the Library of Congress; the Widener, Houghton, and Sprague Libraries at Harvard University; and the Boston Public Library. Collectively, these institutions served as exemplary partners in helping me bring together the material for this book.

Members of an extended network of Bonners, Butlers, Bigbees, and Goodmans lived with this project for the long haul and provided warm encouragement, generosity, and good cheer along the way. Pat Bigbee lent her ear time and again and marveled (without quite saying it) how a single book could take so many different forms. Leslie Butler knows firsthand how hard it is to practice the historian's craft. She also knows how hard it would be for me to express how much I value the life we have made together. For Leslie and for my mom, this book's dedication only hints at the thankfulness and love I have for both of them.

Index

abolition
  1836 postal campaign for, 56, 98, 129
  and Missouri, 12
  and sexuality, 91
  and state sovereignity, 63
  and Texas, 25
  and the military weakness of the South, 35, 157
  and the Pilgrim past, 175
  and the Whig political establishment, 187
  British, 29, 31, 57–58
  constitutional, 58, 62
  nationalist, 67
  evangelical, 131, 134, 145, 164
"Abolition of Negro Slavery" (Dew), 96, 101–02
Adams, John Quincy, 24, 88
Adams, Samuel, 152
Adger, John, 119
Africanization, Cuban, 34, 58
Alabama, 4, 221
  Democratic Party, 71
Alfriend, Frank, 239, 270, 273
Alien and Sedition Acts (1798), 48, 60
Alien Enemies Act (1860), 233, 290
Allen, Henry Watkins, 281, 313
Amazon Valley, 5, 32, 37

American Bible Society, 138
American Colonization Society, 37, 53, 55, 98
American Party (Know-Nothings), 207, 209, 238
American Quarterly Review, 96, 101
American Revolution
  and slavery, 51
  arming slaves during the, 19, 313
  implications of, considered in South Carolina, 150–161
  legacy of during the Civil War, 255–64
  proslavery Unionist interpretation of, 153
  slave defection to British during the, 17, 157
  slaveowner anxiety at onset of, 15
  slavery before the, 4
  slaves liberated after the, 6
American Scholar, The (Emerson), 96
American Sunday School Union, 130
Andrew, James O., 120
Anecdotes of the War for Independence (Garden), 154
Anticipations of the Future (Tucker), 181
Antietam, 234, 241, 249
Arizona, 38, 233
Arkansas, 4, 233, 238

admission to the Union of, 34
Articles of Confederation, 77
Atchison, David, 35
Atkins, John, 315
Atkinson, Joseph, 241
Atlanta Intelligencer, 237
Augusta Constitutionalist, 236, 310
Axson, I. S. K., 123
Ayer, Lewis, 160

Bacon, Nathaniel, 174
Bacon, Thomas, 118
Bagby, George, 69, 225, 237, 242, 246,
    268–269, 300, 302, 321
Bancroft, George, 175, 182
Banks, Nathaniel, 209
Baptist Magazine, 129
Baptists, proslavery, 128–131
Barbé-Marbois, Francois, 84
Barksdale, William, 184, 225
Barnes, Albert, 136
Barron v. Baltimore, 56
Bartow, Francis, 242
Bascom, Henry, 132
Bastiat, Claude-Frédéric, 108
Beauregard, P. G. T., 235
Bee, Bernard, 242
Beecher, Catherine, 195
Beecher, Henry Ward, xvi
Bell, John, 211
Benjamin, Judah P., 39, 64, 211, 303,
    306, 319
Beverley, Robert, 175
Bilbo, William, 238
Bill of Rights, The, 44
"Black Race in North America, The,
    Why was their Introduction
    Permitted?" (1855–56), 37
blacks, free
  and the American Colonization
    Society, 53
  danger posed by, 18
  relocating, 8, 36, 43
  restricted from Missouri, 13
Blake, William O., 178
Bledsoe, Albert Taylor, 41, 112, 313
Bocock, John, 188, 225

Bocock, Thomas, 172
Bolivar, Simon, 311
Bonaparte, Napoleon, 8
"Bonnie Blue Flag", 228
Bourne, George, 134
Boyce, W. W., 287
Boyd, A. H., 275
Boyden, Ebenezer, 123
Bragg, Braxton, 234, 297
Brantly, William T., 128
Brazil, 32, 266, 304, 307
Breckinridge, John C., 212
Bridges, George, 119
Brisbane, William Henry, 129
Brooks, Preston, 157
Brown, John, 22
Brown, Joseph, 227
Brown, William Wells, 90, 175
Bryan, Edward, 34, 103
Buchanan, James, 184, 210, 211, 222
Bunting, Robert F., 317
Burke, Edmund, 87, 140, 177
Burwell, William M., 209, 309
Butler, Andrew, 33

Cairnes, James, 35
Calhoun, John C., 16, 29, 33, 34, 42,
    47, 56, 58–68, 94, 106, 165,
    210, 227, 300, 303
California, 65, 73
  admission to the Union of, 32, 34, 68
Callender, James, 90
Calvin, Jean, 132
Campbell, Charles, 175
Campbell, John Archibald, 70–73, 109,
    123
Campbell, Thomas, 227
Canada, 34
Capers, William, 118, 145
Carey, Henry, 110
Caribbean, 16, 32, 56, 68, 71, 82, 121,
    222, 278
  restrictions against free blacks from
    the, 11
Carlyle, Thomas, 108, 109
Carmichael, Peter, 296
Carroll, B. R., 155, 158

Cartwright, Samuel, 19, 112, 278, 313
Caruthers, Andrew, 136
Cass, Lewis, 71, 73, 189
cavaliers, Virginia, 179, 181, 188
Central America, 32, 34, 38
centralism, 50, 62, 309
  Southern distrust of, 51
Century Hence, A (Tucker), 181
Chalmers, Thomas, 119, 134
Channing, William Ellery, 71, 91
"Character and Capacity of the Negro
  Race, The" (Holcombe), 274
Charleston Courier, 96, 201
Charleston Mercury, 57, 159, 161,
  166, 198, 236, 238, 240, 244,
  287, 289, 292, 299, 305, 321
Charleston Slave Missions' Convention
  (1845), 126
Charlevoix, Pierre, 278
Chesapeake, invasion of (1814), 17, 22
Chesnut, James, Sr., 5
Cheves, Langdon, 106
Chisholm v. Georgia, 45
Christianity
  proslavery, xiii, 114–116, 219
  and nationalism, 116
  reformed slaveholding ethic of, 117
Christy, David, 112
Civil War
  and consolidationism, 44
  and expansion, 33
  arming slaves during the, 19,
    311–22
  as Second American Revolution, 252,
    255–64
  Divine purpose of, 38, 241–51
Claiborne, William, 10
Clarkson, Thomas, 96
Clay, C. C., 49, 171
Clay, Thomas, 122
Clemens, Jeremiah, 242
Clingman, Thomas, 211
Cobb, Howell, 184, 313
Cobb, T. R. R., 178, 231
Cohens v. Virginia, 46
Colonial Union, 120

colonization, African, 16, 60, 101, 112,
  137, 276, 284
Columbia Telescope, 98
Columbia Times, 315
Columbian College, 128
Columbian Star and Christian Index,
  128
Columbus Mississippi Republican,
  236
Common Sense (Paine), 15
compound republic (Madison), 4, 42–78,
  81, 220–28
Compromise of 1850, 70, 207, 209
Conedo, Margarita, 236
confederacy
  partial, and slave insurrection, 16
  proslavery, centered around Texas,
    26, 31
Confederate Congress, 225, 249, 308
Confederate Constitution, 239, 240
Confederate States of America
  and international affairs, 298–322
  boundaries of, 228–41
  committees of safety embraced by,
    290
  conscription adopted by, 227, 233,
    235, 294, 297, 314
  loyalty oaths in, 291
  martial law and, 235, 292, 298
  Montgomery Convention founds,
    223, 243, 301
  passports in, 292
Conrad, Charles M., 249
consolidationism, 13, 44, 46, 64, 179,
  309
  Calhoun, 58
  Jackson's opposition to, 49
Constitution
  and nationalism, 1
  delegation of powers in (Madison),
    51
  eliminating protections for
    African-Americans under the, 56
  three-fifths compromise, 76
Constitutional Convention (1787), 15,
  51, 54, 69, 114, 218, 224, 226

constitutionalism
American versus British, 44, 63
and nationalism, 50
arguments for (1820s–30s), 163
Calhoun's, 58–68
Campbell's, 73
John Scott's, 77
proslavery, 43, 77
and secession, 41
Southern Rights, 43
states rights, 53
Cooper, Thomas, 101, 105, 107, 116
Copperheads, 235, 237
Corn Laws, British, 108
"Cornerstone Address" (Stephens), 269
Cotton is King, 112
Cotton Kingdom, 4
and the Louisiana Purchase, 9
cotton, short-staple, 10, 105
as source of proslavery diplomacy,
311
global demand for, 4
Coxe, Tench, 81
Crawford, Thomas, 166
Crisis, The (Turnbull), 54, 58
Crummell, Alexander, 134
Cuba, 32, 34, 37
free labor economy in, 29
Cunningham, Ann Pamela, 156,
198–199, 202
Cunningham, John, 156, 159
Cushing, E. W., 237

Dabney, George E., 267
Dabney, Robert L., 219
Dahlgren, Charles, 276
Daniel, John M., 267, 293, 305
Dargan, Edmund, 276
Davis, Jefferson, 3, 21, 33, 38, 41, 42,
49, 171, 213, 222, 224, 227,
229, 233, 239, 281, 286, 299,
309, 310, 313, 321
Davis, Mary, 278
De Bow, James D. B., 36, 103, 181,
299, 306, 318
De Bow's Review, xiv, 101, 161, 182,
264, 270, 306

Declaration of Independence,
Mecklenburg, 163
Declaratory Act (1766), 57
Delano, Columbus, 35
Delaware, 34, 237
Della Torre, Peter, 72
Demerara, British, 98, 119
Democratic Party, 191, 208, 210
Dew, Thomas R., 23, 87, 89, 96, 101,
107, 112
Dickinson, S. Henry, 177
Dillard, A. W., 267
*Discourse on the Constitution of the
United States* (Calhoun), 68
Douglas, Stephen A., 212–213, 229
Drayton, John, 18
Dred Scott v. Sandford, 56, 73, 112,
210–212

Eakin, John, 226
Echols, Joseph, 297
Edinburgh Review, 18
Edwards, Bryan, 177
election, presidential
of 1800, 8
of 1836, 91
of 1844, 63
of 1848, 189
of 1852, 206
of 1856, 189, 210
of 1860, 75, 146, 179, 211
of 1864, 240, 309
partisan system of, 64
Eleventh Amendment, 45
Elkison, Henry, 52
Elliott, Ebenezer Newton, 112
Elliott, Stephen, 279, 284
Elliott, Stephen, Jr., 104
emancipation, 317, 319, 321, 326
and Providence, 321
barbarism as a result of, 105
in South America, 4
in the Caribbean, 4, 23, 36, 58, 108,
129
Emancipation
Proclamation, 235, 279, 303
Emerson, Ralph Waldo, 96, 180

enlistment, black, 19, 37, 281, 288, 311–320
equality, 152, 189, 270, 287, 319–321
  and sectionalism, 74
  constitutional, in the territories, 66
  natural, 101
  or independence, 75
  racial, of wartime soldiers, 316
  state, 65
evangelization
  frontier, 133
  household, 124, 126
  proslavery, 123
  slave, 117, 120, 127
Evans, Augusta Jane, 267
Everett, Edward, 169, 170, 200, 205, 211, 213
expansion
  Confederate, 228–41
  results of, 9
  territorial, 34

Falconer, William, 264, 299
Farewell Address (Washington), 165, 185, 186
Faust, Drew, xix
Featherman, Americus, 296
federalism, 48
  Calhoun's, 67
  Scott's, 76
  wartime, 228, 309
Federalist Papers, The, 42
  Federalist 39, 45, 51
Fillmore, Millard, 184, 207, 209
Finley, Robert, 135
Fitzhugh, George, 103, 106, 182, 185, 238, 246, 268, 300, 305, 309, 313
Flash, H. L., 242, 314
Florida, 4, 10, 221
  admission to the Union of, 34
Floyd, John, 184
Fontelle, Lutha, 277
Foote, Henry S., 235
Force Act (1833), 61–63
Ford, Samuel, 248
Forsyth, John, 26

Forsyth, John Jr., 186
Foster, Stephen, 94
Fox-Genovese, Elizabeth, 93
France, 7–10, 57, 304–307
Franklin, Benjamin, 81, 85
Fredericksburg, 235, 241
Free Church of Scotland movement, 134
free soil, 13, 25, 51, 65, 73, 85, 184, 206, 207, 218, 226, 232, 240
French Revolution, 57, 108, 152, 270
fugitive slave clause (in Calhoun's Southern Address), 67
Fugitive Slave Law (1850), 35, 74, 206
Fuller, Richard, 97, 129
Furman Theological Institute, 128
Furman, Richard, 118, 127, 136

Gabriel (Richmond slave), 8, 16
Gadsden, James, 38
Garden, Alexander, 154
Garnett, Muscoe, 34
Garrison, William Lloyd, 187
Georgia, 4, 7, 52
  absorbing Florida, 222
  British attempts to restrict slavery in eighteenth century, 51
Georgia Historical Society, 149
Giddings, Joshua, 199
Gila River Valley, 38
Gildersleeve, Basil, 267
Giles, William Branch, 18
Giles, William Mason, 173
Gilmore, James, 310
Gladney, J. B., 182
Glorietta Pass, 234
Graham, William, 116, 137, 291
Grahame, Robert, 175
Grayson, William J., 222
Great Britain, 17, 28–29, 34, 52, 57, 81, 110, 208, 301–304
"Great Reaction," 18, 97, 152
Green, Duff, 102, 208, 303
Greenville Mountaineer, 154
Gregg, Alexander, 281
Grigsby, Hugh Blair, 179

Grimké, Angelina, 91
Guadeloupe, 57, 306
  French plan to remove black rebels
    from, 8
  restoration of slavery in, 8
Guerrero, Vicente, 25

habeas corpus, 286, 292–294, 313
Haiti, 39, 306
  coverting America to, 201
  failures of black industry in, 107
Hall, William A., 271
Hamilton, Alexander, 7
Hammond, James Henry, 19, 92, 96,
    98, 111, 112, 194, 298, 313
Hamner, James, 273
Hampton Roads Conference (1865),
    310
Hampton, Wade, 10
Hanckel, Thomas, 161
Hancock, John, 88
Harper, John, 99
Harper, William, 19, 88, 92, 96, 98–102,
    104–105, 112, 313
Harpers Ferry, Virginia, 22
Harrison, Jesse Burton, 101
Hartford Convention, 48, 188
Hawes, Richard, 234
Hayne, Isaac, 156
Hayne, Paul Hamilton, 180
Hayne, Robert Y., 17
Hemings, Sally, 90
Henderson, James Pinckney, 28
Henry, Patrick, 44, 69, 152, 167
Hildreth, Richard, 175
Hill, Benjamin, 298, 308
Hilliard, Henry W., 210
history
  and historical consciousness,
    180–183, 324–328
  post-bellum, 273–285, 324–328
  quest for a usable, 183
  Southern colonial, 194–205
  Southern state, 161–171
Hodge, Charles, 112, 135
Holcombe, James P., 165
Holcombe, William Henry, 250, 273

Holden, William, 158
Holland, Edwin, 18, 119
Holmes, George Frederick, 110, 178
Hope, James Barron, 170, 176, 179
Hotze, Henry, 302, 303
Houston Telegraph, 234, 237
Houston, Sam, 29, 207
Howard, C. W., 202
Howe, Julia Ward, 241
Hughes, Henry, 226
Hunt, Memucan, Jr., 23, 25–29
Hunter, Robert, 169, 177, 180, 184
Huston, Felix, 21, 31

identity, territorial, 47
Illinois, 25, 35, 237
imperialism, proslavery, 5, 32–40, 112,
    230–32
Indian removal policies (1830s), 11,
    55
Indians, 52, 231
  as middle ground between whites and
    blacks, 53
Intelligencer, 128

Jackson Mississippian, 236, 240
Jackson, Andrew, 5, 10, 16, 42, 48
Jackson, James, 82, 93, 242
Jackson, Thomas J. (Stonewall), 137,
    220, 279, 302
Jacobins, 18, 152
Jamaica, 57, 57, 119, 219
Jamestown, 174, 178
Jaquess, James, 310, 320
Jefferson, Thomas, 5, 7, 13, 82, 152,
    167, 186
Jim Crow, 328
Johnson, R. W., 232
Johnson, Richard, 92
Johnson, William, 52
Johnson, William Bullein, 128, 128
Johnston, Albert Sidney, 242
Jones, Charles C. Jr., xxii–xxiv
Jones, Charles C., 118, 203
Jones, John Beauchamp, 181
Jones, Mary, xxii–xxiii, 196, 204
Jones, William S., 266

Journal des Economistes, 108
Junkin, George, 136, 138, 260

Kansas, 25, 37, 69, 75, 169, 196
  admission to the Union of, 32, 35
Kansas-Nebraska Act (1854), 185
Keitt, Lawrence, 107, 157
Kennedy, John Pendleton, 75
Kenner, Duncan, 320
Kentucky, 232, 234, 236, 238
King Cotton, 111, 298
Knibb, William, 129
Knickerbocker, 274
Knox, John, 132

Lamar, Mirabeau, 25, 27–28, 30–32
Laurens, Henry, 19
Leavitt, Joshua, 102
Ledger, 201
Lee, Robert E., 220, 234, 279, 319
Legaré, Hugh, 50, 100
Lewis, Meriwether, 167
Liberator, 187
Liberia, 38, 53, 107
Liberty County, Georgia, 116
Liberty Party, 102
Life of Washington (Weems), 154
Lincoln, Abraham, 205, 241, 309
  and the Civil War, 235, 309
  free soil administration of, 39
  free soil platform of, 32
  reaction to his 1860 election, xxi,
    139, 217, 219, 275, 288
Livingston, Robert, 9
London Index, 302
London Missionary Society, 119
London Quarterly Review, 268
Long, Edward, 177
Longstreet, Augustus Baldwin, 132,
  187–89
Lost Cause, 241, 250, 282
*Lost Principle, The, or the Sectional
  Equilibrium* (Scott), 75
Louisiana, 51, 63, 221, 233, 306, 307
  banning slavery in, 25
  Historical Society, 181
  Purchase (1803), 9, 24, 185, 207

withdrawal from the Union,
  implications of, xvi
Lowndes, Rawlins, 54
Lumpkin, Henry, 103

Macarthy, Harry, 74, 228
Macaulay, Thomas Babington, 57, 176
Macon, Nathaniel, 87
Madison, James, 5, 13, 42, 69, 81, 167,
  227
Maine, 13
Manassas, 241, 246, 268
Manly, Basil, 118
Manly, Basil, Jr., 128
Mann, Ambrose Dudley, 301
Marshall, John, 42, 44, 56, 167, 227
Marston Moor, 180
martial law, 286
Martin, William, 158–159
Martineau, Harriet, 91
Martinique, 57, 306
Maryland, 232, 236, 237
"Maryland in Chains", 232
"Maryland, My Maryland", 228
Mason, George, 69, 167, 169
Mason, James Murray, 169, 301, 320
Mason-Dixon Line, 232
Maury, Matthew Fontaine, 37
Maxcy, Jonathan, 128
Maximilian I, 306
McClung, Alexander, 33
McCord, David, 106, 108
McCord, Louisa, 105–113, 195, 203
McCrady, Edward, 145
McCulloch v. Maryland, 45
McCurry, Stephanie, 126
McDuffie, George, 23, 47, 87
McIntosh, Maria, 203
Means, John, 160
Meek, Alexander, 153
Mellichampe, (Simms) 156
Memminger, Christopher, 123
Memoir on Slavery, 101, 104
"Men of Alabama", 228
Methodists, proslavery, 131–132
Metternich, Klaus, 67
Mexican Cession, 11, 32, 34, 71, 207

Mexican War, 13, 29
  southern participation in the, 33
Mexico, 70, 307, 309
Midway, Georgia, 21
Mighty Experiment, 36, 58, 108
Miles, James Warley, 248, 269
Miles, William Porcher, 314
Millar, John, 82
Miller, Stephen, 111
Minnegerode, Charles, 250
Mississippi River, 7
Mississippi River Valley, 13, 33, 39
  1830s slavery in the, 4
  development of, 64
  urgency to control, 8
Mississippi Southern Crisis, 235
Missouri, 4, 35, 51, 232, 236, 238
  statehood, battle over (1819–21), 12,
    15, 34, 46, 51
Missouri Compromise, 13, 14
Mitchel, John, 267
Mobile Tribune, 204
Modern Reform (Stiles), 138
monarchy, constitutional, 266
Monroe Doctrine, 300, 307
Monroe, James, 8, 10, 16, 167
Montesquieu, 85
Moore, John Quitman, 264, 271, 298,
  305
Moore, Thomas V., 132, 246
Morals of Slavery, 91
Morey, Ira, 147
Morris, Thomas, 93
Moultrie, Fort, 158
Moultrie, William, 151
Mount Vernon, 156
  campaign to buy and restore, xxii,
    166, 196–205
  Ladies Association of the Union, 199
Murfreesboro, 241
Murray, John P., 286
Musson, Eugene, 300

Napoleon, Louis, 304–307
Naseby, 180
Natchez, Mississippi, 16
"National Decay" (Hayne), 180

national government, 44
nationalism
  familial, 275
  master class, 21
  partisan, 205–213
  proslavery, 16, 43, 113, 116, 150,
    189, 196, 203, 218, 241, 250,
    288, 312, 322
  versus state sovereignty, 42
nationhood
  and constitutionalism, 42, 50
  and national government, 44
    and James Madison, 45
    and John Marshall, 46
  and South Carolina, 48
  blocking foreign incursions, 11
  Confederate, 217, 220–251, 286–322
    and centralization, 225
    elevated above bondage, 310
    territorial bountries of, 228–251
  self-preservation and, 5
  Virginia constitutionalists denying
    American, 48
Neely, Mark, 290
"Negro Question" (Carlyle), 109
Negro Seamen's Act, 52, 55
Negroe's Catechism, The (Pattillo), 115
Negro-Mania (Campbell), 109
Nelson, Thomas, 167
New England
  and slavery, 184–213
  and western expansion, 33
  social and religious radicalism of,
    190
  Southern perceptions of, 186
  un-American character of, 188
New France, conquest of (1763), 13
New Mexico, 68, 233
New Orleans, xiii–xv 238
  1768 revolt in, 174
  battle of (1815), 10
  New England Society, 181
New Views of the Constitution
  (Taylor), 47
Nicaragua, 31, 34
North Carolina, 65
Northwest Ordinance (1787), 13, 237

Notes on the State of Virginia
   (Jefferson), 15, 82, 84, 86
Nott, Josiah, 109
nullification, 61, 63, 96, 154
  and liberty, 151
  Andrew Jackson's assault on, 48

O'Neall, John Belton, 155
Oglethorpe, James, 174
Ohio River Valley, 13
Ohio Valley Confederacy, 223
Oldham, Williamson, 295
Onuf, Peter, 47
Clotelle (Brown), 90, 175
Oration Delivered Before the
   Washington Light Infantry
   (Trescot, 1847), 1
Oregon, 29
Orr, James, 184
Otis, James, 88

Paine, Thomas, xiv
Palmer, Benjamin Morgan, xiii–xvii, 20,
   135, 141, 145, 244, 247, 276,
   283, 323–328
Palmetto Day, 154, 158, 161
Palmetto Fort, 159
Partisan Leader, The (Tucker), 181
Partisan, The, A Tale of the Revolution
   (Simms), 156
Passenger cases, 56
paternalism, 195, 314
Pattillo, Henry, 114–116
Paulding, James Kirke, 101
Peace Congress, 222
Pellet, Susan, 200
people, the
  and municipal power, 73
  as arbiters of constitutionality, 61
  in the nation and the state, 45, 47
  interpreting the phrase, 44
Perry, Benjamin Franklin, 154, 211
Petigru, James L., 179
Phelan, James, 228
Phillip, Wendell, 70
Pickens, Francis, 231
Pierce, Franklin, 206

Pike, Albert, 210, 288
Pillow, Gideon, 210, 297
Pinckney, Charles, 6
Pinckney, Charles Cotesworth, 121
Pinckney, Maria Henrietta, 50
Plumer, William S., 135, 138
Plymouth Rock, 175
political economy, 36, 38, 101, 105,
   107, 108–111, 129, 195
Political Fallacies (Junkin), 139
Polk, James K., 29
Pollard, Edward, 267, 279
Porcher, Frederick, 173
Porter, Abner A., 125, 144
Porter, William D., 200
Potter, David, 29, 42, 19
Prentiss, S. S., 181
Prentiss, William, 218
Presbyterianism, in the slaveholding
   South, 134–137, 265
presidency, dual (Calhoun), 59, 68, 78
Preston William C., 98, 100, 137
Preston, John, 297
Preston, Margaret Junkin, 137, 250
Pro-Slavery Argument, The, As
   Maintained by the Leading
   Writers of the South, 96, 101,
   112
proslavery polemics, 18, 83, 94, 97,
   116, 152, 177, 321
Protective Tariff, 60, 62
Providential view of history, 36–39,
   241–54, 382–85, 323–25
Pryor, Roger, 170
Pulaski (slave driver), 22
puritanism, English and Yankee, 188
"Python" (John Tyler, Jr.), 190–93,
   305–06

Quintessence of Long Speeches, The
   (Pinckney), 50
Quitman, John, 20, 33

racism
  biological, anticipating, 86
  hierarchical, 4, 106
  materialist, 101

mulattos, eliminating the moral
    difference between races, 92
  scientific, 109, 110
Ramsay, David, 151, 154, 176
Ramsey, J. C. M., 88
Randall, James, 228
Randolph, Edmund, 6, 44
Randolph, John, 17, 54
Rayner, Kenneth, 184
Read, Charles Henry, 265
Rector, Henry, 231
Red River, 4
Religious Herald, 129
religious instruction, for slaves, 115–
    127
Republican Party, 35, 39, 56, 189, 211
republicanism, proslavery, 14, 150,
    218, 231, 238, 240, 290
  and America's domestic mission,
    143
revolt, slave, 15–18, 20, 31
  and evangelicanism, 119
  free state, 35
  in Saint Domingue, Haiti, 7, 15, 17,
    29, 52, 58, 99, 152, 219, 279
  in the Caribbean, 4, 8
"Revolution of 1800", 45
Reynolds, John L., 278
Rhett, Robert Barnwell, 153, 157, 160
Ricardo, David, 106
Rice, John Holt, 118, 119, 120
Rice, Samuel, 208
Rich, Charles, 15
Richmond Daily Dispatch, 267, 292
Richmond Enquirer, 32, 47, 160, 167,
    286, 294
Richmond Examiner, 219, 227, 278,
    292, 293, 305, 310
Richmond Whig, 167, 315
Richmond, Virginia, 171
Rives, William Cabell, 163, 170, 293
Roane, Spencer, 46, 77, 164, 226
Robinson, Conway, 166
Ruffin, Edmund, 98, 181, 317
Ruffner, William Henry, 137
Runaway Scrape, 22
Russell, Lord John, 28

Sabine River, 24
Sabine, Lorenzo, 157
Saint Domingue, (see also Haiti) 18, 38,
    39, 57, 278, 306
  and the Louisiana Purchase, 9
  French plan to remove black rebels
    from, 8
San Domingo (Spanish colony), 300
Savannah Georgian, 160
Say, Jean-Baptiste, 107
"Scene from Southern Life, A", 277
Schlegel, Friedrich von, 142, 147
Schley, William, 238
Scott, John, 75–78, 271
Scott, Thomas, 81
Scott, Winfield, 206, 207, 209
Seabrook, Whitemarsh, 119
secession, 61, 220, 223
  and black violence, 276
  and free state allies, 228
  and inherited rights, 78
  and local history, 158
  and Maryland, 232
  and New England, 187
  and patriotism, 153
  and proslavery constitutionalism, 41
  and reconfederation, 226
  and Southern Rights, 143
  Calhoun's alternative to state
    interposition, 58–68
  Copperhead, 237
  in Kentucky and Missouri, 232
  legitimizing, 47
  ordinance of, 221
  range of options in, 223
  religious sanction for, 144
Second Confederate Congress, 293
sectionalism, 67, 74, 127–140, 153,
    175, 198, 198, 203, 205
  and equilibrium, 33, 65, 66, 76, 76
  and the compound republic, 77
  Calhoun's, 67
self-control, 116
Selma Reporter, 237
Seward, William, 182, 192, 209
sexuality, interracial, 90–93
Sherman v. Booth, 213

Sherman, William T., 289
Shiloh, 249
Silbey, Henry Hopkins, 233
Simms, William Gilmore, 19, 25, 88,
    92, 96, 105, 109, 112, 149–150,
    154–158, 182, 194, 300, 313
"Sketch of Plantation Life in
    Louisiana, A" (1863), 282
Slave Power, The (Cairnes), 35
slave trade
    African, repopulating slave states, 34
    ban on (1808), 16, 34
    Constitutional protection of, 81
    opposition to, 15
    peak of, 82
slaveholders, Southern
    attitude of, toward plantation
        evangelism, 117–127
    economic prosperity of, in the
        1850s, 3, 104–33
    historical consciousness of, 149–150
    narrow identity of, xvi–xvii
    perceived providential mission of,
        283, 288, 312, 13
    response to 1860 election, xxi, 217,
        240, 266, 275, 288
    Southern Rights as proxy for, 68–78
slavery or bondage
    and America's domestic mission, 143
    and animal caste, 101
    and Christianity, 123, 139
    and civilization, 104, 109
    and evangelicanism, 248
    and geopolitical crisis of Missouri
        Compromise, 13
    and human nature, 101
    and human reformation, 269
    and Louis Napoleon, 305
    and pastoral inefficiency, 30
    and population density, 70
    and republicanism, 107
    and reverse reconstruction, 229
    and stadial theory, 89
    and state sovereignty, 48, 212
    and the American continental empire,
        32–40
    and the American Revolution, 51

and the Protestant tradition, 116
and the Westminster Confession, 116
and underdeveloped moral capacities,
    85
as the primary basis of liberty, 290
Biblical sanction of, 123
Brazilian, 117
central to Southern society, 72
Christianized, xxi, 115, 118, 126,
    164, 317, 327
colonial freedom to place persons in, 51
defending, 82, 97, 103, 109, 112,
    218
elevating status of slaveowner and
    freeman, 88
evangelical, 140–148
federal consensus on, 43, 56, 63
fulfilling a divine decree, xiii, 36, 113,
    127, 141, 147, 237, 272
humanized, 95
in Mexico, 305
nationalizing, 210, 212, 224, 310
paternalistic, 31, 133, 274, 275, 281,
    285
perpetuating, 314
republican, xx, xxii, 217
sectional in character, national in
    relations, 79, 81
shaping white character, 177
Southern colonial, 172–180
Southern Union support of, 6
subduing the wilderness through,
    35
transitioning to free labor, 72, 106
volatility of, 15
western diffusion of, 12, 15, 33, 36
slaves
    after the Revolutionary War, 6
    arming, 19–23, 321
    as threat to civilized society, 18
    loyal, myth of, 18–20, 157, 277–279,
        283
    manumitted, removal of, 38
    natural rebelliousness of, 18
    number of
        in 1770, 3
        in 1860–61, 4

wartime redistribution of, to army
   privates, 315
Sledge, William, 318
Slidell, John, 184, 320
Smith, Adam, 106
Smith, Edmund Kirby, 234
Smith, John, 119, 174
Smith, Robert Handy, 229
Smith, Whitefoord, 144
Smith, William, 17, 86
Smith, William A., 79, 265
Smith, William Loughton, 5, 82, 296
Smylie, James, 122
Smyth, Thomas, 132, 141
soldiering, as white slavery, 294–298
South Carolina, 4, 6, 65, 150–161, 221
South Carolina Baptist, 129
South Carolina College, 128
South Carolina Exposition (1828), 60
South Carolina Historical Society, 161
South, The, Its Dangers and its
   Resources (Martin), 158
Southern Address (Calhoun), 67
Southern Aid Society, 138
Southern Colonial, 172–180
Southern Baptist Convention (SBC), 130
Southern Christian Advocate, 312
Southern Convention (1850), 71
Southern Crisis, 236
Southern Field and Fireside, xiv, 225
Southern Illustrated News, The, 239,
   314
Southern Literary Journal, 102
Southern Literary Messenger, 69, 102,
   103, 209, 218, 225, 239, 264,
   268, 273, 275, 282
Southern Magnolia, 154
"Southern Matron", 198
Southern Planter, xiv
Southern Presbyterian Review, 285
Southern Press, 102
Southern Quarterly Review, 96, 102,
   105, 109
Southern Review, 100
Southern Rights, 66, 68–78, 159, 201,
   206, 221, 290
   defining, 75

Southern Rights Associations, 70, 73
Southern Watchman, 128
sovereignty
   popular, 71, 73, 207
   squatter, 212
   state, 46, 96, 144, 226, 228, 239,
     308, 309
   and abolition, 63
   and American liberty, 41
   and secession, 47
   and state equality, 65
   and white power, 50–58
   in a federate republic, 63
   versus nationalism, 42
Spain, 304
Spence, James, 303
*Spiritual Philosophy of African
   Slavery, The* (Holcombe), 274
Spratt, Leonidas, 153
St. Paul, Henry, 293, 304
Stanton, Robert L., 173
state nationalities, 164
Stephens, Alexander, 34, 41, 211, 229,
   231, 249, 269, 287, 289, 308
Stiles, Joseph Clay, 136, 137
"Stonewall's Sable Seers", 279
Story, Joseph, 45
Stowe, Harriet Beecher, 110, 164, 194
Stringfellow, B. F., 88
Stringfellow, J. H., 320
Stringfellow, Thornton, 112, 126, 129
Stuart, J. E. B., 279
suffrage, universal, as subversive to free
   institutions, 269
Sumner, Charles, xvi, 157, 185, 186, 205
Sumter, Fort, 160, 161, 220
Sutherland, Duchess of, 195, 198, 203,
   204

Tallmadge, James, 12
Talmage, Samuel K., 146
Taney, Roger B., 56, 73, 112
taxation, 51, 224, 298
Taylor, John, 42, 43–45, 47, 54, 77, 86,
   164, 226
Taylor, Zachary, 33
Telegraph, 226

Tennessee, 233, 238
Test Oath, during nullification crisis, 100
Texas, 4, 221, 238
  admission to the Union of, 23–32, 34, 37, 208, 307
  free labor economy in, 29
  Revolution, 22
Thanksgiving Sermon, Delivered at the First Presbyterian Church, New Orleans (Palmer), xiv, 143, 148, 276, 283, 323
Thomas, Gertrude Clanton, 218
Thompson, John R., 103, 195
Thornwell, James Henley, 72, 122, 125, 137, 144, 219, 247, 265
Timrod, Henry, 111, 249, 280, 303, 315
Toombs, Robert, 184, 211, 223, 293, 301, 305, 316
Trans-Mississippi Department, 234
Trescot, William Henry, 1, 14, 145, 177, 223, 241
Triennial Convention (Baptist, 1835), 128, 129
Trollope, Frances, 90
Troup, George M., 27, 53
Tucker, George, 181
Tucker, Joseph W., 235, 239
Tucker, Josiah, 89
Tucker, Nathaniel Beverley, 19, 48, 88, 94, 100, 101, 106, 164, 165, 170, 181, 278, 313
Tudor, Thomas, 82
Turnbull, Robert J., 52, 53–55, 58, 61
Turner, James Addison, 318
Turner, Nat, 18, 120
Tyler, John, 176, 190
Tyler, John, Jr., 190–93, 237, 305–06
Tyler, Julia Gardiner, 194, 196

"Uncle Jerry" (Holcombe), 274
Uncle Tom's Cabin (Stowe), 94, 110, 203, 277
Union
  and proslavery buffer areas, 35
  and slavery, 81
  as a federate republic, 63
  dissolution of, 76
  early importance of, to slavery, 3–5
  Jeffersonian, 5–14
United Synod of the South, 135
University of Richmond, 128
Upshur, Abel, 48

Van Buren, Martin, 182
Van Evrie, J. H., 37
Van Zandt, A. B., 123
Vance, Zebulon, 246, 322
Vesey, Denmark, 18, 52, 55, 98, 119, 127
Vicksburg, 240
Vidaurri, Santiago, 309
Virginia, 4, 34, 65, 219, 231, 237
Virginia doctrines, 49
Virginia Dynasty, 11, 16, 167
Virginia Historical Society, 163, 166, 177

Wake Forest, 128
Wakefield, Edward Gibbon, 101
Walker, David, 18
Walker, Robert J., 37
Walker, William, 34
Wallon, Henri, 178
Walsh, Robert, 101
War of 1812, 17
Ward, Edward, 294
Warfield, Catherine, 279
Warren, Joseph, 88
Washington Artillery of New Orleans, 272
Washington College, 137, 139
Washington, George, 7, 185, 186, 311
  immortalizing, 164–170
Washington, Henry A., 176
Washington, Littleton, 268
Watchman, 223
Watts, Thomas H., 228
Wayland, Francis, 91, 97, 129, 135
Weber, Max, 272
Webster, Daniel, 17, 175, 201
Webster-Ashburton agreement, 301
Weems, Parson, 154
Wesley, John, 132
Westminster Confession, 116, 132

Westminster Review, 110

Wharton, Thomas J., 219

Whig Party, 56, 207, 209, 211

Whitaker, Daniel K., 102

White, T. H., 102

Wiecek, William, 43

Wightman, John T., 111, 246

Wild Southern Scenes (Jones), 181

Wiley, Calvin, 268

Williams, David Rogerson, 128

Wilmer, Richard Hooker, 272

Wilmot Proviso, 32, 65, 103, 199

Windward Islands, 57

Winkler, Edwin T., 128

Winthrop, Robert, 165, 172, 175

Wise, Henry, 167, 169, 188, 209,
    223

women's rights
    and free-state individualism, 192
    and slavery, 194–205
    as a threat to republicanism, 194

Yancey, William L., 71, 154, 169, 200,
    210, 226, 301

Yates, Robert, 46

Yeadon, Richard, 3, 201

Zollicoffer, Felix, 242